Trading
in
Commodity
Futures

2ND EDITION

Trading in Commodity Futures

Frederick F. Horn

Victor W. Farah

New York Institute of Finance

Library of Congress Cataloging in Publication Data

Horn, Frederick F
    Trading in commodity futures

    Includes index.
    1. Commodity exchanges.   I. Farah, Victor W.,
joint author.   II. Title.
HG6046.H59   1979   332.6'44   78-27235
ISBN 0-13-925941-4

© 1979 New York Institute of Finance
     70 Pine Street
     New York, New York 10005

Printed in U.S.A.
10   9   8   7   6   5

Contents

Part One
*THE BACKGROUND
AND HISTORY
OF COMMODITIES*

Chapter 1
**THE ORIGINS OF
COMMODITIES, 3**

    COMMODITIES, 3
    THE HISTORY OF FUTURES CONTRACTS, 5
    EARLY ATTEMPTS AT SHIFTING RISK, 5
        To-Arrive Contracts
    THE DEVELOPMENT OF THE COMMODITIES EXCHANGE, 7
    BUYING AND SELLING FUTURES TODAY, 7
    SUMMARY, 9

Chapter 2
FEDERAL LEGISLATION, 10

    THE GROWTH OF COMMODITIES, 10
    THE COMMODITY EXCHANGE ACT OF 1936, 10
    *THE COMMODITY FUTURES TRADING COMMISSION ACT OF
    1974, 11*
        *The Commodity Futures Trading Commission (CFTC) / Powers of
        the CTFC*
    COMMODITIES TODAY, 18

Chapter 3
THE BASICS, 19

DEFINITIONS, 19
    Commodity   /   Futures Contracts   /   The Contract Itself   /
    Trading Hours
PRICE QUOTATIONS AND MINIMUM FLUCTUATIONS, 23
DAILY QUOTATIONS, 33
DAILY TRADING LIMITS, 35
    Maximum Daily Range
ROUNDTURN RATE OF COMMISSION, 39
    Day Trade Commissions   /   Member Rates   /   Foreign Rates
CONCLUSION, 42

Chapter 4
THE OPENING, HANDLING
AND CLOSING OF A
COMMODITY ACCOUNT, 44

TYPES OF COMMODITIES ACCOUNTS, 44
TYPES OF TRANSACTIONS, 45
    Know Your Customer
PROCEDURES FOR INDIVIDUAL SPECULATIVE ACCOUNTS, 46
    Regulations Governing the Opening of a Commodities Account
ADDITIONAL REQUIREMENTS FOR OPENING JOINT OR
BUSINESS ACCOUNTS, 55
    Joint Accounts   /   Sole Proprietorship Company Account   /
    Partnership Accounts   /   Corporation Accounts
OTHER TYPES OF ACCOUNTS, 62
    Trade or Hedge Accounts   /   Guaranteed Accounts   /   Omnibus
    Accounts   /   Unacceptable Accounts
TRANSFERRING (TRADING) ACCOUNTS, 68
HANDLING AN ACCOUNT, 68
    The Duties of the Broker to the Customer   /   Customer Statements
CLOSE-OUT INSTRUCTIONS, 78
ERRONEOUS REPORTS, 78
CUSTOMER GIVE-UP, 79
DEATH OF A CUSTOMER, 79
CONCLUSION, 80

Chapter 5
MARGIN REQUIREMENTS
AND PROCEDURES, 81

SPECULATIVE ACCOUNT REQUIREMENTS, 82
 Minimum Commodity Exchange Speculative Requirements /
 House Requirements / Increases or Decreases in Margin
 Requirements / Concessions in House Requirements
TRADE ACCOUNT REQUIREMENTS, 85
DAY TRADE MARGIN REQUIREMENTS, 88
SPREAD MARGIN REQUIREMENTS, 88
PROCEDURES FOR MARGIN CALLS, 90
 Original Margin Calls / Variation Margin Calls
PROCEDURE FOR A SELL-OUT, 93
RECEIPT OF FUNDS FROM CUSTOMERS, 94
TRANSFER OF FUNDS FROM A STOCK ACCOUNT, 96
TRANSFER OF FUNDS TO STOCKS, 96
PAYOUTS, 97
CONCLUSION, 98

Chapter 6
PLACING AND
EXECUTING ORDERS:
THE MECHANICS, 99

THE ORDER ITSELF, 99
Primary Information / Secondary Information / Account Information
 Information
THE MECHANICS OF PLACING AN ORDER, 103
THE EXCHANGE TRADING FLOOR, 104
PRICE REPORTING AND DISSEMINATION, 104
 Commodity and Delivery Month Symbols / Fast Quotations for
 CBOT Commodities
COMPETITIVE EXECUTIONS REQUIRED, 106
 The Opening . . . / . . . And the Closing Bell / Adjustment of
 Errors
TIME AND SALES, 107
CONCLUSION, 108

Chapter 7
ORDERS, 109

MARKET ORDER, 109
    Market Order to Sell
LIMIT ORDERS, 111
    Limit Order to Buy / Limit Order to Sell
BOARD OR MARKET-IF-TOUCHED (MIT) ORDERS, 113
    MIT Order to Buy / MIT Order to Sell
STOP ORDER, 115
    Stop Order to Buy / Stop Order to Sell / Stop Limit Order /
    Stop-Limit Order to Sell / Stop-and-Limit Orders
TIME ORDERS, 121
    Day Orders / Time-of-the-Day Orders / Off-at-a-Specific-Time
    Order / Week and Month Orders / Open Orders
IMMEDIATE-OR-CANCEL ORDERS, 123
SCALE ORDERS, 124
COMBINATION ORDERS, 125
    Alternative Orders
CONTINGENT ORDERS, 127
ON-THE-OPENING MARKET ORDERS, 128
    On-the-Opening Limit Orders
ON-THE-CLOSE ORDERS, 128
    Limit or Market On-the-Close Order
SPREAD ORDERS, 129
SWITCH ORDERS, 130
CANCELLATIONS, 131
CONCLUSION, 132

Chapter 8
DELIVERIES, 134

BACKGROUND, 134
    Standardization of Contracts / Right of Appeal / The Time
    Element
DELIVERY AT THE SELLER'S OPTION, 137
DELIVERY PERIOD, 138
    Switching Forward
DELIVERABLE GRADES, 141
DELIVERY POINTS, 142
CONCLUSIONS, 143

Chapter 9
THE
CLEARING HOUSE, 144

FUNCTIONS, 145
THE PRINCIPLE OF SUBSTITUTION, 145
GUARANTEEING THE TRANSACTIONS, 146
ORIGINAL MARGIN, 147
    Variation Margin   /   Calculation of Net Positions
SECURITY OF THE COMMODITY CLEARING HOUSE, 150
    The Guaranty Fund / Clearance Fees and the Surplus / The
    Careful Provision Against Loss
MAKING AND TAKING DELIVERY, 152
    Delivery Notice / Transferable versus Nontransferable /
    Delivery Responsibilities / Commissions
CONCLUSION, 156

Part Two
COMMODITIES
TACTICS

Chapter 10
CASH AND
FUTURES PRICE
RELATIONSHIPS, 161

CARRYING CHARGE MARKET OR NORMAL MARKET, 164
    Calculating the Carrying Charges / Convergence of the Prices
INVERTED MARKET, 168
CASH AND FUTURES PRICES IN THE DELIVERY MONTH, 171
RELATIONSHIP OF FUTURES AT DIFFERENT POINTS IN TIME, 173
OPPORTUNITIES IN FUTURES RELATIONSHIPS, 173
OLD AND NEW CROP FUTURES, 178
CROP YEARS, 178
CONCLUSION, 179

Chapter 11
HEDGING, 180

GROWING CIRCLE OF HEDGERS, 182
THE SELLING HEDGE, 183
　　*To Protect Purchases or Inventories　/　To Protect or to Earn an
　　Expected Carrying Charge　/　Hedging to Protect, or to Insure,
　　a Given Price*
THE BUYING HEDGE, 187
　　*To Protect Uncovered Forward Sales of a Commodity or its Products　/
　　To Replace Inventory at Lower Cost　/　To Protect the Price of
　　Stable-Priced Products*
HEDGING IN ACTUAL PRACTICE, 191
　　*Selling Hedge in a Normal Market Followed by a Narrowing in the
　　Basis　/　Selling Hedge in a Normal Market Followed by a Widening
　　in the Basis　/　Buying Hedge in a Normal Market Followed by a
　　Narrowing in the Basis　/　Selling Hedge in an Inverted Market
　　Followed by a Widening in the Basis　/　Buying Hedge in an
　　Inverted Market Followed by a Narrowing in the Basis　/　Buying
　　Hedge in an Inverted Market Followed by a Widening in the Basis*
TRANSFERRING HEDGES, 202
SUMMARY, 204

Chapter 12
FUNDAMENTAL APPROACH
TO FORECASTING
COMMODITY PRICE, 206

THE TWO APPROACHES TO PRICE FORECASTING, 206
FUNDAMENTAL ANALYSIS APPROACH, 207
FUNDAMENTAL MARKET ANALYSIS, 208
THE BASIC MARKET FACTORS, 209
　　*Supply-and-Demand Balance　/　Seasonal Trend Tendency　/
　　Price Levels*
HOW BASIC MARKET FACTORS INFLUENCE PRICES, 213
　　*An Indicated Total Supply Scarcity　/　An Indicated Total Supply
　　Surplus　/　An Indicated Free Supply Scarcity　/　An Indicated
　　Free Supply Surplus　/　Crop Scarce Situations　/　General
　　Inflation and Deflation　/　Normal Seasonal Price Tendencies*
SUMMARY, 222

Chapter 13
TECHNICAL APPROACH
TO FORECASTING
COMMODITY PRICES, 223

IMPORTANCE OF CHART ANALYSIS, 223
HOW CHARTS REFLECT CHANGES IN MARKET PSYCHOLOGY, 224
  How to Construct a Bar Chart   /   How to Construct a Point and
  Figure Chart
BUYING POWER VERSUS SELLING PRESSURE, 228
  An Uptrend   /   Downtrend   /   Congestion Area   /   Support
  Levels
RESISTANCE LEVELS, 238
PATTERN IDENTIFICATION, 239
  Double Top   /   Double Bottom   /   Head and Shoulders   /
  Inverse Head and Shoulders   /   Descending Triangle   /
  Ascending Triangle   /   Symmetrical Triangle   /   Flags   /
  Gaps
SUMMARY, 253

Chapter 14
TRADING TECHNIQUES
FOR THE SPECULATOR, 254

CONSIDERATIONS BEFORE ENTERING THE MARKET, 256
  Adopt and Follow a Definite Trading Plan   /   Trade Conservatively,
  With Money You Can Afford to Risk   /   Never Risk All Your
  Trading Capital on Any One Situation   /   Never Depend on Trading
  Profits to Meet Regular Expenses
LIMIT YOUR LOSSES AND LET YOUR PROFITS RUN, 259
HOW TO INITIATE A POSITION, 261
CONSIDERATIONS ONCE YOU HAVE ESTABLISHED A POSITION, 262
AVERAGING DOWN, 268
PYRAMIDING, 269
LOCKING IN A PROFIT, 270
SELLING THE PREMIUMS AND BUYING THE DISCOUNTS, 272
CONCLUSION, 273

Chapter 15
SPREADING—SOPHISTICATED
SPECULATION, 375

INTERDELIVERY SPREAD, 276
    In a Normal Market   /   In an Inverted Market
INTERMARKET SPREADS, 283
    Transportation Costs   /   Different Deliverable Grades   /   Local
    Supply and Demand Conditions
INTERCOMMODITY SPREAD, 286
COMMODITY/PRODUCT SPREADS, 287
TAX STRADDLES, 292
SPREAD MARGIN REQUIREMENTS, 292
SPREAD COMMISSIONS, 292
CONCLUSIONS, 295

Part Three
COMMODITIES
STRATEGY

Chapter 16
OPEN INTEREST AND
VOLUME OF TRADING, 299

VOLUME OF TRADING, 299
OPEN INTEREST, 300
THE STATISTICS, 301
SEASONAL INFLUENCES ON OPEN INTEREST AND VOLUME OF
TRADING, 302
INTERPRETING CHANGES IN OPEN INTEREST AND VOLUME OF
TRADING, 303
OTHER STATISTICS, 305
CONCLUSION, 308

Chapter 17
GOVERNMENT PRICE SUPPORT
AND DISPOSAL PROGRAMS, 309

THE GOVERNMENT PRICE SUPPORT PROGRAM, 310
HOW PRICES ARE SUPPORTED, 310
    Loans

GRAIN RESERVES, 314
  Farmer-Held Reserve
RESERVE PROGRAM, 315
  Target Price and Loan Program Continues / Price Support Loans
  for 1978–81 Crops / Downward Adjustment in Loans /
  Program Acreages Instead of Allotments / Set-Aside /
  Payment Limits / Soybeans / Purchase Agreements /
  Wool Mohair / Incentive Payments / Price Support for Shorn
  Wool
WHY MARKET PRICES MAY BE LESS THAN SUPPORT PRICES, 321
PRODUCTION ADJUSTMENT PROGRAMS, 323
  Acreage Allotments and Marketing Quotas / Voluntary Diversion
  Programs / The Cropland Adjustment Program and the Cropland
  Conversion Program
COMMODITY DISPOSAL AND INVENTORY OPERATIONS, 324
  Domestic Scale / Export Sale
METHODS OF DISPOSITION, 326
  Sales for Dollars / Credit Sales for Dollars / CCC Credit
  Program / Public Law 480 Credit Program / Sales for Foreign
  Currencies Under Title I, P.L. 480 / Transfers and Donations
THE INTERNATIONAL WHEAT AGREEMENTS, 330
CONCLUSION, 331

Chapter 18
FINANCIAL INSTRUMENTS
AS COMMODITIES, 332

THE GROWING VOLUME OF SUCCESS, 332
THE SWEET QUALITY OF SUCCESS, 333
PRECONDITIONS FOR FINANCIAL FUTURES, 334
HEDGING INTEREST RATE RISK, 335
SELLING HEDGE (GNMA FUTURES), 336
BUYING HEDGE (T-BOND FUTURES), 339
BUYING HEDGE (T-BILL FUTURES), 342
COMMERCIAL PAPER, 345
THE DETERMINATION OF INTEREST RATE LEVELS, 345
  Supply and Demand / Inflation / Governmental Determinants
CONCLUSION, 351

GLOSSARY, 352

INDEX, 367

Preface

The second edition of *Trading in Commodity Futures* has been restructured and rewritten to better acquaint the general public with the mechanics and intricacies of commodity futures trading. This edition serves not only as a primer to the uninitiated but also as a vehicle to broaden the perspective of experienced traders—speculators and hedgers alike.

Covering the basics of sound commodity trading—such as the fundamental and technical analysis techniques, buying-selling terminology, and investment objectives—the book also deals with exchange and federal regulations, hedging and speculation principles, and the intricacies of cash and futures market relationships. Its example material, woven into the text, has been expanded to include many of the new types of contracts available today. One full chapter is devoted to the developments in financial instruments as commodities. A glossary and index aid the reader who wishes to use the book for reference or research.

FREDERICK F. HORN
VICTOR W. FARAH

Acknowledgments

The authors express their grateful appreciation to the following persons and organizations for permission to quote from their works or to reproduce their charts and tables: The Chicago Board of Trade; Chicago Mercantile Exchange; New York Mercantile Exchange; New York Cotton Exchange; Department of Agriculture; Commodity Futures Trading Commission; Chester W. Keltner, President, Keltner Statistical Service for permission to quote from *How to Make Money in Commodities*; Gerald M. Loeb, for permission to quote from *Battle for Investment Survival*; and James S. Schonberg, Exposition Press, *The Grain Trade—How it Works*; T. A. Hieronymus, Professor, Agricultural Economics, University of Illinois College of Agriculture; John Magee, for permission to quote from *Technical Analysis of Stock Trends,* 5th ed.; Frazer Publishing Company for permission to quote from Fred Kelly's *Why You Win or Lose—the Psychology of Speculation;* McCord-Larare Printing Company; *The Wall Street Journal*; the Commodity Research Bureau, Inc., publishers of weekly commodity chart service and publications.

Trading
in
Commodity
Futures

Part One

The Background and History of Commodities

Chapter 1

The Origins of Commodities

COMMODITIES

Commodities trading constitutes an arena of human interaction that is almost as natural as one person greeting another. Just as people need one another for social and psychological benefits, so do they need one another for the many benefits that can be derived from trading in commodities.

Commodities themselves, in their original form as agricultural products, reflect one of the earliest industries—farming. When farmers harvested their crops, they engaged in the buying and selling of commodities—this foodstuff for that.

Today commodities include a much broader spectrum of items and play a much larger role in our economy than ever before. In the last ten years or so, the interest and activity in commodities futures trading has flourished with all the earmarks of a burgeoning area of trading. Unfortunately, not many people know enough about commodities futures trading—or worse yet, feel they know too little—to investigate its possibilities and payoffs, its benefits and advantages.

As in any area of trading, getting to know it better is a way of becoming more comfortable with it. And getting to know the commodity industry as a whole constitutes the subject matter of the pages to follow. It is an exciting industry that can fit many objectives. But making it fit requires a great deal of knowledgeability, a little foresight, a sense of timing, and a touch of common sense.

WHAT IS A COMMODITY?

A commodity, in a general sense, is a basic item, a staple, usually a farm product. Today, however, exchanges are recognizing futures contract markets that trade in products from livestock, mining, forestry, currencies, and financial instruments—all as commodities. (You might flip ahead to Chapter 3 to see Figures 3-1 and 3-2 for an idea of the vast range of commodities available today.)

For our purposes, a *commodity* is any basic item that is bought and sold on an exchange for an agreed-on price and on contractual terms. Since the price is subject to supply and demand factors, a certain element of risk is involved.

Risk is actually what gave rise to trading in commodities futures contracts. For example, farming for subsistence is one thing; farming for a profit is quite another. When a farmer plants corn in the spring, he risks losing his crop to blight, vermin, or bad weather; and if he has a good crop, he then risks losing his profit when an abundance of corn at harvest time drives prices below the breakeven point. Raising livestock and mining precious ores carry similar risks. The investment is made under precarious circumstances, and even if it pays off, the return may not be enough even to offset the costs because of changing market conditions.

Yet the world still needs farm, livestock, and mining products. Despite the risks, people still sow seed, raise herds, and dig holes in the ground. So someone must be assuming the risks.

That someone is the speculator, someone with money that can be used as risk capital and someone with an educated guess. The speculator, in effect, pays the farmer, the herder, or mine owner—or the inevitable middleperson— in return for the "right" to assume the risk. Why would anyone pay for the right to assume risk? Because the speculator has analyzed the prospects of price changes in the commodities and feels that they will be favorable. By means of some type of market forecasting, the speculator not only endeavors to make a profit on the basis of that forecasting but also performs a service in assuming the risks. In so doing, the speculator relieves commodity producers and handlers of some of the burden of risk. The economic value of trading in commodities is therefore tied in with the harvesting of crops, the marketing of industrial products, and the feeding of livestock. The related costs of storage along with the inherent price risks are the primary reasons for the establishment of the futures contract.

A *futures contract* is an agreement for the purchase or sale of a commodity made on an organized exchange under set rules and regulations for the delivery of the commodity, at some future date, for a predetermined amount and quality during a specified time. A futures contract *is* a bona fide contract for actual merchandise. Although related in price to the physical commodity, the futures contract in itself has value, and as such it can be bought and sold as a negotiable instrument.

This contract has roots that go back at least a hundred years in America.

THE HISTORY OF FUTURES CONTRACTS

Around the time of the Civil War, the farmer usually took the brunt of market fluctuations. If he was ready to sell, soon after the harvest, so was everyone else. Consequently, at this time supplies were usually well in excess of immediate requirements, a situation which resulted in depressed price levels. Farmers had several alternatives: accept whatever price they could get for their crops in an already oversupplied market, put their crops in storage (incurring additional costs) and hope prices would improve, or haul their crops back home. Often finding anyone even to make a bid for their hard-earned crop was difficult.

However, the situation reversed itself toward the end of the harvest season, and the produce merchant ran the market gamut. As the season's crop was consumed, available unsold grain became in shorter and shorter supply, and this scarcity resulted in higher prices. Grain merchants were thus forced to buy the bulk of their year's supply (more than they could utilize at the time of purchase) during the harvest period. Or they had to pay exorbitant prices late in the marketing year, before the next season's crops were available, in order to keep their mills running as manufacturers competed with each other for the available supply. On the other hand, during the years of oversupply, producers had to dispose of their goods at fire-sale prices.

EARLY ATTEMPTS AT SHIFTING RISK

To-Arrive Contracts

In order to protect themselves against the seasonal fluctuations, producers and consumers of commodities began to buy and sell for forward delivery. These transactions, which became known as *to-arrive contracts,* involved a binding sale by a farmer to a buyer for a designated amount of grain to arrive ten, twenty, thirty, or sixty days later.

> *Example*: A miller agrees on April 1 to buy 5,000 bushels of corn from a farmer for $2.20 per bushel. The corn is to be delivered on June 1. The buyer and seller both agree on a price for a product "to arrive" two months later.

Contracting for deferred delivery did not, of course, eliminate the risk;

nor did it solve the problem of the market risk. The risk, when you think about it, was not completely off the shoulders of the seller. Admittedly, the producer/seller had estimated sufficient return for a crop before it was even harvested and need be concerned only with the production of the crop and its delivery to the buyer. Yet the seller could still lose. He had to contend with the possibility that the price of the commodity would rise before delivery. If the price of corn advanced to, say, $2.40 by June 1, he stood to lose out on additional profit. The buyer, on the other hand, still had to fear a price decrease. Should the price of corn drop to $2.00 by the time of delivery, the buyer would suffer a 20-cent loss per bushel.

Contracting for deferred delivery did, at least, enable a merchant, a manufacturer, or a processor to schedule raw material shipments for arrival at designated intervals. Insuring their availability for operating needs at all times tended to stabilize the market to a degree, because product prices could be projected on known costs.

Eventually, these forward contracts were bought and sold without waiting for delivery. Many other people who were not in the grain trade were willing to assume the risks but were *not* willing to take the actual delivery. These persons were speculators, not merchants; they were interested in a possible gain on any change in value, not in profits on the sale of the physical commodities themselves. The merchant with a contract, who did not want to absorb the risk at all, could transfer ownership of the contract to a third person (such as a dealer or speculator) who was willing to take a chance solely in the hope of making a profit.

Once speculators became interested in the futures contract market, as such—that is, as a negotiable item on its own—the futures contract market became a viable adjunct to the actual commodities market, or *cash* market as it is sometimes called. Now, the prices in one market generally correspond to the prices in the other, but as trading in futures contracts, as opposed to trading in the commodities themselves, became more and more a practice over the years, the two markets became more and more distinct. (See the chapter on "The Relationship between Cash and Futures Prices.") These daring risk-takers, therefore, served an historic purpose.

The to-arrive contract, although a step forward, still left much to be desired. Often questions arose about the quality of the delivery, the quantities of the contracts varied among the contracting parties, and, of course, defaults on the contracts occurred commonly. These shortcomings eventually led to the formalizing of contracts. These middle men organized themselves into an exchange and set up the needed rules for establishing strict standards for size, quality, and grade; and, among themselves, they mutually guaranteed performance on all contracts. Their agreements constituted not only the formation of the first commodity futures exchange but also one that benefited those in or associated with the marketing of the commodity itself.

THE DEVELOPMENT OF THE COMMODITIES EXCHANGE

A commodity exchange is little more than a central meeting place where buyers and sellers (members of the exchange) meet to transact business. Nonmembers need only open accounts with member firms to deal on the exchange. The exchange merely provides the facilities where the transactions may take place. The exchange itself does not buy or sell commodities or contracts, nor does it establish prices. However, the exchange does promulgate rules and regulations in order to promote uniform practices among buyers and sellers in the market, provide the machinery for facilitating the speedy adjustment of business disputes, and disseminate prices and market information valuable to members and their customers.

BUYING AND SELLING FUTURES TODAY

Today, commodities may be transacted in either the cash or the futures market, two separate but related markets. The establishment of a futures market by no means replaced the cash market; rather, it augmented the cash market.

The *cash market,* sometimes referred to as the *actual* or *spot market,* is where the commodities themselves are bought and sold on a negotiated basis. In almost all cases, the agreement or contract calls for the transfer of a specific quantity of a specific grade of a commodity; it may also call for either immediate or forward delivery. The contract can be cancelled only by the mutual agreement of the two contracting parties.

The *futures market* is distinguished from a cash market insofar as standardized contractual agreements are bought and sold—not the actual commodities themselves. These agreements, more formally called *futures contracts,* provide for the delivery of a specified amount of a particular commodity during a specified future month, but they in fact involve no immediate transfer of ownership of the commodity. In other words, you can buy and sell commodities in a futures market regardless of whether or not you have, or own, the particular commodity. Basically remember this about buying and selling futures:

1. When you *buy* a futures contract, you are *going long.* In so doing, you are simply agreeing to receive delivery and to pay in full for a specific amount and grade of a particular commodity to be delivered to you at a specific place in some designated month in the future.
2. Conversely, when you *sell* a futures contract, you are *going short.* You are agreeing to deliver a specific quantity and grade of a particular commodity at a specific place in some month in the future, at which time you will be paid in full.

The terms and conditions of a futures contract are uniform: the size, the deliverable grades, the place of delivery, and many other specifications are all predetermined and detailed in the rules of the exchange. Consequently, when a contract is negotiated, the seller and buyer need settle on only the month of delivery, the number of contracts (or bushels, if grain), and the price. Price is determined by the competitive bidding and offering, by public outcry, on the floor of the organized futures exchanges.

Contracts may be filled by either delivery or offset. Fulfillment by *delivery* obviously means you either accept or deliver the goods, as contracted. Actually, however, only roughly 2 percent of all futures contracts are ever settled by deliveries. For the most part, they are *offset* (or liquidated) prior to the delivery month. Despite the contract, delivery is *not* mandatory: the participant in the market does not have to take or make delivery unless he or she is able and wishes to. The holder of a contract, either the buyer or seller, has the option of offsetting the contract. Offsetting is accomplished quickly and easily by simply selling or buying a contract of similar size in the same delivery month. For example, a speculator who has purchased, say, one contract of cotton can offset the contract by *selling* another contract of cotton of the same delivery month. Similarly, the one who has sold a contract can offset it simply by buying another contract of equal size and in the same month. Either way, one position cancels out the other, and the difference between the prices of the two transactions represents the speculator's profit or loss. Amazingly, the speculator can offset a position without regard for the other party originally involved in the contract, because at the end of each trading day the *clearing house* assumes the role of the "other party" for *all* transactions by its members. This responsibility on the part of the clearing house enables the participants to buy and sell contracts freely without regard to legal problems normally involved in the "breaking" of a contract. The chapter on clearing houses, later in this book, explains the vital role the clearing house plays in greater detail.

Speculators can make a great deal of money, depending on how right their market projections are. If a person buys a contract at, say, $2.00 per bushel and several weeks later sells it for $2.30, quite a profit can be made: At 5,000 bushels per contract, a 30-cent profit means a profit of $1,500 on the contract! Correspondingly, selling the same contract at $2.30 and then buying it back later at $2.00 again could produce another $1,500 profit! Obviously a speculator can make a profit whether the market is going up or down—the movement itself, in either direction, is what generates the profits. That is the realm of the speculator.

However, not everyone who trades in commodities can be considered a speculator. Some take on contracts simply to protect their commercial interests in the cash market. These people are the *hedgers,* the descendants of the merchants from the days when futures markets did not exist at all. Hedgers buy and sell contracts not so much to make money as *to avoid losing it.*

In this way they use the futures markets as a marketing and/or inventory management tool.

> *Example*: A frozen concentrated orange juice processor maintains an inventory of this product until the new crop of oranges arrives. As long as he holds the inventory, he is subject to the risk of loss because of price decline. For protection, therefore, he sells frozen concentrated orange juice futures contracts in an amount comparable to the quantity of the inventory. In other words, he is buying price insurance.
>
> Selling in the futures market *hedges* the actual inventory. In effect, the futures contract market serves as a price equalizer: Whatever is lost in inventory value is gained on the short position in the futures market. The processor can plan a marketing program without fear of price depreciation. As the processor sells from the inventory, he liquidates (by buying back contracts) the comparable quantity in the futures market.

SUMMARY

As you can see, commodity futures contracts arose from the problem of risk—risk all along the line from the time the seed touched the ground until the bread was on the consumer's table.

But limiting commodities to farm products is, of course, wrong. Commodities trading has steadily expanded to include more and more types of contracts. During the 1960s, dealers in futures markets sensed the public's interest in nonagricultural and nonindustrial commodities. Before long, concentrated frozen orange juice, wood, pork bellies, and other processed or manufactured goods found a niche in the futures marketplace. With their acceptance assured, exchanges developed programs to expand still further. Capping the exchanges' efforts was the incorporation of currencies into the commodities arena in the late sixties and early seventies.

Today the category of commodities futures contracts may include any item that meets the following criteria:

1. bought and sold on a recognized commodity exchange,
2. in a contractual form,
3. at prices determined by bids and offers in the marketplace,
4. for an item that is to be delivered sometime in the future.

That's a futures contract.

Today, commodities exchanges, though hectic and fast-paced, are nonetheless highly regulated and well supervised.

The next chapter tells the story about the legislation enacted to include the ever growing commodity futures industry.

Chapter 2

Federal Legislation

THE GROWTH OF COMMODITIES

During the late 1800s and early 1900s, the tremendous growth of commercial farming gave rise to attempts by the United States government to institute standards for quality and trading. By 1916 the Grain Standards Act was passed. Following World War I, the farm depression caused widespread speculation in grain futures, which brought protests from producers and consumers alike. In 1921 Congress had passed the Futures Trading Act, which was quickly declared unconstitutional by the United States Supreme Court. Congress responded just as quickly by passing the Grain Futures Act of 1922, which the Court upheld the following year.

The Grain Futures Act enabled the government to deal with the exchanges themselves rather than with the traders. Although the Act did provide for fact-finding and investigatory powers by the United States Department of Agriculture (USDA), which was responsible for its enforcement, the powers authorized were inadequate to deal with the excessive speculation, price manipulation, and other abuses.

THE COMMODITY EXCHANGE ACT OF 1936

To cope with the increased problems of futures trading, Congress passed additional amendments in 1936, and the original legislation was renamed the Commodity Exchange Act. The law extended regulatory coverage to cotton and other commodities, as well as grains. It also granted broad additional authority to curb market abuses by traders, to prosecute price manipulation as a criminal offense, to regulate excessive speculation by large market operators, and to extend regulation to previously uncovered commodity brokerage firms to suppress fraud, fictitious transactions, and other misconduct.

THE COMMODITY FUTURES TRADING COMMISSION ACT OF 1974

In 1968 Congress made significant changes in the Act. The most forceful affected the *futures commission merchants* (FCM), that is, any individual, association, partnership, or corporation that buys or sells futures contracts on commission: FCMs must now meet specified minimum financial standards. Other amendments increased the penalties for certain law violations, such as manipulation, and authorized cease and desist orders.

However, the need for closer regulation was apparent even after the 1968 amendments. The dollar value of futures trading in all commodities—those that were regulated and those that were not—rose to $500 billion annually in 1973, thus prompting Congressional hearings for the broader regulation of futures trading.

The Commodity Futures Trading Commission (CFTC)

The result was the Commodity Futures Trading Commission Act of 1974 (CFTCA) signed by then President Ford on October 23, 1974. The new act created an independent Commodity Futures Trading Commission (CFTC), similar to the Securities Exchange Commission, replacing the Commodity Exchange Authority (CEA) of the Department of Agriculture. All CEA records and personnel were transferred to the new commission. The only remaining tie with the Department of Agriculture is a USDA liaison officer appointed by the Secretary of Agriculture and a reciprocal CFTC liaison with the USDA. On April 21, 1975, the CFTC began to exercise its mandate.

The Commission is composed of a chairman and four other commissioners, appointed by the President by and with advice and consent of the Senate. Each commissioner holds office for a five-year term. The major responsibilities of the CFTC, as mandated by the Commodity Exchange Act as amended, are:

1. designation of a board of trade as a contract market,
2. registration of futures Commission merchants (FCM), floor brokers, and *associated persons* (APs),
3. protection of FCMs' customers' funds,
4. periodic auditing of FCMs' books and records,
5. supervision of trading on boards of trade,
6. controlling the excess of speculation by large traders by fixing position and trading limits,

7. investigating questionable practices and violation of the Act, and
8. time-recording the receipt of customers' orders.

The Act now also provides broader authority to the Commission by expanding the definition of commodities to include all goods, articles, services, rights, and interests that are traded for future delivery on a recognized exchange and that are designated as contract markets; anything satisfying that definition is now under federal regulation. Previously unregulated commodities—such as coffee, sugar, silver, copper, gold, other metals, forest products, foreign currencies, GNMA, T bills, and the like—are now regulated. The Commission thus has authority now to regulate transactions for the delivery not only of silver and gold bullion, but of bulk silver coins and bulk gold coins as well.

Powers of the CFTC

The 1974 Act provides the Commission with the exclusive jurisdiction over all futures transactions executed on domestic boards of trade (that is, commodity exchanges).

Registration. Section 204 broadens the coverage of persons associated with commodities futures trading. An *associated person* is defined as anyone associated with a futures commission merchant (FCM) or with an agent of an FCM as a partner, officer, or employee; an AP is also anyone who occupies a similar status or performs similar functions in any capacity that involves:

1. the solicitation or acceptance of customers' orders (other than in a clerical capacity), and
2. the supervision of any person or persons so engaged.

All such associated persons must be registered with the Commission. Registration expires two years after the initial registration unless renewed by the applicant. Under the new Act, APs are subject to administrative disciplinary proceedings.

The CFTCA continued the *annual* registration requirement of FCMs and floor brokers; of course, they are not required to register as APs.

Section 205 amends the previous Act by requiring also the registration and the regulation of Commodity Trading Advisors and Commodity Pool Operators. The commission is empowered to specify persons not within the intent of the two definitions, which are as follows:

A *Commodity Trading Advisor* is any person who, for compensation or profit, engages in the business of advising others, either directly or through publications or writings, as to the value of commodities or as to the advisability of trading in any commodity for future delivery on or subject to the rules of any contract market; an advisor is also anyone who, for compensation or profit and as a part of a regular business, issues or promulgates analysis or reports concerning commodities. Provided that the furnishing of such services is solely *incidental* to the conduct of their business or profession, certain individuals and corporate entities are excluded from this definition, such as:

1. any bank or trust company,
2. any newspaper reporter, newspaper columnist, newspaper editor, lawyer, accountant, or teacher,
3. any floor broker or FCM,
4. the publisher of any bona fide newspaper, news magazine, or business or financial publication of a general and regular circulation that includes their own employees, or
5. any contract market.

However, the new section 4m of the Act spells out that registration does not apply to any trading advisor who, during the preceding twelve months has not furnished trading advice to more than fifteen persons and who does not hold himself or herself out to the public as a commodity trading advisor.

A *Commodity Pool Operator* is any person who is engaged in a business that is of the nature of an investment trust, syndicate, or similar form of enterprise, and who, in connection with such a business solicits, accepts, or receives from others funds, securities, or property, either directly or through capital contributions, for the purpose of trading in any commodity for future delivery on or subject to the rules of any contract market.

Regulation of Transaction Activities. The 1974 legislation greatly expanded the scope of federal regulation:

Contract markets (*exchanges*) are required to demonstrate that futures contracts are not contrary to the public interest and meet an economic need. *Commodity exchanges* must submit, for Commission approval, bylaws, rules, regulations and resolutions relating to contract terms. In addition, the Commission may require an exchange to make any changes in its rules and practices that are in the public interest.

The Commission also has the authority to act in emergency situations and direct an exchange to take such action as is necessary to maintain or restore orderly trading. An *emergency* encompasses any act of the United States or a foreign government or any other major disturbance that prevents the market from accurately reflecting supply and demand.

The Commission may establish additional delivery points for a commodity, or enlarge existing delivery points.

The Commission may authorize the formation of voluntary futures associations, for regulating the practices of the members.

The Commission, taking over the CEA authority to fix trading and position limits, has defined daily trading limits (in contracts or bushels), overnight position limits, and requirements on reportable limits.

The Commodity Exchange Act requires that FCMs report on the activity of each account when the activity in an account reaches a certain level. Parts 17 and 18 of the CEA regulations, as amended, therefore outline the reporting levels for each commodity (Figure 2-1). As soon as the trading activity reaches the levels indicated in their guide, the FCMs are obliged to file a report with the Commission.

The Commission also curtails the amount of speculation that can take place in an account in any one day. Large trading accounts that are strictly speculative, taken collectively, *do* represent a threat to an orderly market. Such accounts must therefore be regulated and monitored. As a result the CTFC has issued a schedule of speculative limits (Figure 2-2), which defines two areas of concern:

1. *Net position* is the extent to which an account is long or short, after all offsetting transactions are figured out, in any one commodity. The net position guidelines are defined in terms of standard trading units.
2. *Daily limit* is the extent to which an account may transact in a given commodity. In day one it, too, is defined in terms of contract units.

Accounts may not exceed the guidelines in either the net position or in the daily trading limit.

Figure 2-1   Guide to Reporting Levels[a]

Commodity	Quantity
Wheat	500,000 bushels
Corn	500,000 bushels
Soybeans	500,000 bushels
Oats	200,000 bushels
Rye	200,000 bushels
Barley	200,000 bushels
Flaxseed	200,000 bushels
Cotton	5,000 bales
Silver bullion	100 contract units
Soybean oil	50 contract units
Soybean meal	50 contract units
Live cattle	50 contract units
Hogs	50 contract units
Sugar	50 contract units
Copper	50 contract units
Gold	50 contract units
Silver coins	50 contract units
All others	25 contract units

[a]Effective June 1, 1977, the quantities fixed for the purpose of reports filed according to Parts 17 and 18 of the Regulations under the Commodity Exchange Act.

Figure 2-2   Commodity Futures Trading Commission's Speculative Limits on Position and Daily Trading Under the Commodity Exchange Act (August 20, 1976)[a]

	Net Position Limits— Long or Short in One Market		Daily Trading Limits on Purchases or on Sales in One Market	
Commodity	One Future	All Futures Combined	One Future	All Futures Combined
Oats, barley flaxseed	2,000,000 bushels in one grain	2,000,000 bushels[b] in one grain	2,000,000 bushels in one grain	2,000,000 bushels[b] in one grain
Rye	500,000 bushels	500,000 bushels	500,000 bushels	500,000 bushels
Corn, wheat, soybeans	3,000,000 bushels	3,000,000 bushels	3,000,000 bushels	3,000,000 bushels
Cotton	30,000 bales[c]	30,000 bales[c]	30,000 bales[c]	None
Eggs—shell	150 carlots	150 carlots	150 carlots	150 carlots
Potatoes: Maine round white	March future, 150 carlots April future, 150 carlots May future, 150 carlots Other futures, 300 carlots	350 carlots	March future, 150 carlots April future, 150 carlots May future, 150 carlots Other futures, 300 carlots	350 carlots
Potatoes: Idaho russet burbank	March future, 150 carlots April future, 150 carlots May future, 150 carlots Other futures, 300 carlots	350 carlots	March future, 150 carlots April future, 150 carlots May futures, 150 carlots Other futures, 300 carlots	350 carlots

[a]Limits do not apply to bona fide hedging transactions or positions. For complete information see specific sections of the Act.

[b]3,000,000 bushels if 1,000,000 bushels or more of total represent spreading or the closing of spreads in the same grain between markets.

[c]Does not apply, except during delivery month, to trades or positions that represent straddles between futures or markets.

Protecting the Investor. CFTC has determined that, effective March 16, 1977, futures commission merchants and associated persons who trade for their own accounts as well as for customers' accounts must meet certain standards:

1. The FCM must establish and enforce internal rules, procedures, and controls to ensure that all customers' orders are transmitted to the appropriate marketplace before transmitting similar orders from:

a. any proprietary, employee, or employee-related account;
b. any account in which an associated person has an interest; or
c. any other account over which the AP has a power of attorney.

2. Registered commodity representatives (also known as associated persons) may not open a commodity account for:

a. any employee of another brokerage house, without prior authorization from the other futures commission merchant,
b. an owner of more than 10-percent equity interest in the AP's brokerage firm, or
c. a member of the same household of (a) and/or (b).

3. The FCM must prevent associated persons from placing orders, directly or indirectly, with another FCM to circumvent the provisions of paragraph one.
4. The FCM must not knowingly take, directly or indirectly, the other side of any customer's order without the customer's prior consent.
5. An associated person shall not disclose the orders being held for customers unless authorized by the customer.

Hedging. The Commission also adopted a new definition of bona fide hedging transactions and position limits that became effective October 1, 1977. Hedging, as mentioned previously, is a procedure widely used in the commodity industry as a protection against the price risks inherent in the handling or processing of commodities. The Commission's revised definition:

1. includes an economic definition of hedging,
2. specifically includes general cross-hedging,
3. allows other transactions and positions as hedging on a case-by-case basis, and
4. establishes new conditions for anticipatory hedging.

All these terms are explained fully in the chapter on hedging.

Protecting the Investor. The Commission has adopted other rules to provide increased protection to customers engaged in commodity futures trading, commodity options, and leverage transactions (that is, transactions usually involving gold or silver bullion and coins that take advantage of rises or declines in the prices of precious metals).

1. *Supervision.* All commodity firms must diligently supervise their employees. FCMs in particular must meet specific supervision requirements, such as the frequent review of customer accounts. The rule does not require the prior approval of commodity-related correspondence sent to customers. It permits branch managers to be supervised by a partner, officer, or qualified supervisory individual, such as a compliance manager.
2. *Discretionary Accounts.* All FCMs are prohibited from executing trades for a customer unless the FCM has the customer's prior, specific instruction or

unless the broker has received a written power of attorney from the customer to execute trades on a discretionary basis.

3. *Advertising of Commodity Market Performance.* Instead of banning the advertisements of *simulated accounts* (accounts appearing in advertising as examples of expected performance), the Commission adopted a strict rule requiring these advertisements to contain such reservations as the limitations inherent in using simulated results as an indicator of actual performance.

   The Commission also decided against banning the advertisement of short-term *actual* results. Instead, it voted to require all such advertisements to contain a prominent warning that past results may not be indicative of future performance. Further, the Commission required any professional who advertises the profitability of past recommendations to include in the advertisement all the recommendations made within at least the past year or at least a summary of those recommendations.

4. *Risk Disclosure.* Futures commission merchants are required to furnish to each new customer a risk disclosure document, to be drafted by the CFTC. This document is explained in Chapter 5.

5. *Suitability.* Correspondingly, the Commission decided that FCMs should be required to inquire of prospective customers, by way of the risk disclosure statement, as to whether futures trading is suitable for them in light of their financial condition and needs. This practice is part of what is called the "know your customer" dictum in the brokerage business.

6. *Confirmation of Trades.* The Commission requires futures commission merchants to confirm all commodity trades in writing to the customer.

As a general "watchdog" procedure, the new act also authorizes the Commission to conduct regular investigations of the futures markets and to furnish reports of its findings to the public on a regular basis. More specifically, the Commission is required to investigate the need for legislation providing an insurance program similar to that for security customers, SIPC.

For still further customer protection, the Act requires each exchange to establish a fair and equitable procedure, through voluntary arbitration if necessary, for settling customers' claims and grievances (not in excess of $15,000) against any member or employee. An important addition to the Commodity Exchange Act enables any person to seek administrative reparation proceedings before the Commission for claims and grievances against FCMs, APs, floor brokers, trading advisors, or pool operators. Any person may file a complaint up to two years after the alleged wrong based on any violation of the amended Commodity Exchange Act. If the Commission determines that reasonable grounds exist for an investigation of the complaint, it notifies the alleged wrongdoer and arranges a hearing before an administrative law judge. The Commission's findings and order, if appealed, are reviewed only in the court of appeals as provided by the procedure under the Commodity Exchange Act.

The Teeth of the Act. The Commission, with injunctive powers, has the authority to go directly into any United States District Court to enjoin an exchange or any person from violating any of the Act's provisions or any rule, regulation, or order set forth by the Commission. If any person has engaged or is engaging in a practice that constitutes a violation, the Commission may legally direct that person to cease and desist. Further, the commission may serve not only a complaint stating the charges, but also a notice of a hearing to be held at a place designated by the Commission before an administrative law judge. Should the person named in the order fail or refuse to cease and desist within fifteen days, the period allowed for appeal, that person is guilty of a misdemeanor.

If the person is indeed found to be in deliberate violation, the Commission is authorized to assess penalties of up to $100,000 for each violation in both administrative and criminal proceedings.

COMMODITIES TODAY

The latest Act, the result of decades of legislative struggle, seems to have the strength to simultaneously restrain misconduct and yet leave the market open to the interplay between supply and demand.

Chapter 3

The Basics

At one time trading in commodities was extremely simple. Since the definition of commodities was for many years confined to agricultural products, understanding commodities was, of course, easy: A grower sold the crop for the best price as soon as it was harvested or stored it until either imminent spoilage forced a sale or until the price was right. Of course, everything was "cash on the barrel head."

Not only does the term "commodities" entail a long list of products that it never did before, but it also involves two markets, one parallel to the other—the cash and futures markets. Like so many other things these days, transacting in commodities is a bit more complicated than the "cash on the barrel head" basis of years gone by. However, you will see not only in this chapter but in most of the others that, although commodities futures trading cannot be termed simple, it is no harder than any other product subject to the law of supply of demand.

DEFINITIONS

Even given their history, commodities futures contracts are no more complicated to buy and sell than any other securities.

Commodity

A *commodity* is any product, service, financial instrument, or foreign currency that is bought and sold on a recognized commodity exchange according to a predetermined contract whose terms are defined in the rules and regulations of that exchange. Of the countless thousands of such items in the world, only some are suited for trading on an organized futures exchange, because to be sold in futures markets, commodities must enjoy competitive conditions in production as well as in distribution. At present there are approximately fifty different commodities traded on twelve different exchanges in the United States (Figure 3-1).

Futures Contracts

A futures contract trades in months that range from a year to eighteen months before the contract expires. Unlike the stock market, for which corporations decide how many stocks will be available for sale, in the commodities futures industry, no contracts exist when the trading begins. And no contracts would exist if no one was interested in trading. But as soon as a buyer finds a seller, a contract is created. All the buyer and seller recognize is that a commodity will be available and they want to speculate in price action.

Even more amazingly, the process of contract creation can go on indefinitely as long as buyers find sellers and vice versa. In fact, the number of contracts can often be larger than the actual supply that exists.

This interesting facet of the commodities market also makes establishing positions easier. As you know, going *long* in the stock market simply means buying stock; going long in commodities means—buying a futures contract that involves the possibility of accepting delivery. However, in stocks selling *short* means selling stocks before the investor actually has ownership; stocks must therefore be borrowed somewhere to cover the short position. But since contracts can be created indefinitely, selling short in commodities may involve two situations: Selling short for the purpose of making delivery or for liquidating a position.

The obvious question is: If there is only so much of a commodity to go around and if the number of contracts exceeds the available commodity supply, how are the contracts filled? Interestingly, as the delivery month nears, the number of contracts tend to decrease rather naturally. The speculators are offsetting, leaving the actual commodity dealers to deal. Those that are remaining at the time of delivery may be honored either through delivery or through offset. If the supply of a commodity is greater than the amount totaled up in all the contracts, then prices tend to drop because supply exceeds demand. The surplus of a commodity brings the buyers of contracts (the *longs*) under pressure to sell off (to *liquidate*) as many and as fast as possible. Needless to say, the speculative longs' selling behavior becomes increasingly aggressive as the delivery month approaches. Because they would have to liquidate (offset) or risk taking a delivery.

On the other hand, if the commodity is in scarce supply, then the sellers (or the *shorts*) would come under pressure to meet their obligations. In simple terms, the shorts would not have enough commodity to fill all the futures contracts. In the cash market, the price would go up, of course, because of the scarce supply. But in the futures market, whatever contracts go unfilled have to be bought back from the longs. Buying a contract back from a long is called *covering.* In such a case the longs could hold out for a favorable price—one probably a lot higher than that anticipated by the shorts.

Figure 3-1 Organized Commodity Exchanges in the United States and the Commodities Traded on Each[a]

Exchange	Commodites Traded
Chicago Board of Trade	Wheat, corn, oats, soybeans, soybean oil, soybean meal, broilers, plywood, stud lumber, silver, MTG (GIUMA), gold, 90-day commercial paper, long-term treasury bonds.
Chicago Mercantile Exchange	Live hogs, pork bellies, shell eggs, live cattle, feeder cattle
Citrus Associates of the New York Cotton Exchange, Inc.	Frozen orange concentrate
Commodity Exchange, Inc.	Copper, silver, gold
International Monetary Market	Gold, T-bills, foreign currencies, silver coins, copper
Kansas City Board of Trade	Wheat, grain sorghum
Minneapolis Grain Exchange	Wheat, oats, rye, flaxseed
New York Cocoa Exchange	Cocoa
New York Coffee & Sugar Exchange	Coffee, sugar
New York Cotton Exchange	Cotton, crude oil, propane gas
New York Mercantile Exchange	Platinum, potatoes, palladium, gold, foreign currencies, imported frozen boneless beef, industrial fuel oil
Mid American Commodity Exchange	Wheat, corn, soybeans, silver coins, gold

[a]Additional commodities may be added to the list traded on most exchanges, or those currently being traded may be discontinued. Any additions or subtractions may be made by a vote of the board of directors and/or a vote of the membership.

Since a contract is eliminated either when a delivery is actually made, when a long liquidates, or when a short covers, all contracts are eliminated—one way or the other—when trading in the delivery month ceases.

The Contract Itself

For each buyer and seller, a futures contract must exist. The contract is a highly standardized document that leaves very little open to negotiation; that is, as much as can be standardized so as to minimize details of trading is included routinely in the contract:

1. the commodity sold,
2. the quantity,
3. the grade, delivery point, and delivery period, and
4. the delivery terms.

About the only thing that has to be negotiated is the price, which is settled on the trading floor (as we will see in later chapters).

Quantity. Each commodity futures contract has a standardized unit of trading. For example, a round lot of grain is 5,000 bushels; two contracts would be 10,000 bushels. In soybean oil, 60,000 pounds constitute a contract; in soybean meal, a 100 tons. As you can also see in Figure 3-2, copper on the Commodity Exchange, Inc. (Comex) is traded in contract units of 25,000 pounds, cocoa in contracts of 30,000 pounds, and so on. Specifying the number of pounds is not necessary. Naturally, other commodities' units of trading are based on the accepted custom and usage of the industrial commodity. For instance, lumber is traded in units of board feet, potatoes in hundredweights, precious metals in troy ounces, eggs in dozens, and so on. All orders for these commodities are entered in contracts. However, when placing orders in grains, traded in multiples of 5,000 bushels, the investor must specify the number of bushels, not the number of contracts.

> *Example*: A client places an order to buy one contract of wheat, which is 5,000 bushels. The broker must enter an order to "Buy 5,000 bushels of May wheat." If the client wants to buy two contracts, the order would then read, "Buy 10,000 bushels of May wheat."

Some exchanges permit trading in *job lots,* which is trading in units smaller than a round lot. A job lot in grains, for instance, is a 1,000-bushel unit. However, job lot sales usually cannot offset or be offset by a round lot purchase; and job lot purchases cannot offset round lot sales. In other words, the purchase of five 1,000-bushel job lots cannot offset the purchase of a round lot of 5,000 bushels. Job lot purchases and sales must be offset by job lots, and round lot purchases and sales must be offset by round lots. Trading in job lots on the CBOT was suspended in October of 1966, but the Mid American Commodity Exchange trade in job lots.

Trading Hours

The hours of trading on each exchange are established by the exchange's board of directors (Figure 3-2). No transactions may take place prior to the opening bell or after the closing bell. At their discretion, the board of directors may shorten the hours or close the exchange on any day or days.

PRICE QUOTATIONS AND MINIMUM FLUCTUATIONS

Prices and fluctuations are quoted in many ways, depending on the type of commodity:

First, grains are quoted in dollars, cents, and fractions of a cent per bushel. Price changes are registered in multiples of ¼ of one cent per bushel, the equivalent of $12.50 per contract. In other words, the minimum fluctuation in the price of wheat, corn, oats and soybeans is a ¼ cent per bushel.

> *Example*: If the last transaction in May wheat was $2.50½, the *minimum* change would be to either $2.50¼ or $2.50¾. Or suppose the price of corn advances from $2.50 per bushel to $2.51. Since there are 5,000 bushels in each contract of grain, a fluctuation of 1 cent per bushel represents the dollar equivalent of $50 (5,000 bushels × $.01 = $50) per contract. Since a 1-cent fluctuation is equal to $50 per contract, a ¼-cent fluctuation is equal to $12.50 per contract (5,000 bushels × ¼ cent = $12.50). Therefore, if the price of corn advances from $2.50 to $2.50¼ per bushel, the price increase would be ¼ cent per bushel or $12.50.

Secondly, most other commodities are quoted in cents and hundredths of a cent per pound. Soybean oil, copper, cocoa, coffee, cotton, broilers, boneless beef, frozen concentrated orange juice, and sugar are quoted this way. Price changes are registered in multiples of 1/100th of a cent per pound, which is called *one point.* Since 1 cent obviously consists of 100/100ths, a fluctuation of 1 cent is equal to 100 points.

> *Example*: An increase in the price of soybean oil from 17.00 to 18.00 cents per pound would be a 1 cent per pound increase. Since there are 60,000 pounds in a contract of soybean oil, a 1 cent per pound fluctuation would be equal to $600 per contract (60,000 × $.01 = $600). Therefore, if a price change in soybean oil of 1 cent per pound is equal to $600 and 1 cent also equals 100 points, then each point in soybean oil is equal to $6.00 per contract unit.

The minimum allowable change in the price of these commodities is one point. If the last trade in soybean oil was 17.25 cents, the minimum change has to be either to 17.24 cents or 17.26 cents.

> *Example*: If the price advanced from 17.25 cents per pound, which is 17 cents and 25/100ths of a cent, to 17.50 cents, the increase is 25 points per pound. Since each point is equal to $6.00, a 25-point move means an increase of $150 per contract.

Third, eggs are quoted in cents per dozen. Price changes are registered in multiples of 5/100ths of 1 cent per dozen, the equivalent of $11.25 per contract. Since a contract of eggs contains 22,500 dozen, a fluctuation of 1 cent is equivalent to $225 per contract (22,500 dozen × $.01 = $225).

Fourth, soybean meal, unlike soybean oil, is quoted in dollars and cents per ton. Price changes are registered in multiples of 10 cents per ton, or $10 per contract. A fluctuation of $1.00 per ton in a 100-ton contract of soybean meal is the equivalent of $100 per contract (100 tons $\times$ $1 = $100).

> *Example*: If the last transaction took place at $70.20, the minimum change in price must be to at least either $70.10 or $70.30 (a 10-cent change per ton). Of if the price of soybean meal advanced from $70.20 per ton to $70.80, the 60-cent advance would represent a $60 increase on the contract, since each 10 cents is equal to $10.00 per contract.

Fifth, potatoes are quoted in dollars and cents per hundredweight. Price changes are registered in multiples of 1 cent per hundred pounds, or $5 per contract. A $1 fluctuation is equivalent to $500 per contract (500 hundredweight $\times$ $1 = $500).

Sixth, pork bellies, hogs, and live cattle are quoted in cents and fractions of a cent per pound. However, price changes are registered in multiples of 2.5/100ths of one cent per pound, which is the equivalent of $9 per contract for pork bellies, $7.50 per contract for hogs, $10 per contract for live cattle.

The arithmetic for these figures is routine. Since a pork belly contract contains 36,000 pounds, a 1-cent fluctuation is equal to $360, and a 1/100ths of one cent (or 1-point) fluctuation equals $3.60 per contract. However, the minimum fluctuation is 2.5/100 of a cent or 2½ points per pound: if 1 point is equal to $3.60 per contract, 2½ points are equal to $9 per contract. The least pork bellies prices may fluctuate is 2½ points at a time.

> *Example*: If the last transaction took place at 36 cents, the minimum amount that the pork bellies price can change is to either 36.02½ cents or 35.97½ cents. The 35.97½-cent price would be shown as 35.97 cents, and 36.02½ cents would be shown as 36.02 cents.

Finally, silver and platinum are quoted in dollars, cents, and tenths of 1 cent per troy ounce. Price changes are registered in multiples of 10/100ths of 1 cent per ounce, which comes out to $50 per contract for silver (5,000 ounces per lot) and $5 per contract for platinum (50 ounces per lot). A 1-cent fluctuation in silver is equivalent to $50 per contract (5,000 ounces $\times$ $.01 = $50). But, a fluctuation of $1 per ounce is necessary in the price of platinum to alter the price of the contract by $50 (50 ounces $\times$ $1 = $50).

Figure 3-2 Trading Facts

Commodity	Exchange	Trading Hours N.Y. Time	Contract Size	Price Quotations	Point Value	Minimum Price Change	Daily Price Limit	Daily Maximum Range
BARLEY**	WINNIPEG GRAIN	10:30 a.m. 2:15 p.m.	100 Metric Tons	cents per ton	1¢ = $1.00 per contract	10¢	$5.00	$10.00
BROILERS	CHICAGO BOARD OF TRADE	10:15 a.m. 2:05 p.m.	28,000 lbs.	¢ and 1/100¢ per lb.	$2.80 per contract	2½ points per lb.	200 points NO LIMITS AFTER FIRST NOTICE DAY	400 points*
CATTLE MIDWESTERN	CHICAGO MERCANTILE	10:05 a.m. 1:45 p.m.	40,000 lbs.	¢ and 1/100¢ per lb.	$4.00 per contract	2½ points per lb.	150 points	300 points
CATTLE (FEEDER)	CHICAGO MERCANTILE	10:05 a.m. 1:45 p.m.	42,000 lbs.	¢ and 1/100¢ per lb.	$4.20 per contract	2½ points per lb.	150 points	300 points
COCOA	NEW YORK COCOA	10:00 a.m. 3:00 p.m.	30,000 lbs.	¢ and 1/100¢ per lb.	$3.00 per contract	1 point per lb.	400 points NO LIMITS ON OR AFTER FIRST NOTICE DAY	400 points
COFFEE "C"	N.Y. COFFEE & SUGAR	10:30 a.m. 2:28 p.m.	37,500 lbs.	¢ and 1/100¢ per lb.	$3.75 per contract	1 point per lb.	200 points NO LIMITS ON OR AFTER FIRST NOTICE DAY	400 points
COPPER	COMMODITY EXCHANGE, INC.	9:50 a.m. 2:00 p.m.	25,000 lbs.	¢ and 1/100¢ per lb.	$2.50 per contract	10 points per lb.	300 points NO LIMITS ON OR AFTER FIRST NOTICE DAY	600 points*

Figure 3-2 (cont.) Trading Facts

Commodity	Exchange	Trading Hours N.Y. Time	Contract Size	Price Quotations	Point Value	Minimum Price Change	Daily Price Limit	Daily Maximum Range
CORN	CHICAGO BOARD OF TRADE	10:30 a.m. 2:15 p.m.	5,000 bushels	¢ and ¼¢ per bu.	¼¢ = $12.50 per contract	¼¢ per bu.	10¢	20¢*
COTTON No. 2	N.Y. COTTON	10:30 a.m. 3:00 p.m.	50,000 lbs.	¢ and 1/100¢ per lb.	$5.00 per contract	1 point per lb.	200 points NO LIMITS ON OR AFTER FIRST NOTICE DAY	400 points*
EGGS (SHELL)	CHICAGO MERCANTILE	10:20 a.m. 2:00 p.m.	22,500 dozen	¢ and 1/100¢ per dozen	$2.25 per contract	5 points per dozen	200 points	400 points
FLAXSEED**	WINNIPEG GRAIN	10:30 a.m. 2:15 p.m.	100 metric tons	cents per ton	1¢ = $1.00 per contract	10¢	$10.00	$20.00
GOLD	COMMODITY EXCHANGE, INC.	9:25 a.m. 2:30 p.m.	100 troy ounces	Dollars and cents per oz.	$1.00	10 points NO LIMITS ON OR AFTER DAY BEFORE FIRST NOTICE DAY	1,000 points	2,000 points
GOLD	NEW YORK MERCANTILE	9:25 a.m. 2:30 p.m.	32.15 troy oz.	Dollars and cents per oz.	$.3215	20 points NO LIMIT DURING DELIVERY MONTH	1,000 points	2,000 points*
GOLD	CHICAGO BOARD OF TRADE	9:25 a.m. 2:30 p.m.	96.45 troy oz.	Dollars and cents per oz.	$.9645	10 points NO LIMIT ON OR AFTER FIRST NOTICE DAY	1,000 points	2,000 points*

Figure 3-2 (cont.)   Trading Facts

Commodity	Exchange	Trading Hours N.Y. Time	Contract Size	Price Quotations	Point Value	Minimum Price Change	Daily Price Limit	Daily Maximum Range
GOLD	INTERNATIONAL MONETARY MARKET	9:25 a.m. 2:30 p.m.	100 troy ounces	Dollars and cents per oz.	$1.00	10 points	1,000 points	2,000 points*
						NO LIMITS ON LAST TRADING DAY		
GOLD	WINNIPEG GRAIN	9:15 a.m. 2:30 p.m.	400 oz. (Standard) 100 oz. (Centum)	Dollars and cents per oz.	$4.00 $1.00	5 points 5 points	1,000 points 1,000 points	2,000 points 2,000 points
						NO LIMITS ON LAST TRADING DAY		
HOGS	CHICAGO MERCANTILE	10:15 a.m. 1:55 p.m.	30,000 lbs.	¢ and 1/100¢ per lb.	$3.00 per contract	2½ points per lb.	150 points	300 points
LUMBER	CHICAGO MERCANTILE	10:00 a.m. 2:05 p.m.	100,000 board ft.	Dollars and ¢ per 1,000 board ft.	1¢ = $1.00	10¢ per 1,000 board ft.	$5.00 per 1,000 board ft.	$10.00 per 1,000 board ft.
OATS	CHICAGO BOARD OF TRADE	10:30 p.m. 2:15 p.m.	5,000 bushels	¢ and ¼¢ per bu.	¼¢ = $12.50 per contract	¼¢ per bu.	6¢	12¢*
ORANGE JUICE FROZEN CONCENTRATE	CITRUS ASSOCIATES OF THE N.Y. COTTON	10:15 a.m. 2:45 p.m.	15,000 lbs.	¢ and 1/100¢ per lb.	$1.50 per contract	5 points per lb.	300 points	600 points
						NO LIMIT ON OR AFTER EIGHTH DAY OF DELIVERY MONTH		

Figure 3-2 (cont'd.) Trading Facts

Commodity	Exchange	Trading Hours N.Y. Time	Contract Size	Price Quotations	Point Value	Minimum Price Change	Daily Price Limit	Daily Maximum Range
PALLADIUM	NEW YORK MERCANTILE	10:20 a.m. 12:55 p.m.	100 troy ounces	Dollars and cents per oz.	$1.00 per contract	5 points per oz. NO LIMIT ON LAST TRADING DAY	400 points	800 points
PLATINUM	NEW YORK MERCANTILE	9:45 a.m. 2:10 p.m.	50 troy ounces	Dollars and cents per oz.	50¢ per contract	10 points per oz. NO LIMIT ON LAST TRADING DAY	1,000 points	2,000 points
PLYWOOD	CHICAGO BOARD OF TRADE	10:00 a.m. 2:00 p.m.	76,032 sq. ft.	Dollars and cents per 1,000 sq. ft.	1¢ = 76¢	10¢ per 1,000 sq. ft. NO LIMIT ON OR AFTER FIRST NOTICE DAY	700 points	1,400 points
PORK BELLIES	CHICAGO MERCANTILE	10:10 a.m. 2:00 p.m.	36,000 lbs.	¢ and 1/100¢ per lb.	$3.60 per contract	2½ points per lb.	200 points	400 points
POTATOES (RUSSET)	CHICAGO MERCANTILE	10:00 a.m. 1:50 p.m.	80,000 lbs. (800 cwt.)	Dollars and cents per 100 lbs.	$8.00 per contract	1¢ per cwt.	50¢	100¢
POTATOES (MAINE)	NEW YORK MERCANTILE	10:00 a.m. 2:00 p.m.	50,000 lbs. (500 cwt.)	Dollars and cents per 100 lbs.	$5.00 per contract	1¢ per cwt. NO LIMIT ON LAST TRADING DAY	50¢	100¢
PROPANE	LPG ASSOCIATES OF THE N.Y. COTTON	9:45 a.m. 2:35 p.m.	100,000 gallons	¢ and 1/100¢ per gal.	$10.00 per contract	1 point per gal. NO LIMIT ON LAST TRADING DAY	100 points	200 points

Figure 3-2 (cont.)   Trading Facts

Commodity	Exchange	Trading Hours N.Y. Time	Contract Size	Price Quotations	Point Value	Minimum Price Change	Daily Price Limit	Daily Maximum Range
RAPESEED**	WINNIPEG GRAIN	10:30 a.m. 2:15 p.m.	100 metric tons	cents per ton	1¢ = $1.00 per contract	10¢	$10.00	$20.00
RYE**	WINNIPEG GRAIN	10:30 a.m. 2:15 p.m.	100 metric tons	cents per ton	1¢ = $1.00 per contract	10¢	$5.00	$10.00
SILVER	CHICAGO BOARD OF TRADE	9:40 a.m. 2:25 p.m.	5,000 troy oz.	¢ and 1/100¢ per troy oz.	50¢ per contract	10 points per oz.	2,000 points NO LIMIT ON OR AFTER FIRST NOTICE DAY	4,000 points
SILVER	COMMODITY EXCHANGE, INC.	9:40 a.m. 2:15 p.m.	5,000 troy oz.	¢ and 1/100¢ per troy oz.	50¢ per contract	10 points per oz. NO LIMIT ON OR AFTER DAY PRIOR TO FIRST NOTICE DAY	2,000 points	4,000 points
SILVER COINS	NEW YORK MERCANTILE	9:35 a.m. 2:15 p.m.	$10,000 (10 bags)	Dollars per bag	$10.00 per contract	1 points per bag NO LIMIT ON LAST TRADING DAY	150 points	300 points*
SILVER COINS (U.S.)	INTERNATIONAL MONETARY MARKET	9:50 a.m. 2:25 p.m.	$5,000 (5 bags)	Dollars per bag	$5.00 per contract	2 points NO LIMIT ON LAST TRADING DAY	150 points	300 points*
SILVER COINS (Canadian)	INTERNATIONAL MONETARY MARKET	9:50 a.m. 2:25 p.m.	$5,000 (5 bags)	Dollars per bag	$5.00 per contract	2 points NO LIMIT ON LAST TRADING DAY	150 points	300 points*

Figure 3-2 (cont'd.) Trading Facts

Commodity	Exchange	Trading Hours N.Y. Time	Contract Size	Price Quotations	Point Value	Minimum Price Change	Daily Price Limit	Daily Maximum Range
SOYBEANS	CHICAGO BOARD OF TRADE	10:30 a.m. 2:15 p.m.	5,000 bushels	¢ and ¼¢ per bu.	¼¢ = $12.50 per contract	¼¢ per bu.	30¢	60¢*
SOYBEAN MEAL	CHICAGO BOARD OF TRADE	10:30 a.m. 2:15 p.m.	100 short tons	Dollars and cents per ton	$1.00 per contract	10 points per ton	1,000 points NO LIMIT ON OR AFTER FIRST NOTICE DAY	2,000 points*
SOYBEAN OIL	CHICAGO BOARD OF TRADE	10:30 a.m. 2:15 p.m.	60,000 lbs.	¢ and 1/100¢ per lb.	$6.00 per contract	1 point per lb.	100 points NO LIMIT ON OR AFTER FIRST NOTICE DAY	200 points*
SUGAR (WORLD) No. 11	N.Y. COFFEE & SUGAR	10:00 a.m. 2:43 p.m. plus call	112,000 lbs.	¢ and 1/100¢ per lb.	$11.20 per contract	1 point per lb. NO LIMIT ON AND AFTER FIRST BUSINESS DAY OF PRIOR MONTH	100 points	200 points*
SUGAR (DOMESTIC) No. 12	N.Y. COFFEE & SUGAR	10:00 a.m. 2:43 p.m. plus call	112,000 lbs.	¢ and 1/100¢ per lb.	$11.20 per contract	1 point per lb. NO LIMIT ON LAST TRADING DAY	100 points	200 points*
WHEAT	CHICAGO BOARD OF TRADE	10:30 a.m. 2:15 p.m.	5,000 bushels	¢ and ¼¢ per bu.	¼¢ = $12.50 per bu.	¼¢ per bu.	20¢	40¢*

Figure 3-2 (cont.)   Trading Facts

Commodity	Exchange	Trading Hours N.Y. Time	Contract Size	Price Quotations	Point Value	Minimum Price Change	Daily Price Limit	Daily Maximum Range
WHEAT (KC)	K.C. BOARD OF TRADE	10:30 a.m. 2:15 p.m.	5,000 bushels	¢ and ¼¢ per bu.	¼¢ = $12.50 per bu.	¼¢ per bu.	25¢	50¢
WHEAT (Minn.)	MINNEAPOLIS GRAIN	10:30 a.m. 2:15 p.m.	5,000 bushels	¢ and ⅛¢ per bu.	⅛¢ = $6.25 per bu.	⅛¢ per bu.	20¢	40¢*

March, 1977

*Variable Limits
**Canadian Funds

Figure 3-3   Sample Financial Page

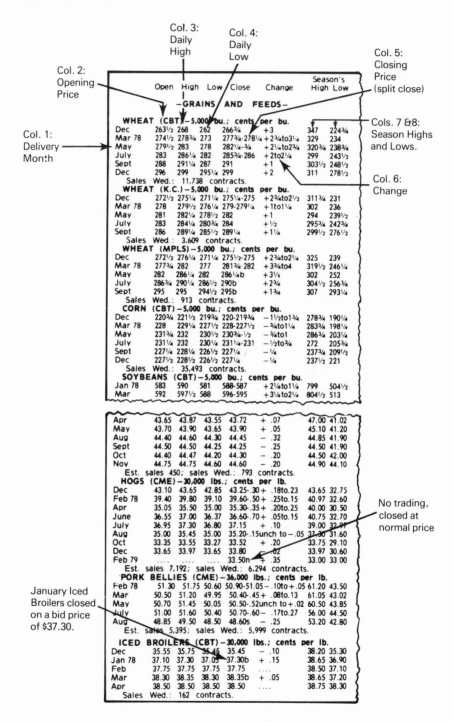

Col. 2: Opening Price

Col. 3: Daily High

Col. 4: Daily Low

Col. 5: Closing Price (split close)

Col. 1: Delivery Month

Cols. 7 &8: Season Highs and Lows.

Col. 6: Change

No trading, closed at normal price

January Iced Broilers closed on a bid price of $37.30.

	Open	High	Low	Close	Change	Season's High	Low
—GRAINS AND FEEDS—						
WHEAT (CBT)—5,000 bu.; cents per bu.						
Dec	263½	268	262	266¾	+3	347	224¾
Mar 78	274½	278¾	273	277¾-278¼	+2¾to3¼	329	234
May	279½	283	278	282¼-¾	+2¼to2¾	320¾	238¾
July	283	286¼	282	285¾-286	+2to2¼	299	243½
Sept	288	291¼	287	291	+1	303½	248½
Dec	296	299	295¼	299	+2	311	278½
Sales Wed.: 11,738 contracts.						
WHEAT (K.C.)—5,000 bu.; cents per bu.						
Dec	272½	275¼	271¼	275¼-275	+2¾to2½	311¾	231
Mar 78	278	279½	276¼	279-279¼	+1to1¼	302	236
May	281	282¼	278½	282	+1	294	239½
July	283	284¼	280¾	284	+½	295¾	242¾
Sept	286	289¼	285½	289¼	+1¼	299½	276½
Sales Wed.: 3,609 contracts.						
WHEAT (MPLS)—5,000 bu.; cents per bu.						
Dec	272½	276¼	271¼	275½-275	+2¾to2½	325	239
Mar 78	277¾	282	277	281¾-282	+3¾to4	319½	246¼
May	282	286¼	282	286¼b	+3¼	302	252
July	286¾	290¼	286½	290b	+2¾	304½	256¾
Sept	295	295	294½	295b	+1¾	307	293¼
Sales Wed.: 913 contracts.						
CORN (CBT)—5,000 bu.; cents per bu.						
Dec	220¾	221½	219¾	220-219¾	−1½to1¾	278¾	190¼
Mar 78	228	229¼	227½	228-227½	−¾to1¼	283¾	198¼
May	231¾	232	230½	230¾-½	−¾to1	286¾	203¼
July	231¼	232	230¼	231¼-231	−½to¾	272	205¾
Sept	227¼	228¼	226½	227¼	−¼	237¾	209½
Dec	227½	228½	226½	227¼	−¼	237½	221
Sales Wed.: 35,493 contracts.						
SOYBEANS (CBT)—5,000 bu.; cents per bu.						
Jan 78	583	590	581	588-587	+2¼to1¼	799	504½
Mar	592	597½	588	596-595	+3¼to2¼	804½	513

	Open	High	Low	Close	Change	High	Low
Apr	43.65	43.87	43.55	43.72	+ .07	47.00	41.02
May	43.70	43.90	43.65	43.90	+ .05	45.10	41.20
Aug	44.40	44.60	44.30	44.45	− .32	44.85	41.90
Sept	44.50	44.50	44.25	44.25	− .25	44.50	41.90
Oct	44.40	44.47	44.20	44.30	− .20	44.50	42.00
Nov	44.75	44.75	44.60	44.60	− .20	44.90	44.10
Est. sales 450; sales Wed.: 793 contracts.						
HOGS (CME)—30,000 lbs.; cents per lb.						
Dec	43.10	43.65	42.85	43.25-.30	+ .18to.23	43.65	32.75
Feb 78	39.40	39.80	39.10	39.60-.50	+ .25to.15	40.97	32.60
Apr	35.05	35.50	35.00	35.30-.35	+ .20to.25	40.00	30.50
June	36.55	37.00	36.37	36.60-.70	+ .05to.15	40.75	32.70
July	36.95	37.30	36.80	37.15	+ .10	39.00	32.97
Aug	35.00	35.45	35.00	35.20-.15	unch to − .05	37.30	31.60
Oct	33.35	33.55	33.27	33.52	+ .20	33.75	29.10
Dec	33.65	33.97	33.65	33.80	−.02	33.97	30.60
Feb 79	....	....	....	33.50n	+ .35	33.00	33.00
Est. sales 7,192; sales Wed.: 6,294 contracts.						
PORK BELLIES (CME)—36,000 lbs.; cents per lb.						
Feb 78	51.30	51.75	50.60	50.90-51.05	− .10to+.05	61.20	43.50
Mar	50.50	51.20	49.95	50.40-.45	+ .08to.13	61.05	43.02
May	50.70	51.45	50.05	50.50-.52	unch to+ .02	60.50	43.85
July	51.00	51.60	50.40	50.70-.60	− .17to.27	56.00	44.50
Aug	48.85	49.50	48.50	48.60s	− .25	53.20	42.80
Est. sales 5,395; sales Wed.: 5,999 contracts.						
ICED BROILERS (CBT)—30,000 lbs.; cents per lb.						
Dec	35.55	35.75	35.45	35.45	− .10	38.20	35.30
Jan 78	37.10	37.30	37.05	37.30b	+ .15	38.65	36.90
Feb	37.75	37.75	37.75	37.75	....	38.50	37.10
Mar	38.30	38.35	38.30	38.35b	+ .05	38.65	37.20
Apr	38.50	38.50	38.50	38.50	....	38.75	38.30
Sales Wed.: 162 contracts.						

DAILY QUOTATIONS

For each commodity that bears trading interest, the broker's quotation equipment generally carries quotations, listed in columns, as follows, reading from left to right: the previous day's closing price, the current day's opening, the high, the low, and the latest quotation. The last quotation is replaced after the close of the market by the current day's closing price. Some quotations boards also show the extreme high and low for the life of each future to date.

The quotations carried on the financial pages of newspapers and in trade papers are usually the daily openings, high, low, close, and change, or previous close, in that order, with highs and lows for the life of each future sometimes shown.

In Exhibit 3-3, the fifth column indicates the price at which the market closed. This is the last price at which each delivery traded during that day. The close may be at a single price; or it may be at two prices, in which case it is called a *split close*. A split close results when there are final trades taking place at different prices. For example, in Figure 3-3, final trades in March wheat took place at 277¾ and 278¼. Other times, the market closes on a bid or an offer (asked) price. In other words, no sales occur at the close: bid and offer prices do not, create a transaction. In such a case, the letter *a* signifies the asked price, and *b* signifies a bid; these letters appear next to the closing price. (See "Iced Broilers" in Figure 3-3.) If a particular commodity or delivery is relatively inactive or has not traded that day, the closing price is a *nominal price*, which is the average between the bid and asked prices. In such a case, the letter *n* appears next to the closing price.

The sixth column indicates the amount of price change in each delivery month from the previous trading session's close. The seventh and eighth columns indicate the highest and the lowest prices for a contract since trading began in that particular delivery month. For example, the life-of-contract high for "Jan. Sugar 1978" delivery was 11.10 cents per pound, or 11 cents and 10 mills; and the life-of-contract low was 7.70 cents per pound, or 7 cents and 70 mills.

Since price tables tend to vary among various publications, of course, you must note the column headings.

Figure 3-4   Daily Trading Limits and Maximum Daily Range

Commodity	Daily Limit	Minimum Daily Range
Barley (Winnipeg)	$5.00 per ton	$10 per ton
Boneless beef (Chicago & NY)	$1.50 per 100 lb.	$3 per 100 lb.
Broilers	2¢ per lb. (a)	4¢ per lb. (a)
Cattle (Chicago)	1½¢ per lb.	3¢ per lb.

Figure 3-4 (cont.)

Commodity	Daily Limit	Maximum Daily Range
Cocoa	4¢ per lb. (c)	4¢ per lb. (c)
Coffee	2¢ per lb. (c)	4¢ per lb. (c)
Copper	3¢ per lb. (c) (a)	6¢ per lb. (c) (a)
Corn	10¢ per bu. (a)	20¢ per bu. (a)
Cotton	2¢ per lb. (c)	2¢ per lb. (c)
Currency		
British pound	$.05 per lb. (a)	$.10 per lb. (a)
Mexican peso	$.00075 per peso (a)	$.00150 per peso (a)
Canadian dollar	$.0075 per CD (a)	$.0150 per CD (a)
Deutschemark	$.0060 per DM (a)	$.0120 per DM (a)
Swiss franc	$.0060 per SF (a)	$.0120 per SF (a)
Italian lira	$.00003 per lira (a)	$.00006 per lira (a)
Japanese yen	$.00006 per yen (a)	$.00012 per yen (a)
Dutch guilder	$.006 per guilder (a)	$.012 per guilder (a)
Eggs, shell	2¢ per doz.	4¢ per doz.
Flaxseed (Winnipeg)	$10 per ton	$20 per ton
GNMA		
Gold		
Hogs	1½¢ per lb.	3¢ per lb.
Lumber	$5 per 1000 bd. ft.	$10 per 1000 bd. ft.
Stud lumber	$5 per 1000 bd. ft. (c)	$10 per 1000 bd. ft. (c)
Milo	15¢ per lb.	30¢ per lb.
Oats	6¢ per bu. (a)	12¢ per bu. (a)
Oranges, concentrate	3¢ per lb. (e)	6¢ per lb. (e)
Palladium	$4 per oz.	$8 per oz.
Platinum	$10 per oz. (f) (a)	$20 per oz. (a) (f)
Plywood (Chicago)	$7 per 1000 sq. ft.	$14 per 1000 sq. ft.
Pork bellies	2¢ per lb.	4¢ per lb.
Potatoes (N.Y.)	50¢ per cwt. (a) (f)	$1.00 per cwt. (a) (f)
Potatoes (Chicago)	50¢ per cwt. (a)(f)	$1.00 per cwt. (a) (f)
Propane	$1 per gal.	$2.00 per gal.
Rapeseed (Winnipeg)	$10 per ton	$20 per ton
Rye (Winnipeg)	$5 per ton	$10 per ton
Silver (Chicago)	20¢ per oz. (c)	40¢ per oz. (c)
Silver (N.Y.)	20¢ per oz. (c)	40¢ per oz. (c)
Silver coins	$150 per bag (a) (f)	$300 per bag (a) (f)
Soybeans (Chicago)	30¢ per bu.	60¢ per bu.
Soybean oil	1¢ per lb. (c)	2¢ per lb. (c)
Soybean meal	$10 per ton (c)	$20 per ton (c)
Sugar	1¢ per lb. (b)	2¢ per lb. (b)
T-Bills		

(a) Variable limits
(b) Limit is removed during month preceding the delivery month
(c) Limit is removed from spot month on first notice day
(d) Limit is removed from spot month on first day of delivery month
(e) Limit is removed from spot month on eighth day of delivery month
(f) Limit for spot month is removed on last trading day of delivery month

Figure 3-5   (a) Example of Daily Trading Limit for Soybeans (30 cents

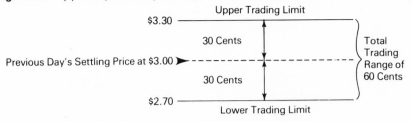

(b) Example of Daily Trading Limit for Cocoa (6 cents)

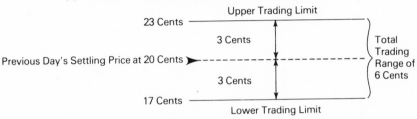

DAILY TRADING LIMITS

Keeping track of prices is important because altogether the daily fluctuation in prices is limited; transactions may take place *only* within certain price limits, fixed by the exchanges' board of directors and set forth in the exchange's rules and regulations. Depending on the applicable rules, the price of a commodity may advance and/or decline only within a prescribed range from the previous day's settlement price. Obviously, the limits, dependent on the exchange directors' decisions, vary from one exchange to another and from one commodity to another. In Figure 3-2, for example, the CBOT limits soybeans to a daily change of 30 cents a bushel, corn to 10 cents a bushel, oats to 6 cents a bushel, soybean oil to 1 cent per pound, and soybean meal to 10 dollars per ton. (See Figure 3-4 for a complete list of daily limits.)

Maximum Daily Range

In addition to limiting daily advances and declines to a specified amount, exchange directors naturally limit the range of permissible daily price fluctuations. The maximum range varies from one commodity to another, but only in two basic ways:

1. The maximum daily range between the high and the low is equal to twice the trading limit. That is, prices may rise above the previous day's settling price by the permissible limit, then decline to the settling price and go below that by the permissable limit.
2. The maximum daily range between the high and the low is equal to the trading limit. That is, prices may rise above the previous day's settling price by the

36

Figure 3-6 The Progress of a Commodity Over One Week, According to the Daily Limit of 20 cents[a]

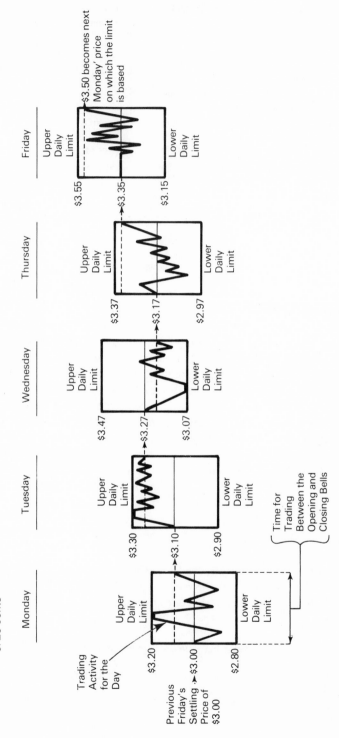

[a] Assuming a "plus-or-minus"-type maximum daily range. The same principles apply to commodities whose limits are equal to their ranges.

permissible limit, then decline only to the settling price. They cannot go below that price during that session. However, should prices rise by half or any part of the limit, they can decline to a level that would constitute the total limit. For example, a commodity whose daily trading limit and maximum daily range is 6 cents, the price could rise 2 cents above the previous day's settling price, then decline 4 cents below it and no further.

The maximum range for grains, for example, between a daily high and low is 40 cents for wheat, 60 cents for soybeans, 12 cents for oats, and 20 cents for corn. The maximum range between the day's high and low for these commodities is twice the daily limit. For other commodities, the maximum range is the same as the daily limit. For instance, the maximum range between the day's high and low for cocoa is 6 cents per pound, the same as the daily limit.

Limits prevent speculative excesses and maintain an orderly market; putting a range on the trading allows traders time to evaluate the factors influencing wide fluctuations that may not be immediately evident in the hubbub of the trading floor.

New limits are set for each trading day, based on the settling price of the day before. Figure 3-5 shows that for the start of the trading day, the upper and lower trading limits are figured from the previous day's closing price. Figure 3-6 demonstrates how a commodity may advance or decline throughout a week, by carrying over the settling price to the next day. Examine this illustration closely. Obviously, the zig-zagging line representing the day's trading can do whatever it wants within the limits. But on Monday, the price hit the upper limit of $3.20 and stayed there. It did the same Tuesday. Wednesday it hit the lower limit and sat there. Thursday it stayed well within both limits, but Friday it neither rose nor sank for approximately half the day before coming active and closing for the week at an all-week high of $3.50. Had the exchange not set limits, the price of the commodity could have skyrocketed early in the week. Or it might have plummeted on Wednesday.

A natural question at this point is why shouldn't the price be allowed to take its "natural" course according to supply and demand? The presence of superimposed limits seems to be a curtailment of free trade. Besides precluding the possibility of foul play, the limits regulate the trading in such a way as to avoid freakish behavior. In most cases, surges of trading, such as occurred in one direction on Monday and Tuesday and in another direction on Wednesday, should not be allowed to set off radical behavior. The market can still advance or decline "naturally," but with the restraint that comes of experience.

However, under certain circumstances, a limit can become an artificial restraint on a commodity that is advancing rapidly on its own merit and not as the result of extraordinary and temporary circumstances. In recognition of this possibility, some exchanges allow greater-than-normal limits during such periods of extended price volatility. These *variable daily price limits* occur in all or specific commodities, and they are subject to the approval of the board of directors or managers of the exchanges. The exchanges that allow variable limits are:

1. Chicago Board of Trade
2. International Monetary Market
3. New York Coffee and Sugar Exchange
4. New York Cotton Exchange
5. New York Mercantile Exchange

To illustrate the mechanics of the variable limits, the Chicago Board of Trade's provision states:

If three or more contracts within a crop year (or all contracts in a crop year if there *are less than three open contracts*) *close* on the limit bid for three successive business days, then the limit becomes 150 percent of the current level for all contract months and remains there for three successive business days.

If three or more contract months (or all contracts in a crop year if there *are less than three open contracts*) in a given crop year close on the limit bid for the next three business days or on the limit sellers for three successive business days, then the limits will *remain* at 150 percent of the original level for *another three day period.*

The limits would remain at 150 percent for successive periods of three business days *until* three or more contracts in a crop year (or all contracts in a crop year if there are less than three open contracts) *do not close* at the limit on one day during that period. If *at anytime during* a three-day business period, the three or more contract months (or all contracts in a crop year if there are less than three open contracts) *do not close* on the limit bid or limit sellers then the limits *would revert to their original level* at the end of the three-day period.

The New York Mercantile Exchange's rules provide:

(a) If the *settling price* for *any month* shall move by the maximum permissible variation the maximum permissible variation for all months during the next business session shall be 50% above the maximum permissible variation that would otherwise be in effect.
(b) If the *settling price* for *any month* for a business session for which the maximum permissible variation has been established in accordance with (a), shall move by the maximum permissible variation in the same direction, the maximum permissible variation for all months during the next business session shall be twice the maximum permissible variation that would otherwise be in effect.
(c) Such increased permissible variation shall remain in effect for all subsequent business sessions of the Exchange until the business session following the first session at which the settling price for NO MONTH shall move by the expanded maximum permissible variation in the same direction, whereupon, the maximum permissible variation for all months shall revert to the original permissible limit.

If that kind of language sounds formidable to you, it has to be. See Figure

3-7 for a "picture" of how such a system works, at least on the CBOT. Basically, all the directors of the exchange want to do is satisfy themselves that the rapid upward (or downward) trend is a genuine trend, borne of the supply and demand counterbalance and not of a quirk in the trading.

Additionally, a trading limit should not be regarded as the end of a commodity's activity for the day as soon as the limit is hit. Activity can and often does continue at the limit, as long as there are buyers and sellers.

Trading ceases only when prices are bid up to the limit and do not meet with corresponding offers within the limit; of course, trading also ceases when prices hit the lower limit with no corresponding bids. (Obviously, when prices are rising, the demand (or the number of buyers) exceeds the supply (or the number of sellers); buyers are therefore *bidding* in a seller's market. On the other hand, declining prices mean that supply (or the number of sellers) exceeds the demand (or the number of buyers); sellers are therefore making *offers* to the buyers.) So if at either limit, the sellers stop making offers or the buyers stop submitting bids, *then* the trading ceases naturally.

At their discretion, the board of directors may also from time to time change or suspend any limit of trading.

The daily limitations on price fluctuations of certain commodities do not apply to trading the current, or *spot,* delivery month, during which time transferable notices for delivery and notices of intention to deliver may be issued. For example, the normal daily limit on soybean oil of 1 cent per pound is removed during the spot delivery month on and after the "first notice day." Though its definition varies among exchanges and commodities, the *first notice day* on the CBOT is the last business day of the month preceding the delivery month. In the case of frozen concentrated orange juice, the daily trading limit is lifted on the eighth day of the delivery month. For potatoes, the daily limit is removed on the last trading day of the delivery month.

Any removal or modification of the daily limit during the spot delivery month after the first notice day or after the specified time applies *only* to the spot delivery month. The regular daily limits remain in effect on *all other* delivery months trading at that time.

Example: On December 31, the first notice day, the daily limit on January delivery soybean meal is removed until the contract expires at the end of January. The daily limit of $10 per ton for the March, May, July, August, September, October, and December deliveries remain in effect.

ROUNDTURN RATE OF COMMISSION

Between September 4, 1973, and March 8, 1978, the commodity futures industry, as a result of antitrust and class action suits against various exchanges, phased out its minimum fixed commission rates on commodity transactions and

Figure 3-7 Example of Variable Trading Limit Due to Extended Price Volatility in Wheat on the Chicago Board of Trade: Normal Trading Limit of 20 Cents Per Bushel.[a]

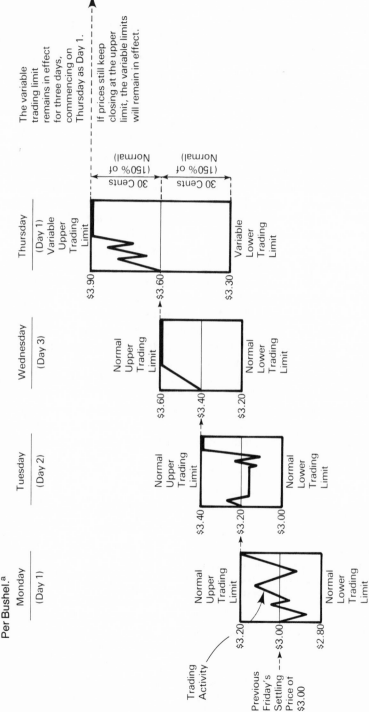

[a]Assuming, once again, a "plus-or-minus"-type limit; again, the principles apply to commodities whose limits equal their ranges.

adopted a system of negotiated commission rates. During the 4½-year phase-out period, fixed rates of commission applied only to a certain number of contracts of a particular delivery that an individual or firm may buy or sell on a particular day. Commissions were negotiated on any contracts bought or sold above the level. As of March 8, 1978, nonmember and, on certain exchanges, member rates of commission are subject to negotiation on all commodity transactions. Each exchange, however, establishes a minimum rate of commission that members must charge when executing orders for either a non-member or another member.

Because of the peculiar nature of commodities, commissions are handled peculiarly. When you buy stocks you pay a commission, and then you pay another commission when you sell those stocks. Generally, commissions in commodities are paid only after both the buying and selling transactions are completed. For this reason, commissions in commodities are referred to as *roundturn*. When you buy a contract, the commission may not be charged until you have liquidated your position by a subsequent sale in the same delivery month or until you take delivery. Conversely, if you sell in expectation of a decline in price, you are not charged a commission until the transaction is completed, that is, until the contract you initially sold is bought back or until you make delivery.

Also in contrast to stock market practices, commissions are usually established on the unit of trading rather than on the dollar value of the contract bought or sold.

> *Example:* Ms. Morris, a nonmember client buys and then sells 5,000 bushels of corn. She pays a roundturn rate of commission of $30 regardless of the price levels.

For some commodities, the roundturn rate of commission varies according to the price level.

> *Example*: The commission on coffee is set on a sliding price scale. The regular nonmember roundturn rate of commission on a contract of coffee is $70 when prices are 50.00 cents to 74.99 cents. When prices are between 75.00 cents and 149.99 cents, the commission is $80. And so the scale slides.

For commodities that have varying commission rates depending on price, roundturn commissions are based on the price of the originating trade. However, if when the contract is offset, the price range is different from the price range when the trade was originated, the commission is half the rate of each price range.

> *Example*: Mr. Bean, a nonmember, buys a contract of December coffee at 68.00 cents, then sells out his long positions at 82.00 cents. He pays a $75 roundturn rate of commission. The $75 commission is derived by adding half the

roundturn rate of $70, the rate applicable when the trade was originated within the 50- to 74.99-cent price range, to half the roundturn rate of 80, the rate when the trade was offset within the 75.00- to 150.00-cent price range.

Day Trade Commissions

Some exchanges allow for a reduced rate of commission for what is called a "day trade." A *day trade* occurs when a position is established and closed out in the same day. In such cases, the commissions are about half the normal roundturn rate.

> *Example*: The normal roundturn rate of commission for a contract of world sugar No. 11 is $62 when the price is 5.50 cents and above, but the commission for a day trade is $31.

Member Rates

When a member acts as a futures commission merchant for another member, the rate of commission is one-half of the nonmember's commission.

> *Example*: Miss Ouay, a member of the CBOT, buys and then sells a contract of wheat (or vice versa). She pays a commission of $15 per contract, which is half the nonmember rate of commission of $30.

Straddles or Spread Commissions. An *intramarket spread* or *straddle* is the purchase of one delivery and the sale of another delivery in the same commodity that is initiated at the same time and closed at the same time (see Chapter 11). On such orders, the rate of commission is higher than the commission for a net long or short position, but it is less than the commission for two contracts (even though two contracts), one long and one short, are involved.

Foreign Rates

Customers residing outside the United States (Alaska and Hawaii are considered outside), Puerto Rico, Mexico, and the Virgin Islands who wish to have orders executed on an exchange must pay a somewhat higher rate than those prescribed for residents of the mainland United States. This higher rate is due to the increased communication expense.

CONCLUSION

This chapter has only roughed out the rudiments of commodities transactions: the many items we call commodities, where they are traded, how quantities are specified, when they are traded, how their pricing works, the extent of the exchange regulations, and how commissions are charged. We have used some briefly defined terms, all of which will be discussed more fully as we go on.

Some very practical questions arise: How is a commodities account opened and handled and closed? What kind of money is needed? How is an order actually placed? What kinds of orders does an investor have to work with? Who takes care of all the criss-crossing paperwork that seems to be involved?

These and many other questions are anticipated and answered in the remaining chapters in this section.

Chapter 4

The Opening, Handling and Closing of a Commodity Account

TYPES OF COMMODITIES ACCOUNTS

CFTC regulations require that commodity accounts be divided into classes. Brokerage firms find that categorizing accounts also helps their book-keeping procedures. Although the actual names and numbers of the classes vary from one firm to another, essentially there are three types:

1. Class 1—regulated
2. Class 2—nonregulated
3. Class 3—spot cash

Class 1 Regulated Accounts. These accounts deal in all commodities that are traded on the domestic boards of trade (that is, on the domestic exchanges) and that consequently come under the control of the Commodity Futures Trading Commission.

Class 2 Nonregulated Accounts. Accounts that deal in nonregulated commodities—those that are *not* under the control of the Commission— are Class 2 accounts. Basically, these commodities are the ones traded on foreign exchanges. For example, gold or flaxseed traded on the Winnipeg exchange or cocoa, coffee, silver, or rubber traded in London are all non-regulated.

Class 3 Spot Cash Accounts. Such accounts are utilized only when an investor actually receives delivery of the cash commodity against a long futures contract or actually makes delivery against a short position during the delivery period. The resulting debit or credit balances are liquidated by transfer to or from the Class 1 or Class 2 account. Most firms discourage clients other than those whose intent is to hedge from taking delivery of spot commodities.

TYPES OF TRANSACTIONS

Transactions are also segregated into types for the purpose of determining margin (discussed in the next chapter) and of reporting.

Type 1—Regular Account. All commodity futures transactions that are *not* part of a spread (or straddle) are considered Type 1, whether they are conducted for the sake of hedging or speculating.

Type 2—Straddle Account. Since straddles/spreads qualify for lower rates of margin and commission than those for outright transactions, they must be kept separate in the records. The only exceptions to the reduced-commission rule is that intercommodity spreads and intermarket spreads are charged a full commission; they are therefore placed in the Type 1 account.

OPENING NEW ACCOUNTS

Though the details of procedure and the specific forms used in opening a new account vary from firm to firm, the general procedure is pretty much the same throughout the industry. The firm's broker should, with or without the customer's request, check the particular procedure and rules and regulations of the firm before opening an account. Since some of the firms soliciting or accepting commodity business from customers are also members of the New York Stock Exchange, for example, they are required to follow the same rules and regulations as in the opening of a stock account. Firms handling commodity business who are not members of the New York Stock Exchange are not necessarily bound by these regulations, but as a general rule they do adhere to the same basic procedures in opening an account. If the customer already has a security account with the firm, obtaining a new account number may not be necessary; the same number may be used for commodity transactions.

Know Your Customer

One such securities regulation that applies to commodities is the NYSE Rule 405. Under this, the so-called "know your customer" rule, a partner or officer of every member organization has the obligation of knowing all the essential facts relative to each customer. Rule 405 also requires a partner or officer to "supervise diligently" all accounts handled by registered representatives, whose responsibility it is to obtain the appropriate facts concerning each customer prior to the opening of an account. Each time a new account is opened, new information should be obtained directly from the customer; information received from an old account of the same customer should not be relied upon.

How much information is needed to "know" your customer? *Knowing your customers* means having enough knowledge about them to determine that they are individuals with whom you want to do business. An agency report on their moral or financial status is not necessarily called for, but someone in the organization should have a personal knowledge of the individual opening an account. If the new customer's occupation or position is one for which the NYSE has outlined special rules when handling such an account, the registered representative must obtain the proper approval and necessary papers to comply with the NYSE requirements formulated for the firm's protection.

Under no circumstances should a new account be accepted that is not desirable in every sense. To determine its desirability, the registered representative (RR) must consider the standard data along with all other information concerning the standing of the customer. A registered representative who has any doubts as to the acceptability of a particular account should refer it to a partner, officer, or branch office manager before executing any orders. The precept of *suitability,* as it relates to commodity trading, has stressed the "know your customer" principle which has been adopted by the majority of FCMs.

The CFTC has also adopted rules that require all commodity sales personnel, under the "suitability" principle, to know their customers.

PROCEDURES FOR INDIVIDUAL SPECULATIVE ACCOUNTS

When opening a new account, a registered representative should adhere to the following procedure:

1. The first step in opening an account is to fill out a *new account report* information form on the day the account is opened (see Figure 4-1). This form not only outlines the questions that should be asked on the opening of any new account (residence, occupation, citizenship, references, and age), it also contains a number of items necessary for correct handling of the account: credit information, instructions on notices and statements, and the account number. Credit references are always required; a bank reference is customary, along with at least one other reference—a business associate, friend, or customer.

This information, any necessary forms, and required legal documents

Figure 4-1   New Account Report

NEW ACCOUNT REPORT

MR.
MRS.
MISS _____
                                                  (NAME OF CUSTOMER)
SOCIAL SECURITY NUMBER OR
TAXPAYER IDENTIFYING NO. _____ . _____ CITIZEN OF _____

ADDRESSES _____
                          (BUSINESS)   (HOME)
TELEPHONES _____ CUSTOMER'S AGE, IF UNDER TWENTY-FIVE _____
                 (BUSINESS)   (HOME)
OCCUPATION AND EMPLOYER _____ POSITION _____

INTRODUCED TO REGISTERED REPRESENTATIVE BY _____ HOW LONG HAVE YOU KNOWN CLIENT? _____

NAME OF BANK REFERENCE _____

OTHER REFERENCES _____

OTHER BROKERS (IF ANY) _____

TYPE OF ACCOUNT ☐ STOCK   ☐ CASH   STOCK TO BE TRANSFERRED?   YES ☐ NO ☐ IF SO, PRINT
                ☐ COMMODITY   ☐ MARGIN   PROPER INSCRIPTION & FORWARDING ADDRESS BELOW

INITIAL TRANSACTION _____

MARGIN DEPOSITED _____

SIGNATURE CARD GIVEN TO _____

STOCK LOAN CARD GIVEN TO _____

CUSTOMER'S AGREEMENT GIVEN TO _____

CUSTOMER OF _____   (USE UNIFORM ABBREVIATIONS WHERE POSSIBLE)

_____   **NEW ACCOUNT REPORT**
(CUSTOMER'S FULL SIGNATURE FOR IDENTIFICATION PURPOSES)
                                              ASEF Form 111

IS ACCOUNT BEING OPERATED BY PERSON OTHER THAN THE OWNER? _____

IF SO, HAS PROPER POWER OF ATTORNEY BEEN EXECUTED AND PLACED ON FILE IN MAIN OFFICE? _____

IF SO, GIVE FOLLOWING INFORMATION FOR PERSON OPERATING ACCOUNT:

    (A)   NATURE OF BUSINESS _____

    (B)   BY WHICH REGULARLY EMPLOYED: _____

    (C)   ADDRESS: _____

SIGNATURE CARD SIGNED BY ALL OFFICERS, ETC.   CORPORATION—RESOLUTION: COPY OF CHARTER

WOMAN'S ACCOUNT—NAME OF HUSBAND: BY WHOM EMPLOYED: OCCUPATION

_____
_____

                        ADDITIONAL   INFORMATION

_____
_____
_____
_____
_____

DATED, _____

_____   APPROVED BY
    (CITY)   (STATE)

_____   _____
SIGNATURE OF REGISTERED REPRESENTATIVE   SIGNATURE OF PARTNER OR OFFICER

should be forwarded to a partner or officer for approval as soon as possible. The purpose of a new account report is to aid a firm in determining whether commodity trading is "suitable" for a potential client and to centralize customer data.

Figure 4-2 Customer Agreement

BROKER & CO.
INCORPORATED

CUSTOMER'S AGREEMENT

1. I agree as follows with respect to all of my accounts, in which I have an interest alone or with others, which I have opened or open in the future, with you for the purchase and sale of securities and commodities:

2. I am of full age and represent that I am not an employee of any exchange or of a Member Firm of any Exchange or the NASD, or of a bank, trust company, or insurance company and that I will promptly notify you if I become so employed.

3. All transactions for my account shall be subject to the constitution, rules, regulations, customs and usages, as the same may be constituted from time to time, of the exchange or market (and its clearing house, if any) where executed.

4. Any and all credit balances, securities, commodities or contracts relating thereto, and all other property of whatsoever kind belonging to me or in which I may have an interest held by you or carried for my accounts shall be subject to a general lien for the discharge of my obligations to you (including unmatured and contingent obligations) however arising and without regard to whether or not you have made advances with respect to such property and without notice to me may be carried in your general loans and all securities may be pledged, repledged, hypothecated or re-hypothecated, separately or in common with other securities or any other property, for the sum due to you thereon or for a greater sum and without retaining in your possession and control for delivery a like amount of similar securities or other property. At any time and from time to time you may, in your discretion, without notice to me, apply and/or transfer any securities, commodities, contracts relating thereto, cash or any other property therein, interchangeably between any of my accounts, whether individual or joint or from any of my accounts to any account guaranteed by me. You are specifically authorized to transfer to my cash account on the settlement day following a purchase made in that account, excess funds available in any of my other accounts, including but not limited to any free balances in any margin account or in any non-regulated commodities account, sufficient to make full payment of this cash purchase. I agree that any debit occurring in any of my accounts may be transferred by you at your option to my margin account.

5. I will maintain such margins as you may in your discretion require from time to time and will pay on demand any debit balance owing with respect to any of my accounts. Whenever in your discretion you deem it desirable for your protection, (and without the necessity of a margin call) including but not limited to an instance where a petition in bankruptcy or for the appointment of a receiver is filed by or against me, or an attachment is levied against my account, or in the event of notice of my death or incapacity, or in compliance with the orders of any Exchange, you may, without prior demand, tender, and without any notice of the time or place of sale, all of which are expressly waived, sell any or all securities, or commodities or contracts relating thereto which may be in your possession, or which you may be carrying for me, or buy any securities, or commodities or contracts relating thereto of which my account or accounts may be short, in order to close out in whole or in part any commitment in my behalf or you may place stop orders with respects to such securities or commodities and such sale or purchase may be made at your discretion on any Exchange or other market where such business is then transacted, or at public auction or private sale, with or without advertising and no demands, calls, tenders or notices which you may make or give in any one or more instances shall invalidate the aforesaid waivers on my part. You shall have the right to purchase for your own account any or all of the aforesaid property at any such sale, discharged of any right of redemption, which is hereby waived.

6. All orders for the purchase or sale of commodities for future delivery may be closed out by you as and when authorized or required by the Exchange where made. Against a "long" position in any commodity contract, prior to maturity thereof, and at least five business days before the first notice day of the delivery month, I will give instructions to liquidate, or place you in sufficient funds to take delivery; and in default thereof, or in the event such liquidating instructions cannot be executed under prevailing conditions, you may, without notice or demand, close out the contracts or take delivery and dispose of the commodity upon any terms and by any method which may be feasible. Against a "short" position in any commodity contract, prior to maturity thereof, and at least five business days before the last trading day of the delivery month, I will give you instructions to cover, or furnish you wih all necessary delivery documents; and in default thereof, you may without demand or notice, cover the contracts, or if orders to buy in such contracts cannot be executed under prevailing conditions, you may procure the actual commodity and make delivery thereof upon any terms and by any method which may be feasible.

7. All transactions in any of my accounts are to be paid for or required margin deposited no later than 2:00 p.m. on the settlement date.

8. I agree to pay interest and service charges upon my accounts monthly at the prevailing rate as determined by you.

9. I agree that, in giving orders to sell, all "short" sale orders will be designated as "short" and all "long" sale orders will be designated as "long" and that the designation of a sell order as "long" is a representation on my part that I own the security and, if the security is not in your possession that it is not then possible to deliver the security to you forthwith and I will deliver it on or before the settlement date.

10. Reports of the execution of orders and statements of my account shall be conclusive if not objected to in writing within five days and ten days, respectively, after transmittal to me by mail or otherwise.

11. All communications including margin calls may be sent to me at my address given you, or at such other address as I may hereafter give you in writing, and all communications so sent, whether in writing or otherwise, shall be deemed given to me personally, whether actually received or not.

12. No waiver of any provision of this agreement shall be deemed a waiver of any other provision, nor a continuing waiver of the provision or provisions so waived.

13. I understand that no provision of this agreement can be amended or waived except in writing signed by an officer of your Company, and that this agreement shall continue in force until its termination by me is acknowledged in writing by an officer of your Company; or until written notice of termination by you shall have been mailed to me at my address last given you.

14. This contract shall be governed by the laws of the State of New York, and shall inure to the benefit of your successors and assigns, and shall be binding on the undersigned, his heirs, executors, administrators and assigns. Any controversy arising out of or relating to my account, to transactions with or for me or to this agreement or the breach thereof, shall be settled by arbitration in accordance with the rules then obtaining of either the American Arbitration Association or the Board of Governors of the New York Stock Exchange as I may elect, except that any controversy arising out of or relating to transactions in commodities or contracts relating thereto, whether executed or to be executed within or outside of the United States shall be settled by arbitration in accordance with the rules then obtaining of the Exchange (if any) where the transaction took place, if within the United States, and provided such Exchange has arbitration facilities or under the rules of the American Arbitration Association as I may elect. If I do not make such election by registered mail addressed to you at your main office within five days after demand by you that I make such election, then you may make such election. Notice preliminary to, in conjunction with, or incident to such arbitration proceeding, may be sent to me by mail and personal service is hereby waived. Judgment upon any award rendered by the arbitrators may be entered in any court having jurisdiction thereof, without notice to me.

15. If any provision hereof is or at any time should become inconsistent with any present or future law, rule or regulation of any securities or commodities exchange or of any sovereign government or a regulatory body thereof and if any of these bodies have jurisdiction over the subject matter of this agreement, said provision shall be deemed to be superseded or modified to conform to such law, rule or regulation, but in all other respects this agreement shall continue and remain in full force and effect.

DATE_____ CUSTOMER'S SIGNATURE _____ _____

LENDING AGREEMENT

YOU AND ANY FIRM SUCCEEDING TO YOUR FIRM ARE HEREBY AUTHORIZED FROM TIME TO TIME TO LEND SEPARATELY OR TOGETHER WITH THE PROPERTY OF OTHERS EITHER TO YOURSELVES OR TO OTHERS ANY PROPERTY WHICH YOU MAY BE CARRYING FOR ME ON MARGIN. THIS AUTHORIZATION SHALL APPLY TO ALL ACCOUNTS CARRIED BY YOU FOR ME AND SHALL REMAIN IN FULL FORCE UNTIL WRITTEN NOTICE OF REVOCATION IS RECEIVED BY YOU AT YOUR PRINCIPAL OFFICE IN NEW YORK.

DATE_____ CUSTOMER'S SIGNATURE _____ _____

KINDLY SIGN THIS FORM IN THE TWO SIGNATURE SPACES INDICATED ABOVE. IN THE CASE OF JOINT ACCOUNTS, BOTH TENANTS SHOULD SIGN IN BOTH SIGNATURE SPACES. RETURN THIS ORIGINAL (WHITE) TO THE BACHE OFFICE WHICH SERVICES YOUR ACCOUNT. THE DUPLICATE (BUFF) SHOULD BE RETAINED FOR YOUR PERSONAL RECORDS.

2. The registered representative secures the customer's signature on the *customer agreement* (see Figure 4-2). Rule x-17, a-3 (a) (9) of Section 17 of the Securities Exchange Act of 1934 is apparently the only regulation that refers to "signature." This rule requires certain records to be kept, including the signature of the owner of a margin account. Although some member organizations rely upon the signature fixed to the customer agreement, others require an additional signature card to be completed for their protection in comparing signatures on written orders and other correspondence. If the account is opened in the name of a corporation, the registered representative should obtain and know specimen signatures of all officers empowered by the resolution of the board of directors to act on behalf of the corporation.

The customer agreement also gives the broker authority to liquidate any positions outstanding if the proper margin requirements are not met.

3. The registered representative secures the customer's signature on the *supplemental commodity customer's agreement* (see Figure 4–3). This form empowers the brokerage firm to transfer from the client's regulated commodity account to another of the client's accounts such excess funds as required either to satisfy margin requirements, to reduce or to pay in full any debit balance, and/or to reduce or to satisfy deficits in other security and/or commodity accounts. A broker may not transfer funds from one of the client's *regulated* accounts to another unless this form is on file. In addition, only an amount sufficient to satisfy a margin call or deficit may be withdrawn; this limitation is a strictly enforced CFTC regulation.

Regulations Governing the Opening of a Commodities Account

Filling out the forms and getting to know the customer, however, do not completely satisfy the CFTC's requirements on opening accounts. Certain other CFTC-inspired exchange regulations must be observed.

Two or More Accounts in the Name of One Customer. Although a customer is not expressly prohibited from opening two or more accounts, member organizations should have the client sign a form similar to ASEF Form 112 (Figure 4-4) stating that no one else has any interest in the account, that the accounts are kept separate merely for the client's convenience, and that each account unreservedly guarantees the other. Of course, this form is unnecessary if similar provisions are incorporated in the customer agreement. Information regarding additional accounts maintained by the same customer must be brought to the attention of the partner or officer for approval of any new account for that customer.

The division of commitments among two or more accounts does not relieve the commission house of the duty to report to the CFTC the name and market position of anyone who has reached the minimum reporting level in any commodity (refer to Figures 3–8 and 3–9).

Figure 4-3   Supplemental Commodity Customer's Agreement

SUPPLEMENTAL COMMODITY CUSTOMER'S AGREEMENT

Account Number _____

Branch Number _____

BROKER & CO.
INCORPORATED
NEW YORK, N.Y. 10011

Dear Sirs:

Until further notice in writing, you are hereby authorized, at any time and from time to time, without prior notice to the undersigned, to transfer from $\frac{my}{our}$ Regulated Commodity Account to any other account, held by you in which $\frac{I}{we}$ have any interest, such excess funds, equities, securities, and/or other property as in your judgment may be required for margin, or to reduce or pay in full any debit balance and/or to reduce or satisfy deficits in such other security and/or commodity accounts. By "Regulated Commodity" is meant any commodity covered by the Commodity Exchange Act at the time of such transactions. You agree, however, that within a reasonable time after making any such transfer, you will confirm the same in writing to the undersigned.

Dated ...., 19.......

....
Customer's Signature

WHITE COPY MUST BE SENT TO MAIN OFFICE.
YELLOW COPY TO BE RETAINED BY CUSTOMER.
PINK COPY TO BE FILED IN BRANCH OFFICE.

Confidential or Numbered Account. The accepted procedure of the majority of firms is to discourage the opening of any account in the name of a person other than that of the customer. However, a firm may designate an account by a number or symbol, provided that it obtains from the customer a written statement attesting to the ownership of such an account. Figure 3-5, an example of such a statement, makes provision for instructions as to where mail and other communications concerning the account are to be sent.

Mail to a Customer in Care of Agent or Attorney or Addressed to Member Organizations. The general rule is that member organizations are prohibited from sending mail, confirmations, and statements to customers

Figure 4-4 Two or More Accounts in the Name of One Client

TWO OR MORE ACCOUNTS IN THE NAME OF ONE CLIENT

Gentlemen:

The undersigned hereby advises you that his............................account and his............................account both belong entirely to him, that no one else has any interest therein, that they are kept separate for his convenience and that each account unreservedly guarantees the other.

Dated,..

....
      (City)   (State)

Yours very truly,

---

in care of an attorney or to an agent with the power of attorney, unless duplicate copies are also sent to the customers at some other address that they designate in writing. In some cases, a customer does not want to receive mail, confirmations, and statements, preferring that the attorney or agent receive all correspondence. This practice is permitted, provided that the customer so instructs the member organization in writing.

As a general rule, member organizations are also prohibited from sending mail, confirmations, and statements to customers at the address of any member organization or in care of a partner, stockholder, or employee of any member organization.

Figure 4-5 Account to be Designated By Number or Otherwise

ACCOUNT TO BE DESIGNATED BY NUMBER OR OTHERWISE

Gentlemen:

The undersigned, for his convenience, hereby requests you to designate his account on your books as Account .... Your Customer's Agreement signed by him, also covers this account; and he hereby declares that this Account .... is his account, and that he is personally responsible for it the same as if it were entered and carried on your books under his own name as signed below.

The undersigned also hereby instructs you to mail all notices of purchases and sales, statements of account and all demands or any other communication bearing upon Account .... to him at

....

....

....

or to

....

....

....

Dated,...

....
       (City)   (State)

Very truly yours,

Accounts Requiring Prior Written Consent.

Employees of the New York Stock Exchange, of member organizations, or of certain non-member organizations must obtain written permission from the NYSE before opening an account. One of the reasons for soliciting information regarding a customer's occupation and employer is to avoid a violation of NYSE Rule 407 or of the trading standards of the CFTC Regulations 155.3 (C).

NYSE RULE 407. No member or member organization shall, without the prior written consent of the employer, make:
1. A cash or margin transaction or carry a margin account in securities or commodities in which an employee of another member or member organization is directly or indirectly interested. Except in connection with transactions of an employee in Monthly Investment Plan type accounts, duplicate reports and statements shall be sent promptly to the employer.

2. A cash or margin transaction or carry a margin account in securities or commodities in which an employee of the exchange, or of any corporation of which the exchange owns the majority of the capital stock, is directly or indirectly interested.

3. A margin transaction or carry a margin account in securities or commodities in which an employee of a bank, trust company, insurance company, or of any other corporation, association, firm or individual engaged in the business of dealing, either as broker or as principal, in stocks, bonds, or other securities in any form, bills of exchange, acceptances, or other securities in any form, bills of exchange, acceptances, or other forms of commercial paper, is directly or indirectly interested.

To comply with this rule, any employee of the NYSE or any of its affiliated companies who wishes to open an account must apply for permission on a form that can be obtained from the NYSE Secretary.

Though NYSE Rule 407(3) applies to all employees of insurance companies without regard to whether they are compensated on a salary or commission basis, it is not considered applicable to independent insurance agents. For the purpose of Rule 407(3), any person who is clearly designated by the charter or bylaws of a bank, trust company, or other financial institution as an officer is not considered an employee.

Under NYSE Rule 406, no member organization shall carry an account:

> ... For a member or allied member of another member organization without the prior written consent of another general partner or officer who is a holder of voting stock in such other organization. Duplicate reports and monthly statements shall be sent to a general partner or an officer who is a holder of voting stock (other than the member or allied member for whom the account is carried) designated in such consent. All clearance transactions for a member or allied member of another member organization shall be reported by the clearing organization to a general partner or officer who has no interest in such transactions.

Briefly, Rule 406 prohibits any member firm from opening an account for another member firm, without prior written consent of another general partner of the other firm or of another holder of voting stock who is an officer of the other firm. Rule 407 explicitly forbids any employees, as defined, from transacting in the market without permission in writing from the employer. Both rules guard against the possibility of securities firms dealing in the market in such a way as to jeopardize their customer's interests.

These rules apply to transactions in commodities as well as to those in securities. In fact the Commodity Futures Act specifically defines the limitations placed on commodity future merchants and associated persons (Figure 4-6). If you refer to this figure, you will see that the intention of the limitations on the FCMs and registered representatives (RRs) is the same as that of Rules 406 and 407.

155.1 Definitions. For purposes of this part, the term "affiliated person" of a futures commission merchant means any general partner, officer, director owner of more than ten percent of the equity interest, correspondent, agent or person associated therewith, associated person or employee of the futures commission merchant, and any relative or spouse of any of the foregoing persons, or any relative of such spouse, who shares the same home as any of the foregoing persons.

155.3 Trading Standards for Futures Commission Merchants.

(a) Each futures commission merchant shall, at a minimum, establish and enforce internal rules, procedures and controls to:

(1) Insure, to the extent possible, that each order received from a customer which is executable at or near the market price is transmitted to the floor of the appropriate contract market before any order in the same commodity for any proprietary account, or any other account in which an affiliated person has an interest, or for which an affiliated person may originate orders without the prior specific consent of the account owner, is transmitted or caused to be transmitted to the floor of a contract market by any affiliated person who gains knowledge of such customer order prior to its transmission to the floor of the appropriate contract market; and

(2) Prevent affiliated persons from placing orders, directly or indirectly, with another futures commission merchant in a manner designed to circumvent the provisions of paragraph (a) (1) of this section

(c) No futures commission merchant shall knowingly handle the account of any affiliated person of another futures commission merchant *unless* the futures commission merchant:

(1) Receives written authorization from a person designated by such other futures commission merchant with responsibility for the surveillance over such account pursuant to paragraph (a) (2) of this section;

(2) Prepares immediately upon receipt of an order for such account a written record of such order, including the account identification and order number, and records thereon, by time-stamp or other timing device, the date and time, to the nearest minute, the order is received; and

(3) Transmits on a regular basis to such other futures commission merchant copies of all statements for such account and of all written records prepared upon the receipt of orders for such account pursuant to paragraph (c) (2) of this section.

(d) No affiliated person of a futures commission merchant shall have an account, directly or indirectly, with another futures commission merchant *unless*

(1) Such affiliated person receives written authorization to maintain such an account from a person designated by the futures commission merchant with which such person is affiliated with responsibility for the surveillance over such account pursuant to paragraph (a) (2) of this section; and

(2) Copies of all statements for such account and of all written records prepared by such other futures commission merchant upon receipt of orders for such account pursuant to paragraph (c) (2) of this section are transmitted on a regular basis to the futures commission merchant with which such person is affiliated.

The point of all these regulations is that neither the customer nor the RR may take advantage of their positions to an unfair extent. The customer must be "known" by the representative.

ADDITIONAL REQUIREMENTS FOR
OPENING JOINT OR BUSINESS ACCOUNTS

In opening accounts for organizations or legal entities other than individuals, additional documents are required. Of course, the forms shown in Figures 4-1, 4-2, and 4-3 must also be prepared for all these accounts.

Joint Accounts

A *joint account* is an account opened by two or more individuals who have a joint interest in the account. All basic requirements that are applicable to an individual account apply also to a joint account: Each participant must sign the individual account forms in addition to a *joint account agreement* form (Figure 4-7).

Accounts may be opened jointly in the name of a husband or wife or in the name of two or more persons, either as joint tenants "with right of survivorship" or as "tenants-in-common." Figure 4-7 is a combination of both types and gives participants the option of opening either type of account by striking out the inapplicable provision.

Right of Survivorship. In this type of account, upon the death of either or any of the joint tenants, the entire interest in the account is vested in the survivor or survivors. In such a case, the estate of the deceased has no claim on the account.

Investors are often unaware that opening a joint tenancy account with right of survivors might result in certain tax disadvantages. For instance, upon the death of a joint tenant, the question arises as to how much of the account's assets belong to the estate. Presumably, *all* the assets in the account are taxable as part of the estate, even though the decedent may have contributed little or none of the funds used for the purchase of the assets. To overcome this presumption, the decendent's estate has to prove how much the survivor or survivors contributed to the account.

In addition to the tax difficulties, other problems have arisen in connection with joint tenancy accounts with right of survivorship. In some states the law regarding the right to create this type of ownership is not clear; in other states, the statutes and court decisions bearing on the subject have created some doubt as to the validity of this form of registration. Registered representatives should not suggest that a customer open a joint account with right of

Figure 4-7   Joint Account Agreement

BROKER & CO.
INCORPORATED

NEW YORK, N.Y. 10011

JOINT ACCOUNT AGREEMENT

Gentlemen: Date ——————————————

We, the undersigned, hereby request you to open a joint trading account in our names, as to which:

Cross out either clause (a) or clause (b)

a) we are tenants in common, each of us having an undivided interest therein.

b) we are joint tenants with right of survivorship and not tenants in common, so that in case of the death of any of us, the entire account shall become the property of the survivor or survivors.

Whether we are joint tenants or tenants in common, our liability hereunder shall be joint and several and shall be binding upon our heirs, successors and assigns.

We ratify and confirm all transactions heretofore entered into for the said account by any of us.

We hereby authorize and instruct you to accept from any one of us any and all orders and instructions for and concerning the said account, as though all of us so ordered or instructed you jointly in regard to the following:

1) The purchase or sale (long or short) of securities, options, and/or commodities contracts.

2) The payment of money.

3) The registration and delivery of securities, options, and/or commodities contracts.

4) Any other action with reference to this account.

Payment of money may be made from time to time by delivering or sending to any one of us a check made payable to any of our individual order or to our joint order.

Confirmations, notices, statements of account and communications of every kind with reference to said account may be sent or given by you to any one of us.

In the event that you shall receive conflicting or inconsistent instructions from any of us, you may follow any of such instructions at your will or you may refrain from executing any of such instructions until they shall have been reconciled in writing to your satisfaction.

We will give you immediate notice in writing of the death of anyone of us. The estate of any one of us who shall have died shall be liable, and the survivor or survivors shall continue liable, jointly and severally, for any debit balance or loss in the account, or which you may sustain, by reason of the completion of transactions initiated prior to the receipt by you of written notice of the death of any one of us, or incurred in the liquidation of the account.

This agreement shall enure to the benefit of your successors and assigns and shall remain in effect until an authorized member of your firm shall acknowledge in writing the receipt of a written statement from one of us that he or she wishes to terminate the account, at which time the party giving such notice will not be bound for any further transactions made for the account thereafter, however, he or she shall remain bound for all prior transactions and for all further deliveries to any of us of any assets in the account, and all communications regarding the account.

Any controversy arising out of or relating to my account, to transactions with or for me or to this agreement or the breach thereof, shall be settled by arbitration in accordance with the American Arbitration Association or the Board of Governors of the New York Stock Exchange as I may elect. If I do not make such election by registered mail addressed to you at your main office within five days after demand by you that I make such election, then you may make such election. Judgment upon any award rendered by the arbitrators may be entered in any court having jurisdiction thereof.

——————————————————————————

——————————————————————————

——————————————————————————

WE REQUIRE TWO SIGNED COPIES — White copy must be sent to Main office.

FORM 2097A-3   Pink copy is to be retained by Branch office. Buff copy to be retained by customer.   PRINTED IN U.S.A.

survivorship or that the customer buy commodity futures with personal funds while they are registered in such an account. The customer should be advised to first consult with an attorney for the possible tax consequences, especially if there is a substantial amount involved.

Tenants-in-Common. In this type of account, each participant has a fractional interest in the account. In the event of the death of one of the tenants-in-common, the estate of the decedent continues to have the same fractional interest in the account. In an account of this type, the survivor acquires no additional interest in the account.

A joint account is sometimes formed so that one participant does the trading while not using his or her own funds or while having only a nominal interest. To transact commodities business on the Chicago Board of Trade in such an account, each participant must complete and sign one copy of the Chicago Board of Trade Regulation 1990 Letter (Figure 4-8). (This letter is not required when the participants in such a joint account are members of the same family—father, mother, sons, daughters, brothers, and sisters.) The letter gets its name from the CBOT Regulation 1990-4, which reads:

> . . . To accept or carry a joint account without determining that it is a bona fide joint account and not merely a discretionary account in which the individual or organization exercising trading authority or control has a nominal interest. Such nominal joint accounts will be considered discretionary accounts and will be subject to the requirements of this regulation.

Sole Proprietorship Company Account

When an individual is the sole proprietor of a company and wishes to open an account under the company's name, an assumed name, a copy of the certificate to do business under an assumed name must be obtained from the customer.

Partnership Accounts

A *partnership,* an association formed by two or more people to carry on a business as co-owners, is liable for all acts or representations by each partner in the course of partnership business. Generally each partner is deemed the agent for all the other partners, and, as such, is empowered to contract and bind the partnership under the rules of agency as to actual and apparent authority.

Before accepting any orders from a partner to buy or sell commodities, a registered representative should obtain a partnership agreement (Figure 4-9), signed by all of the partners. This form permits the trader to act in its behalf—that is, to give orders, receive money, issue notices, and so forth. The form also

Figure 4-8 CBOT Regulation 1990 Letter

CHICAGO BOARD OF TRADE
REGULATION 1990 LETTER

BROKER & CO.
INCORPORATED

NEW YORK, N. Y. 10011

Gentlemen:

      I have carefully examined the provisions of the document by which
I have given trading authority or control over my account to

_____   _____
        (name)   (address)

and understand fully the obligations which I have assumed by executing that
document.

      I understand that your firm is in no way responsible for any loss to
me occasioned by the actions of the individual or organization named above
and that your firm does not, by implication or otherwise, endorse the operating
methods of such individual or organization. I further understand that the Chicago
Board of Trade has no jurisdiction over a non-member who is not employed by one
of its members and that if I give to such individual or organization authority to exercise any of my rights over my account I do so at my own risk.

_____   _____
      (Date)   (Signature of Customer)

---

directs the places where all notices and communications are to be sent. It
further authorizes the member organization, in the event of the death or
retirement of any of its members, to take such proceedings, to require such
papers, and to retain such portions of the account, or to restrict transactions in
it as the member organization may think advisable for its protection.

Figure 4-9   Partnership Account Agreement

BROKER & CO.
INCORPORATED

PARTNERSHIP ACCOUNT AGREEMENT

Date: _____

BROKER & CO.
INCORPORATED
NEW YORK, N.Y. 10011

Gentlemen:

   We, the undersigned, request you to open a partnership account in the name of

_____ ,
a duly organized partnership, of which each of us is a general partner, and of which the undersigned are the sole partners. We jointly and severally authorize and instruct you to accept from
any one of us (each of us being fully authorized to act alone) any and all orders upon said account,
and to act thereon, including (but, not exclusively) any and all orders for the purchase , on cash
and/or on margin, of securities and/or commodities, for the sale of securities and/or commodities,
for the payment of money, including payments to the person giving the order, or any other action
with respect thereto.

   You are hereby further authorized to deliver, from time to time, to any one of us, securities
and/or commodities held to the credit of said account and to pay, from time to time, to any one of us,
moneys held by you to the credit of said account, and each of us likewise consents that confirmations
and notices with reference to said account may be sent or given by you to any one of us. Any one
of us, acting alone, is fully authorized to make any commitments, agreements and/or modifications
thereof, and enter into any transactions of any kind, with respect to this account.

   The authority hereby conferred shall remain in force until written notice of its revocation,
addressed to you, is delivered to your office at Wall St., New York City, and receipt thereof is
acknowledged to us in a writing signed by a partner of your firm.

   "Each of us will sign all agreements as are required in connection with transactions for said
account, all of the terms and provisions of which agreement., in addition to the provisions hereof
shall be binding upon the partnership and upon each of us."

_____

_____

STATE OF   )
COUNTY OF   ) *ss.:*
CITY OF

   On this _____ day of _____ , 19__, before me personally appeared

_____ and _____ ,
to me known and known to me to be the individuals described in and who executed the foregoing
instrument, and they duly severally acknowledged to me that they executed the same.

Corporation Accounts

When dealing with corporations as customers, member organizations must assure themselves by adequate investigation that not only the corporation but the officer desiring to open a commodities account is properly authorized to do so. Since a corporation is an artificial entity recognized as a person only through its agents or officers, who have no authority to bind the corporation merely by virtue of their offices. A corporation may act only within the scope of powers conferred on it by its corporate charter or articles of incorporation. Whenever a corporation desires to open a margin account, the provisions of the articles of incorporation should be carefully reviewed to determine if margin trading is specifically authorized. Because the member organization must have concrete evidence of the authority of the corporation and of its officers, a copy of the corporate charter or articles of incorporation—certified by the appropriate secretary of state—should be obtained.

In addition a *corporate resolution* (Figure 4-10) is required to satisfy the regulations of certain commodity exchanges; it is evidence of authorization given by the corporation to the particular person(s) named therein to act on behalf of the corporation. A corporate resolution should not be substituted for a corporate charter or articles of incorporation. Courts of law have held that a resolution reflects only an act of the directors of the corporation and does not constitute the proper authority to bind the corporation to acts not approved by the stockholders.

The Commodity Credit Division of the firm also determines whether the corporation's articles specifically provide for transactions in commodity futures. Since this judgment must be made as soon as possible, these documents should be received prior to opening the account.

Accounts with Power of Attorney. Any person having the capacity to contract in his or her own right may appoint another person to perform any act that the principal may legally perform. The same requirements and restrictions that apply to an individual as such also apply to an individual when acting as an agent. Because the law of agency governs transactions of this nature, the registered representative must be certain that the agent is carrying out the instructions of the principal and is acting within the scope of his or her authority. The only way to be certain is to require a written original power of attorney, properly executed by the principal.

Two types of power of attorney are suggested for use in connection with margin accounts: a delegation of full trading authority with privilege to withdraw money (Figure 4-11) and an authorization limited only to the purchase and sale of commodities (Figure 4-12). The representative's dealings with the agent are strictly limited to the actual authority conferred by the principal in the power of attorney. For example, member organizations cannot deliver money to an agent unless he or she is authorized to receive it.

Figure 4-10   Corporate Resolution Letter

BROKER & CO.
INCORPORATED

NEW YORK, N.Y. 10011

Gentlemen:

I hereby certify that I am the secretary of ....

a corporation, or association, organized and existing under the laws of the State of ....

that as such secretary I have custody of the records of said corporation, or association, and particularly

the record of the minutes of the meetings of the Board of Directors of said corporation, or association;

that at a certain meeting of said Board of Directors held on the ....day of ....,

19............, of which meeting all the directors of said corporation, or association, were duly notified in ac-

cordance with the by-laws of said corporation, and at which meeting a quorum of such directors was present,

the said Board of Directors passed the following resolution which is now in force:

> BE IT RESOLVED, That...
>
> is ....of this corporation, or asso-
>
> ciation, and ....who is
>
> ....thereof, or either of them, is hereby
> authorized to buy and sell for and in the name of this corporation, or association,
> on the Board of Trade of the City of Chicago, under the rules and regulations of
> said Board, such commodities for future delivery as he or they may deem for the
> best interest of this corporation, or association.
>
> BE IT FURTHER RESOLVED, That ....
> NAME
>
> ....
> MAIL ADDRESS
> who is ....of this corporation, or asso-
> TITLE
> ciation, is hereby designated as the executive officer of this corporation or asso-
> ciation, to whom written notice of each transaction shall be mailed as required by
> paragraph 203, Chapter 7, of the rules of the Board of Trade of the City of Chicago.
>
> BE IT FURTHER RESOLVED, That the secretary of this corporation, or asso-
> ciation, is hereby directed to file a certified copy of this resolution with the
> secretary of the Board of Trade of the City of Chicago, and the filing of such copy
> shall be deemed a written authorization and notice to any of the members of said
> Board through whom we transact business.
>
> BE IT FURTHER RESOLVED, That this resolution shall remain in force until
> notice of its modification or repeal has been given to the secretary of the Board of
> Trade of the City of Chicago.

WITNESS my hand and the corporate seal of said corporation this...

day of ...., 19........

> ....
>
> ....
>
> ....
> P. O. Address

NOTE . . . The executive officer designated to receive
written notices of transactions must be some-
one OTHER than a person authorized to buy
and sell for and in the name of the corporation
or association.

↑
CORPORATE
SEAL HERE

Under ordinary circumstances, the death of the principal automatically terminates the agency. The principal, however, may also revoke authorization to the agent at any time, notifying the firm in writing as provided in the power of attorney. CBOT Regulation 1991 states:

> Every trade in an account over which any individual or organization other than the person in whose name the account is carried exercises trading authority or control shall be conclusively presumed to have been made pursuant to such trading authority or control. The Power of Attorney, trading authorization or other document by which any individual or organization other than the person in whose name an account is carried exercises trading authority or control over such account can be terminated *only by a written revocation* signed by the person in whose name the account is carried or by the death of the person in whose name the account is carried.
>
> In addition to signing the power of attorney, the customer should supply a letter indicating whether or not the attorney participates in any profits accruing to the account. Certain commodity exchanges require that, when the attorney participates in profits, the member firm must notify the exchange and it must also forward to the customer a monthly equity report with open commodity positions calculated to closing prices. Hence such a letter alerts the brokerage firm to such a situation.

If transactions on Chicago Board of Trade and/or Chicago Mercantile Exchange are contemplated and the person holding the power of attorney is not a member of the same family as the customer, a copy of the Chicago Board of Trade Regulation 1900 letter (Figure 4-8) or its equivalent Chicago Mercantile Exchange Rule 942 letter must be obtained. The CBOT requires a minimum equity of $5,000 in Board of Trade commodities in any account over which trading authority or other control is exercised. The CME requires that the account be initiated with a minimum of $5,000 and maintained at a minimum of $3,750.

OTHER TYPES OF ACCOUNTS

Trade or Hedge Accounts

Anyone who handles actual commodities—individuals, proprietorships, partnerships, or corporations—usually maintain trade or hedge accounts to protect their investments. As we have said, their purpose is not to make money necessarily on the hedging process but rather to avoid losing a great portion of their entrepreneurial investments. For example, a cotton mill owner might deal in cotton futures; a feedlot operator might trade in cattle futures.

Since the CFTC has defined bona fide hedging and the Commodity Exchange Act has exempted hedgers from position limits similar to speculators, a hedge letter is required unless:

Figure 4-11   Full Trading Authorization

FULL TRADING AUTHORIZATION WITH PRIVILEGE TO
WITHDRAW MONEY AND/OR SECURITIES

Gentlemen:

The undersigned hereby authorizes .... (whose signature appears below) as his agent and attorney in fact to buy, sell (including short sales) and trade in stocks, bonds and any other securities and/or commodoities and/or contracts relating to the same on margin or otherwise in accordance with your terms and conditions for the undersigned's account and risk and in the undersigned's name, or number on your books. The undersigned hereby agrees to indemnify and hold you harmless from and to pay you promptly on demand any and all losses arising there-from or debit balance due thereon.

You are authorized to follow the instructions of .... in every respect concerning the undersigned's account with you, and make deliveries of securities and payment of moneys to him or as he may order and direct. In all matters and things aforementioned, as well as in all other things necessary or incidental to the further-ance or conduct of the account of the undersigned, the aforesaid agent and attorney in fact is authorized to act for the undersigned and in the undersigned's behalf in the same manner and with the same force and effect as the undersigned might or could do.

The undersigned hereby ratifies and confirms any and all transactions with you heretofore or hereafter made by the aforesaid agent or for the undersigned's account.

This authorization and indemnity is in addition to (and in no way limits or restricts) any rights which you may have under any other agreement or agreements between the undersigned and your firm.

This authorization and indemnity is also a continuing one and shall remain in full force and effect until revoked by the undersigned by a written notice addressd to you and delivered to your office at ...., but such revocation shall not affect any liability in any way resulting from transactions initiated prior to such revocation. This authorization and indemnity shall inure to the benefit of your present firm and of any successor firm or firms irrespective of any change or changes at any time in the personnel thereof for any cause whatsoever, and of the assigns of your present firm or any successor firm.

Dated, ...

....
      (City)   (State)

Very truly yours,

....

SIGNATURE OF AUTHORIZED AGENT:

....

---

1. such customers participate in commodity futures trading that can be identi-fied with their line of business, and
2. their commercial enterprise and financial responsibility have been satis-factorily established.

Figure 4-12   Limited Trading Authorization

TRADING AUTHORIZATION LIMITED TO PURCHASES AND
SALES OF SECURITIES AND COMMODITIES

Gentlemen:

The undersigned hereby authorizes .... (whose signature appears below) as his agent and attorney in fact to buy, sell (including short sales) and trade in stocks, bonds and any other securities and/or commodities and/or contracts relating to the same on margin or otherwise in accordance with your terms and conditions for the undersigned's account and risk and in the undersigned's name, or number on your books. The undersigned hereby agrees to indemnify and hold you harmless from and to pay you promptly on demand any and all losses arising therefrom or debit balance due thereon.

In all such purchases, sales or trades you are authorized to follow the instructions of .... in every respect concerning the undersigned's account with you; and he is authorized to act for the undersigned and in the undersigned's behalf in the same manner and with the same force and effect as the undersigned might or could do with respect to such purchases, sales or trades as well as with respect to all other things necessary or incidential to the furtherance or conduct of such purchases, sales or trades.

The undersigned hereby ratifies and confirms any and all transactions with you heretofore or hereafter made by the aforesaid agent or for the undersigned's account.

This authorization and indemnity is in addition to (and in no way limits or restricts) any rights which you may have under any other agreement or agreements between the undersigned and your firm.

This authorization and indemnity is also a continuing one and shall remain in full force and effect until revoked by the undersigned by a written notice addressed to you and delivered to your office at .... , but such revocation shall not affect any liability in any way resulting from transaction initiated prior to such revocation. This authorization and indemnity shall enure to the benefit of your present firm and of any successor firm or firms irrespective of any change or changes at any time in the personnel thereof for any cause whatsoever, and of the assigns of your present firm or any successor firm.

Dated,....................................

....
      (City)   (State)

                                   Very truly yours,

                                   ....
SIGNATURE OF AUTHORIZED AGENT

....

Certain commodity exchanges require hedge letters to support the customer's treatment as a bona fide hedge account to justify lower margin requirements.

Figure 4-13   Customer's Account Letter

CUSTOMERS' ACCOUNT

DATE_____

ABC & CO.
100 Wall Street
New York 5, New York

Gentlemen:

You are now carrying for us an account designated _____
_____. We will hereafter distinguish the trades in commodities under the Commodity Exchange Act which we transmit to you as between those for our own account and those for our customers. We request that you designate our customers' account as _____ Customers' Account.

Please be advised that all money held by you or hereafter deposited with you to margin trades made for this account, or received by you as a result of profits arising out of trades made through this account, are the funds of our customers trading in commodities under the Commodity Exchange Act.

In carrying this account you agree with us that the funds in said account will not be subject to your lien or offset for and on account of any indebtedness or liability now or hereafter owing by us to your organization otherwise than as the result of transactions made for such account, and shall not be applied by you upon any such indebtedness or liability, except to margin trades made for this account or to pay losses arising out of trades made for this account.

We shall appreciate your confirming this agreement by signing and returning to us the enclosed copy of this letter.

Very truly yours,

(CUSTOMER'S NAME)

_____

We acknowledge receipt of the original of which the above is a copy and agree that the funds held in this account will not be subject to lien or offset.

_____
ABC & CO.

Guaranteed Accounts

A *guaranteed account* is one whose margin requirements are guaranteed by surplus funds in another customer's account. The excess in the guarantor's account may be used—on either a limited or unlimited basis—as margin for transactions in the guaranteed account. The guarantor, however, must sign a *guaranteed account form* (Figure 4-14).

If the guaranteed account effects a transaction that requires additional margin and, in reliance of the guarantee, takes advantage of the excess in the guarantor's account, the broker must keep a memorandum record of such deductions. The excess in the guarantor's account is reduced by the amount required to cover the margin for the transaction in the guaranteed account. This "borrowed" amount may not be decreased in the guaranteed account—that is, it may not be returned to the guarantor's account—until the guaranteed account has a surplus that satisfies its own margin requirements after all deductions.

A guarantee may not be cancelled until the guaranteed account is properly margined. For margin purposes, both accounts are figured as one account only when the guaranteed one needs protection.

Omnibus Accounts

An *omnibus account,* sometimes referred to as a *customer's account,* is an account of one futures commission merchant carried by another in which (1) the transactions of two or more persons are combined rather than designated separately and (2) the identity of individual accounts is not disclosed. When opening an omnibus account, the representative must obtain a letter similar to the one shown in Figure 4-13.

Unacceptable Accounts

Either because of their legal incapacity or because of an expressed or implied legal provision against their holding margin accounts, certain people must be considered unacceptable as commodities customers. The registered representative must be careful when dealing with the following:

1. *Minors.* In most states, people who have not turned twenty-one do not have the legal capacity to contract. An account should not be opened for anyone not of age, even if that person is married, self-supporting, and independent of parental control. A customer who is a minor may repudiate any contracts, including a contract to buy or sell commodities, during his or her minority or within a reasonable time after reaching majority.
2. *Incompetents.* Persons legally adjudged to be insane or incompetent have no legal capacity to contract.

Figure 4-14 Guarantee of Account

BROKER & CO.
INCORPORATED

NEW YORK, N.Y. 10011

GUARANTY OF ACCOUNT

N. Y. S. E. COPY

Gentlemen ·

In consideration of your opening, now or hereafter, and/or continuing, an account or accounts (which, separately or jointly, with any and all renewals thereof, are hereinafter referred to as "said guaranteed account"), with.. ....(hereinafter referred to as the "customer"), or otherwise giving credit in said guaranteed account to said customer, on such terms and conditions as may, from time to time, be agreed to between you and the customer (notice of which is hereby waived), I hereby unconditionally agree to pay to you, on demand, any indebtedness (which term "indebtedness" as used herein also includes interest) which may now or hereafter be owing to you by the customer on said guaranteed account.

I hereby waive notice of acceptance by you of this guaranty, as well as demand, notice of default, and all other notices and confirmations concerning said guaranteed account, including any notices as to the current condition of said guaranteed account, as to any changes therein and as to the manner of conducting or closing the same or otherwise. I also waive any right to require that action be first brought against the customer or any other guarantor of said guaranteed account or that resort be first had to any securities and/or other property and equities in said guaranteed account.

I agree that this guaranty is a continuing one and shall cover any present indebtedness in the guaranteed account, and also all indebtednesses (including indebtednesses on any reopenings of the guaranteed account after it may have been closed or inactive) that may hereafter be created. This guaranty shall continue in full force until you shall receive written notice of cancellation bearing my signature; I, my legal representatives, successors and assigns, shall be and remain fully liable, also, for any indebtedness incurred by the customer after my death or attempted cancellation of this guaranty, but before you have notice of such death or attempted cancellation. I also agree that I shall be liable for any losses incurred in liquidating said guaranteed account during a reasonable time subsequent to your receipt of such notice.

I consent and agree that this guaranty shall be effective not only with respect to said guaranteed account, but also with respect to any and all renewals; that said guaranteed account may be changed from time to time by the purchase and/or sale and/or exchange and/or delivery of securities or other property, or by payments by or to, or upon the order of the customer. I consent and agree that said guaranteed account may be closed out by you at any time, and that you may otherwise, also, deal freely with the customer with respect to said guaranteed account and transactions therein, without notice to me, all without in any way affecting my obligations hereunder.

I agree that as collateral security for this guaranty, and without affecting my obligations hereunder, you may hold any and all securities and/or other property and equities that you may at any time be carrying for me, and you shall have a lien thereon for the amount of the indebtedness in said guaranteed account; also that you may in your discretion transfer to said guaranteed account any equity, or securities, or other property that you may be carrying in any of my accounts, and that you may repledge or rehypothecate any of my securities or other property so transferred by you, separately or together with other securities or property, for more than the amount due you on the guaranteed account, without having in your possession or subject to your control for delivery, securities or other property of the same kind and amount. You shall at no time be required to return to me the identical securities or other property transferred by you, but only securities or other property of the same kind and amount and then only to the extent that said securities or other property shall not have been used by you in payment of any indebtedness due you from the customer.

I agree that the assertion or enforcement by you of said lien or of said right to transfer my equity, securities or other property shall neither release nor affect this guaranty or my liability for the indebtedness guaranteed. I agree that any proceedings on your part to enforce this guaranty shall not cancel, release or otherwise affect the above lien or your right to transfer my equity, securities or other property, but that you shall at all times have and possess both remedies, as well as any other remedies, at law or in equity, for your full protection, all or any of which you may pursue concurrently.

I agree that no agreement on your behalf to waive or modify this guaranty or any provision thereof shall be valid or binding unless evidenced by a writing signed by a partner of your firm.

I agree that this guaranty and its enforcement shall be governed by the laws of the State of New York. Any controversy between you and me arising out of, or relating to this contract, or the breach thereof, shall be determined by arbitration, in accordance with the rules, then obtaining, of either the Arbitration Committee of the Chamber of Commerce of the State of New York, or the American Arbitration Association, or the Arbitration Committee of the New York Stock Exchange, as I may elect. If I do not make such election by registered mail addressed to you at your main office within five (5) days after receipt of notification from you requesting such election, then you may make such election. Any arbitration hereunder shall be before three (3) arbitrators, and the award of the arbitrators, or a majority of them, shall be final, and judgment upon the award rendered may be entered in any Court, State or Federal, having jurisdiction. I agree that notices of, and in, any such arbitration may be sent to me by mail, and waive personal service thereof.

Whenever the first person singular is used herein, it shall include the plural, and if this guaranty is signed by more than one individual, our liability hereunder shall be joint and several.

This guaranty shall inure to the benefit of your firm as now constituted and to any successor firm or firms that may take over or continue your business and/or any of the guaranteed accounts and to the individual partners and assigns of your firm or of any such successor firm and their respective legal representatives, and shall be binding on me, and on my estate and legal representatives in the event of my death or incapacity, and whether or not an executor, administrator, guardian, committee, trustee, or other representative has been appointed for my estate.

WITNESS my hand and seal this...day of..., 19..............

State of	⎫ *ss.:*	....(L.S.)
County of	⎭	....(L.S.)

NOTARY SEAL

On this................day of.., 19 ...., before me personally appeared................................... ...., to me known and known to me to be the individual described in and who executed the foregoing instrument, and duly acknowledged to me that he executed the same.

10–37

(Notary sign here)
....

(Commission expires)

67

3. *Fiduciaries.* Margin accounts should not be opened for administrators, custodians, executors, guardians, trustees, or any other persons acting in a fiduciary capacity. If a fiduciary who desires to open a margin account presents a will or trust instrument specifically authorizing margin transactions, the matter should be referred to legal counsel.

TRANSFERRING (TRADING) ACCOUNTS

Generally, all purchases and sales of any futures contracts are executed openly and competitively; that is, transactions take place as brokers cry out their bids and offers in the trading pit during the regular trading hours as prescribed by the exchange for the given contract market. Competitive executions are required by the CFTC as well as by the exchanges themselves.

The only exception to this requirement are *transfer (office) trades* or trades that involve an exchange of futures for actual commodities. Such trades are known as *ex-pit transactions* because they are transactions that do not have to be made by open outcry of bids and offers in the trading pit or "rings." The transfer of accounts is initiated by a customer who wishes to switch an account or accounts from one brokerage firm to another; to do so, the customer must send written instructions to the brokers of both companies.

In authorizing the exchange of future contracts from one house to another, the customer incurs extra commission expenses. In other words, to transfer a client's open positions, the firm carrying the open positions must sell all the long contracts and buy in all the short contracts; correspondingly, the firm taking over the account picks up the contracts at the original purchase prices. All such trades are conducted ex-pit and at the original prices. Though they do not have to be transacted competitively, these trades are carded and cleared in the usual manner (Chapter 7 explains the functions of the clearing house). The firm losing the account gives the customer a confirmation and statement showing the closing out of the account, charges the regular commission, and issues a check to the other firm for the cash balance in the customer's account. The new firm must *also* charge the regular commission when the trade is completed. Because of this double commission expense, investors usually do not transfer accounts with open commitments.

HANDLING AN ACCOUNT

The Duties of the Broker to the Customer

All the federal regulation, all the exchange rules and regulations, all the policies and practices discussed so far have one overriding purpose: to maintain an orderly commodities market. To accomplish this purpose, the government, the exchanges, and all the many dedicated people who work in the marketplace strive to keep the customer's interest "up front." Failure on any level to protect the commodities customer's interests can lead eventually to the abuse of privileged information and the misuse of customer's funds. And such practices lend themselves to the ultimate breakdown of an orderly market, which in turn benefits no one.

The primary duty of the broker to the customer, therefore, is to handle the account merely as an executor of the client's will. Only on rare occasions should the firm's representative take the responsibility of using the client's funds at his or her own discretion. Accordingly, the CBOT's Rule 151 reads:

> ... no member, registered partnership, or registered corporation shall permit any employee, whether member or nonmember, to exercise discretion in the handling of any transaction for a customer for execution on this Exchange, unless prior written authorization for the exercise of such discretion has been received and unless each such transaction is specifically approved in writing by the employer on the day the transaction is made.

The CME has a similar rule. Obviously, the discretionary use of a client's funds is considered a grave decision, one that is made only at the top of the brokerage firm's organizational level.

Accordingly, perhaps the second most important duty of the broker is to keep the customer informed of the activity in the account. Accurate, up-to-date information not only ensures a strong working relationship between broker and client, but it also enables the customer to make better evaluations of the market and better decisions for his or her account. Obviously, a strict and regular reporting procedure is essential.

Customer Statements

A record of every transaction a broker makes for a customer is entered into the account record; these entries are made immediately upon the completion of the transaction and on the same day as the transaction. At the end of the month, the broker sends a copy of the account record to the customer. In addition, the broker reports the outcome of each transaction to the client immediately, in writing and/or verbally.

Confirmations. Upon the execution of an order, the broker usually reports verbally to the customer; he or she also mails out a *written confirmation* of the transaction on the same day as the trade. The written confirmation, or *confirm,* must indicate:

1. what commodity was bought or sold,
2. the exchange on which the order was executed,
3. the quantity,
4. the contract maturity (delivery month), and
5. the price.

The confirm must also, according to exchange rules, either state the name of the other party to the transaction or contain the words, "Name of other party to contract furnished on request."

A broker must issue a confirm when a client first purchases a contract; and he or she must issue *another* one when the client sells the contract (see Figures 4-15 and 4-16).

> *Example*: Mr. Kawn buys 5,000 bushels of July corn at $1.42 on March 6. The broker mails him a written confirmation on the day of the order's execution. Mr. Kawn then offsets his original purchase by a subsequent sale of 5,000 bushels of July corn at $1.45½ on March 22. The broker sends out *another* written confirmation of the trade, again on the same day.

Purchase and Sale (P&S) Statement.   Whenever a client offsets a position, the contract is said to be *closed out.* In other words, whenever a customer either sells a contract to offset (or close out) a long position or buys one to offset a short position, the transaction calls for additional documentation. In addition to the other confirmations, a *purchase and sale (P&S) statement* must be mailed to the customer; this statement shows:

1. the quantities bought and sold,
2. the prices of the position's acquisition and close-out,
3. the gross profit (or loss) on the price difference.
4. the commission charges, and
5. the net credit (or debit) on the transactions.

> *Example*: When Mr. Kawn offsets his short position by selling 5,000 bushels of July corn at $1.45½ on March 22 (see the previous example), he realized a gross profit of 3½ cents per bushel or $175 per contract. The roundturn commission is $22, which must be deducted from the gross profit, for a net profit of $153. This net amount is credited to Mr. Kawn's account.
>
> Shortly after March 22, Mr. Kawn will receive in the mail not only the written confirmation of the closeout sale transaction (as shown in Figure 4-16) but also the P&S statement for the close-out (as shown in Figure 4-17).

All during the month, of course, the broker keeps close track of all transactions, noting them immediately as they occur and issuing the proper confirmations. At the end of the month, making up the customer's statement is a simple matter of retyping the logged transactions and relevant information onto a standard form.

The monthly statement, however, is more than a simple record-keeping device. It is more like a living history of the account. When either the broker or the customer reviews the statement, the trends, the errors, the successes, the right and the wrong guesses can all be reviewed as lessons for future decisions in the marketplace. It is therefore worthwhile to review the sample statement in Figure 4-18, to get a feel for what can be derived from this report for June of 1978.

Figure 4-15 Written Confirmation of Trade (Purchase)

BROKER & CO.
INCORPORATED

NEW YORK, N.Y. 10011

MEMBERS NEW YORK STOCK EXCHANGE
AMERICAN STOCK EXCHANGE TORONTO STOCK EXCHANGE
AND OTHER LEADING STOCK AND COMMODITY EXCHANGES

NOTIFICATION OF **COMMODITY**
TRANSACTION

P = Statement of
    Purchase & Sale
C = Confirmation

* ★ SEE REVERSE SIDE ★ *

WE HAVE DEBITED OR CREDITED YOUR ACCOUNT WITH THE AMOUNT SHOWN IN THE
NET AMOUNT COLUMN, RESULTING FROM YOUR PURCHASE AND SALE AS FOLLOWS:

DATE	QUANTITY BOUGHT	QUANTITY SOLD	DESCRIPTION	MKT	C L	PRICE	T P	O P	DIFFERENCE	FEES	COMMISSION	NET AMOUNT
032279	5M		BUS JULY CORN	01	1	142		1C				

| AB | 12345 | 9 | | | RATE OF EXCHANGE | U.S. EQUIVALENT | Mar 06 79 |
| OFF | ACCOUNT NUMBER | R.R. | | | | | MONTH DAY YEAR |

FOREIGN TRANSACTIONS ONLY

NAME OF OTHER PARTY IN CONTRACT
FURNISHED ON REQUEST

FORM
936-5

As indicated above we have this day **BOUGHT** OR **SOLD** for your account and
risk, subject to the By-Laws, Rules, Regulations and Customs as now existing or
hereafter amended or adopted, of the Exchange where the transaction was made and
its Clearing House, and subject to all applicable Federal and State laws and to the
regulations of any Government agency having authority with respect thereto:

71

Figure 4-16 Written Confirmation of Trade (Sale)

BROKER & CO.
INCORPORATED

NEW YORK, N.Y. 10011

MEMBERS NEW YORK STOCK EXCHANGE
AMERICAN STOCK EXCHANGE · TORONTO STOCK EXCHANGE
AND OTHER LEADING STOCK AND COMMODITY EXCHANGES

NOTIFICATION OF **COMMODITY** TRANSACTION

P = Statement of
C = Purchase & Sale
    = Confirmation

* * SEE REVERSE SIDE *

WE HAVE DEBITED OR CREDITED YOUR ACCOUNT WITH THE AMOUNT SHOWN IN THE
NET AMOUNT COLUMN, RESULTING FROM YOUR PURCHASE AND SALE AS FOLLOWS

DATE	QUANTITY BOUGHT	QUANTITY SOLD	DESCRIPTION	MKT	CL	PRICE	T/P	DIFFERENCE	FEES	COMMISSION	NET AMOUNT
030679		5M	BUS JULY CORN	01	1	145½	1C				

	RATE OF EXCHANGE	U.S. EQUIVALENT
	FOREIGN TRANSACTIONS ONLY	

Mar 22 '79
MONTH DAY YEAR

AB	12345	9
OFF	ACCOUNT NUMBER	R.R.

•

FORM
936-5

NAME OF OTHER PARTY IN CONTRACT
FURNISHED ON REQUEST

As indicated above we have this day **BOUGHT** OR **SOLD** for your account and
risk, subject to the By-Laws, Rules, Regulations and Customs as now existing or
hereafter amended or adopted, of the Exchange where the transaction was made and
its Clearing House, and subject to all applicable Federal and State laws and to the
regulations of any Government agency having authority with respect thereto:

Figure 4-17 Purchase and Sale (P&S) Statement

NOTIFICATION OF **COMMODITY** TRANSACTION

BROKER & CO.
INCORPORATED
NEW YORK, N.Y. 10011

MEMBERS NEW YORK STOCK EXCHANGE
AMERICAN STOCK EXCHANGE · TORONTO STOCK EXCHANGE
AND OTHER LEADING STOCK AND COMMODITY EXCHANGES

P = Statement of
Purchase & Sale
C = Confirmation

* * SEE REVERSE SIDE *

WE HAVE DEBITED OR CREDITED YOUR ACCOUNT WITH THE AMOUNT SHOWN IN THE NET AMOUNT COLUMN, RESULTING FROM YOUR PURCHASE AND SALE AS FOLLOWS

DATE	QUANTITY		DESCRIPTION	MKT	CLT	PRICE	T	%	DIFFERENCE	FEES	COMMISSION	NET AMOUNT
	BOUGHT	SOLD										
030679	5M		BUS JULY CORN	01	1	142	1P					
032279		5M	BUS JULY CORN	01	1	145½	1P		175.00 CR		22.00	153.00 CR

RATE OF EXCHANGE   U.S. EQUIVALENT
FOREIGN TRANSACTIONS ONLY

Mar 22 '79
MONTH DAY YEAR

AB   12345   9
OFF   ACCOUNT   R.R.
      NUMBER

•

NAME OF OTHER PARTY IN CONTRACT
FURNISHED ON REQUEST

FORM
936-5

As indicated above we have this day **BOUGHT** OR **SOLD** for your account and risk, subject to the By-Laws, Rules, Regulations and Customs as now existing or hereafter amended or adopted, of the Exchange where the transaction was made and its Clearing House, and subject to all applicable Federal and State laws and to the regulations of any Government agency having authority with respect thereto:

The heading of the statement contains the name of the customer, the date of the statement, and, of course, the name of the FMC. It also includes the customer's account number.

The body of this statement is divided into five areas of information (see Figure 4-18):

Part A (Figure 4-18a) contains the activity of the month:

Line 1: The first line in the boxed-in area, dated June 2 reflects a purchase of 5,000 bushels of December wheat at 3.38½.

Line 2: On the same date, a sale of 5,000 bushels was made of December wheat at 3.28½—a day-trade.

Line 3: Also on June 2, the purchase of a contract of July iced broilers at 49.00 cents was made.

Line 4: This is the sale of one contract of July iced broilers, at 50.30 cents, which offsets the purchase four days before on June 2.

Line 5: On June 6, the customer buys one contract of September delivery of copper at 65.40 cents per pound. This is a new position.

Line 6: Another contract of copper is added in the same delivery on June 7, at 64.80 cents per pound.

Lines 7 and 8: On June 12, the customer sells one contract of June fresh eggs at 43.00 a dozen and one contract at 42.20 cents.

Line 9: This is a purchase of one contract of July 1978 fresh eggs at 46.6.

Line 10: Also on June 12, a sale of one contract of September copper at 63.70 cents is made.

Line 11: On the thirteenth, a purchase of 5,000 bushels of December wheat is made at $3.19¼.

Line 12: Another contract of July fresh eggs is sold at 46.80 cents.

Line 13: On June 22, the customer sells one contract of copper for September delivery at 59.80 cents.

Line 14: The customer makes a purchase of one contract of July delivery of iced broilers at 49.70.

Line 15: One contract, 5,000 bushels of December wheat, is sold at 3.19.

Line 16: One contract of July 1978 iced broilers is purchased on the twenty-ninth.

Part B (see Figure 4-18b):

Line 17: The balance forward reflects the money position as of the end of the previous month. In this case, the credit balance of $6,588.25 is brought forward from the May 31, 1978 statement.

Part C: In this section of the statement, all the close-outs (P&Ss) for the statement month are listed, demonstrating the P&S statement number and resultant profit or loss. All money figures reflect the net amounts after commissions and fees.

Line 18: On June 2, a purchase and a sale (a day-trade) of 5,000 bushels of December wheat resulted in a debit of $538.

Line 19: On June 6, a sale of July iced broilers at 50.30 was applied against the purchase made at 49.00 on June 2, giving the customer a profit of $339.50.

Lines 20 & 21: A close-out of two contracts of June fresh eggs, one sold at 43.00 and one at 42.20, takes place, thus offsetting the previously held long position. The result was a gain of $141.25 in one and the loss of $1,096.25 in the other.

Line 22: One contract of September copper sold on June 12 at 63.70 offset the position established by the contract bought on June 6 at 65.40. The loss is $476.50.

Line 23: On June 14, the customer sold one contract of July eggs at 46.80, applied against the contract purchased on June 12 at 46.60. The transaction had a 20-point gain. A debit of $5.00 to the account resulted due to the commission and fee charges.

Line 24: The sale of one contract of September copper on June 22 at 59.80 liquidated the purchase of the one contract at 64.80 on June 7, yielding a loss of $1,301.50.

Line 25: On June 28, the 5,000 bushels of December wheat at 3.19¼ bought on June 13 was offset by the sale of 5,000 bushels of December wheat sold at $3.19, resulting in a loss of $63.00.

June 26: The closing balance figure of a credit of $3,588.75 is the difference between the credit balance of $6,588.25 at the beginning of June and the losses on the transactions during the month of June.

Line 27: This figure is self-explanatory as it reflects the loss of all closed-out transactions for the month of June.

Line 28: This money figure is an important indicator since it allows the customer to appraise his or her trading for the year. In this case, the customer has not fared well.

Part D: This section sums up the open (or nonliquidated) contracts.

Lines 29-31: The customer should always verify this very important part of the monthly statement, checking the trades listed, their dates, the number of contracts, the commodities, and the prices. Also important is the settling prices for the commodities, which project the unrealized (or "paper") profit or loss. In this case, the open contracts show a paper profit of $555.00.

Line 32: Reflects the money figure for the total unrealized profit (or loss), should there have been more than one commodity open at the end of the month.

Line 33: This money figure shows the financial condition of the account as of the end of the month. It is the total of:

$$\begin{array}{l} \text{Actual balance in the account} \\ +(-)\,\text{Unrealized profit (loss)} \\ \hline \text{Total equity} \end{array}$$

In this case, the total equity is a credit that reflects:

	June 30 closing balance	$3,588.75
+	Unrealized profit	555.00
	Total equity	$4,143.75

In appraising this account, however, the customer should not rely on unrealized profit since it can change as the market moves. The status of the account can be fairly and accurately evaluated only on the basis of what is actually in the account, as reflected in the closing balance.

Figure 4-18 (a) A Detailed Monthly Statement

BROKER & CO.
INCORPORATED
NEW YORK, N.Y. 10011
MEMBERS NEW YORK STOCK EXCHANGE
AMERICAN STOCK EXCHANGE CHICAGO STOCK EXCHANGE
AND OTHER LEADING STOCK AND COMMODITY EXCHANGES

STATEMENT B

PERIOD ENDING

MO	DAY	YEAR
06	30	78

FORM 806 P-5

MR DAVID A REIN
6037 HALHAVEN DR.
ALEXANDRIA VA 22310

J. SMITH

KINDLY MENTION
YOUR ACCOUNT NO   R.R
AB 12345 1   09

FEDERAL IDENTIFICATION

WHEN REFERRING TO THIS
OR OTHER TRANSACTIONS.

PAGE 1

STATEMENT OF YOUR
COMMODITY A/C

* TYPE/CLASS
CLASS

DATE	QUANTITY BOUGHT	QUANTITY SOLD	DESCRIPTION	PRICE	AMOUNT DEBITED TO YOUR ACCOUNT	AMOUNT CREDITED TO YOUR ACCOUNT	NET AMOUNT
			MONTH ACTIVITY				
6/02	5M		DEC '78 WHEAT	3.36 1/2			
6/02		5M	DEC '78 WHEAT	3.28 1/2			
6/02	1		JLY '78 ICED BROILER	49.00			
6/06	1		JLY '78 ICED BROILER	50.30			
6/06	1		SEP '78 COPPER	65.40			
6/07	1		SEP '78 COPPER	64.80			
6/12	1		JUN '78 FRESH EGGS	43.00			
6/12	1		JUN '78 FRESH EGGS	42.20			
6/12	1		JLY '78 FRESH EGGS	46.60			
6/12	1		SEP '78 COPPER	63.70			
6/13	5M		DEC '78 WHEAT	3.19 1/4			
6/14	1		JLY '78 FRESH EGGS	46.80			
6/22	1		SEP '78 COPPER	59.80			
6/23	1		JLY '78 ICED BROILER	49.70			
6/28		5M	DEC '78 WHEAT	3.19			
6/29	1		JLY '78 ICED BROILER	49.80			
			BALANCE FWD 05/31/78				
6/02		5	DEC '78 WHEAT	P-5 2483	538.00		6,588.25CR.

KINDLY DIRECT INQUIRIES CONCERNING THIS STATEMENT TO THE BACHE OFFICE WHICH SERVICES YOUR ACCOUNT. SEE REVERSE SIDE.
IMPORTANT — WE URGE YOU TO PRESERVE THIS STATEMENT FOR USE IN PREPARING INCOME TAX RETURNS — IMPORTANT
FOR DESCRIPTION OF TYPE OF ACCOUNT AND EXPLANATION OF SYMBOLS USED, SEE REVERSE SIDE.

Figure 4-18 (b) The Statement Continued

BROKER & CO.
INCORPORATED
NEW YORK, N.Y. 10011
MEMBERS NEW YORK STOCK EXCHANGE
AMERICAN STOCK EXCHANGE · TORONTO STOCK EXCHANGE
AND OTHER LEADING STOCK AND COMMODITY EXCHANGES

STATEMENT C   B 4

PERIOD ENDING — MO 06 | DAY 30 | YEAR 78

KINDLY MENTION — YOUR ACCOUNT NO. AB 12345 2 — R.R. 09 — FEDERAL IDENTIFICATION — TYPE/CLASS * — CLASS

STATEMENT OF YOUR

DATE	BOUGHT	SOLD	DESCRIPTION	PRICE	AMOUNT DEBITED TO YOUR ACCOUNT	AMOUNT CREDITED TO YOUR ACCOUNT	NET AMOUNT
6/06		1	JLY '78 ICED BROILER	P-S 767		339.50	
6/12		1	JUN '78 FRESH EGGS	P-5 1138		141.25	
6/12		1	JUN '78 FRESH EGGS	P-5 1137	1,096.25		
6/12		1	SEP '78 COPPER	P-5 1139	476.50		
6/14		1	JLY '78 FRESH EGGS	P-5 1382	5.00		
6/22		1	SEP '78 COPPER	P-5 516	1,301.50		
6/28		5	DEC '78 WHEAT	P-5 1297	63.00		
			CLOSING BALANCE				3,588.75CR.
			MONTH-TO-DATE PROFIT/LOSS				2,999.50
			YEAR-TO-DATE PROFIT/LOSS				1,411.25
			OPEN CONTRACTS				
6/23	1		JLY '78 ICED BROILER	49.70			
6/29	1		JLY '78 ICED BROILER	49.80			
6/30	2		SETTLE PRICE	50.67			
			UNREALIZED PROFIT				555.00CR.
			TOT UNREALIZED PROFIT				555.00CR.
			TOT EQUITY				4,143.75CR.
							COMPLETE

FORM
808 P-5

KINDLY DIRECT INQUIRIES CONCERNING THIS STATEMENT TO THE BACHE OFFICE WHICH SERVICES YOUR ACCOUNT. SEE REVERSE SIDE.
IMPORTANT — WE URGE YOU TO PRESERVE THIS STATEMENT FOR USE IN PREPARING INCOME TAX RETURNS — IMPORTANT
FOR DESCRIPTION OF TYPE OF ACCOUNT AND EXPLANATION OF SYMBOLS USED, SEE REVERSE SIDE.

CLOSE-OUT INSTRUCTIONS

According to the Commodity Exchange Act, a speculative customer cannot be long or short in the same delivery at the same time. An FMC who executes a sale for a customer must apply that sale, on the same day, against an existing long position. The FMC must also send the customer a P&S statement showing the financial result of the transactions. Of course, the same procedure is followed when an existing short position is offset by a purchase.

Example: Miss Joy Been is long 5,000 bushels of July soybeans, and she subsequently sells 5,000 bushels of July soybeans (same commodity, same delivery month). The sale offsets her original purchase and consequently closes the position. The broker must send out a P&S.

Miss Been has also established a straddle in silver. She has gone long 50 contracts of December against a short position in 50 contracts of March. She then sells 50 contracts December; the same offsets the long position in December silver, even though the position in December silver was part of a straddle. The only way Miss Been could have maintained her straddle is by buying additional contracts in another delivery month.

She is therefore now short in the March delivery, and she has no position in the December delivery.

Sometimes the long and short positions do not balance out perfectly. If so, the client should instruct the broker as to which position the offsetting order should be applied; the customer may want to keep an older position open and close out a more recent (perhaps less profitable) position. If the client does not instruct the FMC in any way, then the FMC is obliged to apply the order against the earliest (or oldest) position in the account.

Example: Miss Been establishes a long position of 5,000 bushels of November soybeans on March 1 and another long position of 5,000 bushels of November soybeans on June 1. She then sells 5,000 bushels of November soybeans on July 1, without giving the broker any instructions as to which contract to close out. According to the law, the broker is mandated to close out the March 1 purchase because it is the earlier position—even if the position is the less profitable one to close out, and even if the close-out spells a loss to the customer.

Miss Been, however, could have specified (and generally the customer should) to the broker which position she wanted to close out. And she is entitled to close out the later, or newer, one, as long as she does not remain both long and short in the same commodity and in the same month.

ERRONEOUS REPORTS

Despite all the controls and supervisory techniques, occasionally a member organization sends out a confirmation or statement that, through a clerical error, does not reflect the true price at which an order was executed.

As long as the actual execution was at the price and quantity in accordance with the customer's order, the member organization must send out—and the customer must accept—a corrected report of the transaction, even when the erroneous report was to the customer's benefit. If the actual execution was *not* at the price and quantity specified by the customer's order, the registered representative should report the error *promptly* to a partner or officer for handling of the correction. Registered representatives (RRs) should not, in the hope that the market itself will correct the mistake, allow any time to elapse once an error is committed.

CUSTOMER GIVE-UP

A *customer give-up* is a contract transaction that is executed by one broker for the client of another broker and then "given up" to the client's regular broker. (This is not a *floor give-up,* which occurs when an independent floor broker "gives up" the names of the firms for which he or she is acting.) Generally, the order is sent over the leased wires of the first broker. The XYZ broker, for example, verifies that Mrs. Grantan is a customer of ABC Company before submitting the order for execution. The only compensation the XYZ broker receives for the courtesy is the wire toll from ABC Company for the use of the wire facilities.

DEATH OF A CUSTOMER

Because many legal complications can arise from this situation, the registered representative should consult with the firm's legal counsel before taking any action with regard to the account of a deceased customer. Many member organizations are protected from some of these legal complications by specific provisions in their customer margin agreement. For example, see paragraph 5 of Figure 4-2.

The general rule, if an individual customer dies, is to cancel all orders and instructions. The account should not, however, be liquidated, nor should any further action be taken, until instructions and necessary documents are obtained from the accredited representative of the estate (the administrator or executor).

Other special cases include:

1. *Joint tenant.* When a joint tenant dies, the survivor must present a death certificate and inheritance tax waivers before the representative can release funds. Upon presentation of such papers, the survivor may be considered the sole owner of the account.

2. *Tenant-in-common.* Upon the death of one of the participants, funds should not be released from the account unless instructions from the survivor and from the executor or administrator of the decedent's estate are obtained, together with the necessary tax waivers. If all the participants die and there are no survivors, the registered representative must obtain instructions from the executor or administrator of each decedent, together with the pertinent documents.
3. *Partner.* When a partner dies, the representative must obtain supplemental authorization from the surviving partners before executing any further orders through the partnership's account.
4. *Principal acting through a power of attorney.* The rule, well established by both common law and statute, is that the death of the principal ordinarily terminates the power of attorney, regardless of whether the agent is aware of the principal's death.

CONCLUSION

Obviously, many rules and regulations restrict the activities of both the customer and the broker. But they are all, as you can see, in the interest of maintaining fair and honest relations between the client and the firm. And they also make for an orderly market in commodities.

Without specific procedures, good faith, and the dedication of the many people in the industry, the marketplace could soon become as precarious as it once did in the twenties—possibly with the same results. Today, legislation and integrity keep the market on a steady pattern of growth, while limiting any freakish price swings.

Chapter 5

Margin Requirements and Procedures

All commodity futures transactions are *margin transactions*. In other words, futures orders are executed by brokers on the guarantee of the client to make good on the contract. The physical embodiment of that guarantee is called *margin*, which is an amount of money deposited with the broker's firm. This money, the margin, is intended to protect the seller against the buyer's default in the event of a fall in price; conversely, it is intended to protect the buyer against the seller's default in the event of a rise in price.

How much money, or the *rate of margin,* that is required of a client who wishes to establish a position in commodities depends on the exchange's regulations, on the type of commodity, on the commodity's contract value, and on its volatility. Perhaps you can see how margin requirements complement the legal requirements for an orderly market. As long as prices do not skyrocket and/or plummet completely out of hand, as long as a ceiling and a floor are put on the daily trading limits, then the amount of money deposited with the member firm *should* cover any unexpected losses on the client's part. The broker normally liquidates the contract, thus closing out the transaction, and then uses the margin in the account to make up for the loss.

If the margin has to be used to honor a contract, or if the market price causes the contract to lose dollar value, the broker will require additional margin if the client wishes to continue trading. This additional margin, called *maintenance margin,* is required—as a general rule—once the account's margin has been reduced by 25 percent or more. Obviously, it is called "maintenance" because the client need deposit only as much as is necessary to bring the account's margin up to the original requirements. The call for the maintenance margin is called a *variation* call, because a variation in the market made it necessary. If, on the other hand, the market price moves in the client's favor, the value of the contract is increased; this increase in value is considered additional equity and it belongs to the customer. Of course, additional equity also accumulates from profitable close-outs. But the position need not be closed out for the investor to enjoy the benefits of the equity. Additional value in the account belongs to the investor and may be either used for other transactions or withdrawn. The position need not be *liquidated*, or sold out, for the investor to use the equity.

> *Example*: Mr. Listalot purchases a contract (5,000 bushels) of soybeans when the margin requirement is $1,000. The price declines by 6 cents a bushel ($300 per contract). If Mr. Listalot liquidates now, the equity in his account is only $700.
>
> Since his equity is below $750—the 75-percent level required—the registered representative calls him for $300 to bring his account back to the required margin. Listalot remits the money. However, since the $300 represents only a paper loss at this point, the actual money balance is $1,300.
>
> Correspondingly, after the remittance, prices rise steadily for an overall increase of 12 cents per bushel ($600 per contract). If Listalot were to sell now, he would realize a profit of $600. If he does not sell, then he has only a paper profit. The actual equity in his account is $1,600 (the original $1,000 plus the $300 in additional margin plus the $300 gain in value over the loss).
>
> Rather than liquidate, he may simply withdraw the excess equity or use it as part of the margin required for an additional contract.

Margin requirements protect the buyer and the seller, help to maintain an orderly market, and tend to prevent an investor from "getting in over the head."

SPECULATIVE ACCOUNT REQUIREMENTS

Margin requirements for speculative accounts fall into two categories:

1. minimum commodity exchange speculative requirements, and
2. house requirements.

Minimum Commodity Exchange Speculative Requirements

Minimum commodity exchange speculative requirements constitute the amount of original margin that the exchange itself requires its member firms to secure from customers whose accounts for futures contracts are executed on the exchange.

> *Example*: ABC Brokerage Co., a member of the Chicago Board of Trade, buys or sells a futures contract of wheat on the exchange for the account of Mr. Listalot. According to exchange regulations, it must require the client to deposit

the minimum speculative margin requirement of 15 cents per bushel. Since 5,000 bushels are in a contract of wheat, the client must deposit $750 as original margin with his broker at ABC Brokerage Co.

The notation of margin requirements varies from one commodity to another. For example, requirements for grains are in cents per bushel—for practical purposes: Contracts of grain vary in size. Although today most grain exchanges, including the CBOT, trade only in round lots of 5,000 bushels, in the past they have allowed trading in odd lots of 1,000 bushels. Multiplying the number of bushels by the margin (in cents) per bushel is simpler than figuring fractions of contract-sized margin requirements. Margin requirements for all other commodities, however, are in dollar amounts per contract unit; all contracts in the same commodity are the same quantity. Margin requirements for some commodities are set at one amount, regardless of price. In other words, the margin for each delivery month of a particular commodity is the same, even though the price of some deliveries may be higher or lower than others. Margin requirements for still other commodities— such as copper, cotton, potatoes, soybean oil—vary according to the level of prices.

Example: The price of the March potato delivery is between $3.01 and $3.05 per hundredweight, and the minimum margin requirement is $250 per contract. At the same time, the price of the May delivery is between $3.51 and $4.00 per hundredweight, and the minimum margin requirement for that delivery is $300 per contract.

Margins for all accounts with positions in the current, or spot, month are automatically increased either on the day prior to the first business day of the delivery month or on the first notice day of the delivery month, at the discretion of the exchange. The current month is the only delivery affected; requirements on other deliveries are not altered.

No member of the exchange is allowed to accept from a customer less than the minimum margin, as fixed by the exchange. These margins are subject to increase or decrease at any time at the discretion of the board of directors of the exchange.

House Requirements

Although the exchange fixes the *minimum* original margin required on each trade, each member firm may impose larger requirements upon its customers. *House requirements* reflect the amount of original margin a brokerage firm requires a client to deposit. Generally, for speculative business, house requirements are higher than the minimum margin established by the exchange. In no case can house requirements be less than the minimum established by the exchanges. For example, an individual brokerage firm can set its house requirements for futures contracts, whether buyer or seller, at $1,000, even though the minimum exchange requirement is only $500. The firm may *not,* however, accept any less than the exchange's requirement of $500.

House margins may be increased or decreased by the commission house at any time, as long as its requirements do not drop below the exchange minimum. For example, the house margin may be increased even though the minimum exchange margin requirement remains the same. Similarly, if the exchange raises its minimum speculative margin to a level that is still lower than the house requirements, the brokerage firm does not have to raise its house requirements. However, brokerage firms usually increase their house requirements by the same amount as the exchange's increase, even though they are already above the minimum.

A brokerage firm naturally can exercise some freedom within its own requirements. Normally the house determines its requirements on the basis of risk, as ascertained by the value of the contract, and/or on the basis of risk exposure, as reflected by the firm's overall open interest in any particular commodity. The overall risk is important because house margin requirements usually apply to all accounts, both commercial and speculative. The house can, at its discretion, make exceptions to its own requirements: However, even though a lower rate may be granted to a client, it can be no lower than the minimum exchange requirement.

Increases or Decreases in Margin Requirements

Unless otherwise indicated, margin increases apply only to new positions, whereas margin reductions apply to both old and new positions.

Examples: The margin for wheat on November 1 is 10 cents per bushel and is subsequently increased to 14 cents on December 1. Clients holding long or short positions initiated at the lower rate are not required to deposit an additional margin of 4 cents per bushel, unless the brokerage house so requires. However, any new positions, long or short, established on December 1 or thereafter require the increased margin of 14 cents per bushel.

On January 1, margin requirements are reduced from 14 cents per bushel to 8 cents per bushel. The requirement of any client who had a position prior to January 1, long or short, is reduced by 6 cents per bushel, thereby freeing equity—assuming the account was properly margined—by the extent of the reduction. For new positions taken on or after January 1, the rate of margin will be 8 cents per bushel.

In other words, the *surplus*—the equity—is increased; or, if the account had been undermargined, the deficiency is lessened.

Concessions in House Requirements

In most commission houses, a production unit manager may request a reduction in house requirements for a particular customer. Reductions in house requirements are normally granted only with the approval of the commodity credit manager or of authorized home office personnel. Requests for reductions are made by sending to the commodity credit manager a wire that contains the client's account number and details of the particular transactions involved. For example, the wire for an established account might say:

RE: 23456 REQUEST HANDLING 10 LONG Q BELLIES @ MINIMUM

This request asks for the exchange's minimum margin requirements on the purchase of 10 contracts of August pork bellies.

Other information, of course, is often needed. For instance, whether the client maintains an open stock account should be included in the wire, since it affords additional protection; its availability might influence the decision by the credit manager. The approximate equity of the stock account should also be included. On new accounts, the client's occupation, name, bank reference, and financial status should also be included. For example, a wire for a new account might read:

RE 33456. JOHN JONES VICE PRESIDENT ABC CORP. WORTH OVER $100M BANKS FIRST NATIONAL. REQUEST MINIMUM RE-QUIREMENTS PURCH 10 AUGUST BELLIES, MGR. KO.

TRADE ACCOUNT REQUIREMENTS

A brokerage firm is usually permitted by the various exchanges to handle *trade accounts,* which are also known as *hedge accounts.* Such accounts deal in certain commodity futures transactions at more favorable margin terms than speculative accounts. The margin rate is lower because the risk is less: A hedge, or a trade, account either sells futures as a hedge against inventory or buys futures as a hedge against forward sales. Since the account is long actuals and short futures at the same time, or vice versa, the risk is usually less than an outright long or short speculative position. Trade accounts for such commodities as grain, sugar, copper, and soybean meal require a lower original margin rate than speculative accounts.

Though the exchange establishes the minimum requirement for hedge or trade margin, the member can request a client to deposit a larger margin. By the same token, some exchanges allow their members to extend credit to their trade or hedge customers on original and variation margin. The exchange, however, fixes a maximum on the amount of credit a member may extend to a customer. Cocoa, for example, requires no original margin, and credit may be extended to cover a limited amount—usually up to $10,000 worth—of adverse market fluctuations. The customer is permitted a deficit of $600 per contract or a limit of $10,000 on all contracts before being called for margin. Otherwise, calls for margins for trade accounts are handled in the same manner as for speculative accounts (see "Procedure for Margin Calls" later in this chapter).

> *Example*: XYZ Company buys 40 contracts of May cocoa against an actual delivery it intends to make in May. The market declines 50 points, and it has a deficit of $150 per contract for a total deficit of $6,000. Since the deficit is less than the $600 per contract limit and less than the $10,000 total limit, the company is not called for margin. However, the market declines another 40 points the following day, creating a deficit of $270 per contract for a total of $10,800. Since this is more than a $10,000 total deficit, it is called for maintenance margin of $10,800—the full amount—even though the deficit per contract is not in excess of $600. If, after the deposit of the margin, the market declined another 90 points, the client would be called for an additional margin of $10,800.
>   To illustrate the $600 per contract credit limit, XYZ buys five contracts of May cocoa on a $10,000 line of credit and the market declines 3 cents: 300 points @ $3 per point equals $900 per contract or $4,500. The account has a deficit of $900 per contract for a total deficit of $4,500, which is greater than the maximum credit allowed on a position of five contracts. The margin clerk therefore calls for $4,500 margin. Although the $10,000 limit was not exceeded, a call for margin is issued because the deficit is greater than $600 per contract.

Although a member may extend credit of only $10,000 to a customer, the customer could obtain a line of credit of $10,000 from each of several different members who are willing to extend the credit. Such a collection of credit lines may sound like the investor is "bending" the rules, but such is not the case. If an investor's financial status warrants such an exception, he or she may obtain $100,000 credit—$10,000 from each of ten different members.

To qualify for these special terms, trade clients must, on most exchanges, also be involved in the industry of the commodity itself. Their operations must represent hedging. For example, a processor of wheat is entitled to trade requirements for wheat futures transactions—as long as such transactions are for hedging purposes. But that processor is not entitled to trade requirements in any other commodity. In other words, an individual or company in the wheat business is entitled to trade requirements in wheat if he or she is hedging—but *not* in soybeans or any other commodity. If the sale of futures is not a bona fide selling hedge against a long position in the cash market, or if the purchase of futures is not a bona fide buying hedge against a forward sale in the cash market, then the client should be required to deposit either the house or minimum speculative exchange requirements.

Figure 5-1   Trade Client Letter Certifying Hedging Operations

---

Date_____

A.B.C. Brokerage Co.
100 Wall Street
New York, New York 10005

Dear Sirs:

        We hereby certify that all orders which we may give you for the sale or purchase of future contracts on any or all of the following Exchanges:

will represent sales or purchases against a corresponding quantity of purchases or sales of

        (a)   spot_____.

        (b)   _____products.

        (c)   future contracts bought or sold simultane-
              ously in different months or markets.

        In case we give you any orders that are not covered by the above, we undertake to advise you at the time the orders are transmitted so that the margin requirements of the Exchange on which said contracts are executed can be fulfilled.

                                        Very truly yours,

    The investor must file a letter stating such involvement and the hedging intention. The signing of a hedge letter (Figure 5-1) by a client normally does not automatically entitle him or her to hedge margins. Usually the firm requires approval from the credit manager for reduced rates. The commodity credit manager, in almost all cases, also confirms the extent of credit or margin basis upon which the account will be handled.

DAY TRADE MARGIN REQUIREMENTS

Commodity day trades are transactions in which a customer establishes and closes out one or more contracts of a future on the same day. A day trade occurs either when an investor buys a contract and offsets it by a subsequent sale in the same day or when he or she sells a contract and offsets it by a subsequent purchase in the same day.

Commodity exchanges do not require members to obtain margin to cover day trades for established accounts. However, most of the firms themselves require that at least 50 percent of the original margin required for an outright position be on deposit, in addition to the margin required for other open positions in the account, prior to accepting day trade orders. But for new clients and for day trades in the current (spot) month, full original margins should be obtained.

> *Example*: The minimum exchange requirement for corn is 12 cents per bushel or $600 per contract. Mr. Stalk buys a contract of 5,000 bushels of corn and tells his broker that he wants to day trade it. Because he plans to sell the contract the same day, Mr. Stalk is required to deposit only $300 margin, the 50 percent of the normal minimum requirement.

The amount of margin for commodities whose margin is based on a sliding scale price range, such as potatoes, is determined by the current market price.

> *Example*: Mrs. P. O. Tatahet wishes to day trade a contract of May potatoes. The current market price of the May contract is $6.25 per hundredweight. Since the price of the May contract is above the $3.51 price, Mrs. Tatahel has to deposit either $150, which is 50 percent of the minimum speculative requirement, or $200, which is 50 percent of the house requirement.

If an established client enters into a transaction that is intended to be a day trade but that, for some reason—a personal decision or market circumstances—is not closed out the same day, he or she must put up the appropriate full rate of margin. In the example on corn, if the transaction was not effected as a day trade, the margin required would be $600. When a registered representative accepts day trades without sufficient margin on deposit and a debit balance is incurred that proves to be uncollectible, some firms charge it to the representative's net commission!

SPREAD MARGIN REQUIREMENTS

Margin requirements for transactions involving *spreads*—that is, the simultaneous purchase of one delivery and the sale of another—are usually smaller than for net long or short positions. The reason for the reduced rate is that fluctuations in the spread *difference* are normally less volatile than fluctuations in the outright price of the commodity. As in other transactions, reductions in house spread requirements are usually arranged only on the approval by a credit manager or some other authorized person.

The exchanges establish the minimum spread requirement, but member firms may impose larger requirements on their customers if they deem them necessary. For example, for spread transactions that involve the same commodity but different delivery months, the CBOT does not require any original margin; however, such transactions must be margined to the market daily. Nevertheless, most firms would probably also request some original margin. For spreads in other commodities, most firms require either one-half of the regular margin if the spread is in the same commodity or the amount required by the exchange. The exceptions to this rule of thumb are spreads with one side in the spot month and "intercrop" spreads, for which the house usually charges one full margin on the higher side.

> *Example*: The house requirement for a contract of cocoa is $1,000 per contract for an outright long or short position. But the margin requirement for a spread that is long one contract in one delivery and short one contract in another is $500. Even though this spread transaction involves two contracts—one long versus one short—the client has to deposit only half of one side of the regular margin. Since the regular margin is $1,000, the spread margin is half, or $500.
>
> At some later date, if the investor "lifts a leg" of the spread—that is, breaks up the spread by liquidating either the long or short position—the margin requirements are increased to whatever the normal speculative requirement would be for the remaining full side. It becomes an outright position.
>
> *Example*: Mr. Bair is long March cocoa and short May cocoa, and he sells his long position in the March delivery. His margin requirements for the remaining short May delivery are increased to the full $1,000.
>
> If one leg of Mr. Bair's spread is in the current (spot month), whether he sells or not, he has to deposit one full margin: $1,000 per spread, rather than the $500 in the previous example.
>
> Or, if one leg of the spread is in a delivery month in the old crop season and one in the new crop season, Mr. Bair might be charged one full margin on the higher side. In other words, Mr. Bair developed a spread between "old" crop cocoa, whose margin is $1,000 per contract, and "new" crop cocoa, whose margin is $1,200, the spread margin requirement would be on the higher of the two. In this case, it would be $1,200.

Margin for those commodities based on sliding price scales, such as potatoes, is half the rate for the higher-priced side.

> *Example*: Mr. Bair is considering a spread long March and short May with the margin requirement on the March delivery at $300 and the margin requirement on the May delivery at $400. His margin requirement for the spread is $200— half the higher-priced side, which is $400 for the May delivery.

PROCEDURE FOR MARGIN CALLS

Registered representatives must give their customers all commodity margin calls orally, both for original and variation margin. Margin calls must also be confirmed in writing, by means of *a call for required margin form* (Figure 5-2).

Original Margin Calls

The required initial deposit is called *standing,* or *original, margin.* A call for original margin cannot be met by liquidation and must be satisfied in full: The rules of the exchanges are explicit in this regard.

> *Example*: Mr. S. Hortarms is advised by his broker that the original margin deposit for the purchase of 5,000 bushels of July wheat, when the original margin is 25 centers per bushel, amounts to $1,250 per contract. But he never

Figure 5-2   Call for Required Margin Form

BROKER & CO.
INCORPORATED

MEMBERS NEW YORK STOCK EXCHANGE
AMERICAN STOCK EXCHANGE TORONTO STOCK EXCHANGE
AND OTHER LEADING STOCK AND COMMODITY EXCHANGES

Branch   19

CALL FOR REQUIRED MARGIN

Your commodity account is in need of margin and we therefore request you to send us immediately a deposit of $_____
in local funds.

Your prompt attention will be appreciated.

BROKER & CO.
INCORPORATED

FORM 1901A—4

CUSTOMER'S COPY

puts up the original margin. Instead, he liquidates his position at a profit. Nonetheless, he is still expected to meet the original margin call. If he liquidates the position at a loss, he must not only make good the loss but also meet the original margin call. If Mr. Hortarms does fulfill the margin requirement after either a profit or loss, he is in violation of the exchange ruling. The position may therefore be liquidated by the broker, and the customer is expected to make up any debit balance incurred.

Calls for original margin from established accounts are expected to be met the day following the transaction; however, it is mandatory in most firms that funds for original margin must be received no later than forty-eight hours after the call. If the funds are not in the broker's possession within forty-eight hours after the call, most firms require that the branch manager wire the commodity margin section and the credit department, giving full details of the reason for the delay. Brokers should exercise caution in ascertaining the reason for a delay in payment. If a client states that a check is in the mail and if it is not received on the following day, the customer should be contacted to determine whether or not the check was actually mailed.

Caution is the watchword in many margin requirements. Some firms require certified checks or bank checks to satisfy calls in which the original call amounts to $10,000 or more. Checks drawn on out-of-town banks must not be accepted because of the delay in collection. Exceptions to either rule can be granted only by authorized personnel. For new commodity accounts, the broker must have for margin purposes a bank cashier's check or certified check before the initial commitment is made. If a new client deposits a personal check, no orders should be accepted until it clears. Of course, a minimum deposit equal to the original margin requirements is mandatory. Exceptions, again, may be granted only with the approval of authorized personnel. If an exception is granted, the funds must be in the firm's possession by the morning following the initial transaction. If the funds are not received by that time, the branch office must wire the commodity margin section and credit department to give full details. If a registered representative accepts an order without following this procedure and if a debit balance is incurred that subsequently proves to be uncollectible, the loss will be charged against the broker's net commission.

Variation Margin Calls

Customarily, most firms call for additional margin, variation margin, when the equity in an account falls below 75 percent of the full margin requirement. Calls for variation margin from established accounts are expected to be met the day following the adverse market movement. It is mandatory, however, that funds satisfying the additional margin be received no later than forty-eight hours after the call.

Example: The original margin for a contract of wheat is 25 cents per bushel, or $1250 per contract, and the market moves against a Miss Chaff by 8 cents. Her margin (or equity) is thus reduced by $400 to $850. Since her equity is less than 75 percent of the requirement, the broker issues a call for additional funds. The broker first calls her for $400 to bring her margin up to the original margin level of $1250, then he sends out a confirmation in writing.

Variation margin calls may be met by liquidation, but liquidation must be accomplished within twenty-four hours of the call and must also be sufficient to put the margin in order.

Example: Miss Chaff buys 25,000 bushels of wheat and deposits her original margin of 25 cents per bushel or $1250 per contract. Since she is buying five contracts at 5,000 bushels each, she deposits $6,250. After the margin has been deposited and the purchase transacted, the market declines 8 cents per bushel. Her equity is reduced by $2,000 to $4,250. Since this figure is less than 75 percent of her original margin of $6,250, the broker phones Chaff for $2,000 to bring her margin up to $6,250. Chaff can either put up the additional variation margin of $2,000, liquidate all of her position, or sell off enough of her position so that her requirements are less than the equity in the account. She chooses to liquidate 10,000 bushels, so her requirements are reduced from $6,250 to $3,750. Since she still has $4,250 equity, she does not have to deposit any additional margin. In other words, although the equity of $4,250 is not sufficient to cover a long position of 25,000 bushels, it is enough to cover 15,000 bushels, for which the requirement would be $3,750, or 25 cents per bushel.

Rule Call.   Though most brokerage firms call for additional variation margin when the client's equity is reduced by 25 percent or more, this practice is a house policy for each firm's own protection. Not all exchanges require as much. They do require, however, that member firms secure additional margin from clients in the event that their client's equity falls below a point specified by the exchange. A call to satisfy these margin requirements is a *rule call*. This level and the consequent amount of additional funds called for varies from one exchange to another. Some exchanges require additional margin to bring a client's equity back up to the original level, whereas other exchanges merely require additional funds to maintain a client's equity at a certain level.

Example: Mr. Paul Pur buys 5,000 bushels of corn on the Chicago Board of Trade through Broker Co. His broker, a member of the exchange, requires that he deposit the minimum exchange requirement of 20 cents per bushel, or $1,000 per contract, as original margin. Although Broker Co. generally calls for additional margin if the client's equity declines 5 cents per bushel, or $250 per contract, the CBOT does not require Broker to call for additional margin unless Pur's equity declines 10 cents per bushel, $500 per contract, or more. As long as Pur's equity remains above 10 cents per bushel, $500 per contract, a rule call is not required. However, if Pur's equity falls below that point, a call for additional funds *must* be made.

Maintenance Requirements. Some exchanges, such as the Kansas City Board of Trade and the Minneapolis Grain Exchange, do not require clients of member firms to bring their margin up to the original level on a variation call. Instead, they require only that clients maintain a certain level as specified by the exchange. These lower requirement levels are referred to as *maintenance requirements,* the minimum equity—as specified by the exchange—that an investor with open positions must maintain.

> *Example*: Mr. Miller purchases 5,000 bushels of December wheat on the Minneapolis Grain Exchange and is allowed minimum speculative requirements of 12 cents per bushel. He therefore must deposit $600 original margin—his equity in the account. If his equity falls below 8 cents per bushel or $400 per contract—the level of maintenance specified by the exchange—must deposit additional funds sufficient to bring his equity up to $400 per contract. He does not have to restore his equity to the original amount of $600, as in the case of a rule call, but he must bring it up to the maintenance level of $400. After making the purchase, if the market declines 5 cents per bushel, $250 per contract, Mr. Miller's equity is reduced from $600 to $350. Since this amount is below the maintenance requirement of $400 per contract, he must deposit an additional $50 to bring his equity up to $400.

PROCEDURE FOR A SELL-OUT

Should a customer fail to meet a call for original or variation margin, the brokerage firm has the right to close out, or sell out, any outstanding contracts of the defaulting customer after due notification to the extent the member firm deems advisable for its own protection. The broker is allowed to take this step because, upon opening an account, the customer signs a customer agreement form that gives the broker the authority to liquidate any positions a client has outstanding if the proper margin requirements are not met.

"Due notification" usually takes the form of a telegram, because a telegram *must* be sent regardless of what other means have been tried to contact the customer. A typical telegram reads as follows:

> DON'T DWR (don't deliver without receipt)
>
> YOUR ACCOUNT REQUIRES (amount) DOLLARS ADDITIONAL MARGIN. IF THIS AMOUNT IS NOT RECEIVED BY (*hour and date*) WE WILL THEREAFTER AT OUR DISCRETION COMMENCE TO LIQUIDATE YOUR ACCOUNT. THIS NOTICE IS WITHOUT PREJUDICE TO ANY OF OUR RIGHTS UNDER YOUR CUSTOMERS AGREEMENT OR OTHERWISE.   ABC & CO.

If a client's position is sold out because he or she is unwilling to meet the call for original or variation margin, the proceeds, if any, of the transaction are credited to the client's account.

> *Example*: Mr. Hudeenee buys one contract of soybean oil and deposits an original margin of $1,200—just before the market declines 80 points. Since each point equals $6, Hudeenee's equity in the account is reduced by $480 to $720. Since his equity is below the $750 maintenance level specified by the exchange, his broker issues a call for additional margin according to the rules of the exchange. Mr. Hudeenee, however, fails to respond to the call for additional funds. The broker—after several calls and a written confirmation long gone in the mail—sends a telegram, and still he receives no reply. The firm liquidates the client's outstanding position to the extent necessary to put the account in order. In this case, after due notification, Mr. Hudeenee is not completely sold out, and the loss incurred on the transaction amounts to $600. The client *still* has a credit balance of $600, less commission.
>
> If, however, the loss incurred had come to more than $1,200, a debit balance would have been recorded. And Hudeenee would be indebted to the firm for the difference between the loss and the $1,200 original deposit. Of course, if the client did not deposit the $1,200 original margin to begin with, he would have been indebted to the broker for the full extent of any loss incurred, plus commissions.

RECEIPT OF FUNDS FROM CUSTOMERS

When a broker receives funds from a customer, he or she should wire the home office commodity clerk and credit department promptly—"promptly" because the current status of commodity accounts must always be maintained by the home office. The wire should contain the account number and the amount received; it should also indicate whether the account is regulated (Class 1) or nonregulated (Class 2). Funds deposited as margin resulting from regulated transactions or funds deposited by the customer for crediting to Class 1 accounts *must be segregated* from "nonregulated" funds: This regulation is strictly enforced by the CFTC.

Though a client may have positions in both regulated and nonregulated commodities, the margin calculations are not distinguished one from the other. In fact, when a broker makes a combined call for regulated and nonregulated funds and receives only one check, the check should be deposited in the nonregulated (Class 2) account. Transferring funds from a Class 2 to a Class 1 account is considerably easier than transferring funds the other way. The broker can transfer from Classes 1 to 2, but only with the Supplemental Commodity Customers Agreement (Figure 5-3). Unfortunately some clients have not signed this form, and the broker must therefore obtain a special letter of authorization from the client before transferring so much as a dime. The law places these restrictions on transferring funds out of a regulated account. However, it places *no* restrictions on the transfer into Class 1 accounts.

Figure 5-3   Supplemental Commodity Customer's Agreement

SUPPLEMENTAL COMMODITY CUSTOMER'S AGREEMENT

Account Number_____

Branch Number_____

BROKER & CO.
INCORPORATED

NEW YORK, N. Y. 10011

Dear Sirs:

Until further notice in writing, you are hereby authorized, at any time and from time to time, without prior notice to the undersigned, to transfer from $\frac{my}{our}$ Regulated Commodity Account to any other account, held by you in which $\frac{I}{we}$ have any interest, such excess funds, equities, securities, and / or other property as in your judgment man by required for margin, or to reduce or pay in full any debit balance and / or to reduce or satisfy deficits in such other security and / or commodity accounts. By "Regulated Commodity" is meant any commodity covered by the Commodity Exchange Act at the time of such transactions. You agree, however, that within a reasonable time after making any such transfer, you will confirm the same in writing to the undersigned.

Dated ...., 19........

....
Customer's Signature

Example: Mrs. Hazalot's combined (regulated and nonregulated) equity is $5,000, and her requirements are $8,000. Her account, 25 percent below house requirements, is "called" for $3,000. The client's regulated account may require $2,000 additional margin, and the nonregulated account may require $1,000 additional margin. Since the client sends in one check for $3,000, it is deposited in the nonregulated account, even though the regulated account requires the greater margin. The home office margin clerk automatically makes the necessary adjustment by transferring funds from Class 2 to Class 1.

TRANSFER OF FUNDS FROM A STOCK ACCOUNT

An associated person in a branch office who receives a request from a customer to transfer funds from a stock account to a commodity account must wire the main office commodity margin clerk and credit department. The wire must include: (1) the client's account number, (2) the amount to be transferred, and (3) the type of stock account. Such a wire might read:

CMDY MGN CA 25-16842 TRFR $2000 FR STX TYPE 1

This request asks the commodity margin clerk to transfer $2,000 from the Type 1 stock account of client 25-16842 to the commodity account. A transfer form is prepared by the commodity margin clerk, and, if approved by the home office, the transfer is effected. There is no restriction on the amount of money that may be transferred. Funds may be transferred to satisfy an outstanding commodity margin call or merely to place funds in the commodity account for commodity purposes.

TRANSFER OF FUNDS TO STOCKS

A transfer of funds from the Class 1 regulated account to a client's stock account is a little trickier. It can be effected only if a Supplemental Commodity Customer's Agreement is on file with the home office commodity margin section and if the debit balance or outstanding margin call in the stock account equals or exceeds the amount to be transferred.

Example: Mrs. Hazalot has a stock account that is in deficit by $4,000. She receives an outstanding margin call in stocks for $4,000. If her commodity account, however, has a surplus equity of $6,000 in a Class 1 account, the margin clerk may transfer $4,000 from the commodity account to the stock account to satisfy the call. The margin clerk may transfer only an amount sufficient to put the stock account in shape, no more than is necessary to cover the debit balance.

If no debit balance exists in the stock account or if the amount to be transferred exceeds the amount of the debit balance, then the Supplemental Commodity Customer's Agreement does not cover the situation. In these cases, a letter must be obtained from the client containing specific transfer instructions. This letter is good for only one transfer. The CFTC regulation governing this point is very strict, and their auditors periodically examine transfers of CFTC funds to insure that the proper form or letter is in the file.

Remember: In the case of the CFTC commodities, all monies received by futures commission merchants to margin or to secure contracts of a commodity customer and all monies accruing to customers as a result of trades are to be separately accounted for and segregated as belonging to the customers. Under no circumstances may any portion of a commodity customer's funds be withdrawn except to margin, secure, or settle trades and contracts made on behalf of that customer. By virtue of the Supplemental Agreement funds from a client's commodity CFTC account may be transferred to a nonCFTC account or to a stock account but only in amounts sufficient to satisfy an outstanding debit balance.

An investor who does not have a debit balance in his or her stock account but merely wants funds transferred from the commodity account to the stock account must send a letter with specific transfer instructions. By the same token, requests for the transfer of amounts from the commodity account to a stock account that are in excess of the debit balance required must be accompanied by a letter giving specific transfer instructions. In other words, if the debit balance in the stock account is, say, $4,000 and the client wants $6,000 transferred to it from the commodity account, he or she must provide a letter containing transfer instructions to that effect.

Transfer from the Class 2 (nonCFTC) account to a client's stock account can be effected upon request to the home office commodity margin clerk from a branch office without special paperwork. Nothing restricts the transfer of funds from a Class 2 (nonCFTC) account, but the CFTC imposes restrictions on the transfer of funds from a Class 1 CFTC account, whether it is to a stock account or to a Class 2 (nonCFTC) account.

PAYOUTS

Requests by clients for payment may not be made before recently deposited checks have cleared. Payments may be made only when the branch office is absolutely certain that all checks deposited by clients have cleared. Needless to say, a customer is not permitted to make withdrawals from an account when the margin (equity) in the account is less than the minimum initial margin or when withdrawals would impair the minimum requirements.

All requests for payment to customers must be approved by the home office commodity clerk. When requesting such approval, the broker must clearly state in the wire the amount to be paid out.

RE: 7-65421 AXP $2,000 CFTC.

This wire requests permission to pay to account 7-65421 the amount of $2,000 from the CFTC commodity account. (The "AXP" stands for "advise if OK to pay.") If this amount is available, the home office margin clerk will wire back:

RE: 7-65421 OK P $2,000 CFTC.   [OK P means "OK to pay."]

CONCLUSION

You are seeing as we progress that the commodities marketplace seems to be filled with innumerable *dos* and *don'ts*. However, each rule, regulation, and restriction is placed upon themarket and upon the people in it for the overall good of the industry and for the general benefit of those who participate in it.

In the next chapter, we will see how orders are placed, how a floor broker executes those orders, and how the orders implement the decisions and plans of the individual trader.

Chapter 6

Placing and Executing Orders: The Mechanics

Placing orders requires a little art and a little science on the part of the commodities participant. Behind the order is the customer's knowledge of the market, the trust in the broker, the experience with past transactions and their outcomes, and above all the confidence that in the long run the market trend will be as forecast.

Placing orders, however, also requires technical and procedural know-how. The interested person should know almost as much as the broker about the types of orders that can be utilized, the situations they suit, the effects they have, and the strategies they fit. Admittedly, most persons use only a few types of orders for the great majority of their transactions, they should be familiar with *all* the various types of orders—with *all* the technical and procedural resources at their disposal. Such familiarity may not only be profitable, but it also may save serious misunderstandings—and the consequent unfortunate results—between the customer and broker. Such familiarity is an excellent illustration that "knowledge is power"—earning power.

THE ORDER ITSELF

An *order* is, simply stated, the client's instruction to the broker to either buy or sell a commodity. Normally, the order contains information relating to the size of the order, the price, and the length of time the order is to remain effective.

To know more specifically what kind of information is needed to place an order, examine the order form in Figure 6-1. This form is typical of the form a broker uses to either execute or cancel an order. Though the form's detail and format of course change from firm to firm, the basic information needs remain the same and are reflected in this figure.

Let's examine the order form in detail. (The boxes in the figure are numbered for your convenience in referring them to the text that follows.)

Primary Information (Boxes 1 through 7)

1. The Exchange.   In this box, the broker has to enter the name of the particular exchange or contract market on which the order is to be executed.

2. Action Code.   This box indicates whether the order is to buy, sell (SL), cancel a former order (CFO), or cancel "straight" (CXL). The buy and sell actions are clear enough.

However, a distinction must be made between the two types of cancellation actions. *Cancelling a former order* is an action taken when the client wants to change the commodity, quantity, price qualification, or duration of an order that has already been placed. A *straight cancel* is the action taken when an entire order is to be cancelled out, if possible, before it has been executed. In other words, a CFO means the customer wants to change something on a previous order and must therefore cancel the former instruction. The straight cancel (CXL) indicates the customer simply wants to call the whole thing off.

3. Quantity.   The exact number of contracts (or bushels, if grains) to be bought or sold is entered in the space marked "Qty." Orders for grains are placed in bushels, whereas orders for all other commodities are placed in contracts. For example, an order to buy one contract (5,000 bushels) of May wheat would read, "Buy 5m May wheat." An order to buy one contract of July soybean oil (60,000 pounds) would read, "Buy 1 July soybean oil."

4. Description.   In this box goes the *complete* description of the commodity and the delivery month to be bought or sold. Symbols are discouraged since confusion may occur.

Figure 6-1   A Typical Order Form

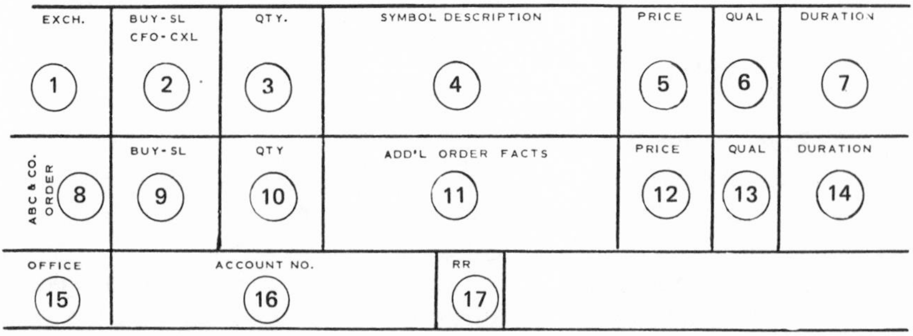

5. Price.   Either the exact price for limit orders or the abbreviation "Mkt" for market orders is inserted into this space. When placing an order, the customer should indicate the price he or she desires, in which case the price is called *fixed.* If the customer indicates *at the market,* he or she is saying, in effect, "whatever the going price is at the market."

6. Qualification.   Any investor's instructions that alter or qualify the manner in which an order is to be handled go here. Such colorful instructions as "fill or kill . . . stop . . . stop limit . . . stop with a limit . . . limit on opening only . . . or limit or market on close"—all discussed in this chapter—place qualifications on the execution of the order.

7. Duration.   Unless indications are made to the broker that the order is to be in effect for more than one day, the broker will consider the order expired at the end of the trading day. Into this box, therefore, goes the instruction as to how long the order is to remain in effect.

a. *Day order:* If nothing is marked in the "Duration" box, then the broker assumes the order expires at the end of the day—a "day" order.
b. *Open order:* This kind of order remains in effect until executed or cancelled by the customer; it is sometimes referred to as *good till cancelled (GTC).*
c. *Good this week (GTW):* The order stands only until the close of the last business day of the week during which it was entered.
d. *Good this month (GTM):* This instruction remains in effect only until the close of the last business day of the calendar month during which it was entered.
e. *Good through date (GT—):* This order stays effective until the close of business on the indicated date.

Secondary Information (Boxes 8 through 14)

The second line of information in Figure 6-1 is not always necessary, and consequently these boxes are not always filled out. When they are to be filled out, of course, they are filled out in the same manner as the first row. This second line becomes necessary if:

1. The abbreviation "CFO" appears in Box 2,
2. a switch or spread order is placed (both of which we will explain later in the chapter), or
3. a contingent order is called for. (Again, this type of order is explained later, along with why some exchanges prohibit them.)

Account Information (Boxes 15 through 17)

15. Production Unit.   Naturally, most firms number or alphabetize their departments or offices. This is a matter of routine to the broker.

16. Account Number.   A customer's account number is therefore the only way, other than the registered representative's personalized familiarity with the customer, to correlate the order to an account. Following the account number itself is either a "1" or a "2," indicating the class of the account.

17. Registered Representative.   Either the initials (in a small firm) or the number (in a large firm) of the RR goes into this box, again for obvious identification reasons.

> *Example:* Mr. Flaiks places an order to buy two contracts of 5,000 bushels each of March corn at the market price. (You will recall that "at the market" means that Mr. Flaiks is prepared to buy the contracts at whatever the price "at the market" is.) Refer to Figure 6-2. Since corn is traded on the Chicago Board of Trade, "CBOT" appears in the first box of the top line. The second box indicates that the order is to "Buy." The third box is the quantity to be bought: In this case, "10,000 bushels" is written as "10M." A description of the commodity, "March Corn," is placed in the fourth box. The price at which the order is to be executed is placed in the fifth box—in this case, at the market. (Mr. Flaiks could have asked for a price to be inserted into that box, thus indicating to the broker that he wants to wait until the market hits that price before buying. If he did so, he would have been setting a *limit price.*)
>
> Mr. Flaiks did not put any qualifications on the order, so that box remains empty. Further, since he did not indicate any specific duration for the order, the broker assumes that the order is a day order. Generally, at the market orders are executed the same day as it is entered.
>
> The second row of boxes is not filled in because none of the conditions are met: This is not a cancellation, switch, spread, or contingent order.
>
> The third row is filled out, as is obvious, for identification purposes.

With the proper information and communication, the mechanics of an order are easy. However, we have used some terms describing the types of orders that can be placed, and the skill of commodities trading actually consists of the artful entering of the right combination of these orders.

Figure 6-2   A Typical Order Form, as It Looks Filled Out

EXCH.	BUY-SL CFO-CXL	QTY.	SYMBOL DESCRIPTION	PRICE	QUAL	DURATION
CBOT	*BUY*	*10M*	*March Corn*	*Mkt*		
ABC & CO. ORDER	BUY-SL	QTY	ADD'L ORDER FACTS	PRICE	QUAL	DURATION
OFFICE	ACCOUNT NO.		RR			
AB	*1 2 3 4 5 - 1*		*9*			

What happens to the actual order once it is filled out? After the AP at the brokerage firm has jotted down this information onto an order blank, he or she gets it to a floor broker who actually fills the order on the trading floor—in a specially designated area, called a "pit" or a "ring."

THE MECHANICS OF PLACING AN ORDER

The order-processing sequence (Figure 6-3) is initiated when a customer gives the registered commodity representative (an associated person), an order. The RCR writes the customer's instructions on the firm's order ticket and submits it to the wire room or order desk where, in compliance with the CFTC regulation, it must be electronically time stamped prior to transmission. From there it is teletyped or telephoned to the firm's representative on the trading floor. A slight delay may occur in entering an order that refers to a previously entered order. In writing, the floor representative relays the order, after recording and time stamping, to the floor broker handling the commodity. Immediately upon execution, the floor broker records (or endorses) the price on the ticket; he or she also records the quantity (if the order is a partial execution. The ticket is then returned to the floor representative.

The executed order (or trade) now travels in the reverse sequence, as shown in Figure 6-35. The entire process, from beginning to end, usually takes a couple of minutes under normal conditions. Should the markets be very active and/or the traffic on the firm's wire system very heavy, a customer might experience a delay in receiving a report.

Figure 6-3   Sequence of Events in Processing an Order

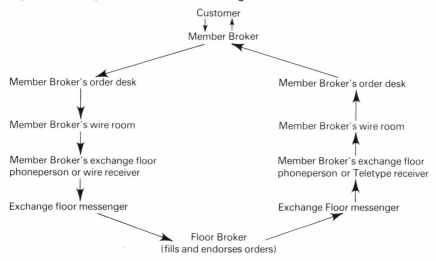

THE EXCHANGE TRADING FLOOR

The exchange trading floor is commonly referred to as *the floor,* where all futures contracts are transacted by open outcry (auction). On the floor of some exchanges transactions in actual or cash commodities are also consummated. The facilities and design of the floors of the various exchanges vary, however the basic arrangements and purposes are similar.

Trading in futures contracts is conducted in octagonal *pits* or around *rings.* Generally, one commodity is traded in each pit or ring. Floor brokers who trade in the specified commodity assigned to each pit stand on the steps of the pit or around the ring, while they aggressively bid and/or offer until a transaction (a trade) is completed.

Anyone who can satisfy requirements regarding his or her financial knowledgeability and reputation as required by the exchanges and CFTC and is accepted may transact business in futures contracts. These members fall into three classifications.

1. A *floor broker* is someone who, for a brokerage fee paid by the respective firms, executes orders for customers of the FCM. Usually they are agents— not employees of the firm they service.
2. A *floor trader* is one who conducts his or her own business in commodity futures contracts either by day trading (getting in and out the same day) or by position trading (holding long and/or short positions overnight or for other durations of time). Traders may or may not clear their own trades; if they do clear, then they must of course satisfy the necessary requirements of the respective clearing houses.
3. A *scalper* anticipates profitable transactions by trading on any small fluctuations and price changes occurring in the market. In many cases scalpers may be the persons generating or supplying the differences for spreads or straddles.

Traders and scalpers contribute tremendously to the liquidity of the market.

PRICE REPORTING AND DISSEMINATION

Adjacent to each pit is a *rostrum* or *pulpit,* occupied by reporters who are employees of the exchange. These reporters record and time stamp each transaction or price change as it occurs. The floor brokers, of course, are also responsible for recording the trade officially. Each transaction must be disseminated to all interested parties: the general public (speculators), hedgers, FCMs, and news media personnel. Each transaction must also be recorded permanently, either by computer or by manual transcription.

Transaction information is also usually displayed on the exchange's visual display system. With an electronic system, strategically located computer terminals, Teletype stations, or telephones on the floor can be used to communicate the transaction results to the main board and to other necessary information-collecting points.

Commodity and Delivery Month Symbols

The use of symbols in commodities trading is in a state of development and change. The many electronic visual systems have brought about the use of varied symbols. Each company with such a system has devised its own combination of symbols, leading to the problem, whenever a change of equipment occurs, of relearning the combinations.

Some display units are programmed to receive ticker tape input from exchanges for direct viewing. Of course, there has to be some common "language." At least the symbols used for the delivery months have been standardized and incorporated into the combinations for the various commodity symbols used by the systems employed. Since the delivery month symbol is standard and accepted by all, Table 6-1 gives each delivery month in the present trading year as well as in the following year, whenever a commodity is traded in the two periods.

Table 6-1   Delivery Month Symbols

	Present Year	Following Year		Present Year	Following Year
F	January	A	N	July	L
G	February	B	Q	August	O
H	March	C	U	September	P
J	April	D	V	October	R
K	May	E	X	November	S
M	June	I	Z	December	T

Fast Quotations for CBOT Commodities

When possible, every price change is reported on the tape. However, if during periods of unusually heavy activity every trade were reported in detail, prices on the tape would be far behind the market. At such times, the tape carries the word "FAST" and shows a range over which prices have traded, such as $4.50-$4.52. When the word "FAST" appears before a quotation, it means that any trades made at intervening prices are to be considered as officially quoted. The market Report Committee of the CBOT has jurisdiction over the price reporting and dissemination functions of the exchange.

COMPETITIVE EXECUTIONS REQUIRED

All futures orders received by member firms are transmitted to the exchange floor for execution and are filled according to bids and offers in the respective trading pits or rings "by open outcry in the open market in the exchange hall during the hours of regular trading." This procedure is an exchange rule as well as a CFTC regulation. *Open market* means a bid or an offer openly and audibly made by public outcry and in such a manner as to be open to all members in the pits or rings at the same time. No transactions may be made by private negotiations. There are no "specialists" on commodity exchanges.[1]

To keep transactions in the open market, brokers on the CBOT are forbidden to *cross orders* as they may on some other exchanges. For example, a broker who has orders to buy and sell in the same delivery at the same price cannot offset ("cross") the buying orders against the selling orders. All bids and offers must be made by open outcry in the pit. The broker is prohibited from guaranteeing a price of execution because no member may act as both principal and agent in a futures transaction.

The Opening . . .

Almost all exchanges initiate the day's trading by an *opening call*. However, the opening call may or may not be at the time trading commences for the day. Usually an exchange official at the rostrum of each pit announces which delivery month (in that commodity) will be traded. When the trading has ceased in that delivery month, the official announces the next month to be traded. Obviously different commodities and different deliveries will "open" at different times.

The first delivery month to be traded is usually the current or nearest delivery month. Subsequent, or more remote, months are then traded until all months are completed. After the opening call, all delivery months commence trading simultaneously. One exception to this procedure occurs on the CBOT on which trading in all deliveries of all grains commences at the same time.

Opening call transactions may be at either single prices or multiple prices. Multiple prices are also known as the *opening range*. This range includes all the prices at which the initial trades are made. For instance, May sugar may open between 9.01 and 8.90. Multiple quantity orders may therefore be filled at different prices. A customer who wants an order filled on the opening call must be content with a price within the range; if that result is not

---

[1]Specialists, in markets where securities are traded, are traders who act as agents on the trading floor. They buy and sell for their own accounts; and in times of freakish markets they often serve to stabilize prices when no one else will.

satisfactory, he or she should place a limit on the price or hold the order until the opening call trading is completed.

No time limit is placed on the opening call. Any broker who has an order to buy or sell a large quantity on the opening may need several minutes—and would be entitled to them—to have the opening range quoted to include every price made in the proper fulfillment of the order.

. . . And the Closing Bell

Likewise, the closing range embraces all final transactions. A broker with a large closing order can tell the pit reporter that he or she is starting a closing order. That broker is then entitled to have the closing range quoted to include all the prices made in the proper fulfillment of the order. However, the order must be completed by the time trading closes. Even though some brokers do not get all their purchases or sales completed, trading must cease once the closing bell rings.

Adjustment of Errors

When a broker commits an error in handling an order, he or she cannot arbitrarily make an adjustment in the customer's favor because such an action can be considered a rebate of commissions, which is illegal according to the bylaws of the exchanges. The price of an order's execution is binding, and no member may make any adjustment with the customer because of an error without first obtaining permission from the officials or committees of the various exchanges.

The general rule of the exchanges follows this rationale: Whenever price fluctuations are rapid and the volume of business large, different prices are bid and offered for the same delivery at the same time—but in different parts of the pit. Since no broker can be at two places at once, orders may be executed at prices not officially quoted or not executed at all even though limits are hit. Occasional errors of this nature are considered inevitable at peak trading times and they are considered no one's fault—merely the natural consequences of the best system so far available for trading.

In view of this possibility, most exchanges forbid member firms from readjusting prices or from reporting orders as filled when they have not been. To do so is considered misconduct and punishable under the exchange's bylaws and regulations.

TIME AND SALES

A customer, upon receiving a report or an execution, may request his or her registered representative to check the *time-and-sales price* on the execution if the report does not seem to coincide with the corresponding prices as reported on the quotation equipment. The discrepancy, as noted by the customer, may be due simply to a lag in reporting as a result of heavy and volatile trading. If such is the case, then the customer will eventually be satisfied that the order was filled according to instructions.

If an error has occurred, however, an employee of the member firm contacts the proper department of the exchange for a record of the transactions at the time of the trade in question, to see if the customer's complaint is justified. If the complaint is legitimate, then the broker must request permission in writing from the exchange to adjust the price of the transaction. If written approval is given, the broker may credit or debit the customer's account accordingly. This procedure usually takes a few days.

Otherwise, the prices of all executions are considered binding.

CONCLUSION

Many people handle the order on a high-pressured and fast-paced basis. With the customer's benefit continually before them, these people on the exchange and in the member firms work day after nerve-jangling day to keep all transactions not only accurate and timely but in accordance with the customer's overall instructions.

When you stop to think about the volume of trading and the number of people involved in each transaction, you can easily marvel at how few errors occur and how rapidly and accurately the action is recorded and supervised.

In the next chapter, we will explore the many types of orders available and to some extent how they suit every objective. A full discussion of tactics, however, is contained in the next section.

For now, let's examine the tools at the disposal of the trader—the various types of orders.

Chapter 7

Orders

If the trader can be considered a kind of craftsperson, and if investing money can be considered analogous to a skill, then the various types of orders available must be considered tools of the trade. They are tools by which the craftsperson builds his or her tactics and strategies.

And if the tool fits the job, the job is done all the better. A knowledge of orders—even though many customers rely on only a few for the majority of their transactions—makes for greater capability and, ultimately, greater financial success.

Let's start with the simplest and quickest type of order and work on through to the more complicated and sophisticated.

MARKET ORDER

A *market order* is an order to be executed at the best possible price at the time the order reaches the trading floor. The price changes, of course, as buyers compete with other buyers and as sellers vie with other sellers. The continuously changing bids and offers persist until a buyer and a seller agree on a price. (Obviously, the *bid* is what a buyer is willing to pay, and the *offer* is what the seller expects to receive for a commodity futures contract.) The best possible "at-the-market" price is therefore an agreed-on price. That results from bids and offers arriving at the same level.

> *Example:* Ms I. N. Vesta is contemplating a purchase of one contract of live cattle futures because of the steady rise in beef prices. However, before she enters her order that morning, she is informed by her registered representative

that cattle receipts at the Omaha livestock terminal are larger than expected. This unexpected supply may have been prompted by the government's decision to allow more imported beef into the country.

Based on this news, the pre-opening futures market indications are that prices could open 30 to 40 points lower. That meant that the August delivery, having closed at 53.40 cents the night before, may open at a level of 53.00. Rather than outguess the market, Ms Vesta places with her representative a market order to buy one contract of August cattle futures. By the time her order reaches the trading floor—a matter of seconds—the abundance of sell orders depresses prices further and Ms Vesta receives an execution of her order at 52.80.

If the market had discounted the report, as it sometimes does, Ms Vesta could have received a price closer to the previous close.

Had she placed a sell order under the same circumstances, she would have been disappointed in the price since she may have expected a price of 53.00 or higher.

Market Order to Buy

Figure 7-1 is a typical market to buy.

Figure 7-1   A Market Order to Buy

EXCH.	BUY · SL CFO · CXL	QTY.	SYMBOL DESCRIPTION	PRICE	QUAL	DURATION
CBOT	BUY	100M	May Wheat	Mkt		

	BUY · SL	QTY	ADD'L ORDER FACTS	PRICE	QUAL	DURATION
ABC & CO. ORDER						

OFFICE	ACCOUNT NO.	RR	
AB	1 ∨ 3 4 5 - 1	9	

Example: Floyd, a floor broker, receives an order to buy 100M (bushels) of May wheat at the market. The May wheat delivery is currently being quoted at $2.60 a bushel bid and $2.60½ offered.

Floyd feels he can get a better price, however, so he shouts out, "One quarter for May!" No one responds on the first bid, so he repeats himself. Someone from another side of the pit responds by yelling out "Sold!" and pointing to Floyd. For some reason, that broker's client is willing to sell at $2.60¼.

If however, no one responded despite Floyd's efforts to do better than the offered price, he would then have had to shout out "Take it!" in response to someone's offer of $2.60½.

Market Order to Sell

Figure 7-2 is a typical order form for a market order to sell.

Example: A cocoa floor broker, Gladys, is given the market order in Figure 6-4 to execute. In the ring, she finds that the July cocoa is going for 160.00 cents bid

Figure 7-2   A Market Order to Sell

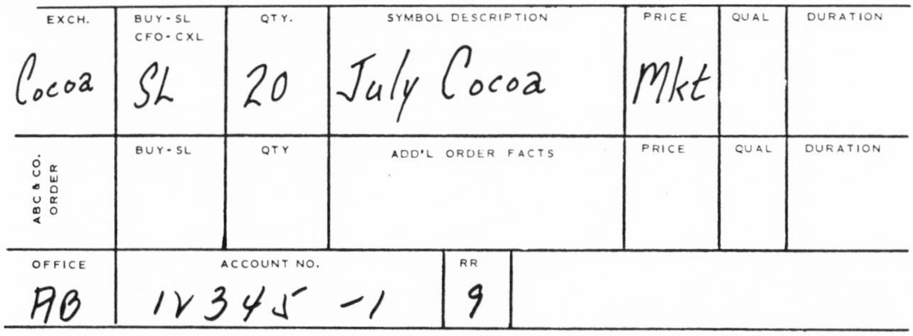

EXCH.	BUY·SL CFO·CXL	QTY.	SYMBOL DESCRIPTION	PRICE	QUAL	DURATION
Cocoa	*SL*	*20*	*July Cocoa*	*Mkt*		

ABC & CO. ORDER	BUY·SL	QTY	ADD'L ORDER FACTS	PRICE	QUAL	DURATION

OFFICE	ACCOUNT NO.	RR	
AO	*IV345 −1*	*9*	

and 160.10 offered. She decides to try to do better and shouts out, "July at 05!" meaning 160.05. Someone on the other side of the ring immediately yells, "Take it!"

If she had no takers, then she would have had to say "Sold!" at 160.00.

After each transaction, each broker records on a trading card the following information:

1. name and number of the opposing broker,
2. commodity,
3. delivery month,
4. quantity, and
5. price.

LIMIT ORDERS

A customer who wishes to either buy or sell *only* at a specified price or at one more favorable has to place a "limit" on the price. A *limit order* is an order that, in effect, tells the broker to execute a transaction only at a specified price or at one more favorable to the client. A *limit order to buy* is placed below the prevailing market price; the order is to be executed at or preferably below the limit. A *limit order to sell* is placed at or above the prevailing market price; the order is to be executed at or, again preferably, above the price limit.

Limit Order to Buy

Figure 7-3 illustrates a typical limit order to buy. This type of order is entered by someone who wishes to establish a long position or to cover a short position at a specific price or at a price somewhat lower than the prevailing market price. In other words, the order would be executed only if the price dropped to or below a certain limit.

Example: The last trade of March oats is at $1.28. Mr. Hoss feels that March oats are an attractive purchase at $1.27, and he therefore places a limit order to buy at $1.27 (Figure 7-3). Floyd, the floor broker, receives the order slip, and he finds that the price is still at $1.28.

Figure 7-3   A Limit Order to Buy

EXCH.	BUY-SL CFO-CXL	QTY.	SYMBOL DESCRIPTION	PRICE	QUAL	DURATION
CBOT	Buy	20M	March Oats	1.27		

ABC & CO. ORDER	BUY-SL	QTY	ADD'L ORDER FACTS	PRICE	QUAL	DURATION

OFFICE	ACCOUNT NO.	RR	
AB	1 V 3 4 5 - 1	9	

The broker does nothing; he does not even bid. The limit order to buy mandates him to buy *only* at or lower than $1.27. His obligation to the customer mandates him to concentrate on getting a price better than the $1.27, if possible.

If the price dips to $1.27 or below, Floyd will buy the 20M bushels called for on his order. If the price stays at $1.28—or goes up—he won't execute that order.

And if the day's trading closes at a price equal to or higher than $1.28, the order will *never* be executed, because Mr. Hoss did not put a duration on the order. Floyd would have to report an "unable" to the client at the close of trading. It is therefore considered a day order.

Limit Order to Sell

Figure 7-4 illustrates a typical limit order to sell. Such an order establishes a short position or liquidates a long position at a specific price or higher; the specific price may or may not be the same as the market price, depending on the customer's intentions.

Example: Gladys receives the limit order to sell (shown in Figure 7-4). In the pit, she finds the price at $1.28. At that point, she does nothing, because the market price is lower than the limit at which the client wishes to sell.

In the meantime, however, she also has several other orders to buy which can be filled immediately. She yells out "Take it!" to two brokers who are offering,

Figure 7-4   A Limit Order to Sell

EXCH.	BUY-SL CFO-CXL	QTY.	SYMBOL DESCRIPTION	PRICE	QUAL	DURATION
CBOT	SL	20M	March Oats	1.30		

ABC & CO. ORDER	BUY-SL	QTY	ADD'L ORDER FACTS	PRICE	QUAL	DURATION

OFFICE	ACCOUNT NO.	RR	
AB	1 V 3 4 5 - 1	9	

and she becomes involved for a few seconds in exchanging the information needed on the cards.

In those few seconds, the bid price rises to $1.35. No sooner does she look up than another broker has yelled "Sold!" She has "missed the market," as the saying goes, because she did not fill her order.

But luckily for her client, the price continues to rise to $1.36—and this time Gladys snaps up the bid.

If, on the other hand, the price dropped quickly below the $1.30 mark, then Gladys would completely miss the market. In such a case, she would have to wait until the price climbed back up over the mark before executing the order.

Again, since this is a day order, if the price stayed below $1.30 for the rest of the day, the order would expire unexecuted.

Obviously, a customer has no guarantee that a limit order will be executed. Much of the success with the order depends on how busy the action gets in the pit, how fast the prices move, and how alert the broker is. For reasons very often far beyond a broker's control, a limit order can go unfilled simply because the broker is not "recognized" by the opposing bidding or offering broker.

The main advantage of a limit order is that the customer determines the price he or she is willing to pay or accept. And the customer does not have to stay continuously in touch with the broker to get the results if the market does move in the right direction. In actuality, the client is instructing the broker as follows: "I expect the market to move in a way favorable to me. So if the market price hits a certain level, tell the floor broker to fill this order at that price or at any price that is better. But *do not* fill the order at any price outside the limit."

No matter what the outcome, though, a limit order never becomes a market order: It is either executed as a limit order or expires.

BOARD OR MARKET-IF-TOUCHED (MIT) ORDERS

A *board,* or *market-if-touched (MIT), order* is an order to make a transaction at the best available price when the market reaches a price specified by the customer. An *MIT order to buy* becomes a market order to buy when the futures sells *at or below the order price.* An *MIT order to sell* becomes a market order to sell when the commodity either sells *at or above the order price.*

The MIT order is therefore like a limit order in some ways but like a market order in others. Like a limit order, the MIT order is not executed until the market price is reached or "touched." Also like a limit order, the MIT may never be filled if the market never touches the order price. But unlike a limit order, the MIT becomes a market order once the price is touched, and it *must* be executed at the best possible price. Even if the price drops back out of the limit indicated on the order, the MIT must be filled. So the best possible price could be inside or outside the limit. The MIT does not regain its limit order characteristics if the broker misses the market. The client *must* get an execution, because the order actually "turns into" a market order once the price is touched.

MIT Order to Buy

A MIT order to buy is used by someone who wants to establish a long position or to cover a short position when the market declines to a specific level; usually, that "specific" level is lower than the current market level. The order does not have to be executed at the MIT price, but it has to be executed when the market trades or is offered at or below the MIT price.

Example: Mrs. Poke wants to buy 10 contracts of July pork bellies at the market when the market declines to 47.75 cents. The market is currently 48.00 cents. She places an order to buy 10 July pork bellies at 47.75 cents MIT, as shown in Figure 7-5. Subsequently, the price of July pork bellies declines and then quickly drops to 47.75 cents. Mrs. Poke's order then becomes a market order, and her broker tries to get the best possible price at the time. Since her MIT order to buy became a market order when the MIT price was touched, her order was executed at 47.75 cents.

Figure 7-5

EXCH.	BUY-SL CFO-CXL	QTY.	SYMBOL DESCRIPTION	PRICE	QUAL	DURATION
CME	Buy	10	July Pork Bellies	47.75	MIT	

ABC & CO. ORDER	BUY-SL	QTY	ADD'L ORDER FACTS	PRICE	QUAL	DURATION

OFFICE	ACCOUNT NO.	RR				
AB	1V 345-1	9				

MIT Order to Sell

An MIT order to sell is used to establish a short position or to liquidate a long position when the market advances to a certain level. Again, the "certain level" is usually higher than the prevailing market price. The MIT, of course, assures the investor of getting the order filled. This person does not want to take the chance of not being able to sell, as could happen with a limit order when the broker is unable to execute the order at or above the limit price.

Example: Ms. Poke buys 10 contracts of December hogs at 37.50 cents and wants to take profits when the market reaches 38.00 cents. She places an order to sell

Figure 7-6

EXCH.	BUY-SL CFO-CXL	QTY.	SYMBOL DESCRIPTION	PRICE	QUAL	DURATION
CME	*SL*	*10*	*Dec Hogs*	*38.00*	*MIT*	

	BUY-SL	QTY	ADD'L ORDER FACTS	PRICE	QUAL	DURATION
ABC & CO. ORDER						

OFFICE	ACCOUNT NO.	RR	
AO	*1 v 3 4 5 -1*	*9*	

10 December hogs at 38.00 cents MIT (see Figure 7-6). The same day, December hogs are traded or bid at 38.00 cents, and her order becomes a market order. The floor broker in the pit gets the best price obtainable at the time. Since Poke's MIT order becomes a market order, it may be filled at 38.00 cents, at a price above 38.00 cents, or at a price below 38.00 cents depending on market circumstances at the time the MIT price is elected.

By the same token, if she wanted to initiate a short position, should December hogs advance to 38.00 cents, she would put in an order to sell 10 December hogs at 38.00 cents MIT.

STOP ORDER

A *stop order,* sometimes called a *stop-loss order,* is an order to buy or sell at the market when the market reaches a specified price. A *stop order to buy,* entered above the prevailing market, becomes a market order when the commodity is either sold or bid at or above the stop price. A *stop order to sell,* entered below the prevailing market, becomes a market order when the commodity is either sold or offered at or below the stop price.

Stop orders differ from MITs principally in the way that they are placed relative to the immediate market conditions (see Figure 7-7). Stop orders to buy are entered above the prevailing market price; stops to sell, below. MITs are entered in an opposite manner, as shown in the figure.

Figure 7-7   The Difference Between a Stop Order and an MIT

STOP ORDER   MIT

$3.10 | Buy order limits entered here   Sell order limits enter here

Prevailing Market Price

$3.00

$2.90 | Sell order limits entered here   Buy order limits entered here

Further, whereas an actual trade has to take place to activate an MIT, a stop order becomes a market order as soon as a bid or offer occurs at or outside the limit on the order.

Like the MIT order, the client is not guaranteed the price he or she is looking for. Depending on the action in the market, the price could be at, higher, or lower than the stop price. All the customer is guaranteed, once the limit is hit, is that the order will be filled at the best possible price.

Stop orders are used basically for three purposes:

1. to minimize loss on a long or short position,
2. to protect a profit on an existing long or short position, or
3. to initiate a new long or short position.

Stop Order to Buy

A buy stop can be used either (1) to protect profits, (2) to minimize losses on an existing short position, or (3) to initiate a new long position.

Example: Mr. de Silva sells short March silver at $4.5900 (i.e., $4.5900 a troy ounce[1]) and wants to limit his loss to approximately 2 cents. He gives the broker an order to buy 10 March silver at 4.6100 stop (see Figure 7-8). If the market advances or is bid at or above the stop price, his stop order to buy becomes a market order to buy at the best possible price obtainable. But the market actually declines, as he anticipates, to $4.5700, and de Silva cancels his stop at $4.6100 and puts in a new stop for $4.5900, this time to protect his profits.

The market subsequently advances; March silver is bid and traded at $4.5900, then $4.600. The stop order to buy becomes a market order and is executed at the best possible price.

A stop order to buy can also be used to establish a long position at a price above the prevailing market.

Figure 7-8

EXCH.	BUY-SL CFO-CXL	QTY.	SYMBOL DESCRIPTION	PRICE	QUAL	DURATION
Comex	Buy	10	March Silver	4.6100	Stop	

ABC & CO. ORDER	BUY-SL	QTY	ADD'L ORDER FACTS	PRICE	QUAL	DURATION

OFFICE	ACCOUNT NO.	RR	
AB	1 r 3 4 5 - 1	9	

[1]Since silver is traded at dollars, cents, and hundredths of cents, the price of $4.5900 is simplified for use in the media.

Example: The market is going through a consolidation period and is moving "sideways" with no clear or evident trend. Although Miss Pink is bullishly inclined, she prudently waits for prices to break out on the top side of the range before buying. More specifically, the market is fluctuating between a range of $4.6100 and $4.5700, and she places an order to buy at $4.6120 stop. As expected, prices break out of the top of this range and reach $4.6120; her stop order to buy becomes a market order, and the broker tries to buy at the best price he can get at that time.

Stop Order to Sell

A stop order to sell is used to liquidate a long position or to institute a short position if the market declined to specific price below the prevailing market.

Example: Mr. Muvrite is long May soybean meal at $147.00, and the price advances to $150.00. Mr. Muvrite feels that prices will move higher, and he wants to hold his position but not lose his profit. To protect the profit, he gives his registered representative an order to sell 10 May soybean meal at $149.50 stop (see Figure 7-9). This order, if May soybean meal is either traded or offered at or below $149.50, becomes a market order, and the broker sells at the best possible price obtainable. However, just because the market trades or is offered at or below the specified stop price, the broker is not compelled to obtain an execution at the exact stop price. Since the stop order becomes a market order, the order may be filled at $149.50 or a price above or below the stop price.

Figure 7-9

EXCH.	BUY-SL CFO-CXL	QTY.	SYMBOL DESCRIPTION	PRICE	QUAL	DURATION
CBOT	SL	10	May SBM	149.50	Stop	
ABC & CO. ORDER	BUY-SL	QTY	ADD'L ORDER FACTS	PRICE	QUAL	DURATION
OFFICE	ACCOUNT NO.		RR			
AB	12345 1		9			

A sell stop can also be used to minimize a loss.

Example: Right after Mr. Muvrite buys May meal at $147.00, he decides to limit his loss to approximately $1. Hence, he places an order with the broker to sell 10 May soybean meal $146.00 stop (see Figure 7-10). If the market is either traded or offered at or below $146.00, Muvrite's stop order becomes a market order. The broker would then sell at the best obtainable at the time.

A third use of a sell stop is to initiate a short position. The customer who

Figure 7-10

EXCH.	BUY - SL CFO - CXL	QTY.	SYMBOL DESCRIPTION	PRICE	QUAL	DURATION
CBOT	*SL*	*10*	*May SBM*	*146.00*	*Stop*	

	BUY - SL	QTY	ADD'L ORDER FACTS	PRICE	QUAL	DURATION
ABC & CO. ORDER						

OFFICE	ACCOUNT NO.	RR	
AB	*1 V 3 4 5 - 1*	*9*	

feels prices will decline to a specific level below the prevailing market level and who wishes to sell at or about that level, perhaps having already made a profit, would initiate such an order. The investor might regard it more prudent to wait for prices to decline to a point below the bottom part of the range before initiating a sale.

> *Example*: The market is fluctuating between $149.00 and $147.00. Muvrite places an order with his broker to sell 10 March soybean meal at $146.90 stop, which means that if March soybean meal is traded or offered at $146.90, his order becomes a market order to sell.

Stop Limit Order

A *stop-limit order* is an order that contains both a stop price and a limit price (Figure 7-11). This type of order, as its name implies, combines the usefulness of a stop order and a limit order. The price indicated, for either a purchase or a sale, is a limit insofar as the floor broker is prohibited from buying over or selling under that level once the stop price has been touched. In other words, the customer is instructing the floor broker that his or her order should be treated as a straight stop order; however, the added instructions are not to pay more if the order is for a purchase or take less if for a sale than the stated price.

This type of order is useful to the customer who wants the advantages of the stop order characteristics but also the restrictiveness of a limit order. The customer, anticipating a sharp and rapid change in the market, wants to participate as long as the market seems favorable. But the customer does not want to enter the market at a random price. Hence the stop-limit order becomes a limit order only after the floor broker exhausts the possibilities of execution at the stop or intervening prices.

Once again, the investor is not guaranteed that the order will be filled; the client can be assured only that, *if executed,* the price will be between the stop and limit levels.

Stop-Limit Order to Buy

A *stop-limit order to buy* becomes a straight limit order to buy as soon as the commodity futures is either traded or bid at or above the stop price; it is executed as a limit order only at the limit price or lower.

This type of order can either cover a short position or establish a long position.

> *Example*: Mr. I. Dajo calls his registered representative to say he wants to buy March potatoes if the market advances to $3.80 a hundredweight, but he *does not* want to pay more than $3.90. So he places an order to "Buy 5 March potatoes $3.80, stop limit $3.90."
> The order form in figure 7-11 tells Floyd, the floor broker, that this order will be activated as a limit order to buy as soon as March potatoes either sells or is offered at $3.80. Floyd will at that point attempt to purchase the 5 contracts before the market hits $3.90. If he cannot by that point, then he cannot attempt to fill the order again until the market comes back down into the $3.80–$3.90 range.

Figure 7-11

EXCH.	BUY-SL CFO-CXL	QTY.	SYMBOL DESCRIPTION	PRICE	QUAL	DURATION
NY Merc	Buy	5	Mar Pots	3.80	Stop Limit	
ABC & CO. ORDER	BUY-SL	QTY	ADD'L ORDER FACTS	PRICE	QUAL	DURATION

OFFICE	ACCOUNT NO.	RR	
AB	1V345 -1	9	

Stop-Limit Order to Sell

A *stop-limit order to sell* becomes a straight limit sell order as soon as the commodity is either traded or offered at or below the stop price; it is executed as a limit order only at the limit price or higher.

A customer uses this kind of order pretty much as a regular stop order to sell, that is, to liquidate a long position at a price that protects his or her profits should the market reverse its uptrend or to institute a short position in anticipation of a declining market.

> *Example*: Mrs. Offa places an order with her registered representative to "Sell 5 March cocoa at 147.00 cents stop limit 146.50." She is instructing her representative to liquidate her long position if the market declines to 147.00 or below, but no lower than 146.50.
> Figure 7-12 shows the resultant order form. The floor broker brings the order

to the pit and finds that the price for March cocoa is 148.00. Of course, he does nothing because the order is not activated until the market declines to the 147.00 level. A sell stop order is always under the prevailing market price.

After a while, the trading hits 147.00, and the broker begins offering at 147.00 and at intervening prices. However, because of the nature of the stop limit order, he cannot sell below 146.50. At that price, he treats the order as a straight limit order to sell.

If the market drops sharply from 147.00 to 146.45 without intervening prices, the broker has to wait until the market recovers to the 146.50 level before offering.

Figure 7-12

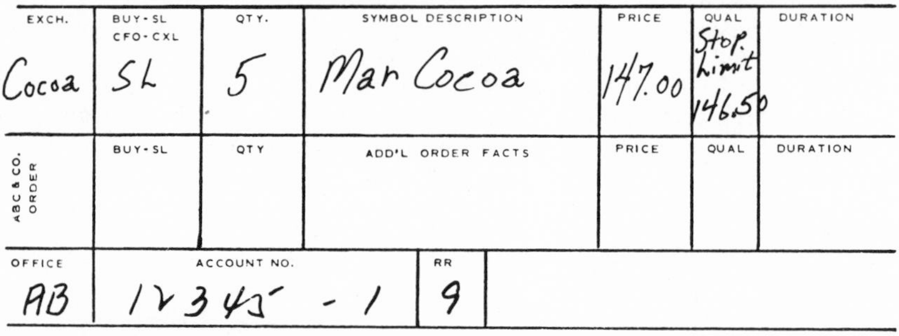

EXCH.	BUY-SL CFO-CXL	QTY.	SYMBOL DESCRIPTION	PRICE	QUAL	DURATION
Cocoa	*SL*	*5*	*Mar Cocoa*	*147.00*	*Stop Limit 146.50*	

ABC & CO. ORDER	BUY-SL	QTY	ADD'L ORDER FACTS	PRICE	QUAL	DURATION

OFFICE	ACCOUNT NO.	RR	
AB	*1 2 3 45 - 1*	*9*	

Stop-and-Limit Orders

A *stop-and-limit* is a stop-limit order in which the stop price and the limit price are one and the same. In other words, the broker has no range to work within. As soon as the stop price is hit, the order becomes a straight limit order, with the limit price the same as the stop price. The broker then attempts to fill a buy order at or lower than the limit level and attempts to execute a sell order at or higher than the limit price. As with any limit order, the broker stops trading on that order as soon as the commodity's price moves outside the limit. Typical stop-and-limit order forms are shown in Figure 7-13.

Figure 7-13   (a) A Stop-and-Limit Order Form to Sell

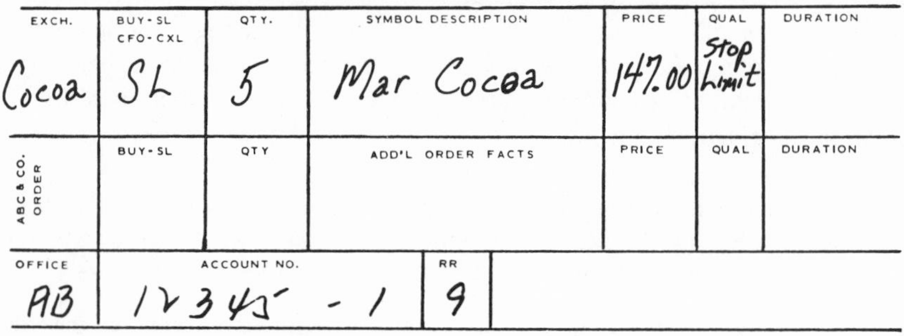

EXCH.	BUY-SL CFO-CXL	QTY.	SYMBOL DESCRIPTION	PRICE	QUAL	DURATION
Cocoa	*SL*	*5*	*Mar Cocoa*	*147.00*	*Stop Limit*	

ABC & CO. ORDER	BUY-SL	QTY	ADD'L ORDER FACTS	PRICE	QUAL	DURATION

OFFICE	ACCOUNT NO.	RR	
AB	*1 2 3 45 - 1*	*9*	

Figure 7-13 (b) A Stop-and-Limit Order Form to Buy

EXCH.	BUY-SL CFO-CXL	QTY.	SYMBOL DESCRIPTION	PRICE	QUAL	DURATION
NY Merc	Buy	5	Mar Pots	3.80	Stop Limit	
ABC & CO. ORDER	BUY-SL	QTY	ADD'L ORDER FACTS	PRICE	QUAL	DURATION

OFFICE	ACCOUNT NO.	RR				
AB	IV345 -1	9				

TIME ORDERS

Orders may be good for specific period of time, or they may be "open," that is, effective until cancelled by the customer. An order may be entered for a day, week, month, or good until cancelled.

Day Orders

A *day order* is an order that expires automatically at the end of the trading session on the day the order is entered, unless it is cancelled or executed before the session closes. Since no period of valid time is stated on these orders, they are called day orders. *All orders are considered to be day orders unless otherwise specified by the customer.* They are good for only the day in which they are entered or for that part of the trading session that remains after the order has been entered (Figure 7-14).

Market orders are obviously day orders. Any other kind of order may be either a day order or an open order.

Figure 7-14 A Day Order

EXCH.	BUY-SL CFO-CXL	QTY.	SYMBOL DESCRIPTION	PRICE	QUAL	DURATION
CME	Buy	10	Feb Cattle	40.50		
ABC & CO. ORDER	BUY-SL	QTY	ADD'L ORDER FACTS	PRICE	QUAL	DURATION

OFFICE	ACCOUNT NO.	RR				
AB	IV345 -1	9				

Time-of-the-Day Orders

A *time-of-the-day order* is one that is executed at a specific time or at specific intervals during the trading session (Figure 7-15).

Figure 7-15   A Time-of-the-Day Order

EXCH.	BUY - SL CFO - CXL	QTY.	SYMBOL DESCRIPTION	PRICE	QUAL	DURATION
CME	*Sh*	*20*	*March lumber*	*Mkt*	@ 11:30 NYT	
ABC & CO. ORDER	BUY - SL	QTY	ADD'L ORDER FACTS	PRICE	QUAL	DURATION
OFFICE	ACCOUNT NO.		RR			
AB	*1 2 3 4 5 - 1*		*9*			

Off-at-a-Specific-Time Order

This is a day order with a time contingency. It remains in effect only until the time indicated under "Duration," whereupon it is cancelled if not executed (Figure 7-16).

Figure 7-16   Off-at-a-Specific-Time Order

EXCH.	BUY - SL CFO - CXL	QTY.	SYMBOL DESCRIPTION	PRICE	QUAL	DURATION
CME	*Buy*	*20*	*Jan Eggs*	*46.30*		*GT 2:00 P.M. NYT*
ABC & CO. ORDER	BUY - SL	QTY	ADD'L ORDER FACTS	PRICE	QUAL	DURATION
OFFICE	ACCOUNT NO.		RR			
AB	*1 2 3 4 5 - 1*		*9*			

Week and Month Orders

In the box marked "Duration," a client can have the broker write down either "week" or "month," indicating that the order should remain in effect until the close of trading on the last trading day of either the week or the month.

Open Orders

An *open order,* also known as *GTC order,* is "good till cancelled." An open order can be good for a week, a month, or longer. However, an open

Figure 7-17 Open Order

EXCH.	BUY-SL CFO-CXL	QTY.	SYMBOL DESCRIPTION	PRICE	QUAL	DURATION
CME	*Buy*	*10*	*Feb Cattle*	*40.50*		*Open GTC*

	BUY-SL	QTY	ADD'L ORDER FACTS	PRICE	QUAL	DURATION
ABC & CO. ORDER						

OFFICE	ACCOUNT NO.	RR	
AB	*1 v 3 4 5 -1*	*9*	

order automatically expires at the end of the trading session on the last trading day when that delivery expires (Figure 7-17).

Open orders remain in effect until the customer explicitly cancels them or until the contract expires. Hence, they are dubbed "good till cancelled." A speculator uses this type of order when he or she feels the market action will eventually bring the desired price, at which time the order will go into effect automatically. This customer is one with the confidence that the market will eventually bring the desired result and is therefore willing to wait.

Note: The CBOT and the Comex have specifically banned time or contingent orders of all kinds. Only market orders to buy or sell, closing orders to buy or sell, spread orders, straight limit orders to buy and sell, and straight stop orders to buy or sell are permitted.

IMMEDIATE-OR-CANCEL ORDERS

An *immediate-or-cancel order* is one that has to be executed upon receipt by the broker or automatically cancelled. In other words, once the broker receives the order, he or she must try to fill the order at the price specified or at a better price. If filling the order is impossible, the broker reports an "unable" to the customer along with the latest quote. If the broker can fill part of the order, he or she will do that and report an unable on the balance. In either case, the broker automatically cancels the order, wholly or partially, and reports the latest quote to the customer.

> *Example*: Mr. Sweet puts in an immediate-or-cancel order to buy 100 July sugar at 9.94 cents. The floor broker is able to buy only 25 at that price and cancels the rest of the order. He reports an unable on the 75 and the latest quote to the customer to see if he wants to put in another order.
> The order form is shown in Figure 7-18.

Immediate-or-cancel orders are also known as *fill-or-kill* or *quick orders*. All three terms are synonymous in the commodities business.

Figure 7-18

EXCH.	BUY-SL CFO-CXL	QTY.	SYMBOL DESCRIPTION	PRICE	QUAL	DURATION
NYC₹S	*Buy*	*100*	*July Sugar*	*9.94*	*FOK*	

ABC & CO. ORDER	BUY-SL	QTY	ADD'L ORDER FACTS	PRICE	QUAL	DURATION

OFFICE	ACCOUNT NO.	RR	
AB	*1 v 3 4 5 - 1*	*9*	

SCALE ORDERS

A *scale order* is an order to buy or sell two or more lots of the same commodity at designated price intervals. If the first part of a scale order is a limit or a stop order at a set price, then all other limits or stop prices are set when the scale order is entered.

Example: Floyd receives an order to buy 10 May cotton at 52.50 cents and 10 each 50 points down for a total of 50 (Figure 7-19). In other words, the customer is giving him an order to buy 10 May cotton contracts at 52.50 cents, 10 at 52.00 cents, 10 at 51.50 cents, 10 at 51.00 cents, and 10 at 50.50 cents—for a total of 50.

Figure 7-19   Scale Order

EXCH.	BUY-SL CFO-CXL	QTY.	SYMBOL DESCRIPTION	PRICE	QUAL	DURATION
N.Y. Cotton	*Scale Buy*	*10*	*May Cotten and 10 each 50 pts. down. Total 50.*	*52.50*		

ABC & CO. ORDER	BUY-SL	QTY	ADD'L ORDER FACTS	PRICE	QUAL	DURATION

OFFICE	ACCOUNT NO.	RR	
AB	*1 v 3 4 5 1*	*9*	

If the first part of the scale order is a market order, the limits or stop prices are then computed from the price at which the first order was filled, but they are considered to have been entered at the same time as the first part of the scale order.

Example: The floor broker receives an order to "Buy 20 September frozen concentrated orange juice at the market and 20 each at 50 points down for a total of 80" (see Figure 7-20). In other words, the customer is placing an order to buy 20 contracts of September frozen concentrated orange juice at the market, then 20 contracts at each 50 points down from the price that the first 20 were executed.

124

Figure 7-20

EXCH.	BUY-SL CFO-CXL	QTY.	SYMBOL DESCRIPTION	PRICE	QUAL	DURATION
N.Y. Cotton	Scale Buy	20	Sept. FCOJ and 20 each 50 pts. down. Total 80.	Mkt.		

ABC & CO. ORDER	BUY-SL	QTY	ADD'L ORDER FACTS	PRICE	QUAL	DURATION

OFFICE	ACCOUNT NO.	RR
AB	IV 345 - 1	9

The market order to buy 20 is executed at 51.50 cents: Therefore the subsequent orders should take place at 51.00 cents, at 50.50 cents, and at 50.00 cents, for a total of 80.

COMBINATION ORDERS

A *combination order* consists of two orders entered at the same time, with one contingent on the other. Sometimes the cancellation of one is contingent upon the execution of the other. Or the purchase or sale of one commodity at a limit in one month is dependent on price action in another delivery month. Combination orders are usually referred to as *alternative orders* and *contingent orders*.

Alternative Orders

A group of orders may be entered all at the same time with the understanding that the execution of any one of the group automatically cancels those remaining. An alternative order is also referred to as an *either/or order* or *one-cancels-the-other order (OCO)*.

The commodity broker, in endeavoring to fill alternative orders, assumes no responsibility. Two groups of alternative orders may even be executed simultaneously—before one or the other may be cancelled.

Example 1: Floyd picks up an order to buy 5 February pork bellies @51.30 cents *or* buy 5 February pork bellies @51.40 cents stop (See Figure 7-21).

The type of order shown in Figure 7-21 is used by a customer who wants either to cover a short position or to establish a long position at a price below the market or at a certain price above the market. The customer is placing a limit order to buy and a stop order to buy, with the understanding that if one of the orders is executed, the other order is immediately cancelled. The customer wants to buy 5 February pork bellies either on a decline to 51.30 cents or on an advance above 51.30.

Figure 7-21 Alternative Order

EXCH.	BUY-SL CFO-CXL	QTY.	SYMBOL DESCRIPTION	PRICE	QUAL	DURATION
CME	*Buy*	*5*	*Feb. Pork Bellies*	*51.30*	*OR 51.40 STP O.C.O.*	

	BUY-SL	QTY	ADD'L ORDER FACTS	PRICE	QUAL	DURATION
ABC & CO. ORDER						

OFFICE	ACCOUNT NO.	RR
AB	*12345 - 1*	*9*

The trader wants to buy if the market drops to a certain level currently below the prevailing market, but he or she does not want to chance missing the market in the event that it does not decline to the limit price. Consequently, the customer still winds up long if the market moves up—without missing the market. On the other hand, if the market dips to 51.30 cents, and the broker who executes the limit order immediately cancels the other order to buy at 51.40 cents stop. Should the market not decline to 51.30 cents but instead advances to the stop price of 51.40 cents, the order becomes a market order to buy and the broker immediately cancels the limit order to buy at 51.30. One cancels the other—"OCO."

Example 2: Broker John receives an order to sell 10 March gold @$163.70 or sell 10 March gold @ $162.00 stop (see Figure 7-22).
    If the market advances to $163.70 and John executes the limit order to sell, he immediately cancels the stop order.
    If the market declines to $162.00 and the stop order is elected, John tries to execute an order to sell. When he does, he immediately cancels the limit order to sell at $163.70. The execution of one, again, cancels the other.

This type of order is used by a customer two ways: (1) to liquidate a long position; or (2) to institute a short position either at a certain price above or below the market. The customer wants to sell 10 March gold either on an advance to $163.70 or on a decline to $162.00 or below. This type of order is

Figure 7-22 Alternative Order

EXCH.	BUY-SL CFO-CXL	QTY.	SYMBOL DESCRIPTION	PRICE	QUAL	DURATION
IMM	*SL*	*10*	*March Gold*	*163.70*	*OR 162.00 STP O.C.O.*	

	BUY-SL	QTY	ADD'L ORDER FACTS	PRICE	QUAL	DURATION
ABC & CO. ORDER						

OFFICE	ACCOUNT NO.	RR
AB	*12345 - 1*	*9*

126

used to sell if the market advances to a certain level currently above the prevailing market but to reduce the risk that the market may decline without advancing to the limit price. Consequently, the client would sell even if the market began to decline and would not have missed the market.

CONTINGENT ORDERS

Contingent orders are grouped orders, entered as one and each of whose execution depends on the execution of the other. In other words, one order is filled if, and only if, the other is; since the subsequent order(s) can be filled only when others are done, the contingent order is sometimes referred to as a *when-done order.*

Principally, contingent orders can be executed in two ways:

1. the simultaneous purchase of one commodity and the sale of another at a stipulated price, or
2. the execution of one order before the execution of the other.

Neither type is acceptable for any commodity traded on the Commodity Exchange, Inc., and on the Chicago Board of Trade. (However, since these and other rules are, as discussed, subject to change at the discretion of the exchanges, you should verify which types of orders are accepted on any given exchange.)

Most importantly, although a broker makes every effort to accomplish the executions in the way the customer desires, he or she can neither take responsibility for the outcome nor offer a guarantee of execution. No broker can be at two places at once.

> *Example 1*: Buy 5 March cocoa @ 147.00 cents; when done sell 5 March cocoa at 146.00 cents stop (see Figure 7-23).

> *Example 2*: Buy March sugar #11 at the market; when done sell 10 March sugar #11 at 10 points higher or above the purchase price.

Figure 7-23   A Contingent Order

EXCH.	BUY·SL CFO·CXL	QTY.	SYMBOL DESCRIPTION	PRICE	QUAL	DURATION
Cocoa	*Buy*	*5*	*March Cocoa* WHEN DONE	*147.00*		
	Sell	*5*	*March Cocoa*	*146.00*	*Stop*	

ABC & CO. ORDER	BUY·SL	QTY	ADD'L ORDER FACTS	PRICE	QUAL	DURATION

OFFICE	ACCOUNT NO.	RR				
AB	*1V 345 -1*	*9*				

ON-THE-OPENING MARKET ORDERS

An *on-the-opening market order* is an order to be executed upon the opening of the trading session at the best possible price obtainable at the time. While an on-the-opening order does not necessarily have to be the first of the session, it must be within the "opening range" as determined by the exchange.

On-the-Opening Limit Orders

On this type of order the customer wants to buy or sell during the opening call—but only at or below a set limit or at or above a set limit (see Figure 7-24). The order is executed within the limit, if market conditions permit, during the opening call. If it remains unfilled at the end of the opening call, it is cancelled.

Figure 7-24   On-the-Opening Limit Order

EXCH.	BUY-SL CFO-CXL	QTY.	SYMBOL DESCRIPTION	PRICE	QUAL	DURATION
NYME	Buy	10	May Potatoes	4.50	Opening Only	

ABC & CO. ORDER	BUY-SL	QTY	ADD'L ORDER FACTS	PRICE	QUAL	DURATION

OFFICE	ACCOUNT NO.	RR				
AB	1V345-1	9				

ON-THE-CLOSE ORDERS

Here the customer desires to buy or sell during the closing call. An on-the-close order does not have to be the final trade of the trading session, but it must be within the closing range as determined by the exchange. For example, if an order is received to buy 5 October platinum at the market on the close, the order form would appear as shown in Figure 7-25.

Figure 7-25   On-Close Order

EXCH.	BUY-SL CFO-CXL	QTY.	SYMBOL DESCRIPTION	PRICE	QUAL	DURATION
NYME	Buy	5	October Platinum	Mkt	On the Close	

ABC & CO. ORDER	BUY-SL	QTY	ADD'L ORDER FACTS	PRICE	QUAL	DURATION

OFFICE	ACCOUNT NO.	RR				
AB	1V345-1	9				

Limit or Market On-the-Close Order

Regardless of price, the customer wants an execution that day. The limit or market on-the-close order permits the broker to try for a set limit during the day, but it mandates the broker to get an execution at some price at or before the end of the day. During the day, the order is executed at its limit if the market permits, as a straight *limit order.* If it remains unfilled at the close of the trading session, it becomes a *market on-the-close order* (MOC), and the commodity is transacted, regardless of the limit on the order.

Example: Floyd receives an order to buy 5 May potatoes at $4.80 or at any price at the close of market. The order appears in Figure 7-26. Floyd keeps the order with him all day, but the market never goes near the $4.80 price the client is looking for. At the closing call, therefore, he is obliged to treat the order as a market order and buys 5 contracts of May potatoes at $4.95.

Figure 7-26   Limit or Market On-the-Close Order

EXCH.	BUY-SL CFO-CXL	QTY.	SYMBOL DESCRIPTION	PRICE	QUAL	DURATION
N.Y.M.	Buy	5	May Potatoes	4.80	Or moc	

ABC & CO. ORDER	BUY-SL	QTY	ADD'L ORDER FACTS	PRICE	QUAL	DURATION

OFFICE	ACCOUNT NO.	RR
AB	1v 345-1	9

SPREAD ORDERS

A *spread order* is an order to buy one futures and to sell another, either in the same or different commodities and in the same or different markets. A spread order can be either at the market or at a specific difference. For instance, an order may read buy 5 March corn and sell 5 September corn at the market. Or a client can place an order for a spread when the September delivery is 5 cents over the March; the order appears in Figure 7-27. Another type of spread order, an *intermarket spread order,* is an order for the purchase of a commodity in one market versus the sale of the same commodity in a different market. An example is the purchase of Chicago July wheat versus the sale of Kansas City July wheat (Figure 7-28).

When entering a spread order, the investor must list the buy part of the order first. Consequently, when liquidating or unwinding the spread, the investor naturally thinks in the reverse order, selling before buying. However, even though the actual procedure is reversed, the order must be written out with the buy segment first, the sell part second (see Figure 7-29).

Figure 7-27 Spread Order

EXCH.	BUY-SL CFO-CXL	QTY.	SYMBOL DESCRIPTION	PRICE	QUAL	DURATION
CBOT	Spread Buy	5	March Corn			

	BUY-SL	QTY	ADD'L ORDER FACTS	PRICE	QUAL	DURATION
ABC & CO. ORDER	SL	5	Sept. Corn	Sept. 5¢ over		

OFFICE	ACCOUNT NO.	RR	
AB	1 V 3 4 5 -1	9	

Figure 7-28 Intermarket Spread Order

EXCH.	BUY-SL CFO-CXL	QTY.	SYMBOL DESCRIPTION	PRICE	QUAL	DURATION
CBOT	Spread Buy	5	July Wheat			

	BUY-SL	QTY	ADD'L ORDER FACTS	PRICE	QUAL	DURATION
ABC & CO. ORDER	K.C. SL	5	July Wheat	K.C. 15¢ over		

OFFICE	ACCOUNT NO.	RR	
AB	1 V 3 4 5 -1	9	

Figure 7-29 Order Form Filled Out to Unwind (Liquidate) a Spread

EXCH.	BUY-SL CFO-CXL	QTY.	SYMBOL DESCRIPTION	PRICE	QUAL	DURATION
CBOT	Spread Buy	5	May Corn			

	BUY-SL	QTY	ADD'L ORDER FACTS	PRICE	QUAL	DURATION
ABC & CO. ORDER	SL	5	Sept. Corn	Sept. 4¢ over		

OFFICE	ACCOUNT NO.	RR	
AB	1 V 3 4 5 - 1	9	

SWITCH ORDERS

A *switch order* is an order for the simultaneous purchase of one delivery month and the sale of another month in the same commodity. It is not a spread or a straddle, because the client must already be long or short in the commodity to conduct a switch.

Example: A client has a profit in an existing long March corn position. He projects the continuance of the price advance and wants to maintain a long position. The March delivery period is near, and the customer must liquidate before notice day. He gives his representative an order to sell March corn and buy May corn. This constitutes a switch.

A switch order can be entered for either the at-the-market price difference or a specified price difference. If the customer indicates an at-the-market difference, then the switch is executed immediately at the best obtainable prices. If a price difference is specified, then the broker must be guided by the going difference before executing the order.

> *Example*: Farnsworth tells his broker to switch from 5 contracts of March corn to 5 of May. He also specifies that the price difference must be 2 cents; he wants the broker to execute his order when the May is 2 cents more than (or "over") the March. Figure 7-30 shows the order form that the broker receives.
>
> The broker asks for the difference for March/May, which at the moment is 1½ cents bid offered at 1¾. If the order reads "at the market," he would have to execute it immediately. But since he is restricted to a 2-cent difference, he remains alert to the "spread difference" in the market. Similar to a spread or straddle, the main concern is the difference between the two months—not with the individual prices.
>
> Eventually, activity develops in the March/May spread and the broker is able to execute the order at the stated difference of 2 cents.

Figure 7-30 A Typical Switch Order

EXCH.	BUY-SL CFO-CXL	QTY.	SYMBOL DESCRIPTION	PRICE	QUAL	DURATION
CBOT	*Switch Buy*	*5M*	*May Corn*			

ABC & CO. ORDER	BUY-SL	QTY	ADD'L ORDER FACTS	PRICE	QUAL	DURATION
	SL	*5M*	*March Corn*	*May 2¢ over*		

OFFICE	ACCOUNT NO.		RR			
AB	*12345*	*1*	*9*			

CANCELLATIONS

Inasmuch as orders are actually instructions from the customer to the broker, changes in these instructions must be handled through the cancellation of prior instructions. The customer may want to cancel the whole order or just part of it; he or she may also want to alter some part of the order. Whether the change of mind involves the whole order or just part of it, it has to be implemented by means of a cancellation notice. An investor may therefore use two types of cancellation orders:

1. A *straight cancel order (CXL)* is an order that cancels the whole previous order without replacing it with a new order. The investor has, perhaps,

changed the basic decision to buy or sell. The broker kills the order or, if it is already partially executed, kills the unfilled balance. (See Figure 7-31).

2. A *cancel former order (CFO)* is an order that not only cancels a previous order but also replaces it with a new one. Generally, the investor has still decided to buy or sell but on slightly different terms; usually, a CFO is used to alter the price on a previous order. For instance, a customer first orders 10 contracts of May coffee at 158.00 cents on a limit order; a little later in the day, that same person cancels the order and replaces it with one exactly the same except that it becomes a market order. (See Figure 6-32.)

Figure 7-31   A Straight Cancel Order Form (CXL)

EXCH.	BUY·SL CFO·CXL	QTY.	SYMBOL DESCRIPTION	PRICE	QUAL	DURATION
Comex	*CXL-Buy*	*20*	*March Copper*	*58.00*		
ABC & CO. ORDER	BUY·SL	QTY	ADD'L ORDER FACTS	PRICE	QUAL	DURATION
OFFICE *AB*	ACCOUNT NO. *IV345-1*	RR *9*				

Figure 7-32   A Cancel Former Order Form (CFO)

EXCH.	BUY·SL CFO·CXL	QTY.	SYMBOL DESCRIPTION	PRICE	QUAL	DURATION
N.Y. COS	*CFO Buy*	*10*	*May Coffee*	*158.00*		
ABC & CO. ORDER	BUY·SL *Buy*	QTY *10*	ADD'L ORDER FACTS *May Coffee*	PRICE *mkt*	QUAL	DURATION
OFFICE *AB*	ACCOUNT NO. *12345-1*	RR *9*				

Obviously, cancellations that reach the floor after a specified time on the last day of trading in an expiring future may involve extraordinary problems. The broker therefore accepts such orders with the understanding that the customer assumes the sole responsibility for whatever results.

CONCLUSION

If all this sounds complicated, it is. But thousands of people all across the country—employees of brokerage houses, workers on exchanges, and customers from their homes and places of business—all deal in these orders daily with a minimum of confusion and error.

One question that might be on your mind, however, is: With all the orders that are passed daily and with all the types of orders available, who keeps track of all the trading? Of course, the exchanges and the member firms keep track of what is going on in the pits, but they do not actually handle the transferral of ownership as transactions are made. To do so, of course, would be impossible.

The task of allocating ownership and of totalling up all the transactions in a trading session for a net outcome is the duty of the clearing house—which is discussed in Chapter 9.

Chapter 8

Deliveries

Perhaps one of the greatest misconceptions about commodities regards taking deliveries. Certainly many a potential commodities customer has shied away from the area because somewhere deep in the subconscious, he or she pictures a large truck dumping 50,000 bushels of soybeans on the front lawn.

Actually taking a delivery is a lot easier. Although approximately only 2 percent of the open contracts are actually settled by delivery, the delivery must nonetheless sooner or later be made. Its inevitability imbues the industry with a natural time mechanism that starts ticking when the first two parties get together to make a contract and that stops only shortly before the actual delivery is made. The element of time and the procedures of delivery are therefore two areas of concern to the investor.

BACKGROUND

For many years grain organizations tried to bring about a more consistent application of uniform standards, but the results were disappointing. The lack of an effective agency to establish a single set of standards for grain that would be applicable throughout the United States and that would insure uniform application kept the grain-grading system ineffective during this period of localized and unrelated grain inspection.

The demand for uniform grades and inspection resulted in the introduction, in the Fifty-Seventh to the Sixty-Fourth Congresses, from years 1903 to 1916, of twenty-six different bills providing either for federal supervision of grain grading or for outright federal grain inspection. The United

134

States Grain Standards Act was finally passed August 11, 1916. The act provides in part for:

1. the establishment of official grain standards,
2. the federal licensing and supervision of the work of grain inspectors, and
3. the entertaining of appeals from the grades assigned by licensed inspectors.

The Secretary of Agriculture is authorized to make investigations and to establish federal standards for the most common grains. That is, the Secretary of Agriculture is empowered by the act to establish classes and subclasses for each grain and to establish a numerical grading schedule for each class or subclass to determine its quality, condition, and characteristics. The grade designation of a particular class of grain determines its value. Grain of superior quality commands premium prices, whereas discounts are paid for grain of inferior quality. Federal standards under this act are now in effect for wheat, corn, barley, oats, feed oats, mixed feed oats, rye, grain sorghums, flaxseed, soybeans, and mixed grain.

Standardization of Contracts

The establishment of standard grades has often been said to be the single most important contribution to the development of futures trading. Futures trading on its present scale would be impossible without the existence of standard grades and without an accompanying system of inspection to determine the standards of lots of a commodity offered for sale. Prior to contract standardization, both dealers and processors were reluctant to buy until merchandise was available for physical inspection. They were reluctant to take a seller's description at face value, and, for safety's sake, they were compelled to inspect carefully every lot offered for sale. Such conditions obviously limited the volume of forward sales; hence, producers were obliged to assume all price, transportation, and other risks up until the time that they could deliver their products to primary markets, where large dealers and manufacturers could inspect and sample. Dealers who occasionally did "speculate"—that is, bought for forward delivery—took on much greater risks than they need to assume today under conditions of contract standardization.

The advent of contract standardization greatly stimulated trading for forward delivery and thereby reduced dependence upon consignment as a means of disposing of goods. It made it possible for anyone engaged in trade to buy and sell for forward delivery with confidence that the buyer would receive what was contracted for. For such a system to function presupposes a means for sampling and certifying, by an outside party, individual lots as proper for delivery under contract standards. Sampling is undertaken by licensed inspectors; the buyer is freed from performing this function himself. Commodities that are to be delivered against the exchange contract are inspected and assorted in accordance with standard grade criteria, and grade certificates are then issued. Once a contract has been made, neither the grades, nor points of delivery, nor any other important element may be changed.

An integral part of the system of grading and inspection are exchange licensed warehouses, in which all lots intended for delivery must be stored. The warehouse receipt, issued by approved or bonded warehouses, certifies that the commodity exists in the warehouse; grade and weight certificates certify its quality and weight.

Only certified stocks are deliverable against a futures contract—that is, stocks of a commodity that have been graded, and been found to be of deliverable quality, and are stored at the delivery points and in warehouses designated regular for delivery by the exchange.

Right of Appeal

When a difference of opinion arises as to the grade assigned by a licensed inspector there are several methods available for settling the controversy. Either the buyer or seller may request that the grain be resampled and reinspected by the original inspector; should disagreement still persist, an appeal may be made for federal inspection. The initial sampling and grading is done by state employees licensed by the federal government. However, in the case of appeals, all questions of grade are decided by federal agents. Three appeals can be made.

First: An appeal may be made to a local federal grain supervisor employed by the U.S.D.A. These federal grain supervisors are stationed at all important grain centers. A new sample is drawn, and the federal grain supervisor examines it and either affirms or rescinds the grade previously assigned by the licensed inspectors. If the federal supervisor rescinds the grade determined by the licensed inspectors, the supervisor indicates a new grading that supersedes the licensed inspectors' grading.

Second: If either party to the transaction is not satisfied with the grade assigned by the federal supervisor, an appeal may be made to the U.S.D.A. Grain Division, Board of Appeals and Review, located in Chicago or Portland, Oregon. A new sample is usually not drawn for this purpose. Rather, the sample and findings of the federal supervisor are reviewed by the board of review.

Third: A third and final appeal may be made to the Secretary of Agriculture.

The Time Element

The year designation for a futures contract always denotes the year in which the futures expire, not the year in which trading commences. Commodities are therefore traded up to one year ahead of delivery and in some cases as far as eighteen months ahead of delivery. Thus, the maximum lifespan of a commodity futures contract is a year to eighteen months. (Trading in the same delivery month of a different year is an accepted practice.) Trading, for instance, in May wheat to be delivered in May of 1980 usually commences in April 1979, shortly before trading has ceased for May 1979 wheat, and it continues until it expires in May 1980. In other words, the May 1980 wheat "comes on the board" after the May 1979 wheat "goes off the board" (that is, expires). The May delivery usually commences trading in April and continues until May of the following year.

Trading in commodity futures customarily occurs in only a few delivery months, not for every month in the year. Market custom, based on trade needs and harvest time, has evolved this system. For example, wheat, corn, and oats are traded for deliveries in March, May, July, September, and December. Soybeans are traded for March, May, July, August, September, and November. Besides, trading that is concentrated in a few select months, instead of spread out over a whole year, tends to enhance the liquidity of the markets.

DELIVERY AT THE SELLER'S OPTION

Delivery of the actual commodity is at the seller's choosing, as long as he or she remains within the ranges prescribed by the exchanges' standard contract. The contract specifies a range of deliverable grades, a place of delivery, and a delivery period. But the seller may choose the particular grade, the exact place, and the specific day. And the seller does not even have to decide any of these matters upon making the contract; all the decisions can be made during the delivery period. The buyer has no say at all in these matters.

The buyer seems to be at an unfair advantage, but the apparent lop-sidedness of the deal is for good reasons. For one thing, if the delivery dates were at the discretion of the buyers, possibly all buyers in a particular delivery period could demand delivery all at once, placing an abnormal demand on what could be an unnaturally limited supply, forcing prices up and creating a "false" market in that delivery. Flexibility on the delivery date also gives the seller the chance to move the commodity into an approved warehouse or other shipping point. Further, unless the seller has a little leeway on the delivery grades, a slightly short supply in a particular grade could create a monopoly and possibly a price-manipulation situation for those who could gain control of the supply. For instance, suppose that only one grade of a given commodity, which accounts for only a small portion of the output for the year, is in short supply because of crop failure. If the seller is not permitted to substitute another grade of the same commodity, anyone who can control the short supply of the necessary grade has an unfair advantage and can exert an unnatural control over the prices. Sellers would be forced either to purchase the deliverable grade in the cash market to fill the orders or offset their contracts by purchases in the futures market—either way at what would most likely be exorbitant prices. The futures prices would reflect the price of only one grade, a small part of the total yield. This result would defeat the use of the future contract as a hedging instrument and thus defeat the purpose for which it was created.

The flexibility therefore has to be given to the seller.

DELIVERY PERIOD

Ultimately all futures contracts must be settled on or before the last trading day, which is the day designated by the exchange that a futures contract may be liquidated by an offsetting transaction. To expedite liquidating both long or short positions in the expiring month, the exchange's rules also provide for specific days on which *notices of intention to deliver* are submitted to the clearing houses. The initiation of the delivery period is known as *first notice day,* which also varies among the exchanges and among the commodities: This day may be one to seven days prior to *first delivery day* (see Table 8-1). Some commodities' delivery periods occur after the last trading day.

Though the seller can make delivery during any business day from the first notice day, he or she does not necessarily have to deliver on the first day, the second, or any day. While the sellers can tender their notices of intention to deliver on each and every day of the delivery period, they need not deliver every day. In fact, none of the sellers have to make delivery; rather, they may all choose to offset their contracts by purchases in the futures market. (Speculators, of course, will always opt for offsetting whenever possible before the first notice day, since their goal is not to make or take deliveries, but profits.)

Switching Forward

Approaching the delivery month, the customer may still wish to keep a position in the market but does not wish to take or make delivery. If so, he or she could transfer the contracts prior to their maturity date into a more distant delivery. This tactic, called *switching forward,* is accomplished by simultaneously liquidating the commitment in the near delivery month and assuming an equivalent commitment in a forward month. If the client is long, he or she places an order to sell the existing position in the nearby maturing delivery and simultaneously buys another contract in a more distant delivery month.

Most firms request their clients to give them instructions regarding the disposition of long positions in the near month before the first notice day. Should they not receive timely instructions, brokers reserve the right either to

liquidate long contracts—when tenders are received—or to accept delivery of
the actual commodity in accordance with the terms of the contract, for the
account and at the risk of the client. Furthermore, most firms require that their
clients who are short contracts in the current month give them definite
instructions about liquidation no later than the day before the last day of
trading in the contracts; they must advise of their intention either to deliver or
to buy in.

Table 8-1   Listing of Representative Commodities from Each Exchange and Relevant
Delivery Facts

Exchanges and Commodity	First Notice Day	Last Trading Day	Last Notice Day	Notices Transferable
CBOT Broilers	Last business day prior to delivery month	4th last business day of delivery month	2nd last business day	No
Grains: corn-oats-soy-bean-wheat	Last business day prior to delivery month	8th last business day	2nd last business day	No*
Plywood	Last business day prior to delivery month	8th last business day	6th last business day	*
Silver	Last business day prior to delivery month	4th last business day of delivery month	2nd last business day	No*
Soybean meal and oil	Last business day prior to delivery month	8th last business day	6th last business day	No*
GNMA	1st business day after last trading day	8th last business day of delivery		No
CME Cattle (live)	6th calendar day of delivery month	20th calendar day of delivery month	2nd last business day	No
Eggs (shell)	Last business day prior to delivery month	8th last business day	Last business day	No
Gold (IMM)	See schedule			
Hogs (live)	6th calendar day of delivery month	20th calendar day of delivery month	2nd last business day	No

Table 8-1 (cont.)

Exchanges and Commodity	First Notice Day	Last Trading Day	Last Notice Day	Notices Transferable
Lumber **	1st business day after last trading day	Last business day preceding 16th calendar day of delivery month	3rd last business day	No
Pork bellies	1st delivery day is 1st business day of delivery month	6th last business day of delivery month	2nd last business day	No
N.Y. Cocoa	7 business days prior 1st business day of delivery month	8th last business day	Last trading day	Yes
N.Y. Coffee and Sugar Coffee	5 days prior 1st business day of delivery month	5 days before last business day of delivery month	Last trading day	Yes
Sugar	1st full business day prior to 15th calendar day of preceding month	Last business day of delivery month	Last notice day is 2nd notice day— 1st business day of delivery month	Yes
CME T Bills (IMM) Foreign Currency (IMM)	1st business day after last trading day	Wednesday after 3rd auction in delivery month		No
Citrus Assoc. of N.Y. Cotton Exchange*	1st business day after last trading day	10th last business day	3rd last business day	No
Commodity Exchange Copper	2nd last business day of month prior to delivery month	20th calendar day if holiday next business day	3rd last business day	No
Gold	2nd last business day of month prior to delivery month	4th last business day	3rd last business day	No

Table 8-1 (cont.)

Exchanges and Commodity	First Notice Day	Last Trading Day	Last Notice Day	Notices Trans- ferable
Silver	2nd last business day of month prior to delivery month	4th last business day	3rd last business day	No
N.Y. Cotton Cotton	5th last business day of month prior to delivery month	17th last business day of delivery month	Last business day	Yes
N.Y. Merchant Potatoes**	1st business day after last trading day	10		No
Platinum**	1st business day after last trading day	14th calendar day of delivery month		No

Note: *Long receiving notice while market in session may sell the same day and retender.
**First notice day after the last trading day.

DELIVERABLE GRADES

Most commodity futures contracts call for delivery in one grade of the commodity, which is called the *basis* or *contract grade,* but they also allow other specified grades to be delivered at the seller's option at premiums or discounts to the contract price. Superior grades are deliverable at a premium, and grades of a lesser quality are deliverable at a discount to the contract price. For example, various grades of corn are deliverable against the futures contract: No. 2 yellow corn and substitutions at differentials established by the exchange.

Premiums and discounts are established on the basis of the differentials that normally exist in the cash market between the various grades. The grades that are allowed to be delivered on futures contracts, together with the corres- ponding premiums and discounts, are fixed by the Board of Directors of the exchange. The seller has the choice of delivering any one of the grades specified by the exchange.

The exchange, however, must guard against having too many deliverable grades. Certainly an overabundance would adversely affect the price of all the deliverable grades because buyers would fear getting the least desirable grades. As a result, the prices of futures might be unduly depressed. On some futures contracts, such as silver, gold and financial instruments, no such problem exists because only one grade is deliverable. However, since the deliverable grade of many commodities accounts for such a large percentage of production or supply, there is little likelihood of a possible squeeze or corner.

The differentials at which grades other than the contract grade are deliverable are either fixed in the contract (and consequently cannot be changed during the life of the contract) or established daily on the basis of differentials in the spot market. In those commodities—such as grains, soybean meal, and soybean oil—where the differentials are fixed, they cannot be changed during the life of any specific contract even though the differentials in the cash market change—to either the advantage or disadvantage of the hedger. In other words, because of changes in the supply and demand for the various grades, the differentials in the cash market for a time may be different from those in the futures market. If these differences exist for any length of time, the exchange usually changes the differentials in the futures contract to conform with those currently existing in the cash market.

DELIVERY POINTS

The exchange designates points from which commodities may be shipped. They deem as *regular* certain warehouse facilities, grain elevators, depositories, or other places of storage. Commodities traded on the given exchange may not be shipped from any other point.

The seller holds only a negotiable *warehouse receipt,* which is issued by the storage point authorized by the exchange and which is evidence that the seller "has the goods." Only receipts from storage facilities approved and licensed by the exchange are deliverable, but the seller may select any one of a number of these, as long as they are authorized by the exchange.

The delivery, or the transfer of ownership, is accomplished by the endorsement of the receipt by the seller over to the buyer. Accompanying the receipt is a certificate of weight and grade issued by the exchange. Delivery of grains, for example, is made by tendering a registered warehouse receipt from an approved Chicago grain elevator, with the barge or rail billing attached. In return, the buyer pays in full with a certified check.

The CBOT designates all points from which meal deliveries can be made. Generally, shipments are from Midwestern manufacturing plants. Sellers make delivery with shipping certificates to either Eastern Trunk line Territory or, at a premium, to semi-unrestricted territories. Meal is loaded in bulk, F.O.B. rail cars, basis Decatur, Illinois. The shipper prepays the freight and charges the owner as specified in the rules and regulations. Delivery points for soy products are located primarily in the soybean-producing areas of the Midwest, but sellers usually furnish rail billing with adjustments to Decatur, Illinois.

CONCLUSION

You can see that the soybeans will not end up on the customer's front lawn. The most he or she will wind up with is a receipt, which is negotiable and can therefore be sold. Only now, the commodity is no longer a future; it is now an actual physical item. The futures trading is ended.

Chapter 9

The Clearing House

During the course of a trading day on an exchange, many transactions are consummated. These transactions have to be "matched up" according to the delivery months and prices—a difficult job. To facilitate this task, all trades are cleared through an organization called a clearing house or clearing association.

Each clearing house is an adjunct of the exchange and therefore works closely with it. The primary job of the clearing house is to net out all the criss-crossing transactions of each day, offsetting contracts of one clearing member with those of others. The function is similar to that of the clearing house that banking firms utilize—namely, to offset and settle the contractual obligations with a minimum of handling of cash transfers and actual deliveries.

Of course, all the transactions of one day's trading session have to be "cleared" before the start of the next—a difficult and indispensable function.

But the clearing house does still more.

It also guarantees performance for each transaction that it clears. In other words, it guarantees proper and timely delivery to every buyer (if the buyer wishes to take delivery) and payment upon delivery to every seller (if the seller wishes to make delivery). It further guarantees payment, whenever a net position warrants payment, on any contracts that are to be closed out by offsetting transactions.

In a word, the clearing house frees up the FCMs to conduct business in behalf of their customers with the confidence that any transactions that are conducted in accordance with exchange regulations will be honored one way or the other. The clearing house is a source of confidence and integrity for the exchange.

MEMBERSHIP

In order for the clearing house to do its job and fulfill its obligations, each member of the exchange must perform according to the rules of the exchange. Anyone who buys a "seat" on the exchange is a member of the exchange; however, not all exchange members are clearing house members. Clearing house membership is not compulsory. Any exchange member who transacts business on the exchange for his or her own account or in behalf of a customer must have those transactions cleared through a member of the clearing house.

Rigid financial and other types of qualifications must be met before approval as a clearing house member. One qualification requires the clearing house member to have an office within a short distance of the clearing house. This requirement expedites the handling of delivery notices and the daily pickup of transaction sheets.

From the clearing house's point of view, only their members' names appear on the transaction documents. The name of the client does not appear on the contract. Anyone who is not a clearing house member and who is clearing transactions through a member is responsible to the member, not to the clearing house itself.

FUNCTIONS

In commodity trading, the clearing house therefore serves three functions:

1. It provides a quick and simple way of settling contracts by offset, allowing traders to initiate and liquidate positions with ease.
2. It greatly simplifies deliveries against futures contracts by allocating them to qualified longs.
3. It provides uniform and continuing protection against default on contracts.

Obviously, the exchange would become bogged down within a day without such an organization to "clean up" after a day's session.

THE PRINCIPLE OF SUBSTITUTION

Once all the contracts are accepted by the clearing house, the original parties to the transaction cease dealing with one another. From the time that the trade is turned over to the clearing house, the member firm deals only with the clearing house. In turn, the clearing house assumes the role of the other party in the transaction: It becomes the "buyer" of all contracts that were sold and the "seller" of all contracts that were bought. Obviously, the clearing house—in this role—winds up buying and selling many contracts from and to "itself."

In assuming this role, the clearing house accomplishes two things:

First, since the contract is between the member firm and the clearing house, the firm (or its client) can offset the contract at any time without obtaining permission (to "break" the contract) from the originating party. "The other party" is, of course, the clearing house through which all trades are cleared and guaranteed anyway. Obviously the clearing house renders the futures markets a great deal more flexible and convenient by assuming this role. Trading can be conducted more freely and with far less legal difficulty.

Secondly, since traders are buying and selling identical contracts, the contracts are easily matchable and therefore can be substituted. Once the customer buys back the contract that was originally sold or sells one that was originally bought, he or she no longer has a contractual obligation.

> *Example*: ABC Company, a member broker, buys a contract from XYZ Company. At the end of the trading session, the clearing house substitutes itself as the other party to the contract: It becomes the seller of the contract that ABC bought and the buyer of the contract that XYZ sold.
>
> The next day ABC decides to sell the contract to EFG Company. In so doing, ABC merely transfers its contractual obligations to EFG. The clearing house again substitutes itself as "the other party" to each side of the transaction: It becomes the buyer of the contract that ABC sold and the seller of the contract that EFG bought. See Figure 9-1. ABC, in effect, bought from the clearing house and then sold to the clearing house. ABC's obligation to the clearing house is finished. The difference between the buying price and the selling price, less commission, is ABC's profit or loss. XYZ is still short with the clearing house, and EFG is now long with the clearing house.
>
> If EFG were covering a previously established short position when it bought the contract that ABC was selling, the number of contracts outstanding would have been reduced by one, XYZ would, however, still be short and someone else would be long.

GUARANTEEING THE TRANSACTIONS

In addition to making possible the direct settlement of all offsetting contracts, the clearing house guards against the slightest possibility of financial

Figure 9-1   Example of a Clearing House Substitution Function

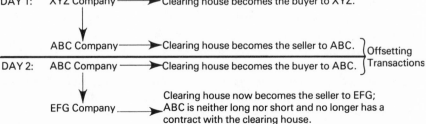

loss to any member or the clearing house itself. When the clearing house stands in the shoes of every buyer and of every seller, bound thus to fulfill all contracts, it also guarantees performance on all of them. To be able to do so, it must obtain some form of guarantee from its member firms. It therefore requires of each member a money deposit for each contract that is cleared *but not offset.* The performance money deposited by the member firms is called *original margin.*

ORIGINAL MARGIN

Actually, the original margin is not deposited with the clearing corporation. It is instead deposited in escrow with an approved bank for the account of the clearing member and for the joint benefit of the member and the clearing house. The member retains the original proof of deposit, while the clearing house holds a duplicate.

Only three types of security may be used as original margin:

1. *Obligations of the United States government*: Since a clearing member does not receive interest on cash deposited as margin, some members deposit Treasury bills, bonds, and notes, which earn interest anyway from the government.
2. *Stock in the clearing house:* Members must purchase clearing house stock when they join; how much they buy depends on the volume of trades cleared and the number of positions carried. The stock is valued at the latest book value of the shares.
3. *Cash:* As the members' margin needs permit, the cash must be deposited or may be withdrawn.

Variation Margin

When an individual customer opens an account with a brokerage firm, he or she is expected to maintain a certain level of margin in order to do business. The member firm has the same obligation to the clearing house. As the market moves against the member's net position, additional *variation* margin must be called for and deposited. Even if a customer defaults on his or her obligation to meet a margin call, the brokerage firm cannot default on its obligation; it must pay the clearing house out of its own capital. For this reason, firms are very strict regarding margin calls: hence the sell-out clause in the customer's agreement. Unlike the customer, however, the firm cannot meet the variation margin call by liquidation.

To determine the amount of margin due from each member, the clearing house records the reports of all trades, offsets as many as possible, and strikes a balance at the end of the trading day. The total contracts bought, of course, must equal the total sold; that is, the total of longs has to equal the total of shorts on the exchange as a whole. Besides totalling out the transactions for the entire exchange, the clearing house also breaks down the long and short positions for each member. Any firm that has completely offset all its positions owes the clearing house nothing in way of margin, because it has no open positions to which the clearing house can be "the other party." Any firms that have a net long or short position, however, must make deposits with the clearing house if its present margin deposit is not sufficient. (See Table 9-1.)

Table 9-1   Example of Net Positions at the End of the Day

	ABC Company		DEF Company		GHI Company		JKL Company		MNO Company	
Position	Bought	Sold	Bought	Sold	Bought	Sold	Bought	Sold	Bought	Sold
Recorded contract transactions	5	10	10	15	10	5	10	10	10	15
Net long					5					
Net short		5		5						5
Offset completely							-0-			

Summary:
ABC is short 5.
DEF is short 5.
GHI is long 5.
JKL is completely closed-out.
MNO is short 5.

After determining a member's net position, the clearing house must next determine the member's margin requirements to see whether variation margin must be deposited. Variation margin is calculated as being equivalent to the difference between the price at which the contract was traded during the day and the settlement price at the close of the day—*if* the settlement price indicates a loss in value. In simple terms, with the price of a contract going up and down all day, any given contract is likely to be traded at a price different from the market price in effect at the closing bell. If the closing price is higher, then the contract has gained in value; if the closing price is lower, then the contract has lost value. The difference in value determines the variation margin.

The closing price determines the *settlement price,* which is computed daily by the clearing corporation personnel for each delivery month of each commodity traded on the exchange. Based on the closing prices or closing ranges, it is consistent with the maintenance of prevailing spread differences. For example, in grains and soybeans the settlement price is determined to the nearest quarter-cent, in potatoes to the nearest cent per hundredweight, and in cattle to the nearest hundredth of a cent per pound.

All trades therefore are compared against the settlement price, which is released shortly after closing. The net figure is either a *pay,* which is an amount the member must pay the clearing house, or a *collect,* which is an amount the clearing house must pay the member. In effect, a "pay" is the equivalent of variation margin.

> *Example*: The price of March wheat declines 1 cent during the course of trading in one day. All members with a net long position in March wheat now owe the clearing house 1 cent per bushel, or $50 per contract. The market has moved unfavorably for March wheat, bringing about a difference in the opening and closing prices of 1 cent, which is equal to the variation call.
>
> Early that morning, ABC Company buys 20,000 bushels (four contracts) of March wheat—and watches the price decline gradually all day long. Since at the start of the day, it had no open position with the clearing house, its net position with the house at the end of the day is net long 20M March wheat. Since ABC bought at $2.50 and the price declined to $2.49 (a decrease that works out to $50 per contract), ABC owes the clearing corporation $200 in variation margin. It is a "pay" situation for the ABC Company.
>
> On the other hand, EFG Company sold 20,000 bushels of March wheat on the opening call at $2.50 per bushel. On the closing call, it bought back the four contracts at $2.49 per bushel, making $200 profit. The transactions proved profitable, of course, but since one transaction offset the other, EFG simply pockets $200—the clearing corporation does not require any additional margin.

Since the settlement price and all variation calls are made daily, margin is kept up to its original levels—"to the market"—on a day-to-day basis thereby shielding both members and the clearing house from losses.

As an even greater protection in times of volatile trading, when prices are fluctuating dramatically, the clearing house can make variation calls during the trading hours to bring a member's position approximately to the market. In such situations, the variation margin is based on the amount of funds on the commitment outstanding at the close of the preceding day.

Obviously, the clearing corporation makes no investment profits on its activities. Its position is always the equal and opposite to each of its members. And since the total long position for the whole exchange is always equal to the total short position on the exchange, the clearing house's position has to be always "net even" on the market. Its prime concern is balancing out the transactions and guaranteeing performance.

Calculation of Net Positions

Clearing members submit special cards for each trade, giving such data as the commodity, delivery month, price, quantity, whether bought or sold, whether for house or customer account, and so on. Assuming that the opposite clearing member submits an offsetting card or cards that agree on these particulars, the trade is accepted by the Clearing Corporation for clearance.

Daily, the Clearing Corporation renders to each clearing member a *trade register,* which summarizes by delivery month the previous net position and all the day's trade of the clearing member, with the pay or collect on each figured to the settlement price. The net pay or collect on all positions and trades for the day is also provided. Payment for a net pay must be made prior to the opening of the business day following. A margin statement is also given to each clearing member showing net positions for all commodities with an open position, standing margins required for each, and the amount of margins on deposit. The excess on deposit or the amount to be deposited by 9:15 A.M. the business day following is also provided. Trade registers and margin statements are provided separately for *house* and *customer accounts.* House or proprietary accounts are those representing transactions made by a brokerage firm or its employees. Most firms do not trade for their own account unless an error is made by a clerical employee that cannot be rectified the same day. The Commodity Exchange Act requires employee trading accounts to be designated as house accounts, separate and distinct from customer accounts. This strengthens the requirement for the segregation of customer funds. The day's pay or collect cannot offset standing margins: For example, a collect cannot offset an increase in standing margin requirements, nor can a pay offset a reduction in standing margin requirements. Obviously, no offsets are allowed between house and customer accounts.

THE SECURITY OF THE COMMODITY CLEARING HOUSE

The Guaranty Fund

The clearing house itself, as well as each of its members, apparently has ample protection against default as a result of original and variation margin requirements. Margin deposits, however, form only the foundation for an impregnable financial bulwark that makes it possible for the clearing house to guarantee all cleared contracts for both delivery and payment. As a further safeguard and as a condition of membership, a clearing member contributes to the guarantee fund of the clearing house. Though the amount required of each clearing member varies among different clearing houses, throughout the period of membership the deposit stands as a share in the financial stability and integrity of the organization. The guarantee fund is not even lodged with the clearing house; it is deposited in the form of cash or government securities in an approved bank. The cash or bonds cannot be withdrawn for payment or delivery either to the clearing house or to the clearing member except on an order bearing the signatures of three of the clearing house directors. Not only does the deposit of each member firm into the guarantee fund guarantee its individual transactions with the clearing house, but also the aggregate fund, when necessary, absorbs losses on any one member's account that may exceed all the credits to that member's account. In other words, all the members guarantee the accounts of all other members.

Clearance Fees and the Surplus

Still another financial source of the clearing house—one that in some clearing houses is continually augmented—is the *surplus fund* accumulated from fees charged for clearing each contract and billed to each member monthly. In comparison with the services that the clearing house renders, these clearing fees are small; but small fees paid on the many contracts cleared by all clearing members every business day of the year amount to impressive totals at the end of each year.

The surplus fund also serves as a financial guarantee. The funds are usually invested in United States government bonds, and the interest is usually applied to the operating expenses of the clearing house. As time goes on, the income from the surplus fund may even become sufficient to meet the major part of the operating expenses, a factor that will keep the clearance fee at a nominal figure.

The Careful Provision Against Loss

Clearing house bylaws and rules set forth the procedure in case recourse to the guarantee and the surplus funds should ever be necessary. In the event of a default by a member, the clearing house must close out all the member's contracts with the clearing house within a reasonable time by purchase or sale on the exchange floor. The closed account must be debited or credited with the resulting losses or profits. If, when the contracts of a failed member are closed out, a deficit is owed to the clearing house, then the deficit is made good first by recourse to the member's margin account and then to its contributions to the guarantee fund.

If these measures prove insufficient to make good the deficit, the surplus fund is applied to an extent determined by the Board of Directors. If the loss is so great as to exhaust the surplus fund, the general guarantee fund stands as a second reserve. If the guarantee fund is drawn upon, it must be immediately restored by assessment on all clearing members. This assessment, according to the usual bylaws, would be levied according to the equitable principle that those who have benefited most from the clearing house must contribute most, should the failure of a co-member draw heavily upon its resources.

These elaborate safeguards indicate sufficiently the formidable financial strength of the commodity clearing house. Though the financial resources in the guarantee fund and in the surplus fund are strong bulwarks in themselves and though the right of assessment of all members is also fully enforceable and effective, the right to call for variation margin deposits—hourly, if necessary—is the greatest possible and most effective insurance against both minor and heavy losses.

Admittedly, failure of clearing house members has occurred from time to time, but the margins on deposit have always been sufficient to absorb market differences and to protect the clearing house against loss. Nor is financial solidarity a benefit to the clearing house alone. With the safeguards that a clearing house provides, no member can suffer a loss through another member's default except through assessment. Indeed, the clearing house performs a credit insurance function by which every commodity operator who is a member of the clearing house may insure that every sale will be paid for at the contract price and that every purchase will be delivered at the contract price. No one loses.

MAKING AND TAKING DELIVERY

The clearing house also distributes notices of delivery. As a seller to all buyers and as a buyer to all sellers, through substitution, the clearing house permits deliveries to be made directly from a short wishing to make delivery to the oldest eligible outstanding long. Interim buyers and sellers are not involved in the ultimate settlement, since, through offset prior to maturity, they fulfill their contractual obligations.

Example: In February Mr. Kawn sells 25,000 bushels (5 contracts) of corn for delivery the following September. During the months that follow, he does not offset his contracts by a subsequent purchase, and he is therefore still short when the delivery month (September) arrives. The seller is obligated either to make delivery of the quantity he contracted to sell or to buy back the contracts he sold. Mr. Kawn elects to make delivery. He has the choice of making delivery during any business day during the month of September. On September 10 he decides to make delivery and issues five notices, one for each contract sold, since a separate notice is required for each contract.

Delivery Notice

When the seller decides to make delivery, the clearing broker issues a form known as a *delivery notice* to the clearing house of the respective exchange during any trading day. The notice is sent initially to the clearing house because the deliverer is short with the clearing house, the substitute buyer. The delivery notice has all the essential facts regarding the delivery: the grade of the commodity, its price, the place of delivery, and the day on which delivery will be made. But *it does not give the name of any specific person to whom delivery is to be made.*

Figure 9-2 (a) A Transferable Delivery Notice: On the back of this sheet is a log for keeping track of who accepted the notice, when, and to whom it was transferred.

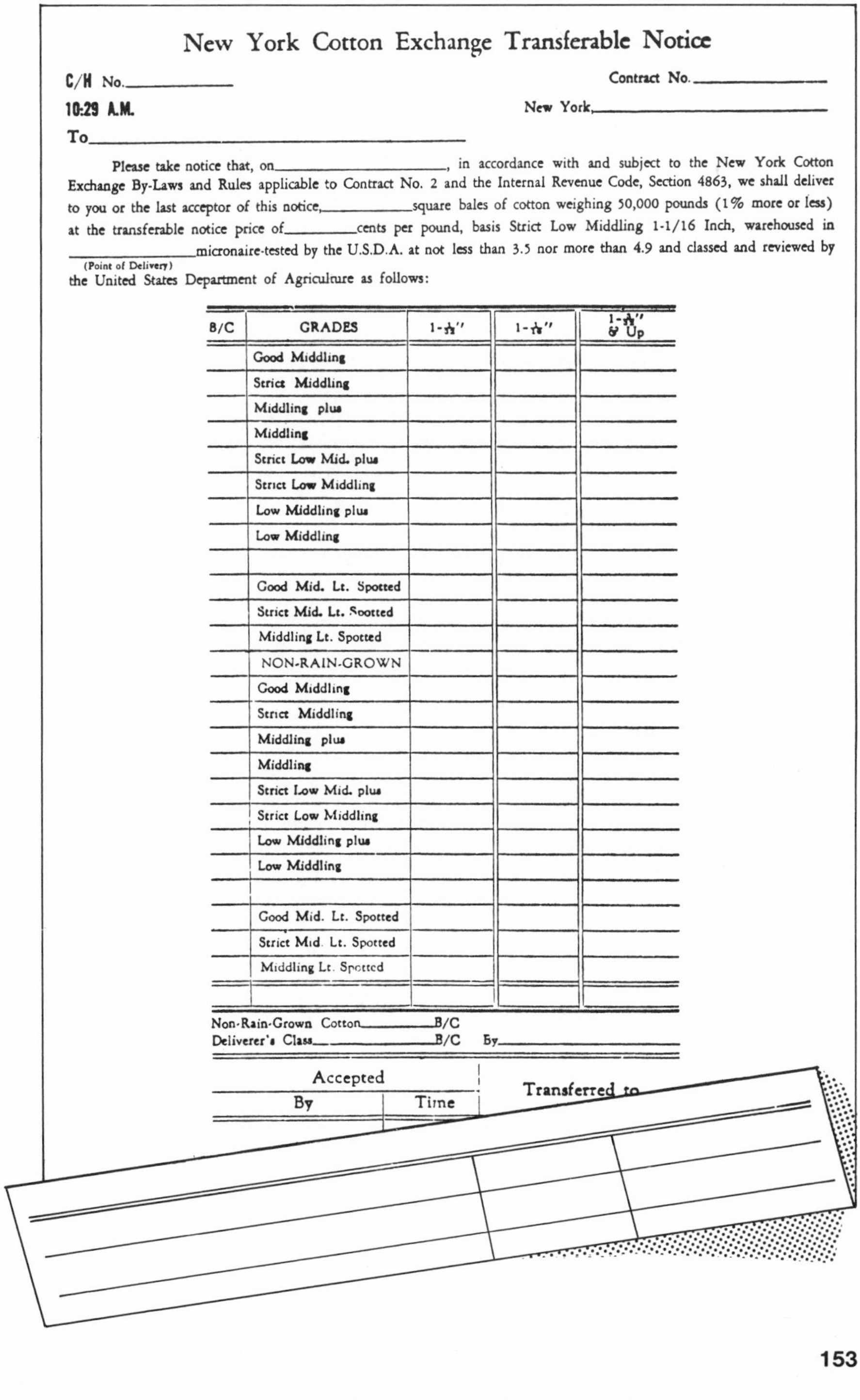

New York Cotton Exchange Transferable Notice

C/H No._____   Contract No._____

10:29 A.M.   New York,_____

To_____

Please take notice that, on_____, in accordance with and subject to the New York Cotton Exchange By-Laws and Rules applicable to Contract No. 2 and the Internal Revenue Code, Section 4863, we shall deliver to you or the last acceptor of this notice,_____square bales of cotton weighing 50,000 pounds (1% more or less) at the transferable notice price of_____cents per pound, basis Strict Low Middling 1-1/16 Inch, warehoused in _____micronaire-tested by the U.S.D.A. at not less than 3.5 nor more than 4.9 and classed and reviewed by
(Point of Delivery)
the United States Department of Agriculture as follows:

B/C	GRADES	1-$\frac{1}{32}$''	1-$\frac{1}{16}$''	1-$\frac{3}{32}$'' & Up
	Good Middling			
	Strict Middling			
	Middling plus			
	Middling			
	Strict Low Mid. plus			
	Strict Low Middling			
	Low Middling plus			
	Low Middling			
	Good Mid. Lt. Spotted			
	Strict Mid. Lt. Spotted			
	Middling Lt. Spotted			
	NON-RAIN-GROWN			
	Good Middling			
	Strict Middling			
	Middling plus			
	Middling			
	Strict Low Mid. plus			
	Strict Low Middling			
	Low Middling plus			
	Low Middling			
	Good Mid. Lt. Spotted			
	Strict Mid. Lt. Spotted			
	Middling Lt. Spotted			

Non-Rain-Grown Cotton_____B/C
Deliverer's Class_____B/C   By_____

Accepted		Transferred to
By	Time	

153

Figure 9-2 (b) A Nontransferable Soybean Meal Delivery Notice

No._____

SOYBEAN MEAL DELIVERY NOTICE

BROKER & CO.
INCORPORATED

NEW YORK, N.Y. 10011

_____ 19_____

BOARD OF TRADE CLEARING CORPORATION

We have on hand ready for delivery the following described Soybean Meal Shipping Certificate, and hereby made tender to you for the same, in fulfillment of contract of sale to you of 100 tons (2,000 pounds each) of Soybean Meal of Standard of Board of Trade of the City of

Chicago at_____44% Protein Soybean Meal.

Soybean Meal Shipping Certificate, Registrar's Number_____

registered on_____, 19_____, issued by Shipping plant of

_____Located at_____

_____, 100 tons at Delivery Price_____

per ton $_____, Less premium_____days @_____

cents per ton per day $_____

ETL Certificate (delivery price)

Semi-Unrestricted Certificate, premium of $3.25 per ton - $......................................
                    Amount due upon surrender of Soybean Meal Shipping Certificate

$ _____

BROKER & CO.
INCORPORATED

By _____

Premium charge paid to and including_____,19_____
Number of days from date of registration or date to which premium paid to date of delivery (not counting date of registration or date of payment of charges but counting day delivery made)

_____days.

E. & O.E.

The delivery date that appears on the notice is the business day following the issuance of the notice. If the notice is issued on a Monday, the delivery has to be made on Tuesday, unless a holiday intervenes. If it is issued on Friday, the commodity is delivered on the following Monday. The price that appears on the notice (the price the deliverer is to receive from the long who accepts the notice) is the settlement price of the previous session. In other words, if the notice is issued on Monday, the notice price is the settlement price of the preceding Friday.

When the notice is delivered to the clearing house, the house ascertains from its books the names of those clearing members who are long the given contracts and passes the notices along to them. The methods of distributing the notices of the holders of long positions vary among exchanges. On most exchanges, notices are apportioned on the basis of the oldest longs. On some exchanges they are apportioned, as far as practical, on the basis of the percentage of gross long contracts held by a member in the spot month. The brokerage firms receiving the notices usually distribute them, in turn, to their clients who hold the oldest long positions.

Transferable versus Nontransferable

Some notices are transferable and some are nontransferable. On the New York Cocoa Exchange and the Cotton Exchange, for example, they are transferable. On the CBOT, they are not.

If a holder of a long position, a so-called "long," receives a transferable notice—even while the contract is still trading, before the end of the delivery month—he or she must accept it. However, all the long has to do is sell it and pass the notice on or "transfer" it to the buyer. Since the commodity is in the warehouse, certified as to grade and ready for delivery, a time limitation is set on the transfer. Delivery must be made the next day, so anyone who does not wish to accept delivery must sell it within a half-hour. On the notice itself are lines for the endorsement by each long and a box for the time it was received. (See Figure 9-2a.) If the notice remains in the long's hands for more than a half hour, it is considered accepted, or *stopped*. The long must then take delivery.

A nontransferable notice, on the other hand, is handled differently. The long, upon receiving the notice, can still sell the contract to avoid delivery. But the notice cannot be transferred to the buyer immediately. The receiver of the notice, the long, must keep it overnight and absorb one day's charges: He is "stuck," as the saying goes. However, since he has sold out the long position, he now causes a new notice to be issued and sent to the clearing house after the close of the market. In so doing the long is said to be "retendering" the notice. The following morning the clearing house resumes the procedure. The long has two transactions in the account, one for the futures position and the other for the cash or actual position. The gain or loss in the actual position is the difference between the selling price and the settlement price of the retendered notice.

Delivery Responsibilities

One way or the other, once a long accepts the delivery notice—or *stops* it, as is the phrase—the clearing house's obligation is ended. The seller is informed of the buyer's identity, and then the two parties take all the arrangements from that point. They may also make certain adjustments, if necessary, in accordance with the certified grade and weight of the commodity.

The delivery is considered complete and the contract closed when the buyer accepts a warehouse receipt (indicating the storage of the commodity) from the seller and in turn pays in full with a certified check. Payment is *not* made through the clearing house. The only link the clearing house maintains with the contract is that it retains the margins on account until the actual delivery is made.

The futures contract is settled separately. All intervening buyers have been eliminated—with their profits or losses—by their sales upon receipt of the notices.

Commissions

No additional commission is charged on a retender and a redelivery on the CBOT if they are accomplished within the same delivery month in which the notice was originally stopped. However, on most other exchanges an additional commission is charged when a person resells and redelivers. Figures on the number of notices and retenders for each commodity are made known by the clearing house during each trading session of the delivery month.

CONCLUSION

The clearing operation is vital to the commodities industry. Without it, the trading would quickly collapse into a chaotic jumble of errors and confusion. And if it could survive—if only briefly—the transactions would undoubtedly bog down in one legal sandtrap after another.

The average customer barely gives a thought to the behind-the-scenes activity that guarantees performance on his or her contract.

In this section, we have reviewed the basics of the commodities industry: a little of its background, its regulation by government, the duties of the brokers and exchange officials, the rights and obligations of the investors, and finally the dedication of the clearing personnel.

In effect, we have described a huge machine, with complicated gears and levers, that starts up abruptly and snaps off sharply at the clanging of a bell. While it is working, it is capable of doing many things, of accomplishing many tasks, but like any machine it works only under human guidance and control.

That guidance and control constitute the tactics of commodities transactions—the day-to-day buying and selling that accomplishes the short-term goals. And tactics is the subject of the next section.

Part Two

Commodities Tactics

Chapter 10

Cash and Futures Price Relationships

Commodities can be bought and sold in two separate but related markets—the cash market and the futures market. The *cash price* is the price of the actual commodity in the commercial marketplace. The *futures price* is the price of the futures contract on the exchange. These two markets tend to parallel one another and to converge as each delivery month expires. The parallel movement occurs because factors that effect either a rise or a fall in cash prices usually affect futures prices in much the same manner. This strong parallel relationship makes hedging possible and advantageous; because both markets move together, the losses incurred in one are offset, for the most part, by the profits made in the other. The convergence of the two markets as the delivery draws near occurs because carrying charges decline, as we shall see.

The term "basis" arises from its usage by the trade in determining prices at which cash sales are made, "based" on futures. The *basis* is the price of the cash commodity at the delivery point in relation to the nearby or dominant futures. Basis prices are modified also by the location and quality of the commodity.

However, the difference between futures and cash prices, called the *basis,* is not constant. Although prices in the cash market and prices in the futures market tend to rise and fall together, the correlation is not exact. As shown in Figure 10-1, the cash and futures prices are constantly fluctuating. Hence, unless each changes by *exactly* the same amount, the basis tends to widen or narrow. During some periods, cash prices *advance* somewhat faster than futures or they *decline* faster than futures—or futures prices outpace cash prices in either direction.

The basis is thus subject, for one thing, to the law of supply and demand. When the price of futures is higher than the cash price, this type of basis is referred to as a *normal* or *carrying charge market.* (You'll see why it is called a "carrying charge" market in the chapter on hedging.) A normal market indicates that more than adequate supplies for full seasonal needs appear to be available. Conversely, when the price of futures is lower than the cash price, this type of basis is referred to as an *inverted market,* and it is usually an indication of intense demand for immediate delivery—demand motivated by fears of a possible shortage. (See Figures 10-2 and 10-3.)

Whether the cash price is higher or lower than the nearby futures price, at the local delivery point, is largely determined by the amount of commodity available on the market relative to demand at that time. For example, if at the delivery point the available supply appears large enough to take care of prospective requirements until the next futures delivery period, the cash price

Figure 10-1   The Difference Between Futures and Cash Prices (Basis)

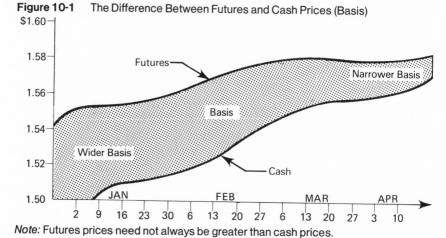

Note: Futures prices need not always be greater than cash prices.

Figure 10-2   A Normal Market in which Futures Prices Are Higher than Cash Prices

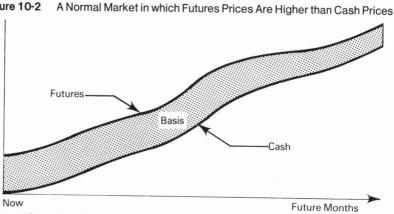

Futures prices are said to be "at a premium to" cash prices. Cash prices are said to be "at a discount to" futures prices.

Figure 10-3 An Inverted Market in which Cash Prices are Higher than Futures Prices

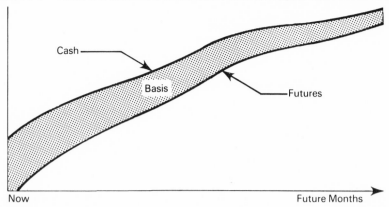

Cash prices are said to be "at a premium to" futures prices. Futures prices are said to be "at a discount to" cash prices.

is lower than (or *at a discount to*) the price of the nearest futures delivery. If prospective requirements appear to be larger than the supplies coming onto that market until the next delivery, the cash price is said to move to a *premium* above the futures prices. In other words if the immediate demand is in excess of available supplies, the cash price turns out to be higher than (at a premium to) the price of the nearest futures, regardless of the cost of carrying (or storing) the commodity from one point in time to another.

The basis is also subject to seasonal influences. The basis tends to widen at certain times during the marketing season and narrow at other times. The premium of futures over cash prices and the discount of futures under cash prices tend to shift back and forth during the overall season. The widening and narrowing reflect the relative surplus during one part of the season and the relative depletion during another. For example, in a normal market the cash price tends to decline faster than the futures price during the harvest period because of the abundant supplies coming onto the market over a short period of time. Thus the basis widens. Once the harvest has been completed and harvest pressures abate, the basis usually begins to narrow; that is, the cash price gains faster than the price of futures. As a season's supplies are used up, the quantity available at some locations may become short, and cash prices at those locations tend to strengthen relative to the futures price. Thus, supply and demand patterns change according to seasonal demands.

This changing basis provides the hedger with the opportunity to make an additional profit, while securing protection from a change in the price level—if he or she correctly anticipates the change in the basis. Even though the difference between the cash and futures price may widen or narrow, the risk of an adverse change in the basis is generally much less than the risk of a change in the overall cash price structure; that is, a merchandiser's risk of going unhedged is greater than the risk of an adverse change in the basis. Though the

163

basis is variable, it is quite predictable, because cash and futures have a tendency to adjust to each other during the delivery period at the delivery point.

CARRYING CHARGE MARKET OR NORMAL MARKET

Under normal circumstances, with what appears to be an adequate supply, the price of a commodity for future delivery should be equal to the present cash price plus the amount of carrying charges necessary to carry (or to store) the commodity from the present until the month of delivery. Theoretically, an "old" crop future—one representing a crop already in storage as contrasted to a crop yet to be harvested—should sell at a higher price than when it was harvested; the higher price includes a carrying charge. The futures price is therefore at a premium over cash price of the basic deliverable grade. The premium, equivalent to the *carrying charges,* results from *the costs of warehousing, insurance, and interest incurred during storage.* For more distant futures months, storage is naturally longer and the costs of storage, insurance, and interest are higher. Consequently, the premium of the futures contract over the cash price of the commodity must be higher. Thus, in October, the price of the December delivery should be above the cash price by an amount equal to the cost of carrying the actual commodity in store from October until December. The March price should be even farther above the December price because of the greater cost of storage from December to March.

Calculating the Carrying Charges

To determine carrying charges, multiply the monthly carrying charges by the number of months that the actual commodity is to be stored. If it costs 5 cents per bushel per month to carry corn in storage, the full carrying charges between November and March are 20 cents (4 months × 5 cents = 20 cents). The actual commodity is carried for a maximum of four months—November, December, January, and February. Do not include March in your calculations because the actual grain can be delivered against the March contract on March 1. When figuring carrying charges, always assume that delivery will occur at the earliest possible time.

The cash price at any given time should therefore sell at a carrying charge discount to the futures contract. The extent of the discount depends on the time interval between the cash and futures. As time passes, the discount should narrow; cash should gain on futures until the futures contract expires, at which time the cash and futures prices usually turn out to be equal. So the maximum premium that March futures could be above the price of the cash commodity on November 1 is 20 cents. If cash corn is purchased and March corn futures are sold when futures are at full carrying charges to cash corn, the hedger is completely protected whether cash prices advance or decline.

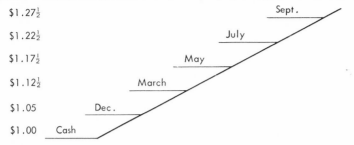

Figure 10-4   Cash/Futures Relationship in a Carrying Charge or Normal Market

$1.27½

$1.22½

$1.17½

$1.12½

$1.05

$1.00

Sept.

July

May

March

Dec.

Cash

Example: In October, the cash price of corn is $2 per bushel. The carrying charges for a bushel of corn is running about 5 cents per month. (These costs naturally vary with changes in storage costs and with interest rates, as well as with changes in the value of the grain itself.) In October, therefore, the December futures delivery, an old crop future, sell for roughly 10 cents over the cash price. March corn, another old crop future, sells at the same time for 25 cents over the cash and 15 cents over the December futures. Refer to Figure 10-4: Each successive price represents additional carrying charges for each month. (These figures are actually theoretical to a large extent, because they reflect the full carrying charges, which are seldom attained.)

This principle rests on three facts:

1. Grain is produced at one time of the year, but it is used at a fairly regular rate so that inventories *must be carried* from harvest time forward.
2. Costs are incurred in storing and maintaining the quality of grain.
3. Virtually no cost is incurred in holding futures contracts.

These three facts cause cash prices to increase in relation to futures prices as the season progresses. Logically, the closer you get to a remote delivery date, the *longer* you've carried the commodity. Hence the charges should increase the price continuously until a new harvest is in—What takes place to make the carrying charges break and start downward? When does that happen? If you buy a July corn futures contract in October with the intention of taking delivery for commercial purposes, you incur only the cost of the small margin deposit required to guarantee the contract. On the other hand, if you buy the corn itself in October for sale or use the following July, you must store it, thus running up expenses like full investment value, depreciation, and maintenance. But because holding cash grain costs money, an increase in price during the season equal to the cost of storage only makes sense. In other words, the cash price of the grain should gain faster than the futures price, as the season progresses, by the amount of the carrying charges.

As long as the crop is either normal or over-abundant, the formation of carrying charges is more or less assured. They are assured because merchandisers, the people who deal in the actual commodity, do not buy and store the commodity in quantity until the cash price has worked its way down to an acceptable discou it to futures. At that level, wherever it lies, the cash price makes it profitable for merchandisers to store the commodity; in trade parlance, the cash price is said to *reach a hedgeable basis.* This rather natural inclination on the part of merchandisers by itself tends to assure the development of what is called a "carrying charge relationship" between the cash price and the futures prices. However, as the season progresses, the cost of holding the actual commodity until delivery becomes smaller; therefore, the difference between the cash and futures price should become smaller until it ultimately disappears.

Convergence of the Prices

Eventually futures must decline to the cash price, or the cash price must advance to the futures price. They must, in one way or the other, converge. As time passes and the delivery period draws near, the difference between the cash and futures prices tend to narrow by reason of the lessening carrying charges. Whether prices advance or decline, the cost of carrying the commodity becomes less and less. For instance, if it costs 20 cents to carry corn from November to March, it costs only 15 cents from December to March. By March 1, the first day of the delivery period, the two prices should be just about equal because the carrying charges are by then reduced to zero.

A Declining Market   If as March approaches the spot price declines, then the futures price, formerly at full carrying charges, *may* decline to the spot price, but it cannot decline to a level below the spot price. In other words, the futures price has to decline at least as much as the cash price, if not more. If the futures price does not decline as much as the cash price, then it is selling at more than a carrying charge premium. This is a guaranteed profit situation for anyone who buys cash corn, sells futures, holds the actual corn in storage until March, then delivers it against the short March futures position. Since in such a situation the cost of carrying the corn until March is less than the premium at which the March futures is sold, the seller makes a profit: The profit is the difference between the premium and the cost of carrying the corn until March, which is approaching zero anyway. Such a condition cannot endure for very long because, as firms buy cash and sell futures to take advantage of the abnormality, a normal carrying charge relationship is reestablished.

Generally, if a cash market declines, futures have to decline more than cash prices because they start at a higher price. If the market advances, cash prices have to advance further to catch up with futures because they start from a lower price.

Example: On November 1 the price of cash corn in Chicago is $2.10 per bushel, whereas at the same time March futures are $2.30. Cash is 20 cents under

Figure 10-5   Illustration of Cash and Futures Convergence in a Declining Market

	Cash	*Futures*	*Basis*
November 1	$2.10	$2.30	20 cents
December 1	$2.00	$2.15	15 cents
January 1	$1.90	$2.00	10 cents
February 1	$1.80	$1.85	5 cents
March 1	$1.70	$1.70	————

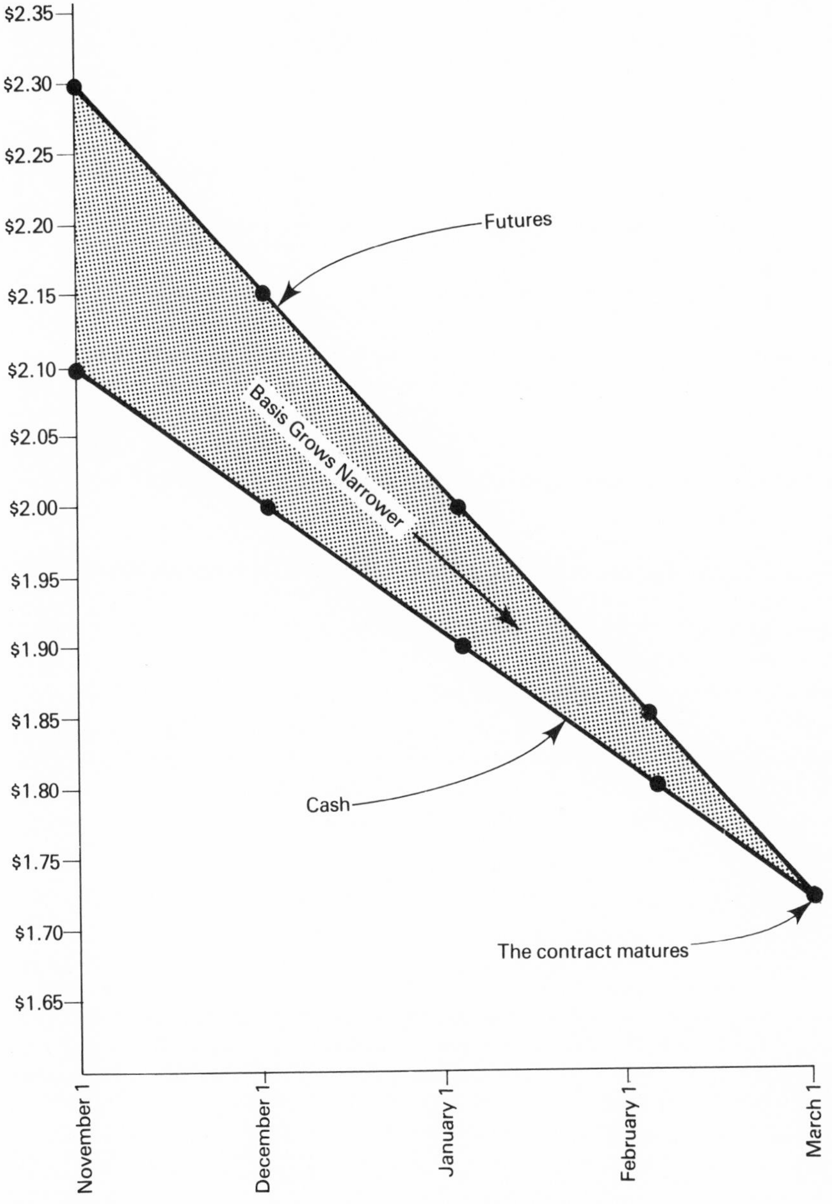

March, a difference that represents the full carrying charges between November and March. Regardless of whether the market advances or declines, by January 1, the difference between the cash and the futures prices is no more than 10 cents. By February 1, it is 5 cents. And by March 1, the cash and futures price are approximately the same. In this case, the cash price declines to $2.00 by December 1. Consequently, the futures price must decline by 15 cents to $2.15, because the most that March can be at a premium to cash is the full carrying charges. The cash price continues its decline and falls 10 cents to $1.90 by January 1; and the price of futures therefore declines to $2.00 because the carrying charges from January 1 to March 1 equal 10 cents. The cash price declines still farther to $1.80 by February 1; futures follow by 15 cents to $1.85, now at a premium of only 5 cents, the carrying charge between February 1 to March 1. The cash price finally drops to $1.70 by March 1, where it converges with the futures price which has dropped by 15 cents to $1.70. The two prices thus equal each other at the delivery point, in March. To converge, the price of cash corn declined 40 cents from $2.10 on November 1 to $1.70 on March 1, and futures dropped 60 cents from $2.30 to $1.70. (See Figure 10-5.)

Although in this example hedgers who were long cash suffered a 40-cent loss, they realized a 60-cent profit from their short futures position. They thus earned the carrying charges of 20 cents, which was the basis when they established the selling hedges (see Figure 10-5 again). In addition to protection against a 40-cent decline in the price of cash corn, they earned an additional 20 cents because of a favorable change in the basis. Thus when futures are at a premium to the cash, buying the actual commodity and selling futures pays for the cost of carrying the actual commodity.

An Advancing Market.   On the other hand, if cash prices advance, the results are the same. As the spot price advances, the futures price may advance to a level below the spot price, but it cannot advance to a point higher than the spot price. If futures prices advance more than the spot price, again they represent more than a carrying charge premium. Thus traders would quickly buy the cash and sell the futures until the normal relationship was reestablished. For instance, although March futures may be 17 cents higher than cash on November 1, they cannot maintain this premium over the long run because the March delivery cannot exceed the cash price by more than carrying charges, which are 15 cents.

Example: The cash price advances 10 cents to $2.20 between November 1 and December 1. Futures can advance only 5 cents to $2.35 because they can be above cash on December 1 only by the carrying charges between December and March, which is 15 cents. Thus, while both cash and futures advance, cash prices must advance more than futures because they started at a lower level.

The cash price extends its advance another 10 cents to $2.30 by January 1. The price of futures can advance only to $2.40 because the March futures may exceed cash prices on January 1 by only 10 cents, the carrying charges from January 1 to March 1. The cash price advances still further to $2.40 by

February 1, and futures advance only 5 cents to $2.45. Only one month to go before the contract matures—5 cents worth of charges. Finally, the cash price advances to $2.50 by March 1, and futures advance only 5 cents to $2.50.

Thus if the price of cash corn advanced 40 cents from $2.10 on November 1 to $2.50 on March 1, futures can advance only 20 cents from $2.30 to $2.50. (See Figure 10-6.)

Even though those who were short futures incurred a 20-cent loss, they realized a 40-cent profit from their long cash positions, thus earning the carrying charge of 20 cents, which was the basis when they established the selling hedges.

Naturally, these premiums of futures over cash and of one future over another do not always exist in precisely this manner in actual markets. The "hard" triangles in Figures 10-5 and 10-6 would be more like the zig-zag hills and valleys of the market's actual daily performance. For one reason, the cash commodity may be in short supply at the present time, but the trade might anticipate that the commodity will be in abundant supply later on. Under such circumstances, the carrying charge premium is typically smaller than normal; in fact, it might be eliminated together.

INVERTED MARKET

As long as the upcoming supply of commodities is equal to or greater than the demand, then the market tends to remain normal: Futures tend to be higher than cash prices. Approaching the delivery period, the two prices gravitate toward equality; this tendency is, as you have seen, considered normal.

However, when supplies on hand are inadequate to meet seasonal needs, cash prices could rise above futures prices, and the nearby futures go to a premium over the distant months, creating what is called an *inverted market*. Under such circumstances, the commodity moves rapidly into the marketing channels eliminating the storage process, and in turn the carrying charges.

An inverted market develops because of (1) an urgent demand for immediate delivery to meet sales agreements and to maintain declining inventories, and/or (2) expectations of an increase in future supplies. The prices of various futures contracts reflect the action taken by users of the cash commodity based upon their current needs and their expectations of the coming price trend. (See Figure 10-7.) They need the commodity now, so they have to buy at any price. As the cash price increases, the nearby futures price advances concurrently.

When the nearby delivery is at a premium, the premium adjusts demand to compensate for the available supply. When cash prices go up, the less

Figure 10-6   Illustration of Cash and Futures Convergence in an Advancing Market

	Cash	*Futures*	*Basis*
November 1	$2.10	$2.30	20 cents
December 1	$2.20	$2.35	15 cents
January 1	$2.30	$2.40	10 cents
February 1	$2.40	$2.45	5 cents
March 1	$2.50	$2.50	————

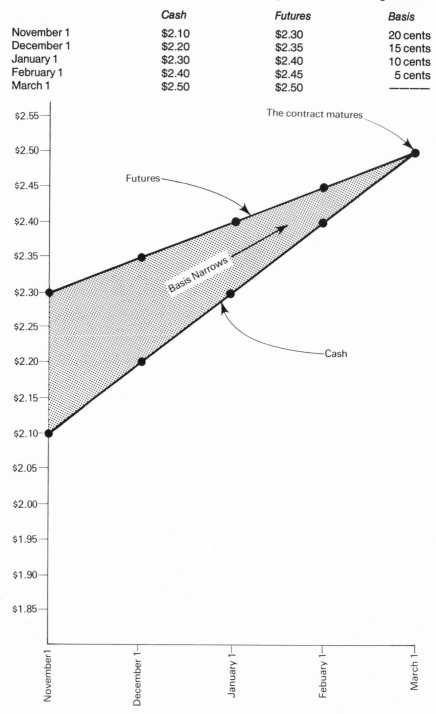

urgent buyers simply do not buy. The more needy buyers buy at any price, just to have the commodity. Thus the premium advances to a limit that curtails buying for demands of lesser importance, and the available commodity satisfies the more urgent requirements. If more of a commodity is put on the market than is currently needed, the premium either narrows and discourages selling or it narrows and encourages demand until a proper supply-and-demand balance results. In this manner, so far as is possible, a reduced supply is stretched for use throughout an entire season. When supplies are small, the more urgent type of demand keeps storage stocks low, and buyers are willing to absorb the cost of carrying the grain in order to have some of it available when needed. As withholding of stocks occurs when supplies are small, the development of a premium price for the nearby delivery acts as a deterrent for carrying large inventories except by those who have a definite need for the commodity.

CASH AND FUTURES PRICES IN THE DELIVERY MONTH

Regardless of whether the cash market is inverted or normal prior to the maturity of a futures contract, the cash and the futures prices will in all probability converge during the delivery period at the delivery point. Since the foundation of the futures contract is the delivery process, impending deliveries act as the equalizer. Whether the futures or the cash price is at a premium does not matter. Neither does the amount or the direction of change. By the time a futures delivery becomes the current or spot delivery, its price will approximate the price of the deliverable grade of the actual commodity.

Here's why. In a normal market, with cash prices lower than the price of futures as the contract approaches expiration, commercial firms buy the actual commodity, sell the futures, and make delivery against their short positions in futures. By the same token, those who are long futures tend to liquidate their futures positions, because for them taking delivery of the futures contract is uneconomical. They can purchase the actual commodity at a price lower than that in the futures market. These developments force the price of futures down to the level of actuals.

On the other hand, in an inverted market with futures prices lower than the price of actuals, merchants buy futures and stand for delivery, thus forcing the price of futures up into line with cash. Then, too, those who are short futures tend to buy back contracts, then sell the actual commodity in the higher-priced cash market; this tactic is more advantageous than to deliver against the lower-priced futures contract. This "buy-back" or covering also contributes to forcing the price of futures into line with the cash price.

Example: The price of No. 2 yellow corn in Chicago during the month of February is $2.40 per bushel, while at the same time the March corn futures sell for $2.50. Anyone who owns or who can buy corn (at $2.40) in Chicago can make 10 cents by selling the March futures (at $2.50) and delivering the actual corn against the futures sale during the month of March. Naturally, anyone who has the choice of selling either in the cash market for $2.40 or in the futures market for $2.50 chooses to sell in the higher-priced futures market. Thus, the selling of futures—combined with the buying of cash by those who did not own the corn but who wanted to take advantage of this disparity—tends to force the price of futures into line with the cash price.

On the other hand, if the cash price of No. 2 yellow corn in Chicago is $2.50 while the March futures price is $2.40, anyone who needed cash corn would buy in the futures market rather than in the cash market. The futures market is the cheaper source of supply. The buyer purchases March futures and then stands for delivery in March. The purchase of futures and the lack of demand for the actual commodity forces the two prices into alignment.

This process continues until the premiums or discounts eventually disappear. Thus, arbitraging between cash and futures markets forces the two prices more or less together. You must say "more or less" because although the two prices tend to converge during the delivery period, they are rarely, if ever, identical. This discrepancy in practice does not violate the principle. Rather, it results from certain technical differences between the value of cash grain in boxcars and the value of grain taken on delivery of futures. These differences have to do with the time of delivery, the quality of the commodity, the place, loading charges, and freight structure. Usually, the cash prices wind up slightly higher than futures.

Even the mere possibility of arbitraging is usually sufficient to keep cash and futures prices in line. Occasionally, however, situations arise in which a disparity develops between the spot and futures market prices. For example, bringing supplies into deliverable positions may be impossible because of a lack of storage space at delivery points, because of a lack of time to ship the commodity to delivery points from outlying areas, or because of the commodity's ineligibility for delivery. In such cases, the cash price remains below the futures. Such instances, however, are definitely the exceptions rather than the rule.

Obviously, even though the prices of the cash and futures markets converge to within close range of one another, cash prices will not be the same—in all geographic locations. The cost of transportation and other factors cause price differentials from one locale to another.

Example: In February, the cash basis is "3 over," meaning that No. 2 yellow corn in Chicago is selling for 3 cents more than the March futures. At the same time, the East-Central Illinois basis is 7 under and the New Orleans basis is 14 over. In these instances, the basis prices differ according to location, but they all refer to the same nearby future.

Sometimes the cash price refers to a more distant future. In October, a buyer may be concerned with the price of corn at local elevators in relation to the May futures. In this case, the farm basis may be "30 under May."

The only important basis is the one that applies to the individual user, who must become familiar with the changes in his or her own local basis.

Because hedging is so extensively practiced by people who market commodities, futures have become the central focus and pricing point of their system. Futures prices represent the general level of the price of the commodity, and the multitude of cash prices that exist at any given time are established in relation to the futures. But even though futures prices are the central reference point and even though cash prices are quoted in relation to futures prices, *futures prices do not determine cash prices.* On the contrary, futures prices are determined by the conditions (and the speculative judgments about the conditions) of supplies and of the requirements prevailing in cash markets. Cash prices determine futures prices, but at the same time cash prices are stated or are "based" on futures prices.

RELATIONSHIP OF FUTURES AT DIFFERENT POINTS IN TIME

The same basic relationship that exists between the cash and futures market also exists between one futures contract and another, except that different delivery months do not converge with each other at delivery time. When the nearby futures are lower in price than (at a discount to) the more distant deliveries, the market is considered a carrying charge market or normal market.

> *Example*: See Figure 10-8. Chicago wheat is a normal market. The December wheat delivery on December 1 closed at $2.66¾ per bushel; the March closed at $2.78; the May closed at $2.82½; the July closed at $2.85¾; and so on. Each subsequent delivery is progressively higher in price than the previous delivery. The March is at a premium to the December, the May is at a premium to the March, and the July is at a premium to the May.

When nearby deliveries are higher in price (or are at a premium) to deferred deliveries, the market is referred to as an *inverted market.*

> *Example*: The January delivery of orange juice closes on December 1 at 124.50 cents. The March delivery closes at 121.25; May, at 119.50; July, at 118.65; and September, at 117.70 bid.
> In this case, each succeeding delivery is *lower* in price than the one before. The March delivery closes at a discount to January; May closes at a discount to March—and so on.

OPPORTUNITIES IN FUTURES RELATIONSHIPS

Wherever differences in prices exist, interest in arbitrage or spreading is also present. Spreading—a kind of sophisticated speculation—is discussed in

Figure 10-8   A Page Showing Commodity Prices

Futures Prices
Thursday, December 1, 1977

—GRAINS AND FEEDS—

WHEAT (CBT)—5,000 bu.; cents per bu.

	Open	High	Low	Close	Change	Season's High	Low
Dec	263½	268	262	266¾	+3	347	224¾
Mar 78	274½	278¾	273	277¾-278¼	+2¾to3¼	329	234
May	279½	283	278	282¼-¾	+2¼to2¾	320¾	238¾
July	283	286¼	282	285¾-286	+2to2¼	299	243½
Sept	288	291¼	287	291	+1	303½	248½
Dec	296	299	295¼	299	+2	311	278½

Sales Wed.: 11,738 contracts.

WHEAT (K.C.)—5,000 bu.; cents per bu.

	Open	High	Low	Close	Change	Season's High	Low
Dec	272½	275¼	271¼	275¼-275	+2¾to2½	311¾	231
Mar 78	278	279½	276¼	279-279¼	+1to1¼	302	236
May	281	282¼	278½	282	+1	294	239½
July	283	284¼	280¾	284	+½	295¾	242¾
Sept	286	289¼	285½	289¼	+1¼	299½	276½

Sales Wed.: 3,609 contracts.

WHEAT (MPLS)—5,000 bu.; cents per bu.

	Open	High	Low	Close	Change	Season's High	Low
Dec	272½	276¼	271¼	275½-275	+2¾to2¼	325	239
Mar 78	277¾	282	277	281¾-282	+¾to4	319½	246¼
May	282	286¼	282	286¼b	+3¼	302	252
July	286¾	290¼	286½	290b	+2¾	304½	256¾
Sept	295	295	294½	295b	+1¾	307	293¼

Sales Wed.: 913 contracts.

CORN (CBT)—5,000 bu.; cents per bu.

	Open	High	Low	Close	Change	Season's High	Low
Dec	220¾	221½	219¾	220-219¾	-1½to1¾	278¾	190¼
Mar 78	228	229¼	227½	228-227½	-¾to1¼	283¾	198¼
May	231¾	232	230½	230¾-½	-¾to1	286¾	203¼
July	231¼	232	230¼	231¼-231	-½to¾	272	205¾
Sept	227¼	228¼	226½	227¼	-¼	237¾	209½
Dec	227½	228½	226½	227¼	-¼	237½	221

Sales Wed.: 35,493 contracts.

SOYBEANS (CBT)—5,000 bu.; cents per bu.

	Open	High	Low	Close	Change	Season's High	Low
Jan 78	583	590	581	588-587	+2¼to1¼	799	504½
Mar	592	597½	588	596-595	+3¼to2¼	804½	513
May	599	603¾	595	601-600	+¾to-¼	807½	520
July	601	609½	601	608-607	+2¼to1¼	807	526½
Aug	603½	607½	607½	606½	+1	652	529¼
Sept	588	591½	586	589	+1	631½	523
Nov	581	588½	581	586	+1¾	625½	535
Jan 79	588	592½	588	591	+1½	620½	585½

Sales Wed.: 31,416 contracts.

SOYBEAN MEAL (CBT)—100 tons; $ per ton

	Open	High	Low	Close	Change	Season's High	Low
Dec	155.00	156.00	153.80	154.80-155.-	-.50to.30	212.50	134.00
Jan78	157.50	158.30	156.00	157.30-.10	-.30to.50	212.00	136.50
Mar	161.00	162.00	159.20	161.-160.80	unch to-.20	214.50	140.00
May	162.50	164.50	162.00	163.00-.50	-.10to+.40	216.50	143.50
July	166.50	167.00	164.50	165.50-165.-	.70to1.2	218.50	147.00
Aug	166.20	167.53	166.00	167.00-.50	-.50to unch	181.00	148.00
Sept	163.00	165.50	163.00	164.-163.50	unch to-.50	180.50	149.50
Oct	164.00	164.00	162.50	163.50	....	178.50	150.50
Dec	164.00	165.50	164.00	165.00b	....	179.00	156.00

Sales Wed.: 11,476 contracts.

SOYBEAN OIL (CBT)—60,000 lbs.; cents per lb.

	Open	High	Low	Close	Change	Season's High	Low
Dec	20.75	21.40	20.75	21.25-.40+	.52to.67	29.18	17.37
Jan 78	20.40	21.15	20.40	20.95-21.05+	.47to.57	28.71	17.50
Mar	20.50	21.05	20.45	20.80-.85+	.35to.40	28.65	17.75
May	20.45	20.85	20.40	20.80-.70+	.35to.25	28.35	18.00
July	20.40	20.75	20.30	20.65-.70+	.27to.32	28.15	18.13
Aug	20.40	20.65	20.30	20.55	+ .20	21.60	18.13
Sept	19.90	20.20	19.85	20.20-.15+	.45to.45	21.20	18.13
Oct	19.80	20.00	19.80	19.95b	+ .20	20.50	18.40
Dec	19.75	19.90	19.60	19.90	+ .30	20.35	18.50

Sales Wed.: 11,897 contracts.

OATS (CBT)—5,000 bu.; cents per bu.

	Open	High	Low	Close	Change	Season's High	Low
Dec	133½	135½	133½	135½	+2	173	107¼
Mar 78	139¼	141½	139	141-141¼	+2to2¼	172	112¼
May	140¾	142½	140½	142	+2	146	115
July	141	143	141	142½	+2	145	115
Sept	139½	141¼	139¼	141¼b	+2	114¾	131

Sales Wed.: 2,795 contracts.

OATS (WPG)—20 metric tons; $ per ton

	Open	High	Low	Close	Change	Season's High	Low
Dec	75.20	75.30	74.00	74.00	....	90.00	60.70
May 78	72.30	72.30	71.50	71.50b	....	73.40	63.10
July	....	....		70.00a	+ .20	68.80	68.50

Est. sales 390; sales Wed.: 512 contracts.

RAPESEED (WPG)—20 metric tons; $ per ton

	Open	High	Low	Close	Change	Season's High	Low
Jan78	301.50	307.50	301.50	307.50	+4.00	339.90	252.50
Mar	295.00	299.50	294.00	299.50a	+4.00	303.00	247.00
June	288.50	291.10	288.50	291.10b	+1.10	297.00	243.20
Sept	....	....	....	282.60b	+1.60	285.50	247.50

Est. sales 1,310; sales Wed.: 1,561 contracts.

RYE (WPG)—20 metric tons; $ per ton

	Open	High	Low	Close	Change	Season's High	Low
Dec	108.20	108.20	107.50	108.20b	- .10	116.50	79.00
May78	111.20	111.30	110.60	111.00	....	117.00	82.30
July	....	....	108.10n	....		113.50	110.30

—FOODS AND FIBER—

FRESH EGGS (CME)—22,500 doz.; cents per doz.

	Open	High	Low	Close	Change	Season's High	Low
Dec	45.50	46.50	45.30	46.20-.10+	1 00to.90	62.90	45.10
Jan 78	46.30	46.90	46.10	46.80-.75+	.95to.90	60.00	43.90
Mar	44.80	44.80	44.30	44.50	+ .50	49.00	43.85
Apr	....	....	....	42.45b	+ .45	48.00	42.00
May	42.00	42.50	42.00	42.00	+ .25	45.00	41.75
June	....	....	....	43.10n	....	43.50	42.80

Est. sales 917; sales Wed.: 928 contracts.

MAINE POTATOES (NYM)—50,000 lbs.; cts. per lb.-s

	Open	High	Low	Close	Change	Season's High	Low
Mar 78	3.80	3.80	3.67	3.69	- .11	7.10	3.67
Apr	4.09	4.15	4.05	4.05	- .03	8.95	4.02
May	4.71	4.72	4.57	4.59	- .13	9.19	4.57
Nov	4.88	4.89	4.86	4.88	+ .02	5.10	4.75
Mar 79	5.84	5.84	5.84	5.84	+ .04	6.77	5.80
Apr	....	....	....	6.35	....	6.75	6.75
May	7.04	7.04	7.04	7.00	....	7.75	6.90

Est. sales 2,714; sales Wed.: 1,285 contracts.

COFFEE (CSE)—37,500 lbs.; cents per lb.

	Open	High	Low	Close	Change	Season's High	Low
Dec	217.00	219.00	217.00	218.00b	+1.50	334.00	141.00
Mar78	169.75	171.00	168.30	170.25	- .08	329.05	132.51
May	158.00	159.25	157.50	158.75-159.25+	.12to.62	314.5	132.00
July	150.50	152.25	150.50	152.25	+1.00	238.00	128.00
Sept	143.25	146.00	143.25	145.00b	+ .25	243.00	127.50
Dec	....	....	....	130.50b	- .25	155.50	121.75
Mar79	....	....	....	128.50b	-1.50	137.00	119.00

Est sales 572; sales Wed.: 442 contracts.

SUGAR, WORLD (CSE)—112,000 lbs.; cents per lb.

	Open	High	Low	Close	Change	Season's High	Low
Jan 78	8.60	8.60	8.60	8.55b	+ .05	11.10	7.70
Mar	9.28	9.38	9.24	9.27-.28	unch to+.01	11.06	7.96
May	9.70	9.77	9.66	9.66-.68	-.05to.03	11.00	8.28
July	9.94	10.01	9.90	9.90	-.03	11.00	8.45
Sept	10.10	10.20	10.10	10.10	....	10.93	8.65
Oct	10.25	10.32	10.18	10.18-.19	-.05to.04	10.32	8.80
Jan 79	....	....	....	10.41n	+ .03	10.65	10.65
Mar	10.70	10.75	10.67	10.67	+ .03	10.75	9.95

Est. sales 3,820; sales Wed.: 4,087 contracts.

COCOA (CEX)—30,000 lbs.; cents per lb.-s

	Open	High	Low	Close	Change	Season's High	Low
Dec	171.20	171.20	168.50	170.00	-1.20	206.00	69.25
Mar78	147.50	147.50	145.70	147.05	-1.15	195.25	92.25
May	138.00	138.70	137.05	138.10	- .80	188.25	117.00
July	134.26	134.79	133.25	134.25	- .85	181.40	122.75
Sept	132.00	132.30	131.00	132.00	- .80	174.50	119.25
Dec	128.25	128.40	128.25	128.15	- .85	165.00	122.25
Mar79	125.75	125.75	125.75	126.00	- .25	127.00	120.00

Est. sales 675; sales Wed.: 1,268 contracts.

ORANGE JUICE (CTN)—15,000 lbs.; cents per lb.

	Open	High	Low	Close	Change	Season's High	Low
Jan78	124.60	126.40	124.10	124.50	-1.10	139.75	43.50
Mar	121.50	123.25	120.70	121.25-.30	-.75to.70	138.00	45.00
May	120.30	121.90	119.00	119.50	-1.00	135.00	67.30
July	119.60	120.60	118.30	118.50-.80	-1.55to1.25	134.00	68.25
Sept	118.00	119.25	118.00	117.70b	- .70	132.60	83.00
Nov	114.25	114.25	114.25	112.70b	- .30	128.50	85.45
Jan79	101.50	102.25	101.25	101.25b	-1.25	119.00	81.00
Mar	....	....		99.75b	- .25	116.60	91.75

Est. sales 1,375; sales Wed.: 4,377 contracts.

COTTON (CTN)—50,000 lbs.; cents per lb.

	Open	High	Low	Close	Change	Season's High	Low
Dec	51.40	51.42	51.30	51.38	+ .03	72.54	49.75
Mar 78	51.70	51.80	51.65	51.77-.78+	.01to.02	72.55	50.55
May	52.43	52.58	52.41	52.52-.53	unch to+.01	72.65	51.28
July	53.26	53.40	53.20	53.35	+ .03	71.80	52.15
Oct	54.25	54.35	54.20	54.25	+ .15	68.40	53.18
Dec	54.75	54.90	54.70	54.80b	- .02	62.00	53.82
Mar79	....	....		55.10b	- .05	56.00	54.90

Est. sales 2,450; sales Wed.: 2,163 contracts.

—METALS—

a later chapter. Our concern here is what effect the availability of the actual commodity may have on price differences of futures delivery months.

The trader in spreads knows, for instance, that, when available supplies are larger than the anticipated demand, they put pressure on cash prices. He or she also knows that they also weigh upon the price of the nearby futures deliveries to a level where they are at a discount to the deferred deliveries.

If your appraisal is that actual supplies are more than ample to satisfy immediate demand, then the sale of the nearby delivery month against the purchase of the distant month is justified. Supporting your analysis, you would sell March corn and buy May corn, expecting the premium of May over March to become larger. If your judgment is correct and March declines in price more than May, then you can close out at a profit.

Example: Ms Grane, in checking the closing prices of the corn market, notices that the March/May difference is 3 cents premium for May. The next day, in line with her analysis, she instructs her broker to sell 5,000 March and buy 5,000 May at the market. The execution she receives is March at $2.28 and May at $2.31.

Over the next two months, the March delivery declines to $2.18 and May to only $2.28. She closes out the spread at a 10-cent difference, the premium for May.

Her profit is calculated as follows:

Sold March at	$2.28	Bought May at	$2.31
Bought March at	$2.18	Sold May at	2.28
Gain	$ .10	Loss	$ .03

Her net profit is 7 cents, or $350, less commissions.

If, on the other hand, you believe that the available supplies are scarce relative to the prospective demand and that the prices of the nearby delivery months will gain on the deferred months, then you should buy the nearby and sell the distants. Your analysis that tightness in available supplies will cause cash prices to rise because of an upsurge in demand should influence your action in the futures market. Determining you are right, you buy March, the nearby delivery, and sell May, the distant. With May at a premium to March, you expect the price difference between March and May to get smaller; you expect the spread to narrow.

Example: In the same situation as in the previous example, Ms Grane now expects the spread to narrow even to the point that March will go to premium. Fortified by her analysis, she buys March corn at $2.28 and sells March corn at $2.31.

Over the next month, the March delivery gains rapidly on May to a level where it is 15 cents over the May. Ms Grane liquidates the spread and receives $2.51 for March while May is bought at $2.36.

Her profit is calculated as follows:

Bought March at	$2.28	Sold May at	$2.31
Sold March at	2.51	Bought May at	2.36
Gain	$ .23	Loss	$ .05

Net profit on her transaction is 18 cents, or $900. less commissions.

The examples illustrate profitable situations. The market, however, could have reacted contrary to expectations, with negative results for Ms Grane.

Although the distant deliveries may be higher-priced than the nearby deliveries, the premium is limited to carrying charges—the cost of carrying a commodity in store from one point in time to another. The May delivery in our first examples could not differ from the March delivery by more than the cost of carrying the cash article from March to May. If the maximum carrying charge on corn is approximately 5 cents per bushel per month, the most that the May delivery price could rise above the March delivery price is 10 cents.

If at any time the May delivery exceeds the March delivery by more than the carrying charges, an *automatic* profit situation is set up: A trader simply buys the March delivery, sells the May, and takes delivery against the March contract; after holding the actual commodity in storage until May, he or she than redelivers it against the short May position.

> *Example*: The May delivery goes to a 15-cent premium to the March delivery. Ms Grane buys the March at $2.85 and sells the May at $3.00. A profit, less commissions, of at least 5 cents is assured as long as 5 cents per month covers all the carrying charges. Any favorable move in the market would add to this profit of $250. per contract.

When large firms start taking advantage of this opening, however, the situation soon reverts to a straight carrying charge market. So, in effect, the premium on distant deliveries over nearby deliveries is limited to the carrying charges.

But there is no limit on how much the nearby deliveries can go over the deferred, depending on the acuteness of the scarcity and on the buyers' willingness to pay to obtain immediate supplies. This situation was illustrated in the second example.

Between Different Futures Markets.   In addition to price relationships between various delivery months within a market, relationships also exist between the prices of the same commodity in different markets; that is, wheat futures may sell on the CBOT at a price different from that on the

Kansas City Board of Trade or on the Minneapolis Grain Exchange. Although the price of wheat in each of the three markets advances or declines simultaneously, the parallel movement is not exactly uniform. As the price of wheat in Kansas City, in Chicago, or in Minneapolis fluctuates, the price differences among them widen or narrow. This changing price relationship provides speculative opportunities for those who correctly anticipate the change. The factors that primarily influence the relationship between markets are the cost of transportation from one market to another, along with the local supply and demand conditions in each market. In addition, different classes and grades of the commodity deliverable on each contract might be a factor.

Between Different but Related Commodities.   The changing price relationships between different commodities, such as corn and oats or wheat and rye, also offer spreading opportunities. Although they are different commodities, they are used for similar purposes; for example, corn and oats are both used for feed. Since one can be readily substituted for the other, their respective prices are functionally related. If the price for oats were lower than the price of corn, the demand for oats increases and corn usage slackens. Consequently, the price of oats advances, and the price of corn declines until their normal relationship is reestablished. If you are speculating, then you sell the commodity that seems overpriced and purchase the one that seems underpriced. The relative supply and demand conditions of each must be analyzed individually.

Between Raw Materials and Products.   Changes also occur in the relationship between the prices of raw materials and their products— between soybeans and soybean oil and soybean meal, for example. But though soybeans are naturally closely related to the products soybean oil and soybean meal, each reacts to changes within its own group. These influences may affect one but not necessarily either of the others. As a consequence, oil and meal values change in relation to soybeans, and the value of oil sales varies in relation to the meal. In times past, oil from a bushel of soybeans has brought about twice as much money as the meal; at other times, the meal has brought twice as much as the oil. The combined value of oil and meal fluctuates against the soybeans anywhere from dropping below the cost of soybeans without any provision for conversion costs to rising by a sizable manufacturing profit over the cost.

Each of these futures markets follows the dictates of carrying charge (or inverse) conditions as required by supply and demand within each trade. Soybeans reflect the overall demand for the exports of soybeans and for their conversion to products. In the course of merchandising, hedges can be placed in the futures market representing the product in which the risk lies and in the delivery month judged to offer the greatest price protection. As always, speculative opportunities exist in correctly analyzing the commercial potentialities.

OLD AND NEW CROP FUTURES

Simultaneous trading in both old and new crop futures takes place in most commodities. Such commodities are the ones produced annually, such as wheat, corn, oats, soybeans, cotton, and potatoes.

An *old crop futures* is one that expires prior to the harvesting of the next crop, and because of its expiration date, requires deliveries (if any) to be made from the existing, old crop supply. A *new crop futures,* on the other hand, is one that expires during a month sufficiently far distant to permit deliveries from the new crop supply.

> *Example*: On February 1, when the March, May, July, and September wheat futures are quoted, the first two are old crop futures, and the last two are new. The wheat harvest in the United States usually does not start soon enough to make new crop wheat available in quantity for delivery in May. The harvest is sufficiently advanced, however, to make new crop wheat available for delivery in July.

CROP YEARS

For purposes of statistical analysis, agricultural commodities are discussed on the basis of crop years, not calendar years. These *crop years*— sometimes referred to as crop seasons, seasons, marketing years, or marketing seasons—begin with the first of the month during which the bulk of the crop is harvested and extend to the same date the following year. For example, the crop year for wheat and oats in the United States begins on July 1 and extends through June 30 of the following year. For cotton, the crop year begins on August 1. For soybeans, it begins on September 1; and for corn, October 1. With these dates in mind, you know that reference to the 1979–80 crop year for wheat, for example, means from July 1 to July 1 of these two years. The 1979–80 season for corn runs from October 1, 1979 to October 1, 1980.

Old crop supply and demand statistics largely determine the price of old crop futures, and new crop supply and demand statistics largely determine the price of new crop futures.

An interesting point is that although September corn is technically old crop futures, inasmuch as it expires just prior to the start of the new crop season, it actually sometimes qualifies as new crop futures—at least in a limited sense. Improved seed varieties and earlier maturing crops, combined with better harvesting methods, occasionally make it possible for deliveries of new crop corn to be made in September. Such deliveries are most likely when the September futures is selling at a wide premium over the new crop price due to a scarcity of old crop supplies. For the most part, however, you can classify a futures as being an old crop futures or a new crop futures depending on whether it expires before or after the beginning of the new crop season.

CONCLUSION

If you understand the relationships between cash and futures prices, then you understand a lot about the opportunities for and the potentials of hedging, speculating, and spreading. You have seen these terms sprinkled throughout the previous chapters, but now we will treat each in greater detail—a chapter for each.

Chapter 11

Hedging

In a general sense, *hedging* is the counterbalancing of market commitments or positions to avoid or to lessen financial loss. In commodities, a rather natural hedging opportunity is built into the relationship between the futures market and the cash market. Since the prices in either tend to rise or fall more or less together, their parallel behavior can be used to lessen the risk of any dealer in commodities.

Hedging, like the futures contract, was born of risk. Anyone who has to grow, process, or in any way handle a commodity for eventual sale runs a risk as long as the materials are in his or her possession. If during the period of possession, the market price declines sharply, the eventual sale could be a price far lower than anticipated—lower perhaps than the total of the purchase and handling costs. In a word, the eventual sale could be a clear-cut loss.

Correspondingly, anyone whose business relies on a steady supply of commodities at a fairly steady price runs a similar risk even though he or she does not actually *possess* the materials. If a manufacturer, for instance, can inventory only so much of a raw material at one time and yet has to purchase, say, every quarter, then the company's budget is based on a certain cost—even given inflation—of raw materials. If radical market price changes drastically alter the costs of these materials over a quarter of a year, the company could be facing costs that would either eat into their profits or drive the company's prices up.

Both parties may prefer to avoid the speculative risk and to simply take a normal service charge or markup on the goods. If so, both can protect themselves by taking a position in the futures market opposite to their positions in the cash market:

1. *Selling hedge*: Anyone who owns a commodity in the actual market and who is considered long (a buyer) simply sells a contract in the futures market (that is, becomes a short).
2. *Buying hedge*: Anyone who is expecting to purchase an actual commodity or who is committed to perform on a forward sale simply goes long (that is, buys a contract) in the futures market.

As you can see, the hedger merely does what he or she intends to do eventually—buy or sell—but does it in the futures market.

Why?

Because the actual cash price of a given commodity usually runs roughly side-by-side, up or down, with its counterpart price in the futures contract market, the commodity user can rely on this rule of thumb: *A loss in one market means a profit in the other, as long as opposite positions are maintained, one in each market.* Prices in both markets run parallel because both respond to the same stimuli of supply and demand. If the commodity owner sells the goods for a cash market loss, the futures position can probably be closed out for a profit. Likewise, the manufacturer who has to pay exorbitant cash prices for raw materials keeps the commercial deal profitable by closing out the futures position for a gain. The rule of thumb is rooted in the relationship of cash-to-futures prices, called the "basis." The basis widens or narrows as the cash and futures prices fluctuate independently. It is this change that provides the foundation for hedging.

To a certain extent, selling hedges are matched one for one by buying hedges. However, in actual practice, seldom are two parties ready at precisely the same moment to initiate a futures contract. And to further complicate the trading, the quantities of the two parties may differ. Or both may want to sell or to buy at the same time. Some hedgers therefore may not find others whose interests are in hedging. Who assumes the risk by taking the other half of the contract?

For the most part, the speculator carries the hedging load. The speculator bridges the gap between the buying and selling hedgers. Further, when a hedger uses the many speculators in the market as underwriters and the contract as an insurance policy: The risk is shifted from one person's shoulders and distributed in many smaller parts among the many speculators.

Example: A wheat dealer is long 5,000 bushels in his inventory. He sells an equivalent quantity, 5,000 bushels, in the futures market. He is now long and short at the same time—long in the cash market and short in the futures market.

Prices decline in both markets, just when the dealer is ready to sell. He sells the wheat for a cash market loss, but then closes out the futures position for a corresponding gain. His inventory has been sold and his futures position closed out.

Example: Shutterbug Films Company sells a large order of photographic film on a contract; it will take the company roughly nine months to fill the whole order.

Mr. Shutterbug, however, is worried about the increasing cost of silver and wants to make sure that when he buys the silver necessary to make the film that the cost will be within the range on which the contract was estimated and ultimately awarded. He therefore authorizes his financial officer to buy enough silver futures contracts to cover the needs of all outstanding production estimates.

Should the price of silver keep going up—out of the range of profitability for Mr. Shutterbug—the profits from the closed-out futures can make up for the losses in the cash market.

THE GROWING CIRCLE OF HEDGERS

Hedgers are no longer a small group confined to producers or users of agricultural items: Today, their circle includes manufacturers and other users of forest products, processors of precious and base ores, livestock feeders and herders, corporate financial managers, bank officials, and other inventory managers. As the number of tradable commodities grows, so does the number of hedgers as they find they can protect themselves against large losses.

However, in order to qualify as bona fide hedgers, investors must meet certain requirements as specified by the Commodities Futures Trading Commission. As of October 1, 1977, The CFTC has defined bona fide hedging in such a way as to broaden the scope of risk-shifting transactions in the futures markets: A hedger is defined as someone who opens a futures contract:

... where such transactions or positions normally represent a substitute for transactions to be made or positions to be taken at a later time in a physical marketing channel, and where they are economically approximate to the reduction of risks in the conduct and management of a commercial enterprise ...

The hedging definition consists of three main elements:

First, it explains the type of futures transaction and the position assumed that is considered bona fide hedging. Under economically appropriate conditions, such transactions and positions arise from the potential change in value of:

1. assets that a person owns, produces, manufactures, possesses, or merchandises—or of any anticipated assets;
2. liabilities that a person owes or anticipates owing; or
3. services that a person provides, purchases, or anticipates performing. However, transactions for this purpose must be to offset price risks associated with actual commercial operations and such positions are initiated and liquidated so as not to disrupt the orderly marketing process.

Second, purchases and sales for futures delivery are limited for certain commodities to the following specific conditions:

1. *sales* of any commodity for future delivery on a contract market must not exceed in quantity:
   a. the fixed price purchases or ownership of the same cash commodity by the same person; or
   b. the twelve-month unsold anticipated production of the same commodity by the same person, provided that no such position is maintained in any futures during the five last trading days of that futures.
2. Purchases of any commodity for future delivery on a contract market must not exceed in quantity:
   a. the fixed-price sale of the cash commodity by the same person;
   b. the quantity equivalent of fixed-price sales of one cash product and by-products of the same commodity by the same person; or
   c. the twelve-month unfilled anticipated requirements of the cash commodity for processing, manufacturing, or feeding by the same person, provided that such transactions and positions in the last five trading days of any one futures do not exceed the person's unfilled anticipated requirements.

The definition also contains a provision for *cross-commodity* hedging: This kind of hedging consists of purchases and sales for futures delivery that are not the same quantity of the same cash commodity, provided the fluctuations in value of the cash and the offsetting futures positions are substantially related and that the futures positions are not maintained beyond the last five trading days of any particular futures contract.

Third, the expanded definition of bona fide hedging exempts from limits certain transactions and positions previously fixed by the Commodity Exchange Act.

THE SELLING HEDGE

Most business persons are not in business to speculate on the rise or fall of commodity prices. Their profit is derived from some service they render that requires the handling of a commodity: To protect their profit margin, therefore, against a decline in the price of the actual commodity while it is in their possession, they hedge by selling the number of futures contracts approximately equivalent to the amount of actuals held. *Selling hedges* are used for basically three purposes:

1. To protect inventories of commodities not covered by actual sales or by sales of its products.
2. To protect, or to earn, an expected carrying charge on commodities stored.
3. To protect, or to insure, a given price for prospective or estimated production of commodities.

The seller can—if doing so is profitable—deliver the actual commodity in fulfillment of the sale in the futures market or sell the actual commodity in the spot market and simultaneously offset the short position in futures by a subsequent purchase in futures. Most commercial people offset their positions.

Note: Liquidating both the cash and the futures sides of a hedge *simultaneously* is imperative. Leaving either part of a hedge uncovered by the other is inviting risk.

To Protect Purchases or Inventories

The great bulk of the farmer's surplus grain moves through the country elevator on its way from the farm to the processor and then to the ultimate consumer. Unless the grain has been contracted for prior to delivery, the elevator buys the grain upon its arrival or receives it from the farmer for storing with the sale to take place at a later date. As soon as title to the grain passes to the elevator, the elevator is exposed to risks of adverse price changes.

Deferred Shipment Agreements. However, the country elevator may hedge its purchases through sales for deferred delivery to terminal market buyers. Hedging in this way is made possible by the fact that the price is agreed on at the time the contract for the deferred shipment of the grain is made, thus relieving the elevator of the risks incident to price fluctuations. The deferred shipment contract also specifies the terms of sale, the grade, and the time of shipment, which may be 5, 10, 20, 30, or even as much as 120 days.

Deferred shipment sales may be arranged "on track" or "on board" at the source or "to arrive" within a given time at some designated destination. In the *on track sale,* the price is set F.O.B. source: The supplier agrees to load the railroad car or boat within a specified period, and the buyer pays the cost of shipping the commodity to the destination. But in *to-arrive* sales, the price is based on delivery at the destination point, and the supplier pays the cost of shipping the commodity to the destination.

Consignment. In any event, the on-track and to-arrive methods of selling may not always prove satisfactory. For example, in the case of grain, to-arrive bids may prove to be too low in the event that terminal market buyers have sufficient grain already on hand. The country elevator may then decide to consign its grain. Much grain is sold in this manner, and in some sections of the country this practice is followed almost exclusively. But here again, the elevator must either bear the risk on price movements until the grain is sold in the terminal market or hedge these price risks in the futures market.

The Mechanics of the Hedge. A hedge against cash purchases may be obtained by selling futures contracts equivalent in amount to the cash purchases. Such a hedge is, as a general rule, placed in the nearby future, as this delivery is normally expected to follow more closely the spot or cash commodity price. In the final analysis, the object is to insure the country elevator of the price that prevails in the terminal market at the time the elevator buys the cash grain, because the price paid to the farmer ordinarily is based upon the terminal market price.

Example: In late October a country elevator operator, Mr. Upton Lifta, buys 5,000 bushels of corn. He pays a price that, when added to the freight charges to his terminal market at Chicago, to the terminal handling charges, and to his own operating margin, approximates the Chicago spot corn price at that particular time of $2.50 per bushel. Bearing in mind that Mr. Lifta wants to insure himself this price, he immediately sells 5,000 bushels of the December *futures* at the then prevailing price of $2.52 per bushel. Whether corn prices move up or down is of no consequence to him now, as long as the cash price and the futures price move in unison, because a loss in one market will be offset by a gain in the other.

Mr. Lifta then consigns his corn to Chicago, and it is sold on the market at $2.45 per bushel, spot prices having declined 5 cents in the interim. But during the same period the futures price declined 5 cents a bushel also, thus permitting the elevator operator to remove his hedge through a purchase of 5,000 bushels of the December corn futures at $2.47 per bushel. The elevator's loss of 5 cents a bushel on the cash transaction is offset by a profit of 5 cents a bushel in the futures market, thus providing 100 percent protection against price risks.

	Cash	*Futures*
Oct. 15	Buys 5,000 bu. corn @.............$2.50	Sells 5,000 bu. Dec. corn @.........$2.52
Nov. 1	Sells 5,000 bu. corn @.............$2.45	Buys 5,000 bu. Dec. corn @.........$2.47
	−$ .05	+$ .05

Yet, if prices had advanced following the purchase of the actual commodity and the sale of futures, the operator would have encountered a loss on his short futures position. However, he would have made an offsetting profit by being able to sell his actual inventory at a higher level.

Example: He consigns his grain to Chicago, and it is sold on the market at $2.55 per bushel, spot prices having advanced 5 cents a bushel. The futures price also advanced 5 cents, permitting him to remove his hedge through a purchase of 5,000 bushels of December futures at $2.57 per bushel. The elevator's loss of 5 cents a bushel on the short futures position is offset by a profit of 5 cents a bushel in the cash market.

	Cash	*Futures*
Oct. 15	Buys 5,000 bu. corn @.............$1.50	Sells 5,000 bu. Dec. corn @.........$1.52
Nov. 1	Sells 5,000 bu. corn @.............$1.55	Buys 5,000 bu. Dec. corn @.........$1.57
	+$ .05	−$ .05

In foregoing example, the elevator operator obviously would have made an additional profit by not hedging because cash prices advanced. However, at the time of buying the actual commodity, he had no way of knowing for sure which way prices would move, so he hedged. He waived one opportunity to make an additional profit in order to protect his operating margin against a speculative loss. The elevator operator makes a profit on the original purchase. He did not actually pay the terminal market price of $2.50 but an amount less than that, say $2.35. The 15-cent difference is presumably enough to cover his elevator and shipping expense and leave him with a profit.

The elevator operator should, as a general rule, select the delivery month that is closest to the time that the grain is to be sold. A hedge against corn purchased in November, for example, for consignment sale shortly thereafter ordinarily would be covered by a sale in the December futures, as this delivery is normally expected to follow more closely the cash grain price. However, if an abnormal situation in the December futures is likely to cause the price of this future to rise relative to the spot price, a more deferred delivery could possibly afford better protection.

Hedging by Manufacturers and Processors. Flour millers, corn and soybean processors, distillers, feed manufacturers, and other processors of grain and its products—in order to do business—must accumulate substantial inventories of grain, particularly in the period of heavy movement following harvest. They must insure adequate supplies of raw materials for the continuous, year-round operation of their businesses. The necessity of a large stock of grain becomes quite evident in the instance of a flour miller who produces flour for a popular trade name that is expected to maintain the same quality at all times. Obviously, to maintain and protect the quality and uniformity of the product, the miller finds it necessary to accumulate substantial inventories of wheat.

A processor of a commodity or a product manufacturer can protect against losses in inventory value, to a large extent, through forward sales of the finished product or hedges in the futures market. Forward sales furnish protection against inventory value losses due to price changes on raw materials because the price of the finished product is directly related to, and based on, the purchase price of the commodity.

A coffee roaster may have accumulated inventories of (or purchased) green coffee beans in excess of estimated forward sales. To protect these purchases or inventories, the roaster can sell the number of futures contracts approximately equivalent to that amount. As the roaster uses the inventory for coffee production, he or she buys back the futures contracts, thereby closing out the hedge on that portion of the inventory.

To Protect or to Earn an Expected Carrying Charge

A country elevator operator with adequate storage space and grain of a grade deliverable on futures contracts may decide against selling immediately.

Instead the operator stores the grain and sells a futures contract roughly equivalent to the grain stored. The contract is supposed to earn a *carrying charge,* that is, a reasonable return for storage, for certain costs in carrying the grain, and for interest, insurance, and shrinkage. The carrying charge is earned, of course, only if the futures contract price is far enough above the actual purchase price of the grain. Also, the hedge would ordinarily be placed in the deferred futures of the same crop year, as opposed to the nearby delivery. The deferred futures contract, under normal conditions, sells at a premium over both the near future and spot grain prices, and the price difference normally approximates the cost of carrying the grain to the deferred delivery month.

The object of this kind of hedge is to cover the carrying charge anticipated at the time the hedge is placed. Although in some instances the actual grain is delivered against the futures contract to close out the hedge, in most cases delivery is not intended at all when the hedge is placed. For as soon as the elevator operator can find a profitable deal, he or she sells the grain and simultaneously buys back (or takes off) the hedge.

Hedging to Protect, or to Insure, a Given Price

Agricultural producers, or farmers, are exposed to rapid changes in demand for their products, and they are hard put to increase or decrease production to conform with changing economic conditions. Unlike manufacturers, who may slow down in periods of depression, farmers must continue to produce. At best, they may shift from one crop to another.

Risks are inherent in farming, and producers often look toward the futures market for price insurance on their prospective crops of, say, grain. Grain prices, for example, are higher on the average near the end of the crop year than immediately after the harvest. In late August, a farmer, estimating the upcoming crop to yield 20,000 bushels and satisfied with the prevailing price at that time for the December corn futures, can insure the value of the crop—approximately—by selling 20,000 bushels of this futures. When the crop is harvested and delivered for sale to the local elevator, the farmer removes the hedge by buying in the futures.

BUYING HEDGE

A buying hedge is intended to protect against an advance in the price of the cash commodity, or its products, that has already been sold at a specific price but not yet purchased. Exporters and manufacturers commonly sell commodities or their products at a stipulated price for forward delivery. The forward delivery is said to be *uncovered* if the commodity is not on hand. The secret of success in a buying hedge is that initiating a futures position should coincide as closely as possible with the signing of a contract for actual forward sales. Timing is *very* important.

Insofar as buying hedges allow firms to make long-term commitments without having to carry large inventories, they prevent the tie-up of working capital for long periods of time and thus free these funds for other productive uses. Interest charges are also lower, because a firm needs to borrow less to meet its everyday needs. Buying hedges can therefore be considered a healthful stimulus to the economy as a whole.

Buying hedges are used for basically three purposes:

1. To protect uncovered forward sales of a commodity or its products.
2. To replace inventory at a lower cost.
3. To maintain prices on stable-priced products.

To Protect Uncovered Forward Sales of a Commodity or its Products

The demand on manufacturers and processors often requires them to enter into contracts for the forward sales of their products, sales in advance of actual production. A copper fabricator, who makes forward sales of rolled sheets, finds that he lacks the required inventory for production needed for the forward sale. To insure a supply of copper at the price estimated in the sale, he hedges by buying futures contracts equivalent to the required amount of actual copper.

Example: On June 15, Mr. Coprola obtains an order for a quantity of rolled sheets to be delivered on September 15. Based on the current price of merchant copper and his processing costs, he quotes a fixed price for the copper sheets and signs a contract for its delivery.

However, the actual price of copper on June 15—the cash price—will not, in all probability, be the same three months later. In the interim, demand may improve, or labor or political problems may curtail delivery of copper. Any number of events may raise the price of copper between June 15 and September 15. Enough of a rise could wipe out the profit margin. The forward sale that once looks so profitable could become a substantial loss.

Of course, the fabricator may purchase the copper when he first makes the contract, but he would have to tie up considerable working capital or pay interest charges for a bank loan; he would also have to pay insurance costs for three months. Naturally, these costs would have to be included in the price of the sheets and would therefore raise the price of the finished consumer product.

The fabricator might also decide to speculate: He may have reason to believe that the price of copper will decline before the commodity is needed. Therefore, he would decide not to hedge. If prices decline, he would make a windfall speculative profit. However, if prices advanced, he could suffer a sizable loss.

In this case, however, the mill holds only two months' worth of production and the fabricator is not the speculative type. So he looks for price protection in the purchase of futures. Mr. Coprola utilizes the futures market and buys futures contracts in the amounts necessary to fill the order. Therefore, on June 15, he instructs his broker to buy 5 contracts of September copper at the market. He pays a price of 61.50 cents per pound for the futures contract, and the fabricator uses this price to establish a cost for the delivery of the rolled sheets in September. The fabricator, an experienced hedger, knows that the grade of copper he utilizes is one of the basic grades in the futures contact and the futures price will fluctuate with the cash price. The fabricator knows that the charges associated with a futures contract usually make acceptance of delivery uneconomical. More important, he cannot be sure that delivery against the futures contract will be in time for his production, since delivery is at the seller's option during the delivery period.

On August 4, one of his suppliers of copper offers him an attractive price of 64 cents per pound for the quality and quantity he requires. He accepts the offer and simultaneously sells his 5 contracts of September futures at 64.50, the going price. Copper prices rose during this period and the results of his hedge proved to be profitable. Although he loses 2½ cents on the forward sale transaction, this loss is more than offset by a 3-cent gain in the futures.

	Cash		*Futures*	
June 15	Sells rolled sheets that equate to 5 contracts of copper futures based on a price of	61.50	Buys 5 contracts of September futures at	61.50
August 4	Buys 125,000 lbs. of merchant copper at	64.00	Sells 5 contracts of September futures at	64.50
	Loss	2.50 ($3125)	Gain	3.00 ($3750)

The net profit is $625, less commissions.

If the price of copper had declined instead of advancing, the fabricator still would not lose. He incurs a loss on his long position in futures, but he can buy the actual copper at a lower price. The gain in cash offsets the loss in futures.

Feed manufacturers, corn and soybean processors, distillers, and other manufacturers and processors of grain and its products may use the futures market in a similar fashion to hedge uncovered forward sales of their products. A distiller, for example, who knows that a bushel of whole corn yields 2.5 to 2.6 gallons of 95 percent alcohol, that wheat yields 2.4, and that rye yields 2.2, can readily calculate the number of futures contracts necessary to offset, or to cover, a forward sale of alcohol.

Example—Hedging by an Exporter.
The export trade uses the futures market extensively to hedge uncovered commodity sales to foreign buyers. On any given day an exporter may receive a bid from a foreign buyer for acceptance immediately or by the close of the market that day. To accept

such a bid on such terms, the exporter must actually have the commodity on hand. Obviously carrying the necessarily large inventories involves tremendous risks were it not for the hedging facilities of the futures markets. An exporter may buy a commodity in anticipation of future sales, particularly to take advantage of favorable cash prices. But more often the exporter meets such orders by purchasing an equivalent quantity of futures contracts. Later, when the exporter buys the actual commodity to cover the sales made abroad, he or she removes the hedge in the futures market in either of two ways:

1. by selling out the futures contracts; or
2. by giving up, or exchanging, the futures with the dealer from whom the commodity was bought, an "ex-pit" transaction.

Ex-Pit Transaction. Closing out a hedge by exchanging futures for cash, is referred to as an *ex-pit transaction.* "Ex-pit" means "outside the pit, which is where this transaction takes place. It thus also takes place outside the regular procedure of competitive bidding and offering by open outcry. For example, an exporter purchases grain from a terminal elevator operator and at the same time hedges it by a sale of futures. Meanwhile the grain dealer buys hedging futures to cover the forward delivery. When buying the grain, the exporter may enter into an agreement with the elevator operator whereby the operator agrees to take over the exporter's futures contract purchases. Such an agreement enables both the exporter and the dealer to remove their hedges in the futures market *simultaneously*: In taking over the exporter's futures purchases, the dealer, in effect, buys in the hedge, since these futures contract purchases offset futures contract sales against the cash grain sold. At the same time, the transfer of the exporter's futures to the dealer enables the exporter to close out his or her hedge also.

To Replace Inventory at Lower Cost

A buying hedge has another use. When distant-month futures are selling below the spot or below the nearby futures price, the merchant can sell off inventories at the relatively high spot price and replace them with lower-cost futures contracts for more remote deliveries.

To Protect the Price of Stable-Priced Products

A buying hedge can also be profitable for processors or manufacturers of stable-priced goods. Certain breakfast cereals, for example, show little price variation at the retail level. If distant deliveries are selling at discounts, producers can purchase their future raw material needs at levels that guarantee their normal business profit. In other words, futures trading permits processors to cover their raw material needs at their convenience and to their advantage instead of being forced to make purchases only at the particular time the actual commodities are available. This type of hedge also avoids storage costs and ties up only a minimum of working capital, because of the relatively small margin outlay required for futures transactions.

HEDGING IN ACTUAL PRACTICE

All the examples so far have turned out perfectly. Not surprisingly, then, these examples are called *perfect hedges*—perfect in the sense that the cash and futures prices moved up and down by exactly the same amount, thus providing complete protection regardless of how high or low prices moved. The difference between cash and future prices, the *basis,* remained constant. However, the basis does change from time to time and from one location to another. Consequently, the changing relationship between cash and futures prices may at times result in additional profits or losses, depending on whether the basis changes in or against the hedger's favor.

Though the basis is variable, it is quite predictable. Cash and futures prices have a tendency to adjust to each other during the delivery period at the delivery point, because of the pressure caused by deliveries in the expiring futures.

The effectiveness of the hedge is governed by the cash-futures relationship at the time the hedge is established and by the subsequent narrowing or widening in the basis during the life of the hedge. Explanations of how the basis affects hedging is best demonstrated by an example.

Selling Hedge in a Normal Market Following by a Narrowing in the Basis

Example: On October 1, a cotton spot merchant buys 100 bales (50,000 pounds) of cotton from a farmer at 60.00 cents a pound based on prices at a futures delivery point. He sells one contract of December futures at 62.00 cents a pound. The equivalent amount in the futures unit of trading is 100 bales of 500 pounds each. In grading the cotton the merchant determines it should be worth 75 points off (under) the December futures. The merchant's buying basis is said to be 200 points (2 cents) off December. He is unable to sell the cotton at his estimate of 75 points off at this time. By November 1, the merchant finds a buyer at his price of 75 points off December futures, which is now selling at 60.00 cents. The cash transaction is therefore priced at 59.25 cents per pound. He "buys in," or covers, his short hedge at the current futures price of 60.00 cents. Calculations for the transactions are:

	Cash		*Futures*	
October 1	Buys 50,000 pounds cotton at 60.00 cents a pound	30,000.00	Sells 1 contract December futures	62.00 cents
November 1	Sells 50,000 pounds cotton at 59.25 cents a pound	$29,625.00	Buys 1 contract December futures	60.00 cents

				2.00 cents
			(2 cents = 200 points with each point = $5)	
	Loss	$375	Gain	$1000

Net profit is $625 less futures commissions.

The merchant fairly predicted what his profit would be because he bought at 200 points off and sold at 75 points off the basis, or 125 points at $5 a point equals $625.

In actual business conditions, considerations to delivery point differentials and detailed costs would apply.

His profit developed as a result of a narrowing in the basis, that is, a narrowing in the difference between the cash and futures prices. Although both the cash and futures prices declined, the cash price did not decline as much as the futures price. The cash market (in which he was long) declined 75 points (75/100 of a cent), while the futures market (in which he was short) declined 200 points (2 cents). He bought spot cotton and sold futures when cash was 200 points or 2 cents off (under) futures; then he sold cash and bought futures when cash was 75 points off the futures. The basis narrowed from 200 points to 75 points. The difference between his buying and selling basis is his profit, 125 points.

Thus, even though he sold the actual cotton for less than the purchase price, he made a profit because he used the futures market. If he had not hedged, he would have incurred a straight $375 loss on the cash transaction.

If cash and futures prices advance instead of decline the results are basically the same *as long as the basis narrows.*

Selling Hedge in a Normal Market Followed by a Widening in the Basis

In the previous example, the futures price was always at a full carrying premium in relation to the cash price. In other words, the premium price of futures always covered the cost of the monthly charge for storing the cotton. But this is not always the case. At times the premium price of the futures (over the cash price) is not at full carrying charges. Therefore the selling hedge does not give complete protection, and it may result in temporary losses if the basis widens.

Example: On August 1, cash cotton is 200 points (2 cents) off (under) December futures. The cash price is 61.50 cents a pound, and the December futures price is 63.50 cents a pound. If carrying charges on cotton are approximately 75 points or $375 per contract per month and if the cotton is stored (carried) for 4 months, theoretically the maximum premium December futures could go over cash is 300 points, the full carrying charges between August and December.

Mr. Baler buys spot cotton on August 1 and sells December futures when the price of spot is 200 points off December. Should the December futures premium on (over) cash widen to 300 points, he faces a near term loss of 100 points. *A loss results if the cash price advances less than the futures price or the cash price declines more than the futures price.* However, a sell hedger's risk is limited to the difference between the current basis and the carrying charges. And that risk diminishes as time passes; that is, it decreases by 75 points each succeeding month: On September 1 it is 225 points, 150 points on October 1, 75 points on November 1, and zero on December 1. Mr. Baler bought spot cotton and sold December futures on August 1 at 200 points off. His theoretical maximum risk, if he sells the cotton on September 1 and covers his hedge, is 25 points, the carrying charges between September and December. The buying basis is 200 points off, and his selling basis is 225 points off. The difference of 25 points between the buying and selling is the loss.

Assuming the grade of cotton bought is the same as the futures grade.

	Cash	Futures	Basis
August 1	Buys 50,000 pounds spot cotton @ 61.50 cents a pound $30,750	Sells 1 contract December futures @ 63.50	200 under December
September 1	Sells 50,000 pounds spot cotton @ 60.75 cents a pound 30,375	Buys 1 contract December future @ 63.00	225 under December
	−$375	+ 50 points +$250 @ $5 a point	−25 points

The net loss is $125, plus commissions.

The basis loss developed because the cash market in which the hedger bought initially declined further than the futures market in which he sold. Although the selling hedge protected the merchant against 50 points of the 75 points (75/100 of a cent) decline in the cash price, it could not offer full protection against the basis change of 25 points. The sell hedger, though eliminating risk as far as price change is concerned, still faces the risk of an adverse change in the price relationship. This hedger lost $125 plus commissions on the transaction, but the loss was still less than it would have been without the hedge. The loss would have been $375 instead of $125.

On the other hand, if the merchant had kept the hedge for two months longer (that is, until November 1), he would have made a profit on the hedge and thus earned part of the carrying charges in addition to protecting himself against a price decline. By November 1, the maximum premium on the December futures over cash would have been 75 points, the full carrying charges for one month. Since he put on the hedge when futures were 200 points on (over) the cash price, he would have made 125 points or $625 profit in addition to protecting himself against the 75 points decline in the spot price.

Even if cash prices advance, a loss on the sell hedge would have also resulted if the cash price did not gain as much as the futures price. If prices advance, the calculations are as follows:

	Cash	*Futures*	*Basis*
August 1	Buys 50,000 pounds spot cotton at 61.50 cents a pound $30,750	Sells 1 contract December @ 63.50	200 points under
September 1	Sells 50,000 pounds spot cotton at 61.60 cents a pound $30,800	Buys 1 contract December @ 63.85	225 points under
	Gain $50	−35 points Loss. . . . . $175 (@ $5 a point)	−25 points

The net loss is $125, plus commissions.

In this case, the merchant would have been better off not hedging, because cash prices advanced. However, Mr. Baler had no way of knowing that prices would advance after he purchased the commodity. Consequently, he sold futures as a hedge to protect his operation margin against a decline in the price of the actual commodity. Even though the hedge resulted in $125 loss, if his operating margin, included in his original purchase price, was sufficiently large to absorb the loss, he would still have made a profitable sale. Even though the futures market did not give full protection and did not completely pay for the cost of carrying the physical article until the delivery period, hedging can still be advantageous to protect the value of inventory against a significant price decline.

Also, if you can merchandise the cash commodity at a better basis than that at which you bought, you should hedge. In other words, if you anticipated a change in basis, the hedge is still profitable even though futures are not at a full carrying charge premium when the sell hedge is initiated.

Example: Mr. Baler's buying basis is 200 points *under* December in August and his selling basis is 50 points *over* December on November. He makes a 250 point or $1250. profit because of a favorable change in the basis, which is more than enough to pay for the cost of carrying charges from August to November (225 points or $1125.) in addition to protecting his operating margin against a price decline.

Although a selling hedge at less than full carrying charges may be profitable and gives full protection over the short run, it may also be unprofitable and only result in partial protection against a price decline. Over the long run, however, the hedge is generally profitable, but it results in only a partial recovery of the carrying charges.

Buying Hedge in a Normal Market
Followed by a Narrowing in the Basis

If an elevator operator purchases futures as a hedge against a forward cash sale when futures are at a full carrying charge premium to cash, the hedge provides only partial protection against a price advance. The difference between the cash and futures prices must narrow by the amount of the carrying charges as the delivery period approaches. However, in this instance the basis movement is less important than the hedger's ability to anticipate basis when cash grain is acquired. Futures cannot maintain their premium above cash over the long run: Either they must move down into line with the cash prices, or the cash prices must advance to the futures prices. And the adjustment between cash and futures can take place in an advancing or declining market: If the market advances, cash prices must advance further than futures because they began from a lower level; conversely, if the market declines, futures must decline more than cash.

Example: A miller buys March futures as a hedge on November 1, when futures are 10 cents above the cash price. The most that March futures can be at a premium to cash on December 1 is 15 cents, which is the cost of carrying from December to March. The price of cash advances from $2.10 to $2.20 by December 1, and the most that March futures can advance is from $2.30 to $2.35. The miller's buying basis is 20 cents under March futures and his selling basis is 15 cents under March futures, which results in a 5-cent loss in the basis. The loss in the basis develops because the cash price advances more than the futures price. Thus, as time passes, the buy hedger loses the equivalent of carrying charges. The purchase of futures protects the miller against 5 cents of the 10-cent advance in the cash price, but it does not protect him against the 5-cent change in the basis. Despite the 5-cent loss on the hedge, his profit margin on the forward cash sale may be large enough to absorb this loss, and he may still make a profitable sale. At any rate, a 5-cent loss is better than a 10-cent loss, which is what he would have encountered if he had not hedged by buying futures.

	Cash	Futures	Basis
November 1	Sells 5,000 bushels No. 2 corn @ $2.10	Buys 5,000 bushels March corn @ $2.30	20 cents under March
December 1	Buys 5,000 bushels No. 2 corn @ $2.20	Sells 5,000 bushels March corn @ $2.35	15 cents under March
	−$ .10	+$ .05	

Net loss is 5 cents per bushel, which is equivalent to $250, plus commission.

The results are the same even if prices decline.

Example: The miller buys March corn futures at $2.30 against a forward sale at a price of $2.10, and the market subsequently declines. The futures price has to decline farther than the cash price, because the premium on the futures above the cash must decrease by the equivalent of carrying charges as times passes. Thus, the price of cash corn declines 10 cents to $2.00 by December 1, and the price of futures declines 15 cents to $2.15. The 15-cent difference represents the full carrying charges between December and March.

	Cash	Futures	Basis
November 1	Sells 5,000 bushels No. 2 corn @ $2.10	Buys 5,000 bushels March corn @ $2.30	20 cents under March
December 1	Buys 5,000 bushels No. 2 corn @ $2.00	Sells 5,000 bushels March corn @ $2.15	15 cents under March
	+$ .10	−$ .15	

Net loss is 5 cents per bushel, which is equivalent to $250, less commission.

Although a buying hedge in a normal market protects against a price advance, it cannot give full protection over the long run because of the tendency for cash and futures prices to converge as the delivery period approaches. Large premiums on futures over cash spell the potentially large losses. In addition, the longer the hedge is held, the more unprofitable it will be.

Buying Hedge in a Normal Market
Followed by a Widening in the Basis

A buying hedge in a normal market affords only partial protection over the long run. But it can be profitable and provide full short-term protection if the premium on futures is less than the full carrying charges and if the basis widens; that is, if cash prices advance less than futures or if cash prices decline more than futures, a profit results.

Example: Mr. Miller buys March futures at $2.20 on November 1 as a hedge against a forward sale, which was made in the cash market at a price of $2.10. His selling basis is thus 10 cents under March. The most that the March futures can be at a premium to the cash market is 20 cents, the carrying charges between November and March. He intends to make a maximum profit of 10 cents on the hedge, if the basis widens to 20 cents. But obviously by December 1, the most that the premium can be is 15 cents, the carrying charges from December 1 to March 1. Therefore, although the price of cash corn advances from $2.10 to $2.20 between November 1 and December 1, futures advance to only $2.35. The maximum possible profit is 5 cents, because the hedge was put on a 10-cent difference. Thus the basis subsequently widens to 15 cents by December 1, and Mr. Miller buys his physical requirements to deliver. At the same time, he liquidates his hedge in futures, making a profit of 5 cents.

	Cash	Futures	Basis
November 1	Sells 5,000 bushels No. 2 corn @ $2.10	Buys 5,000 bushels March corn @ $2.20	10 cents under March
December 1	Buys 5,000 bushels No. 2 corn @ $2.20	Sells 5,000 bushels March corn @ $2.35	15 cents under March
	−$ .10	+$ .15	

The profit in basis developed as a result of the fact that the cash market, in which he was short, advanced less than the futures market, in which he was long. When cash prices advanced from $2.10 to $2.20, the miller incurred a 10-cent loss in filling his order because he had to purchase his physical requirements for more than he had calculated. On the other hand, his long position in futures advanced from $2.20 to $2.35 and thus resulted in 15-cent profit. Even though both cash and futures prices advanced, the futures market, in which he was long, advanced more than the cash market, in which he was short. Therefore, his profit was larger than his loss. The buy hedge, in addition to protecting him against a 10-cent advance in the cash price, also resulted in an additional profit of 5 cents. If the hedge were held until February 1, however, it would have resulted in a loss because the most that March could be above cash is 5 cents. Since the hedge was established at a 10-cent basis, the miller would incur a 5-cent loss.

The results would be approximately the same, even if prices declined, as long as the basis widened—that is, as long as cash declined more than futures. In this case, the cash and futures price both declined, but the cash market, in which the miller was short, declined more than the futures market, in which he was long. Therefore, he made more on the cash position than he lost on the futures position.

Example:

	Cash	Futures	Basis
November 1	Sells 5,000 bushels No. 2 corn @ $2.10	Buys 5,000 bushels March corn @ $2.20	10 cents under March
December 1	Buys 5,000 bushels No. 2 corn @ $1.90	Sells 5,000 bushels March corn @ $2.05	15 cents under March
	+$ .20	−$ .15	

Net profit is 5 cents per bushel, which is equivalent to $250, less commission.

Although a buying hedge in a normal market can be profitable in the short run, the profit potential is limited to the difference between the basis when you put the hedge on and the full carrying charges. Consequently, since carrying charges decrease each month, the chances of profit also decrease.

Selling Hedge in an Inverted Market
Followed by a Widening in the Basis

Example: Mrs. Olivia Perator buys cash beans when they are 10 cents over the November futures, which she sells as a hedge. By September 1, when she sells the cash beans, the basis has widened to 12 cents over November. She makes a profit of 2 cents per bushel on the basis, as well as protecting herself against a price decline in the value of her cash inventory.

	Cash	Futures	Basis
July 1	Buys 5,000 bushels soybeans @....... $6.00	Sells 5,000 bushels November soybeans @ $5.90	10 cents over November
September 1	Sells 5,000 bushels soybeans @....... $5.80	Buys 5,000 bushels November soybeans @ $5.68	12 cents over November
	−$ .20	+$ .22	

Net profit is 2 cents per bushel, which is equivalent to $100, less commission.

The basis profit developed as a result of the fact that cash prices declined less than futures. The cash market, in which the elevator operator was long, declined less than the futures market, in which she was short. Consequently, her profit was larger than her loss. She bought cash beans at $6 and sold them at $5.80, for a loss of 20 cents. On the other hand, she sold November beans at $5.90, covered at $5.68, and realized a profit of 22 cents. The profit of 22 cents on the futures side of the transaction more than offset the loss of 20 cents on the cash side of the transaction. A 2-cent profit resulted on balance.

Similarly, the sell hedger makes a profit on the hedge if the cash and futures price advance, as long as the basis widens. In other words, a sell hedger can make a profit on the hedge even in an advancing market if the cash price widens its premium over futures—that is, if the cash advances farther than futures.

Example: Mrs. Perator originally buys cash beans at $6.00 and simultaneously sells November futures at $5.90. On September 1 she sells cash beans for $6.20 and realizes a profit of 20 cents on the cash transaction. Since she no longer needs a hedge, she covers her short futures. However, in the interim, the futures price also advances, but not as much as the cash price. On July 1 she sells November futures at $5.90 and purchases November futures at $6.08 on September 1, which results in an 18-cent loss. Even though she incurs an 18-cent loss on the futures side of the transactions, she makes a profit of 20 cents on the cash side and thus realizes a 2-cent profit on balance.

	Cash	Futures	Basis
July 1	Buys 5,000 bushels soybeans @.......$6.00	Sells 5,000 bushels November soybeans @ $5.90	10 cents over November
September 1	Sells 5,000 bushels soybeans @.......$6.20	Buys 5,000 bushels November soybeans @ $6.08	12 cents over November
	+$ .20	−$ .18	

Net profit is 2 cents per bushel, which is equivalent to $100, less commission.

Although a sell hedger can make a profit on the basis in an inverted market in the short run, the longer she keeps the hedge on, the less her chances of profit become and the greater her chances of a loss. The cash and futures prices ultimately converge as the delivery period for November futures approaches. Although futures are sold at a discount to cash, they cannot remain at a discount over the long run, because the cash and futures prices must converge during the delivery month. Either the cash must decline to the level of futures, or futures must advance to the price of cash. If the market advances, futures must advance farther than cash. Conversely if the market declines, cash must decline farther than futures, because they began at a higher price. Therefore though a selling hedge in an inverted market can prove profitable over the near term if the basis widens, it will provide only partial protection over the long run.

Example: Mrs. Perator buys cash beans in July at 10 cents over November futures, which she simultaneously sells as a hedge. She buys the cash beans at $6.00 and sells the November futures at $5.90. The market subsequently declines and the basis narrows to 6 cents by the time she finds a buyer for her cash beans and can lift her hedge.
She incurs a loss of 4 cents. Her buying basis is 10 cents over November, and her selling basis is 6 cents over November.

	Cash	Futures	Basis
July 1	Buys 5,000 bushels soybeans @.......$6.00	Sells 5,000 bushels November soybeans @ $5.90	10 cents over November
September 1	Sells 5,000 bushels soybeans @.......$5.80	Buys 5,000 bushels November soybeans @.......$5.74	6 cents over November
	−$ .20	+$ .16	

Net loss is 4 cents per bushel, which is equivalent to $200, less commission.

The loss on the basis developed as a result of the fact that cash prices declined farther than futures. She bought cash beans on July 1 at a price of $6.00 and sold them on September 1 at a price of $5.80, which resulted in a 20-cent loss. On the other hand, she sold November futures on July 1 at $5.90 and bought them back on September 1 at $5.74, realizing a profit of 16 cents. She had a loss of 20 cents on the cash sale but made a profit of 16 cents on the futures side, for an overall loss of 4 cents. The short futures position protected the elevator operator against 16 cents of the 20-cent decline, but it could not protect her against the basis change of 4 cents.

The results are the same, even if prices in the cash and futures market advance, as long as the basis narrows—that is, as long as the cash advances less than the price of futures.

Example: Mr. Beansley buys cash beans on July 1 at a price of $6.00, and at the same time sells November beans at a price of $5.90. His buying basis is thus 10 cents over November futures. By September 1, when he finds a buyer, the price of cash beans has advanced to $6.20, which results in a 20-cent profit on the cash sale. When he lifts his hedge by purchasing futures at $6.14, he incurs a 24-cent loss on the futures side of the transaction. He makes 20 cents on his cash sale, but he loses 24 cents on the futures transaction, for an overall loss of 4 cents on the transaction. The loss on his short futures is greater than the gain on his cash inventory. Thus, the hedge results in a loss.

	Cash	Futures	Basis
July 1	Buys 5,000 bushels soybeans @....... $6.00	Sells 5,000 bushels November soybeans @ $5.90	10 cents over November
September 1	Sells 5,000 bushels soybeans @....... $6.20	Buys 5,000 bushels November soybeans @ $6.14	6 cents over November
	+$ .20	−$ .24	

Net loss is 4 cents, which is equivalent to $200, plus commission.

In this case, the processor not only missed an additional profit of 20 cents, but he also incurred an additional loss of 4 cents because of a narrowing in the basis. Obviously, he would have fared better if he had not hedged at all. However, if his operating margin is large enough to absorb the loss, the cash sale will still be profitable. If the market declines, the cash declines farther than the futures; consequently, the short hedge protects against at least part of the decline in cash.

Buying Hedge in an Inverted Market
Followed by a Narrowing in the Basis

Example: Mr. Oberzeez buys futures as a hedge against a forward cash sale when futures are at a discount to the cash price, a practice that is referred to as *going short the premium.* On July 1, he sells soybeans at $6.00 per bushel and buys November futures at $5.90. Though the November futures are 10 cents lower than cash, they cannot maintain this discount over the long run because the cash and futures prices converge during the delivery period: Either futures must advance to the cash price, or the cash price must decline to the futures price. If the market advances, futures must advance farther than cash because they started at a lower price level; conversely, if the market declines, cash prices must decline more than futures.

Cash prices advance from $6.00 on July 1 to $6.20 by November 1, when he purchases his physical requirements to fulfill his forward sale. He thus incurs a loss of 20 cents on the forward sale. In the meantime, futures advance from $5.90 to $6.20, because the price of cash and futures must approximate each other at the delivery point during the delivery period. Hence, while he incurs a 20-cent loss on the forward cash sale, he makes a profit of 30 cents on his long position in futures, for a 10-cent overall profit.

	Cash	*Futures*	*Basis*
July 1	Sells 5,000 bushels soybeans @.......$6.00	Buys 5,000 bushels November soybeans @ $5.90	10 cents over November
November 1	Buys 5,000 bushels soybeans @.......$6.20	Sells 5,000 bushels November soybeans @ $6.20	—
	−$ .20	+$ .30	

Net profit is 10 cents per bushel, which is equivalent to $500, less commission.

In addition to protecting against a 20-cent advance in the price of the cash commodity, the hedge resulted in an additional profit of 10 cents because of a favorable change in the basis.

The results are approximately the same even if prices decline.

Example: The price of cash beans declines by 20 cents to $5.80 by November 1; futures decline only 10 cents to $5.80. Thus, while the exporter loses 10 cents on his long position in futures, he is able to buy his actual requirements to fill the forward sale at a lower price and thus compensate for the loss in futures.

	Cash	*Futures*	*Basis*
July 1	Sells 5,000 bushels soybeans @.......$6.00	Buys 5,000 bushels November soybeans @ $5.90	10 cents over November
November 1	Buys 5,000 bushels soybeans @.......$5.80	Sells 5,000 bushels November soybeans @ $5.80	—
	+$ .20	−$ .10	

Net profit is 10 cents per bushel, which is equivalent to $500, less commission.

Buying Hedge in an Inverted Market
Followed by a Widening in the Basis

A buying hedge in an inverted market ultimately proves profitable because the discount must disappear as the distant delivery becomes the spot delivery. However, over the short run, this type of hedge may prove unprofitable if the basis widens—that is, if either the cash price advances more than futures or if it declines less than futures.

> *Example*: On July 1, Mr. Oberzeez makes a forward sale of soybeans at a fixed price of $6.00 for shipment in mid-November and buys November as a hedge at a price of $5.90. His selling basis is 10 cents over on July 1. If the basis widens to 12 cents by the time he buys his physical requirements and liquidates his hedge, he encounters a loss of 2 cents. The cash price advances 20 cents, but the futures market advances only 18 cents.

	Cash	Futures	Basis
July 1	Sells 5,000 bushels soybeans @ $6.00	Buys 5,000 bushels November soybeans @ $5.90	10 cents over November
September 1	Buys 5,000 bushels soybeans @ $6.20	Sells 5,000 bushels November soybeans @ $6.08	12 cents over November
	−$ .20	+$ .18	

Net loss is 2 cents per bushel, which is equivalent to $100, plus commission.

Although the buying hedge protected him against 18 cents of the 20-cent advance in the cash price, it could not protect him against the 2-cent change in the basis. Thus the hedge resulted in a 2-cent loss. But if his margin of profit is large enough to absorb this loss, the transaction can still be profitable. To lose 2 cents is better than to lose 20 cents, as he would have done had he not hedged.

The results are the same if prices decline as long as the basis widens, that is, as long as cash declines less than futures.

TRANSFERRING HEDGES

If an attractive enough market develops for the cash grain, the hedger may at any time sell the stored grain prior to the expiration of the futures and immediately remove the hedge. However, such markets don't always develop. In that event the hedger, anticipating a better market later, can hold the grain beyond the delivery month in which the hedge was originally placed by *transferring the hedge* to a deferred futures.

The transfer must be done before the expiration date for trading in the month of maturity. (Current Board of Trade Rules forbid futures trading in the last seven days of the spot month for grain or soybeans.) It is accomplished by buying in the hedge in the maturing futures and simultaneously selling a like quantity of futures in a deferred month. Closely watching all factors that are likely to influence changes in the spread between the different futures, the hedger strives to make the transfer at the time at which the deferred futures reflect the best possible carrying charge obtainable.

> *Example*: Mr. Lifta wishes to hold grain, which was stored for carrying charge purposes, beyond the month in which the original hedge was placed, in a December futures contract. In late November this delivery weakens relative to the May futures so that the price difference widens to 7 cents per bushel. Mr. Lifta decides that this is about as wide a spread as can be expected to develop and transfers his hedge to the May futures contract. He buys in the hedge in the December futures and simultaneously sells an equivalent quantity of the May futures at a premium, or price difference, of 7 cents per bushel.

This mere explanation of a transfer offers no formula to calculate precisely the timing of the transfer. The hedger can only strive to select the time when the deferred futures reflect the best possible premium over the original hedging futures. The matter is a responsibility of the hedger, requiring the best judgment.

Such transfers may involve futures contracts either for the same market that mature in different months or for different markets that mature in the same or different months. The transfer of hedges from futures contracts that mature in near months to those that mature in more distant months in the same market are made for long-basis positions (long actuals, short futures); you buy nearby futures contracts and sell, as simultaneously as possible, futures contracts that mature in more distant months. For short-basis positions (short actuals, long futures), sell nearby futures contracts and buy, as simultaneously as possible, futures contracts for the more distant months. Similarly, transfers may be made involving futures contracts for different markets but maturing in the same or in different months.

If you switch a selling hedge (long cash, short futures) when the distant futures is higher-priced than the original future, you improve your buying basis. However, if the deferred delivery is at a discount to the original futures you jeopardize your buying basis. On the other hand, if you transfer a buying hedge (short actuals, long futures) when the distant futures is at a premium to the nearby futures, you weaken your selling basis. Conversely, if the deferred future is at a discount to the nearby futures, you improve your selling basis.

> *Example*: Mr. Lifta buys cash on November 1 at a basis of "20 cents under"; that is, he buys cash corn at $2.10 and sells March futures $2.30. The July delivery at that time is $1.48. Although the March futures are at full carrying charges premium to cash on November 1, July is not at a full carrying premium

to March futures or to cash: The full carrying charges between March and July would be 20 cents, between cash and July would be 40 cents. However, by February 1, July goes to a full carrying charge premium to March. Since March cannot decline any farther relative to July, Mr. Lifta decides to transfer the hedge from March to July at a 20-cent difference. The cash price on February 1 is $1.90. At this point, he has made a profit of 15 cents because the basis narrowed from 20 cents under March to 5 cents under March. On June 1, he sells his cash corn and lifts his hedge at 5 cents under July. Since he put the hedge on at 25 cents under July, he has made a basis profit of 20 cents. This plus a profit of 15 cents on the March, results in an overall profit of 35 cents.

He bought cash corn for $2.10 on November 1, sold it for $1.70 on June 1, and thus incurred a loss of 40 cents on the cash sale. On the other hand, he sold March futures at $2.30 on November 1 and bought them back at $1.95 on February 1, realizing a profit of 35 cents. He also sold July futures on February 1 at $2.15 and repurchased them on June 1 at $1.75, realizing a profit of 40 cents. He made a profit of 35 cents on the short March future and a profit of 40 cents on the short July futures, for a total profit of 75 cents, which more than offset the 40-cent loss on the cash sale.

	Cash	Futures	
November 1	Bought 5,000 bushels No. 2 corn @ $2.10	Sold 5,000 bushels March corn @ $2.30	
February 1		Buy 5,000 bushels March corn @ $1.95	+.35
February 1		Sold 5,000 bushels July corn @ $2.15	
June 1	Sold 5,000 bushels No. 2 corn @ $1.70	Bought 5,000 bushels July corn @ $1.75	+.40
	−$ .40		+.75

In this example, cash corn was bought at 20 cents under the March future, then the hedge was moved forward to the July at a premium of 20 cents. The cash was sold at 5 cents under for a gain of 15 cents plus 20 cents, the difference at which the hedge was transferred, or a total profit of 35 cents.

SUMMARY

In hedging, these are important points to remember!

1. When hedges are placed in a normal market and the spread narrows, the selling hedger gains and the buying hedger loses.
2. When hedges are placed in a normal market and the spread widens, the selling hedger loses and the buying hedger gains.
3. When hedges are placed in an inverted market and the spread narrows, the selling hedger loses and the buying hedger gains.
4. When hedges are placed in an inverted market and the spread widens, the selling hedger gains and the buying hedger loses.

Because of the narrowing tendency of the spread, premiums of futures over cash are generally favorable to the hedge seller and discounts unfavorable. The reverse is true for the hedge buyer.

That is what hedging is all about, a close and conservative game whose end is to avoid losses. Chapter 14 will deal with speculators, those who deal in commodities in expectation of a profit. But before you can truly appreciate the speculator's role and aims, you must understand a little about evaluating the commodities market itself. Two different approaches are therefore discussed in the upcoming chapters.

Chapter 12

Fundamental Approach to Forecasting Commodity Prices

THE TWO APPROACHES TO PRICE FORECASTING

Those who trade in commodities, whether as their principal business or as an investment sideline, usually use one of two basic approaches to forecast prices and arrive at buying and selling decisions:

1. the *price movement analysis,* or *technical approach*; or
2. the *fundamental analysis approach.*

Any commodity trader who hopes to be successful must understand the principles underlying these two basic approaches to price forecasting and then learn how to apply them to actual markets. This done, he or she will, in a sense, have accomplished what the successful businessperson accomplishes in learning and applying the operating principles necessary for success in business.

Since the two basic approaches are founded on two entirely different concepts, traders are usually inclined to be strongly in favor of either one approach or the other, and to consider the approach they do not favor as having little merit. As natural as this reaction is, there is no reason why anyone should have to use either approach exclusively. Common sense advises that the best possible trading results with the least amount of risk should be obtained by combining the good points of both approaches. How much combination is practicable depends on the market situation and also to some extent on the circumstances and objectives of the individual trader. In this chapter, we will discuss the merits of the fundamental approach; in the next chapter, we will deal with the technical approach.

You can decide which is best for you.

FUNDAMENTAL ANALYSIS APPROACH

In this approach the trader bases buying and selling decisions on a study of the factors that are likely to shape the trend of prices. Whereas the technical trader is concerned only with the movement itself—not with the factors that cause price movements—the fundamental market student studies market influences in detail. On the basis of these factors, he or she determines ahead of time whether prices are more likely to advance or decline. The factors taken into account include many market influences, such as supply and demand statistics, normal seasonal price trends, domestic government farm programs, international commodity agreements, comparison of present prices to prices during past similar conditions, political developments, general inflationary or deflationary tendencies, and so forth.

The theory behind the fundamental approach to commodity trading is that, in the final analysis, supply compared to demand determines prices. A supply scarcity, relative to less demand, results in a higher price level than a supply surplus, relative to a large demand, all other factors being equal. Generally speaking, all "other factors" are important only to the extent that they affect or alter this basic supply-demand balance. Inasmuch as the supply-demand relationship principally determines prices, the fundamental market student evaluates the existing or probable supply-demand balance, takes into account any other existing factors that affect it, and then assumes a market position. That position is usually long-term.

Actually, the fundamental analysis approach to commodity trading is tied in closely with normal seasonal price tendencies. For example, the fundamental market student knows that Chicago December wheat usually reaches a summer low sometime in July or August—possibly even as early as June— and that from this low a seasonal price advance normally extends into at least November or December. The fundamental market student also knows that Chicago July corn normally stages an advance from a fall or winter low to a May, June, or July high and that Chicago November soybeans usually stage a decline from a spring or summer high to a fall harvest-time low. By knowing these seasonal tendencies and by fully understanding the factors and the particular situations responsible for each, the fundamental market student is likely to fall into a normal seasonal price pattern or run an irregular path.

In either event, the fundamental trader is usually able to take full advantage of the major price moves. Actually the fundamentalist is in a better position to do so than the technical trader. The technical trader, who is not so concerned with such factors, does not take a position until after the market itself confirms that a move is underway. Furthermore, during periods of erratic or indecisive market action, the technical trader, depending on the particular system in use, may be forced to change positions several times. Conversely, the fundamental trader, who has studied and understands the factors involved in the situation, is less likely to lose perspective and abandon a position that is actually sound and that, if maintained, will prove profitable in the long run.

Of course, the fundamental market analyst may also, along with an appraisal of market factors, give some consideration to the behavior of the market itself. In so doing, he or she is actually using some of the techniques employed by the technical market student. But this practice is not incompatible with fundamental market analysis. As a matter of fact, the good fundamental market analyst continuously observes and interprets market action. Market action often provides an actual checkpoint as to whether the market is performing as expected; it is a double-check of the analysis. By giving consideration to price movement, the fundamental trader often improves the timing of purchases and sales based principally on the original fundamental analysis.

The fundamental analysis approach to commodity trading appeals to many traders for several reasons. For one thing, it permits a trader interested only in longer-term price swings to take a position and maintain it with a minimum of attention to day-to-day market action. Also, many traders prefer to have a full understanding as to precisely why prices are moving higher or lower, and they gain such an understanding only by studying the factors that cause price changes.

Briefly, the principal difference between the technical and fundamental approaches is that the technical trader makes no attempt to study fundamental factors. The price-movement analyst is content merely to follow the moves as they occur, relying on the action of the market itself to determine when to buy and sell. The fundamental trader, on the other hand, studies market factors in detail. By appraising situations and by studying all factors, he or she determines in advance whether prices seem likely to move higher or lower and then takes a position in the market accordingly.

FUNDAMENTAL MARKET ANALYSIS

Fundamental analysis is, rather obviously, based on a study of fundamental, or basic, market factors—factors such as supply-and-demand statistics, seasonal price tendencies, and price levels. The fundamental analyst's premise is that, from a study of how fundamental market factors gave rise to certain price levels and patterns in the past, a trader can predict with a reasonable degree of accuracy a price trend and price range. Therefore, the fundamental market student appraises a situation and establishes a position in the market based upon an opinion, or a prediction, as to what will probably result from the existing factors.

THE BASIC MARKET FACTORS

Which factors? What statistics are used in figuring supply-and-demand balances? What are the seasonal price tendencies for various commodities and what causes them? What do you look for when comparing current and past price levels?

Your success in applying the fundamental analysis approach depends primarily on your ability to evaluate the basic market factors. In other words, you must be able to separate the basic, or important, factors from the vast amount of day-to-day market information that is important only as it relates to and affects these factors.

Supply-and-Demand Balance

The most influential factor in determining the price of a commodity is the supply-and-demand balance—the amount of a commodity that is available in relation to requirements. To figure supply-and-demand balances, you rely principally on government statistics. With government statistics continuously available, figuring supply-demand is a lot easier. With few exceptions these statistics, both with repect to supply and utilization, are issued by the U.S. Department of Agriculture (USDA) and are commonly referred to as *official estimates*. Sometimes you may feel that a government estimate is too high or too low. In such cases, the procedure is not to ignore the estimate but rather to adjust it in making supply-and-demand computations.

In domestically produced agricultural commodities, preliminary government crop estimates are issued well ahead of the actual harvest. These, plus private reports and perhaps personally recording crop conditions, make it possible to forecast probable supply-and-demand balances well in advance. For information on the various govenment reports that are available on both supply and utilization, write to the U.S. Department of Agriculture in Washington and ask for a complete list of such reports.

Supply-and-demand balances are statistics based on a crop year or marketing period, not a calendar year. (See the last section of "Cash and Futures Price Relationships.") A crop season begins on the first-of-the month date closest to the harvest period. For statistical purposes, a new crop is assumed to be fully available at the start of the new crop season.

In figuring the *total supply* of a commodity for a particular season, three categories of supply must be taken into account:

1. the new crop;
2. the old crop carryover; and
3. probable imports.

The old crop carryover consists of all unused stocks (from either the previous or earlier crops) that remain at the end of the immediately preceding season; these unused stocks are sometimes referred to as *reserve stocks*. Since the supply of a commodity is comprised of inventories plus current production, nonstorable commodities have no inventories and therefore current production is the sole supply: For example, live cattle and hogs, iced broilers. The supplies of other commodities that are by-products, while they may or may not be storable, depend on the production of raw materials from which they are processed. The marketable supply of soymeal, plywood and lumber and eggs is considered the current production, and their prices may be influenced by the supply and price of the "parent" commodity. Frozen pork bellies (raw bacon) and frozen concentrated orange juice are storable, and inventories must therefore be considered. However, they too rely on the production of "parent" commodities.

Seasonal production and price patterns also appear in commodities other than grains. Hog production (pig births or farrowings), for example, is the largest during the spring months of March, April, and May. These newborn pigs are brought to market during the period of August through December. Cattle also go through a production cycle inasmuch as heifers are not bred until they are approximately three years old. The "fattening" process of a yearling calve runs six to nine months. The length of time required from breeding to the "finished product" has a large impact on supply and price cycles. One of the most important fundamental factors that influences production and supply—particularly in livestock—is the feeding costs. This cost of feed is expressed in terms of a ratio, such as the hog/corn ration or the steer/corn ration. Corn is a very important component of the feeding cost. This ratio is expressed as the number of units of corn *equal* in value to 100 pounds of pork or beef. The ratio expressed is high when the value of corn is low relative to the sales value of beef. In other words, a ratio of 20 to 1 (20/1) indicates that corn is inexpensive relative to the sales value of livestock and that feeding is profitable. These ratios are calculated and released monthly by the USDA.

With respect to *utilization,* or disappearance, there are two principal categories of usage:

1. domestic utilization, and
2. exports.

Under domestic utilization, usage breakdowns are more detailed; in the case of wheat, for example, the breakdown is wheat used for food, seed, industry, and feed.

Free Supply-and-Demand Balance.   The government supports the prices of six important farm commodities, five of which are traded in futures markets: Those five are wheat, corn, oats, soybeans, and cotton. (See the chapter, "Government Price Support and Disposal Programs.") When substantial amounts of these commodities are owned by the government or are under government loan, appraising the supply-and-demand balance solely on the basis of overall statistics is not enough. In such cases, an allowance must be made for the portion of the supply owned by the government and under government loan, including impoundings, if any. Impoundings represent that part of the *current* crop placed under the loan. This allowance is for the portion of the supply that will not be available to the market except at a stipulated government sales price. The supply-and-demand balance arrived at after adjusting for this allowance is called the *free supply-and-demand balance.*

The free supply-and-demand balance may be computed in several ways, but the answer should be the same, or at least approximately the same, regardless of the method used. Examples of supply/demand balance use grain as the commodity for clarity on all points presented. One way to figure the total free supply surplus, or excess, is to add together (1) the new crop, (2) imports, (3) free stocks in the beginning of a season carryover, and (4) the estimated Commodity Credit Corporation (CCC) sales for domestic use. On the utilization side, add domestic requirements to the portion of exports that you estimate will be filled from free supply stocks to arrive at a subtotal of free requirements; to this figure, add the amount of impoundings for a total free disappearance. This utilization figure is then subtracted from the total free supply figure to determine the size of the free surplus (or deficit). This method of computation is ideal in the case of wheat, wherein CCC sales for domestic use are usually small and how much free wheat is required for export can be determined with reasonable accuracy. But these conditions do not exist in all supported commodities as a breakdown of CCC sales that show the amount used domestically and the amount that goes into export is not always available.

When this information is lacking, the following method for figuring the free supply-and-demand balance should be used. Add together the (1) new crop, (2) estimated imports, (3) free stocks in the carryover at the start of the season, and (4) estimated total CCC sales for the season. From this figure then subtract the total estimated usage (or disappearance) for the season, including impoundings if any. The difference is the free supply surplus or free supply deficit.

The ratio of government-controlled versus free supply and demand varies. When large stocks of a commodity are owned by the government and/or placed under loan, the free supply-and-demand balance obviously must be given greater weight when forecasting a logical price level than when government stocks and loan impoundings are small. During the late 1950s and early 1960s, when a large percentage of the wheat and corn surpluses were in government hands, it was necessary to rely almost entirely on free supply and utilization figures to forecast prices. The old-school fundamental analyst who

insisted that total supply-and-demand balances were the key factors in judging
market values did not fare very well during this period.

In those cases in which the government owns no part of the supply and
none is under loan, the entire supply is considered "free," and so are requirements. In such cases the "free" supply-and-demand balance is the same as the
total supply-and-demand, and, of course, the term "free" need not be used. The
only reason for using "free" in connection with supply-and-demand analysis is
to distinguish the portion of a supply that is isolated from the market—because
of the government support program from the portion that is available to the
market. And, of course, with respect to requirements, "free" is used to
distinguish between the portion of requirements that is filled through regular
market channels and the portion that is filled from government stocks or from a
part of the isolated current supply (impoundings).

Seasonal Price Tendency

There is a tendency, more pronounced in some commodities than in
others, for prices to follow an established seasonal pattern. The tendency in
wheat, for example, is for prices to go through two cycles of advance and one
of decline all in a twelve-month crop season. These seasonal price cycles
move as follows: a moderate to broad advance from the July-August low to the
following November-December high; a moderate to substantial decline from
the November-December high to the following February low; a recovery from
the February low to the March-May high; and then a decline to the July-
August low, thus completing the full twelve-month cycle. Corn and soybean
prices tend to reach a seasonal low sometime in the October-December
period, with seasonal highs reached sometime between May through July.
Potatoes start from a low in January to a high in the May/June period and
recede to a September-December low. Pork bellies run up from a March low
to a July peak and resume the slide to a November low with a gradual recovery
in December.

Some market analysts prefer not to regard a seasonal price tendency as a
basic market factor in itself but rather to consider the separate influences that
cause seasonal price tendencies as basic factors.

Seasonal price patterns may be disrupted by extraordinary external
forces such as unusual export demand (Russian wheat sales), abnormal
weather, or labor disruptions.

Price Levels

An extremely important factor to the fundamental market analyst is the
price level. In fact, in fundamental market analysis the level at which a
commodity is selling is a continuous consideration. After everything else is

considered, the level at which a commodity is selling is usually the deciding factor as to whether a bullish or bearish stand is warranted.

Three types of price comparisons must be made in determining whether the price of a commodity is too high or too low: First, observe the price level at which a commodity is selling in relation to the current (or anticipated) government loan rate. Second, mark the selling level compared to prices in past seasons when similar conditions prevailed. Third, note whether the price of a commodity appears to be too high or too low compared to the price of competing commodities. (*Note*: When a new crop substantially exceeds probable requirements and a sizable surplus is to go under loan, the level of prices in relation to the government loan rate is far more important than the level at which a commodity is selling in relation to prices in past seasons or in relation to other commodity prices.)

HOW BASIC MARKET FACTORS INFLUENCE PRICES

The basic market factors, or their various combinations, normally lead to definite types of market situations. Actually, what the fundamental market analyst does is to appraise the basic factors that exist and then decide what type of situation will likely result. The ability to classify situations depends upon his or her knowledge of how basic factors influence prices.

An Indicated Total Supply Scarcity

A total supply scarcity is basically the most bullish of all situations. In such a circumstance, you don't turn bearish, or sell, until prices have become high enough to discount the bullish supply situation. How far prices advance before leveling off, of course, depends on how acute the scarcity is. Bullishness also depends on whether commodity prices as a whole are advancing or declining. All these considerations taken into account, you will find that predicting the peak is extremely difficult in a scarcity situation.

In fact, predicting the level at which the bull market will top out is probably tougher in a total supply scarcity situation than in any other. There is no reserve supply that will become available "at a price." The market has no ceiling, no top. In such a market, the fundamental trader should rely more on price movement analysis to determine when the bull move has topped out. In other words, follow the market rather than try to outguess it.

Example: The 1973–74 wheat season was an extremely inflationary period in general. It was also a time of total supply scarcity. Under the circumstances, you would expect prices to advance to a very high level. And in fact they did: In Chicago, March wheat hit an extreme high of $6.45 per bushel in February of 1974. This high was $5.20 over the then prevailing Chicago loan rate—the most that any wheat future had ever sold above the loan up to that time. (See Table 12-1).

Table 12-1   Breakdown of Supply and Requirements (Disappearance) for the
1973–75 Seasons*

	1973-74	1974-75
Supply:		
Carryover July 1	200	200
Production	1,200	1,200
Imports	10	10
Total supply	1,410	1,210
Requirements (Disappearance):		
Exports	400	450
Domestic usage	810	875
Total disappearance	1,210	1,325
Carryover June 30	200	—

*Quantities are in millions of bushels.

Supplies were expected to be less than demand during the 1974–75 marketing season because of smaller production and larger prospective usage compared to the 1973–74 season. You would therefore expect prices to rise—obviously. With a requirement of 1,325 million bushels, only 1,210 million bushels were available. So price, the great equalizer, had to advance until demand was sufficiently curtailed so that available supplies would be enough to satisfy the more urgent requirements.

Preliminary estimates may indicate that demand during a particular season may be in excess of available supply. When such a situation occurs, prices tend to advance and thereby curtail purchases for demands of lesser importance, so that the available grain satisfies the more urgent requirements. As prices move higher, buyers become more reluctant to purchase; instead, they seek substitutes where feasible, postpone buying, or purchase only requirements necessary to maintain a working inventory.

An Indicated Total Supply Surplus

When production is substantially in excess of requirements, resulting in a total supply surplus, prices generally decline to, and average out at, a relatively low level during the entire crop season. In such situations, to lay the groundwork for a sizable and extended advance, a wider-than-average discount below the loan rate, preferably during the early part of the crop season, is needed.

Example: Table 12-2 shows that for the 1973–74 season, supplies were in excess of demand by some 200 million bushels. During the 1974–75 season, supplies are again in excess of demand, but this time by an even larger surplus of 285 million bushels. Even though prospective disappearance is expected to increase to 1,325 million, up 115 million from the 1973–74 season level of

1,210 million, supplies will still exceed demand. Imports total up to 10 million bushels and another 200 million are carried over from 1973–74. These two factors serve only to augment the surplus already achieved by the 1,400 million bushels produced—by itself more than enough to satisfy the prospective disappearance of 1,325 million.

With such a large surplus, prices will decline below the loan level, ultimately inducing farmers to apply for government loans, putting up their grain as collateral rather than selling it in the open market.

Table 12-2   Breakdown of Supply and Requirements (Disappearance) for the 1973–75 Seasons*

	1973-74	*1974-75*
Supply:		
Carryover July 1	200	200
Production	1,200	1,400
Imports	10	10
Total supply	1,410	1,610
Requirements (Disappearance):		
Exports	400	450
Domestic usage	810	875
Total disappearance	1,210	1,325
Carryover June 30	200	285

*Quantities are in millions of bushels.

As the production surplus of 75 million bushels is placed under loan, it is temporarily removed from the market, thereby reducing the quantity available somewhat. If a sufficient quantity is artificially removed from the market in this manner, the available supply moves into better balance with prospective demand. As the supply-and-demand relationship improves, prices begin to advance again.

An Indicated Free Supply Scarcity

A *free supply scarcity* is an artificially created scarcity that results from the federal government's program aimed at stabilizing farm prices. Under a congressionally authorized program, the U.S. Department of agriculture can make loans to farmers at a designated loan rate, taking the farmers' surplus inventory as collateral.[1] In this way, in times of great surplus, the government can in effect hold back some of the surplus until prices rise enough to warrant selling it on the open market. The loans are available only on certain

---

[1]The government farm policy was a major factor in controlling prices and supplies through the loan programs, acreage diversion, and price supports until recent years when world shortages began to appear, principally in wheat and corn.

commodities and only for a limited time after the harvest (called the *impounding deadline*). The loans are called *nonrecourse loans,* because they give farmers the choice of default without penalty or of paying off the loan prior to maturity and redeeming the commodity.

Since it is artificial, the free supply scarcity is not as bullish as a total supply scarcity. An adequate supply exists, but not all of it is immediately available; part of that supply is owned by the government and some of the current crop may have been placed under loan (impoundings). The bullishness is limited to a certain price range. The top of the range is the premium of the market price over the loan value necessary to make paying off the loans profitable and placing the grain into supply channels. The lower limit is the discount necessary to draw the surplus portion of the supply under loan. Obviously, the USDA carefully regulates the resale or other disposition of these surplus stocks, so as not to unduly suppress free market prices. This situation is encountered very often in markets heavily dominated by surpluses and government support programs.

> *Example*: Mr. Sowphorty, a farmer, has produced 2,000 bushels of wheat on his allotted wheat acreage, and the government loan rate for wheat that year has been set at $2 per bushel. If the overall supply-and-demand balance is such that the free market price is above $2 per bushel, the producer can be expected to sell his crop outright rather than store it for a loan; he can get a higher price by selling in the marketplace than he can get from the government. But on the other hand, if the overall supply-and-demand balance is such that the free market price is depressed—below the loan rate of $2—many producers will store the yield for a loan rather than sell because they can get a higher price from the government than they can get in the free market. So prior to the impounding deadline, which for wheat is March 31, many producers will store their wheat in approved warehouses or in farm storage and take a loan on it; they, in effect, sell it to the government at the loan rate, or loan price.

As farmers apply for government loans, they pledge a sufficient portion of their crop as collateral. The pledges temporarily remove some of the supply from the open market. If a sufficient portion of the crop becomes unavailable for sale on the open market, free supplies—those not owned or controlled by the government—will become artificially scarce, which will cause free market prices to advance.

After free market prices move up above the loan rate—up to where producers can get more by selling in the free market than they can get from the government—they may redeem their loans. They can remove the grain from the loan program, sell it at the higher market price, and pay off the loan. If free market prices do not move up above the loan price prior to the deadline for making such redemptions, which in the case of wheat is April 30, the producers, instead of redeeming their wheat, merely deliver it to the government. Hence, the government owns grain and has, at times, accumulated huge quantities of wheat, corn, and cotton.

Not to disrupt our domestic industry, the government is usually restricted from selling commodities acquired from defaulted loans in the domestic market except at a stipulated price, which is usually 115 or more percent of the loan price in that particular season, plus reasonable carrying charges.

> *Example*: The national loan average for wheat in 1971–72 was $1.25 for No. 2 soft red winter wheat. The Chicago equivalent of the loan, the loan level for No. 2 soft wheat at Chicago, was $1.46. The government selling price was $1.83. Farmers could apply for loans and receive $1.46 for their wheat. The government inventories, however, would not be available for domestic sale until the market advanced to $1.83.
>
> Holding back for the $1.83 price prevents the government from supporting prices through the availability of loans while at the same time depressing them to a point below the loan rate price by reselling them too soon. Although the government stocks are made available to the market if a shortage develops, thus increasing the free supply, they have to be at a price high enough above the loan level to permit redemptions from the loan and sales of all free commercial supplies to take place before government commences selling.

Thus, if free supplies are not sufficient to satisfy prospective requirements, prices will rise to the government selling price to attract the necessary supplies. If the government has a sufficient inventory in its possession to sell at its price, it will augment available supplies and thus satisfy requirements. The government selling price may thus become an effective ceiling over which prices cannot advance.

> *Example*: In a certain commodity, the total supply for the season—carryover, imports, and production—is 1,500 million bushels. (See Table 12-3.) But the estimated requirements are only 800 million bushels. From a total supply standpoint, the supply *far* exceeds probable needs. From a free supply standpoint, however, the picture is a little different. The government owns 500 million bushels of the carryover, reducing the free supply to 1,000 million bushels. Of the total requirements, probably 50 million bushels will be filled from government stocks, leaving 750 million to be filled from free stocks. Therefore, whereas the total supply exceeds requirements by 700 million bushels, the free supply exceeds free requirements by only 200 million bushels. This 200 million bushels is the *free supply margin*. If more than this margin is placed under loan, thus reducing the free supply, a shortage of free stocks will occur in relation to free requirements. Hence, the free supply scarcity.
>
> This artificial scarcity results in a bullish situation, because in order for requirements to be met, prices must move up to where the free supply is increased either by stocks coming back out from under loan (redemption) or by CCC sales for unrestricted use.

Table 12-3   Comparison of Total and Free Supplies

Total Supply and Usage		Free Supply and Usage	
Supply:			
Carryover July 1	600*	Free carryover July 1	100*
Production	890	Production	890
Imports	10	Imports	10
Total supply	1,500	Total free supply	1,000
Disappearance:			
Exports	300*	Exports	300*
Domestic usage	500	Domestic usage	500
Total disappearance	800	Total disappearance	800
Carryover June 30	700*		200

*Quantities are in millions of bushels.

If the government does not have enough inventory to satisfy additional demand, prices will continue to rise until the less urgent demands are curtailed and the available supplies are enough to meet the more critical requirements.

Example: Total supplies are 1,500 million bushels, and prospective requirements are 1,200 million bushels. (See Table 12-4.) Total supplies are some 300 million in excess of estimated needs. However, 500 million bushels of the 600 million bushel carryover is in CCC hands. Hence free supplies are 1,000 million, 200 million less than estimated requirements. Although supply in existence is enough to satisfy the prospective demand, it is not available except at a higher price. Consequently, prices must rise to the government selling level to attract the necessary supplies to satisfy demand. If the government's inventory cannot satisfy this additional demand, prices will continue to rise until demand adjusts to the existing supplies.

Table 12-4   Comparison of Total and Free Supplies

Total Supply and Usage		Free Supply and Usage	
Supply:			
Carryover July 1	600*	Free carryover July 1	100*
Production	890	Production	890
Imports	10	Imports	10
Total supply	1,500	Total free supply	1,000
Disappearance:			
Exports	450*	Exports	450*
Domestic usage	750	Domestic usage	750
Total disappearance	1,200	Total disappearance	1,200
Carryover June 30	300*	Free supply deficit	−200*

*Quantities are in millions of bushels.

An Indicated Free Supply Surplus

This is the most bearish supply and demand situation, because a free supply surplus usually means an even larger total supply surplus. In other words, even after allowing for all that is owned by the government and all that is under loan, there is still a sizable surplus on the basis of free supply calculations. How bearish a free supply surplus is depends on the size of the surplus. When an indicated free supply surplus exists (such as in Table 12-5), prices will always have to sell at a sufficiently wide discount under the government loan price to draw the free surplus, or at least most of it, under loan. A small discount should be enough to cause a small free surplus to be impounded, but if the free surplus is large, you may be reasonably certain that a wider-than-average discount is required.

Table 12-5

*Total Supply and Usage**		*Free Supply and Usage**	
Supply:			
Carryover July 1	400	Free carryover July 1	100
Production	1,200	Production	1,200
Imports	10	Imports	10
Total supply	1,610	Total free supply	1,310
Disappearance:			
Exports	410	Exports	410
Domestic usage	800	Domestic usage	800
Total disappearance	1,210	Total disappearance	1,210
Carryover June 30	400	Free supply surplus	100

*Quantities are in millions of bushels.

If the price of the commodity is at a small discount to the government loan price, then some or all of the free supply surplus may be impounded. For purposes of illustration, if impoundings totaled up to 55 million bushels, then the free supply surplus would be reduced by 55 million bushels, as shown in Table 12-6.

Table 12-6

*Total Supply and Usage**		*Free Supply and Usage**	
Supply:			
Carryover July 1	400	Free carryover July 1	100
Production	1,200	Production	1,200
Imports	10	Imports	10
Total Supply	1,600	Total free supply	1,310

Table 12-6 (cont.)

*Total Supply and Usage**		*Free Supply and Usage**	
Disappearance:			
Exports	410	Exports	410
Domestic usage	800	Domestic usage	800
Total disappearance	1,210	Total utilization	1,210
		Impoundings	55
		Total disappearance	1,265
		Free supply surplus	45

*Quantities are in millions of bushels.

Crop Scarce Situations

Damage to a growing crop or even the fear of serious damage can sometimes be a strong bullish influence. The influence is particularly strong when the supply-demand relationship is already in close balance and when a sizable redution in the new crop promises to further tighten the balance in the season ahead. Usually the crop scare bull moves extend farther than warranted, because crop scares are typically given wide publicity and damage reports are more often than not exaggerated. But with enforced acreage curtailment—due to the government support program—the danger of extensive and severe crop damage is less than when seeded acreages were larger. The least productive acres, those most subject to crop losses, have been taken out of cultivation. Also, better farming methods and improved seed varieties have reduced crop losses during recent years. Even extensive crop damange has little bullish effect on the price of a commodity in which there is an existing large surplus—unless the damage is so severe that a part of the existing surplus is needed to meet requirements and unless higher prices are required to make surplus stocks available.

Actually, of concern to the fundamental analyst is the simple fact that, during the growing season, *concern* over crop progress can in itself become a dominant market influence, so much so that this concern temporarily overshadows everything else in the situation and leads to a price advance. Usually such advances tend to be short-lived, because in the final analysis crop damage is important only to the extent that it actually changes the supply-and-demand balance. At the same time, however, maintaining a short position during the crop growing season if an important crop scare develops is usually not advisable. Also, because of the possibility that a crop scare may develop, a short position during the crop growing season always carries relatively more risk than does a short position after the supply-and-demand balance has become well established.

General Inflation and Deflation

During periods of extreme inflation a commodity normally sells higher than ordinarily warranted on the basis of supply-and-demand statistics. During periods of extreme deflation the reverse is true. In forecasting highs and lows and in forecasting a logical price level for a commodity, you must consider the general commodity price level and the general commodity price trend.

Normal Seasonal Price Tendencies

Seasonal price tendencies, quite obviously, should not be relied on alone as a basis for making purchases and sales. They should serve as a guide only and be considered in conjunction with other factors. If an average supply-and-demand balance exists, you would expect prices to probably follow a normal seasonal pattern. On the other hand, if the fundamental supply-and-demand situation is either extremely bullish or extremely bearish, or if some unusual special influence is affecting the situation, you can reasonably assume that the seasonal price pattern will be distorted.

Also to be considered in conjunction with seasonal price tendencies is the prevailing price level, both in relation to the level that has existed in past seasons when conditions have been similar and in relation to the government loan rate. If, for example, the price of a commodity appears to be unusually depressed at the time of the year when a seasonal low is normally reached, you could expect that prices might undergo a broader than average seasonal advance. On the other hand, if the market appears to be overpriced at the time when a seasonal low is normally reached, you would logically anticipate a smaller-than-average seasonal price advance. In fact, if the market appears to be sufficiently overpriced, you might conclude that prices should actually decline during the period of normal seasonal advance.

You should not attempt to lay down a hard-and-fast rule that will apply in all cases. But a good general rule for the fundamental trader is that you should avoid being long during periods of the year when seasonal price declines usually occur, and you should avoid being short during periods of the year when seasonal price advances usually occur, unless you have a particularly good reason for doing otherwise.

Table 12-7 Basic Guide for Applying Fundamental Market Analysis

1. Calculate the total supply-and-demand balance.
   a. Determine whether carryover stocks are being increased or decreased.
   b. Determine what price pattern has resulted from similar situations in the past.

2. Calculate the free supply-and-demand balance.
   a. Determine whether there is an indicated free surplus or an artificial scarcity.
   b. Determine how much must be impounded to absorb the surplus or how much must be redeemed, or sold by the CCC, to alleviate the scarcity.
   c. Determine what discount under the loan or what premium over the loan has been necessary in past seasons to cause similar impoundings or redemptions.
3. Consider seasonal tendency.
   a. Determine whether the situation is such that prices should logically follow the established tendency, and then, on the basis of this, decide whether to take a position immediately or to wait for a better buying or selling opportunity.
   b. Always try to trade with the established tendency. Establish a position against this tendency only when an excellent reason exists, such as a distorted seasonal pattern or when the market is being dominated by a factor of a special nature.
4. Observe price level.
   a. Determine whether prices are already too high or too low with the result that the situation may already have been discounted.
   b. If the price level indicates that the normal seasonal tendency has been distorted by an advance during the normal period for seasonal weakness, or by a broad decline during the normal period for seasonal strength, look for, or at least allow for, the possibility of another counter-seasonal move to follow, irrespective of the situation.
5. Give consideration, as seems warranted, to any existing factors of a special nature.

SUMMARY

If the fundamental approach can be summed up in a phrase, it is a *long-term* forecasting approach. Fundamental analysis attempts to predict long-range effects of basic market influences.

The next chapter deals with technical forecasting, which—if it can be summed up in a phrase—is a *short-term* approach that, in a sense, almost follows the market rather than tries to predict it. In a way, it is a little more empirical than the fundamental approach, taking the market behavior at what it is, not questioning what it should be. If differs in this respect from the fundamentalist's technique which is more rational, dealing in the market as it "should be."

Chapter 13

Technical Approach to Forecasting Commodity Prices

IMPORTANCE OF CHART ANALYSIS

The second approach to forecasting commodity prices, *technical analysis* or *chart analysis,* is a study of the price movement itself that seeks to determine the probable future course prices will take by appraising the past and present action of the market.

Regardless of the opinion held as to the value of charting, many traders use this technique, and their market influence therefore must not be ignored. In the United States during the past decade and in Europe more recently, technical analysis has attracted an ever-increasing following among speculators. Their individual positions may be small in relation to the total number of contracts traded, and these speculators may have little market influence in and by themselves. Yet, when tens of thousands of these individuals act in unison when certain price levels are penetrated, their actions can have a very potent influence upon the market.

A knowledge of chart analysis may even at times save you from making an unfavorable commitment or provide you with a better opportunity to make a more favorable commitment. For example, if you are contemplating embarking on a large-scale selling program but are near a point where chartists would be buying because of a technical signal, wait for the chart buying to run its course before you initiate your selling program. This rule also applies if you are contemplating buying futures when you are at or near a chart selling point.

Further a purely fundamental approach is a very logical approach. But logic doesn't always prevail. Many times a strong market, one that has been moving steadily upward, fails to respond to unfavorable news almost as if it never happened. The majority of traders apparently either choose to ignore the news (because of their overwhelming optimism) or place little importance upon it at the moment. In a weaker market, when prices have been moving downward, the same news may cause a sharp sell-off. This seemingly illogical process cannot be explained by the simple economics of the situation. An additional tool to gauge the market's performance is required.

Fundamental analysis is further complicated by the tendency of a market to discount known factors and adjust to anticipated conditions. This tendency destroys much of the synchronization between the market and current economic conditions. For instance during the marketing season the USDA periodically releases production and demand estimates that are usually quite significant in shaping the future course of prices. Yet often a market goes up despite a bearish report—or down despite a bullish one. Why? Simply because the market has probably anticipated such a report. Traders apparently reason that there is little percentage in holding the commodity any longer because the gain they expected, and which the commodity itself anticipated by gradually appreciating in value, has now happened. Consequently, when the news becomes public, sellers are more aggressive than buyers and prices decline.

In addition, traders respond differently, with varying reaction times, to news. Some require much more convincing than others; perhaps particular tax considerations or other special factors inhibit others in buying and/or selling. Whatever the cause, be it a psychological factor, the slow dissemination of information, or laws regulating transfer of wealth, the lag between the first recognition of a change and the reaction to it is the dominant factor in all profitable trading.

Establishing market positions, therefore, solely on fundamentals may put you into or take you out of the market too soon or too late. You might have the right idea, but if you come in at the wrong time you may encounter heavy losses. Likewise, you may get out of a situation too quickly, before it has a chance to mature. Deciding when to buy or sell is as important as, if not more important than, deciding what you should buy or sell.

HOW CHARTS REFLECT CHANGES IN MARKET PSYCHOLOGY

As Bernard Baruch once said, markets are people. Consequently, their buying and selling decisions—based on their changing ideas of supply and demand, on their varying opinions and attitudes, or on a combination of all these—cause prices to rise or fall.

Make every effort to determine what the tendencies of the public are (right or wrong) and profit from them. The buying and/or selling power of the public, once on a stampede, is almost beyond calculation. The fact that the stampede will probably turn out to be an eventually costly move does not in any way decrease your loss in fighting it, nor does it make up for the possible profits lost in not taking advantage of the trend. Theorists may claim that commodities are "too high" or "too low," based on their individual and varying ideas of what people should pay in a given situation at a given time. But the real price of a commodity is based on the majority appraisal of the moment. If the public's pocketbook is longest and widest open, its appraisal goes—for a time anyway.

At times the fundamentals are strong, and optimism is overwhelming. Then prices suddenly reverse themselves for no apparent reason. There is no major news nor a change in fundamentals, but there is a change in trader sentiment. These seemingly favorable fundamental factors make it difficult— almost impossible—for one to make a decision to sell. However, if the majority of traders no longer feel that the price level is justified, begin to liquidate, and become more aggressive than buyers, prices will decline.

At other times, when the fundamental factors are weak, nothing among the fundamental factors will apparently restore confidence or generate suffi- cient optimism to produce a decision to buy a commodity. Then suddenly prices begin to rise. There is no major news or change in the fundamentals, but once again the traders' attitude changes. In such a case, traders apparently either feel that the worst is known or that the decline has been overdone. If the majority of traders feel that the prices are too low, then the buyers become more aggressive than the sellers. Hence prices advance. A trader needs to know the factors already included in the market price level.

No man, no organization can hope to know and accurately analyze the infinite factual data, mass moods, individual necessities, hopes, fears, esti- mates, and guesses that, with the subtle alterations ever going on in the general economic framework, combine to generate supply and demand. But the summation of all these factors is reflected virtually instantaneously in market prices. They are a built-in, natural indicator of all things together.

Since the price of a commodity at any given time has, in effect, taken everything into consideration, the price movement itself should provide a good clue to changes in public opinion or trader psychology. To know which developments prompted buyers and sellers to act the way they did is not necessary. However, to recognize the pattern and understand what results may be expected from it is important. For this task charts are the most satisfactory tool yet devised. By observing how commodity prices really act, rather than how economists think they should act, the trader acquires a new grasp on market strategy.

How to Construct a Bar Chart

A *bar chart,* also referred to as a *vertical line chart,* shows the daily trading range (the high, low, and close) for a particular day's trading. The price

Figure 13-1   Daily Trading Range Expressed in a Bar Chart

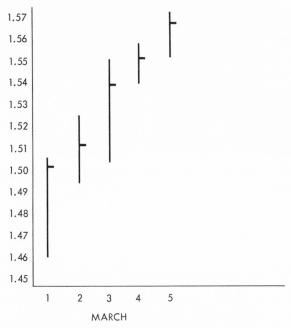

scale is placed vertically on the left-hand side of the graph paper. The time sequence is placed on the horizontal axis (see Figure 13-1).

Let's say the prices—high, low, and close—for five days' trading are as follows:

	High	Low	Close
March 1	$1.50½	$1.46	$1.50¼
2	$1.52½	$1.49½	$1.51¼—$1.51¾
3	$1.54¾	$1.50½	$1.53¾B—$1.54A
4	$1.55¾	$1.54	$1.55¼
5	$1.57¼	$1.55	$1.56¾

You indicate the high of the first day's trading (March 1) by placing a dot at the $1.50½ level. Then you place a dot at the $1.46 level. Next you draw a line connecting the high and the low. Finally you draw a line sideways at $1.05¼ indicating the close. The same procedure is repeated for each subsequent day's trading. Sometimes when a split close occurs (when two different final trades take place at different parts of the ring at different prices), some chartists draw both lines sideways or use just the lower close.

By plotting the daily range of prices in this way you can obtain a graphic picture of the trend of the market and the movement of prices over a period of time, which is helpful in determining the probable future course of prices.

How to Construct a Point and Figure Chart

Another type of chart is called a *point and figure chart,* which shows the intraday movement rather than just the overall range. For example, the bar chart shows only that on March 1 the market traded over a range of $1.50½ to $1.46. All we know is that the highest price attained that day was $1.50½, the lowest price was $1.46, and the close was $1.50¼; it gives no indication of the price movement within that range during the course of the day, which would, in turn, give us a clue to a reversal in trend. For example, the market may have opened at $1.50½, then declined to $1.47¾, later advanced to $1.49¼, declined again to $1.47, advanced to $1.49¼, next declined to $1.47¾, advanced again to $1.49¾, declined to $1.46, then advanced to $1.49½, later declined to $1.48, and finally advanced to $1.50¼, which was the close that day. Although a bar chart is useful in showing you the overall price range it does not demonstrate at which price levels the changes took place, which is helpful in determining shifts in buying power and selling pressure.

Figure 13-2 is an illustration of a 1¢ reversal chart. When using a 1¢ reversal price chart, fractions such as ¼ and ½ are disregarded. Only each full 1¢ change is recorded in this case. For example, if the first trade is at a price of $1.50½ and the market subsequently declines to $1.47⅞, you plot from $1.50 to $1.48, not to $1.47⅞ or to $1.47. If the market then advances from $1.47⅞ to $1.49⅛, you plot from $1.48 to $1.49, since that is the nearest full 1¢ change. You do not plot to $1.50. However, remember that reversal charts can be smaller or larger—a ⅜¢, ½¢, or 3¢ reversal, for instance.

Start with the first trade of the day at a price of $1.50, represented by placing an O in the first column at the $1.50 price level. The next full 1-cent price change is to $1.48, which is 2 cents lower. As long as the change is in the same direction, continue to plot Os in the same column. When there is a reversal in price, you cannot go up in the same column—the square has already been filled in. Consequently, you must move over one column to the right and up one square to begin plotting. For example, the next price change is upward to $1.49. Since we have already plotted down from $1.50 to $1.48, we must now move over to the second column and up one square to $1.49 because the space above $1.48 in the first column is already filled. The next price reversal is to $1.47. In this case, continue to plot downward to $1.47 in the

Figure 13-2   One Cent Reversal Chart (Point and Figure Chart)

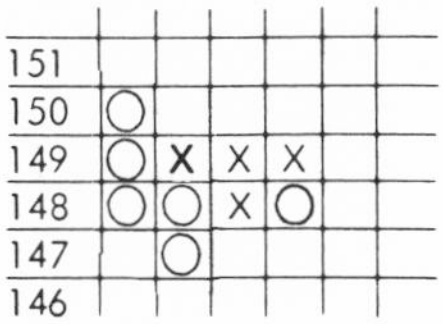

same column, the second column, because the boxes below the $1.49 level have not been filled in yet. Even though there may not be any trades between two prices, each box is filled. In the previous entry, for example, the market advanced from $1.48 to $1.49. The next sale was recorded at $1.47. Although no sales intervened between $1.49 and $1.47, each square between $1.49 and $1.47 is filled in. The market next advances from $1.47 to $1.49. Since the squares above the $1.47 have already been filled in the second column, move over to the third column and fill the $1.48 and $1.49 square. The market then declines to $1.48. Since the square below the $1.49 has already been filled in the third column, you must move over to the fourth column and plot $1.48. The market now advances to $1.49. In this case continue to plot in the fourth column because the square above $1.48 is not filled yet. In order to keep track of the "ups and downs," some chartists mark an X for "up" prices and O for "down" prices. Both are shown in the tables.

The figures in Table 13-1 are a practice set figures. Practice plotting these figures on a piece of chart paper; then compare your chart with the one in Figure 13-3.

Table 13-1   Sample Data for Plotting on One Cent Chart

First Day: 150¼–147¾–149–147–147¾–149¼–149–148–148–146–147–149½–148–152¼

Second Day: 151¼–150¼–151¼–152¼–151¼–154

Third Day: 153–151¼–152–154–153–155¼

Fourth Day: 154–156¼–155–157¼

Fifth Day: 156¼–157

BUYING POWER VERSUS SELLING PRESSURE

Although many people claim that they can predict price movements from a chart, we regard charts as a method of *following* the market. By

Figure 13-3   One-Cent Reversal Chart Plotted on Prices Given in Text

1.60														
1.59														
1.58														
1.57													X	5
1.56												X	X	X
1.55											X	4	X	
1.54									X		X	3	X	
1.53									X	O	X	X		
1.52							X		X	2	O	X		
1.51							X	X	X	X	O			
1.50	O				1	X								
1.49	O	O	X	X		X	X							
1.48	O	O	X	X	O	X	X							
1.47	O			O	X									
1.46				O										
1.45														

recording price movements as they develop, charts provide a continuous picture of the internal forces causing commodity price movements. Therefore, they enable you to detect and evaluate promptly any significant changes taking place. For example, if buying power and selling pressures are about equal at a particular price level, prices move *sideways*—a situation referred to as a *congestion area* or *trading range*. The market tends to meet support on *dips* (declines), but *encounters* resistance on *rallies* (advances). In other words, if buyers are no more aggressive than sellers, prices fluctuate within a limited range horizontally. On the other hand, if buying power is stronger than selling pressure at a particular price level, prices rise. As long as buying power (demand) continues in excess of selling pressure (supply), prices proceed in an upward trend. If selling pressure becomes stronger than buying power at a particular level, prices decline. Uptrends indicate that at a given price level, buyers are being more aggressive than sellers; a downtrend indicates sellers are more aggressive than buyers at a particular price level.

> Example: Fifty lots are being offered for sale, and several buyers are bidding for quantities totaling 150 lots. Obviously all the buyers cannot be satisfied. In competing with one another to obtain what is being offered, the buyers begin to bid the price up. Some buyers are willing to pay a higher price than other buyers in order to get the lots being offered. As the price goes higher, some buyers become less inclined to make a purchase.
>
> Conversely, as the price rises, some sellers are stimulated to offer larger quantities. When buyers become reluctant to pay higher prices and sellers become more willing to sell, sellers become more aggressive than buyers at a particular price level, and prices begin to decline. If 150 lots are offered for sale, buyers are bidding for only 50 lots, and the sellers are anxious to sell, they will reduce their asking price in an effort to dispose of their lots.
>
> As the price becomes lower, sellers become more reluctant to offer and the buyers become more willing to buy. Thus the trend of prices reverses itself once again. As this tug of war between buyers and sellers takes place, this constant shifting process (either from down to up or up to down) is reflected in the price movement itself.

Although a trend can come to an end at any time without warning, it must first reveal itself in the price movement, which the alert trader observes. In short, the object of chart analysis is to attempt to follow a trend until it is concluded and to ascertain when such a trend has changed.

An Uptrend

An *uptrend* in the price of a commodity is characterized by a series of highs and lows that attain levels generally higher than previous highs and lows. (See Figure 13-4.)

Drawing a line connecting the low points of several moves to determine the trend is usually helpful. The trend line points in the direction in which prices are moving. Prices that continue above the upward trend line constitute an indication that buying power is more aggressive than selling pressure, and you should maintain a long position. As a general rule, your chances of success are usually better if you trade from the long side when the trend is up.

The end of an uptrend is indicated when a high fails to exceed the peak of the previous high. This indicator does not necessarily mean that a downtrend is imminent, but it does suggest that a considerable amount of sideward activity may be needed for supply and demand to adjust to the new price level. In due course, either a new uptrend will start, or else a downside breakout will occur. If a break in the uptrend is followed by a succession of lower highs and lower lows, a down trend has been established. When the uptrend is broken, it is an indication that selling pressure is overtaking buying power. If you are long, this trend is your cue to liquidate your position. If you had been bearish on this commodity, based on your fundamental analysis, but had hesitated in initiating a short position (because prices were in an uptrend), this may also be your cue to establish your short position.

For instance, Figure 13-4 shows that the market has been in a clearly defined downtrend and has begun to advance (rally). Whether the rally is just a temporary interruption in the downward move or the beginning of a significant reversal in trend is difficult to determine at the time. However, when the downward trend is broken, a trader should cover short positions but not necessarily establish long positions without further confirmation that the trend has changed. Some chartists feel that the market should be able to "set back" (that is, react or decline) from the high and then advance above that high before a trader contemplates buying.

Example: The market has just made a low of $1.50, then rallied to $1.56 penetrating the downtrend line, and closed at $1.54 on that day. Before buying, you should wait for a move above $1.56 ($B_1$ in Figure 13-4) as confirmation that the trend has truly turned up. This may happen the next day, or it may take several days before the market can advance above $1.56, if at all. At that point, you establish a long position and place stop protection (SS)—that is, a stop order to sell—just below the previous low point of the move, which in this case was (1). If the market reacts to that point, the uptrend is considered broken and your long is automatically stopped out of the position.

If the market proceeds upward, as you expect, and then begins to react, you can use subsequent reaction points—(2), (3), (4), (5)—to buy additional quantities. Or you can wait for additional confirmation, such as the market's advancing above the previous high of the move (B_2 and B_3), then raise sell stop protection to SS_2 and SS_3 respectively, just below the previous low points of the moves (2) and (3) respectively, and so on.

Buying on dips enables you to add to the position at more favorable price levels. However, buying on a dip leaves you vulnerable to the possibility that it may not be just a minor dip, but rather the beginning of a significant reversal. Although buying on the breakout requires that you pay a higher price than if you bought on the dip, the market is moving in the direction you want it to be moving.

When the market declines below the trendline, you are automatically stopped out of your position. In other words, when the market declines below the

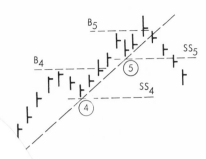

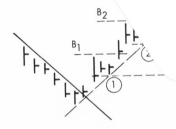

uptrend line and penetrates SS_5 on the downside, your stop order to sell is activated and becomes a market order to sell at the best possible price your broker can obtain at that time.

Downtrend

A market is in a *downward trend* when the highs and lows of the move get progressively lower. When each price decline reaches a lower level than the previous decline and each rally falls short of the previous high, the market is considered in a downtrend. A line should be drawn connecting high points of several moves to determine the downtrend. As long as prices continue below the downtrend line, the trend may be considered down, indicating that selling pressure is more aggressive than buying power. You would thus maintain a short position.

The end of a downtrend is indicated when a low fails to penetrate a previous low. This failure does not of itself indicate that a trend reversal is an early prospect. The downtrend may be resumed or a new uptrend started, but a new trend will not occur until either buying power or selling pressure dominates and determines the direction of the new trend. When the downtrend is broken, it can be a sign that an uptrend is beginning.

If you are short, this penetration should be your signal to cover your position. If you had been *fundamentally* bullish on this commodity but had hesitated in establishing a long position because prices were in a downtrend, this may be your cue also to initiate your long position.

Example: Figure 13-5 shows that the market has been in an uptrend and is now beginning to react. When the uptrend is penetrated on the downside, anyone with a long position should liquidate but not necessarily establish a short position without further confirmation that the trend has reversed itself. You should wait for the market to rally and subsequently decline below the previous low before considering selling short. In the figure, the market just made a new high for the move at (1a), then reacted to S_1 penetrating the uptrend, and finally rallied to (1b). You should wait for confirmation that the trend has turned down, a subsequent move below the S_1 level. When the market does penetrate the S_1 level on the downside, establish a short position and place a stop order to buy (BS_1) either above the high of the move (1a) or just above the trendline (1b). If the market rallies to (1b), the downtrend is broken, and your short position is stopped out with a relatively small loss.

If the market proceeds downward as you expect and then rallies, you could utilize these subsequent rallies—(2a), (3a), and (4a) respectively—to sell additional quantities. On the other hand, you could wait for the market to decline below the previous lows of the move—S_2, S_3, and S_4—then lower your stop protection to BS_2, BS_3, and BS_4 respectively, which is just above the previous highs of the moves (2a), (3a), and (4a) respectively.

When the market advances above the trendline, you are stopped out of your position. In other words, when the market advances above the downtrend line and penetrates BS on the upside, you are stopped out of your short position; that is, your stop order to buy is elected and becomes a market order to buy at the best possible price at that time.

That the downtrend has been broken is not necessarily an indication that an uptrend has been established. To confirm that an uptrend has been established, you should wait for the market to advance above the previous rally.

Swings occur within swings. Reactions happen in bull markets and rallies in bear markets. But these intermediate movements do not alter the

Figure 13-5   Example of Downtrend

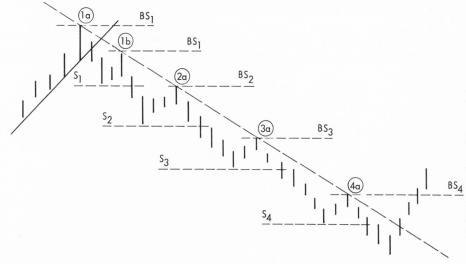

trend of the market; they merely temporarily interrupt it. You can assume as much as a rule of thumb, but note: All markets have experienced extreme limit moves at one time or another.

In commodities, an old adage says: "Bulls make money, bears make money, and hogs get slaughtered." When the trend is upward, traders are tempted to take advantage of these intermediate movements by selling a commodity that has already advanced considerably, in the belief that it can be picked up again at a lower price during a brief reaction. By the same token, after a market has been declining, some people attempt to buy in the hope of selling it on a quick rally. Either practice is usually unwise. When you try to sell in a rising market or buy in a declining market, you are, in effect, trying to pick an *exact* top or bottom, a goal that is not necessary to be successful. You can avoid the risk of a bad guess and still profit if you just try to catch the major portion of the move. Assuming prices advance from $1.50 to $1.80, for example, a prudent trader is content to get in at $1.55 and out at $1.75. But the "hog" isn't satisfied—he is unhappy if he doesn't catch the full advance of 30 cents. Don't try to buy at the very low and sell at the very top.

Traders have found that their chances of success are better on the average when they trade with the trend, not against it. Don't try to anticipate a trend. Wait until the trend has been started before initiating a position, then trade with it. Don't attempt to forecast what will happen; be guided by what has already begun to happen.

In way of analogy, one of the most successful commodity traders tells the story of how, as a boy, he used to test the tide in the river. From the Ninth Street pier in the East River in New York, where he normally swam, he could swim to two points: either the Eighth Street dock or the Tenth Street dock. Before deciding which course to take, he threw a piece of cork into the water to see which way the current was going. Then he swam in that direction, figuring it was easier to swim with the current than against it. His testing the tide is analogous to commodity speculation. Before the plunge into the speculative tidal waters of commodity trading, see which way the current is moving. Then swim with it.

Congestion Area

Congestion areas are periods of trading during which the market reacts in alternating directions with great frequency; such areas are characterized by small dips and peaks without a clear-cut trend in either direction. Advances fostered by aggressive buying are leveled off by sales resistance, and declines are well contained by buying power.

At some point in the trading of a commodity, usually at the tail end of an extended advance, buyers start to lose interest in the prices and sellers become more eager to sell. As a result the market reacts by declining slightly. This small decline is met by still-bullish buyers who, for whatever reasons, are not convinced that the advance is over. As they drive prices up again with their buying power, the market meets the same resistance it did before. And so the prices bounce back and forth within a narrow range. With rallies limited and dips well contained, the market is said to be moving *sideways,* in no clearcut direction either up or down.

Buying power and selling pressure are at a rough equilibrium.

Of course, a congestion area can develop during a downtrend as well. If at some point, prices encounter support and begin to rally, some traders may still feel a little bearish and continue to sell, exerting a downward pressure. This downward selling pressure, in turn, encounters the enthusiasm of bullish buyers who feel that the market is turning up. Thus the same sideways movement continues, only at a lower range, as long as the buyers' collective power more or less equals the sellers' cumulative pressure.

A congested area, wherever it appears, does not necessarily mean that the upward or downward trend is reversed. All it means is that the trend, whichever it was, has paused because of a temporary balance of buying and selling pressures. To determine whether a trend is indeed established, use the methods described under "Uptrend" and "Downtrend."

However, you can learn something from a congestion area. Generally accepted is the rule that the longer the duration of the congestion period (or the "wider" the congestion area on the chart), the more extensive the ensuing trend. The reasoning behind this rule is that more and more trades accumulate as the congestion area continues. When prices eventually break out of the range either way, they mark the end of a period during which both buyers and sellers have experienced relatively small gains and losses. Each side is eager to do some "real business."

When prices break out of the congested range on the downside, those who are short are making money and those who are long are losing money. The longs are therefore more eager to liquidate their positions by selling their contracts. As an increasing number of contracts are liquidated, the downward pressure accelerates the decline. In addition, those who had considered selling short during the congested phase but who awaited further confirmation of the downtrend begin selling short as prices move toward the downside. Thus they add fuel to the fire.

The same reasoning is applicable to shorts who are losing money as prices start an upward trend.

Although the width of a congestion area is to some degree correlated to the extent of a subsequent move, either up or down, the subsequent trend does not exactly equal the lateral movement. The extent of a move is not necessarily proportional to the width of the congestion area. Nevertheless, many traders employ this ratio to determine the approximate extent of a move that is getting underway.

Taking a Count. To estimate the extent of a move following a breakout, measure the width of the congestion area. The measurement should extend from the beginning of the congestion area (that is, the point at which it began) to the end of the congestion area (that is, where the market finally broke out of the range). When the congestion area has two perfectly vertical "walls," such as in Figure 13-6, the measurement is made between the walls; the walls are the two columns that have five Xs.

The upside count, the count to estimate the duration of the trend, is made from the *bottom* of the vertical walls; the horizontal line, from which the count is taken, must touch both vertical walls. The count is made across the line with the greatest number of Xs. In Figure 13-6, the horizontal line adjacent to $1.51 has more Xs (14) than any of the other lines. You then count 14 squares up from the $1.51 level, which gives you a price objective of $1.65.

The same procedure is followed in taking a count of the downside objective. In Figure 13-7, since the line adjacent to $1.64 contains the greatest number of Xs (13), it is the line from which the downward count begins. When taking a count from the line with the most Xs, note that each box of that line should be included in the count—even those that have no Xs. Although only 13 squares are filled in on the line next to $1.64, the line contains 15 squares (13 filled and 2 unfilled), if you measure from one vertical wall to the other. So you then count 15 squares *down* from $1.64, which gives you a downside objective of $1.49.

Although taking a count is fairly simple when the congestion area has two vertical walls, counting is somewhat more difficult when one or both sides of the congestion area are slanted (such as in Figure 13-8). In this type of congestion area, make the count from a line between the top and the bottom of the slanting line—that is, from a line approximately the width of the congestion area. The line with the fewest number of unfilled squares is usually a

Figure 13-6   Determining the Upside Objective

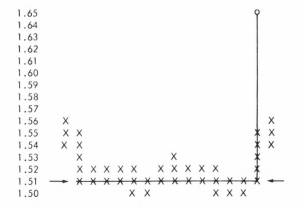

Figure 13-7 Determining the Downside Objective

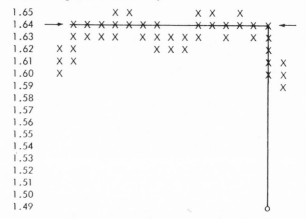

Figure 13-8 Determining the Price Objective when the Congestion Area Slants

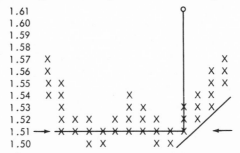

good choice: In Figure 13-8, it is the line adjacent to the $1.51 level. Since that line measures 10 squares across, count 10 squares upward from the $1.51 level, which gives you a price objective of $1.61.

Either up or down, the count can be helpful in determining the approximate extent of a move. But remember that the object of chart analysis is to follow a trend until it is concluded and to ascertain when such a trend has changed. Consequently, if the trend begins to reverse itself at a level below your objective, you should abandon the position because your objective has not yet been realized.

Support Levels

A *support area* is a price range in which you may expect a possible increase in the demand for commodity. A support area is not difficult to find on a chart. When the market is in an uptrend, any previously established congestion area in the uptrend is an area of support (see Figure 13-9).

Why is the congestion area regarded as a "support"? The answer is largely psychological in nature. When prices are fluctuating in a narrow range, moving sideways, buying power and selling pressure are about equal. When prices break out of the congestion area on the topside, the longs—the people who bought—are making money, but the shorts—the people who sold—are losing money. As a natural although quite often damaging, reaction, the shorts maintain their positions in the hope that the market will react and decline again to the price at which they sold. But more often than not, sellers are happy just to break even. Consequently, if (after advancing) prices return to a previous congestion area, people who had sold in that area are inclined to buy back the contracts—just to "get out." If enough sellers feel this way, a considerable amount of buying power may develop as prices recede to that level. As prices draw closer to this level they are stemmed more and more. The decline grinds to a halt at this, the "support" level. Another possible source of increased buying power consists of people who regretted not going long during the original congestion period after watching the breakout and subsequent advance. When prices return to the level at which they wanted to buy, they are not going to "miss the boat" again. Again, the support grows from a psychological reaction.

A third source of buying develops from traders who bought in the congestion area and then took profits when prices advanced. When prices react to the same level, the traders may want to try the same operation again.

These three sources of increased buying *may* be sufficient to check the decline. We say "may" because you can never be sure just how many traders are still in the market. Many shorts may have already offset their contracts,

Figure 13-9   Support Levels

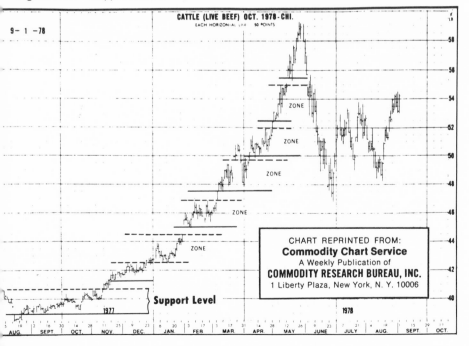

and the longs may have already sold their contracts. Or those who had contemplated buying may no longer be interested in buying because of changing circumstances. As a general rule, however, purchasing a commodity at a price close to a support level is considered wiser than at a price level considerably above a support area.

If, on the other hand, you are fundamentally bearish on a commodity and prices are right on top of a support area, wait for prices to penetrate a support level on the downside before establishing a short position. If a support area is penetrated, buying power at that price level is not sufficient to stem the decline. The market will probably decline to the next support area, wherever that may be.

In planning your positions, always consider the nearest area of support, and then the next, and so on. Usually, the wider areas of support provide more buying power, more support.

When a support area is penetrated on the downside, it then becomes the nearest "area of resistance" to a subsequent advance.

RESISTANCE LEVELS

A *resistance area* is a price range characterized by increased selling pressure or increased offerings of a particular commodity, which tend to level off advances. A resistance level is not difficult to find on a chart. If the market is in a downtrend, any previously established congestion area in that downtrend is an area of resistance (see Figure 13-10).

Pretty much the same psychology applies to resistance levels as applies to support areas, only the shorts and longs are reversed in their roles. Anyone who bought a commodity in the congestion area and then watched it decline might be inclined to hold on to it, hoping that it would come back and show a profit. However, human nature being what it is, that long would probably be glad to sell out at a breakeven price. Consequently, if prices rally and begin to move upward, the longs tend to sell out as they get closer to their breakeven point. Thus increasing selling pressure from this source offers resistance to further advance. Also, traders who previously sold at that level and then took profits when prices decline may want to repeat the process. Traders who had contemplated selling but had done nothing about it now have another opportunity to sell.

If a sufficient amount of selling is generated by these three groups, and if they are more aggressive in their selling attitude than the buyers at that level, prices will be forced to decline. Again, we can never say with any degree of certainty how many such traders are still in the market. Longs may have already offset their contracts. The shorts or "should-have" shorts may no longer be interested in selling because of changing circumstances. As a general

Figure 13-10 Resistance Levels

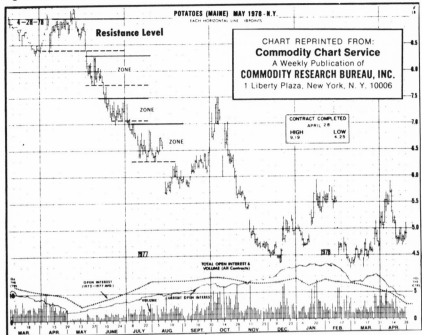

policy, however, it is better to sell a commodity at a price closer to a resistance level rather than at one well below a resistance area.

If, on the other hand, you are bullish because of your fundamental analysis and prices are just below a resistance area, wait for prices to penetrate the resistance level on the upside before establishing a long position. If a resistance area is penetrated, selling pressure at that level is not sufficient to check the advance. The advance will probably continue without resistance to at least the next resistance level.

Always plan your positions in relation to the nearest area of resistance, and then the next, and so forth. Usually, the wider areas of resistance provide more selling pressure.

In addition, once a resistance area is penetrated on the topside, it becomes the nearest area of support to a subsequent decline.

PATTERN IDENTIFICATION

Even though seeing a trend is usually fairly simple once it is underway, identifying a turning point in a trend is often much more difficult. Top and bottom patterns take on many different forms. But no matter which form they take, several things are characteristic. A reversal is in the making; the trend is changing, whether it be slow and gradual or sudden and swift.

A *bottom* is the area within which buying power begins to absorb all offerings and demand begins to exceed supply. On the other hand, a *top* is an area within which selling pressure intensifies and buying power is insufficient to absorb the offerings.

Between the tops and the bottoms, buyers and sellers struggle at a perpetual tug of war—a constant and shifting match that thrusts prices every which way. The net influences of buyers and sellers is reflected in the patterns that prices develop. These patterns, laid out on the graph, give us additional indications as to whether the market is building a bottom or top. Let's take a look at some of these patterns.

Double Top

The *double top* (or *M*) *formation* is usually indicative of a reversal in trend—that an uptrend is leveling off and a downtrend is beginning.

In Figure 13-11, the market in an uptrend makes new highs at B, then declines to point C. Prices react from B to C because sellers are more aggressive than buyers at that general level. However, when the market reacts to point C, support responds. Buying power once again intensifies and selling pressure slackens, causing prices to rise again to D. On this rally from C to D, the market cannot penetrate the previous high, point B. So it reacts once again, indicating that in and around that area selling pressure is increasing and buying power decreasing. This time, as prices react toward point C, buying power is no longer evident. Prices penetrate the previous low and continue downward. This type of pattern following an uptrend is usually a fairly good indication that the market has topped out and that the trend is reversing itself. Long positions should be liquidated either when the uptrend is penetrated on the downside or after the second decline at point C.

Even after prices break below C's level, fundamentally bearish investors who hesitated to sell because the trend of prices was up may now consider establishing short positions. A stop order to buy should then be placed above the D and B level to minimize your loss in the event the decline does not follow through. Though a short sale when the market advanced to B or when it rallied from C to D would turn out satisfactorily in the long run, a more prudent move is to await further confirmation of the trend, such as a reversal of the uptrend and/or a decline below C. Although you are selling at a lower price than you would have received if you had sold on the rally from C to D, the situation

Figure 13-11   Double Top

Figure 13-12   Double Top Indicating a Market Downturn

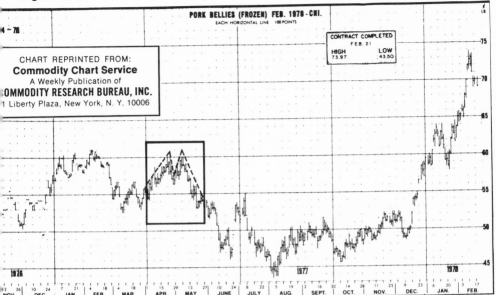

after point D is a good indication that the market has indeed reversed itself and your chances of success are better.

Double Bottom

A *double bottom* (or *W*) *formation* usually signals the termination of a downtrend and the beginning of an uptrend. A double bottom is also called a *fulcrum* (see Figure 13-13).

Figure 13-13 shows the market in a downtrend from A to B, hitting a low at B. It then rallies to C, but selling pressures bounce it back to D. However, on this decline the market fails to penetrate the previous low and rallies again—an indication that buying power is becoming stronger than selling pressure in this area. When the price penetrates the level of C, where it had previously been set back, it indicates to the trader that an established advance has likely begun.

Long positions may now be established with greater safety than if they had been established at the fulcrum, or between points B to C, C to D, or D to C again. A stop order to sell, placed just below the previous lows (B or D)

Figure 13-13   Double Bottom

Figure 13-14   Double Bottom Indicating Market Upturn

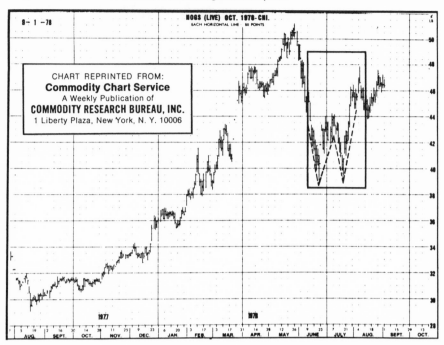

minimizes the risk. By the same token, those who had been short should cover (buy back) their contracts when the market advances above point C. Although you are buying at a higher price by awaiting a breakout above C, your chances of success are better. Figure 13-14 shows a double bottom charting of an actual market situation.

Head and Shoulders

Another type of top is a *head and shoulders formation,* or the *triple-top formation.* Usually occurring after an extensive advance, this formation ordinarily heralds a major top and portends a decline of major proportions: The longer the head and shoulders formation takes to develop, the greater the ensuing decline (see Figure 13-15).

The first sign that a head and shoulders formation may be developing is a sharp rally followed by an extended advance and a subsequent reaction. The market usually reacts somewhat to the influence of a lot of profit-taking after a sustained advance (points A to B in Figure 13-15); when an uptrend is drawn out, traders start closing out positions to cash in. If enough of them do so, the market starts turning downward a bit as a result of this sudden tendency to liquidate (B to C). Other traders, sensing a top, sell in order to "short the market," that is, sell at a top price and buy in at a lower price on the decline to come.

242

Figure 13-15   Head and Shoulders, or Triple-Top Formation

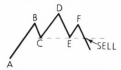

Of course, a certain amount of buying power develops in reaction to this decline. Some traders may wish to use this opportunity to add to their existing long positions; and others, who failed to take advantage of the advance earlier, may establish new long positions. The downward reaction (or correction) is thus arrested, and the market moves upward again (C to D).

The renewed advance exceeds the high of the previous move, gaining momentum as previous short sellers (who are losers at this point) begin to cover (buy back their contracts) and thereby accelerate the upswing. But, as the market moves upward again, it encounters renewed profit-taking as well as new selling, which induces another reaction (D to E).

This reaction carries below the uptrend line. At this point longs start selling again, and possibly new sellers give the downward swing an extra push. Prices usually carry to the most recent support level, which in this case is the low of the previous move (E).

Traders, recalling that this was a support area before, begin to buy again; and recent sellers, realizing that the downward reaction is not following through (even though the uptrend was broken), begin to buy back their short positions. The market subsequently begins to rally (E to F), but falls short of the previous high and eases under increased selling pressure.

Figure 13-16   Head and Shoulders Top

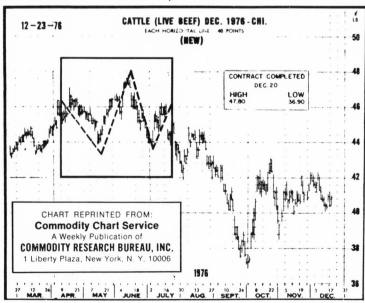

243

This time the price breaks through the support level, because the selling pressure has become so much greater than the buying power.

A major reversal ensues. When prices penetrate the level of the two previous lows, the horizontal line on the graph defined by points C and E (often referred to as the *neckline*), the market *is* reversing itself from up to down. If you are long, you should liquidate your position. If you were contemplating a short position but had hesitated because the market was in an upward swing, this is your cue to establish short positions and place a stop order to buy above F, or perhaps D, to minimize your loss.

Following a penetration of the neckline, an approximation of the possible extent of the downside move may be made by measuring the distance between the high of the head (D) and the neckline below the top of the head. Then extending this distance from the point at which the neckline was penetrated should lead you to the downside objective.

Figure 13-16 shows the charting of an actual market head and shoulders top situation.

Inverse Head and Shoulders

The opposite of a head and shoulders formation is an *inverse head and shoulders*. This type of bottom usually develops after an extensive decline and, when completed, usually portends a sizable advance (see Figure 13-17).

The first sign that an inverse head and shoulders formation may be in the making is a sharp sell-off. After a sustained decline, a market usually rallies somewhat under the influence of profit-taking (points B to C in Figure 13-17). The market rallies as the shorts buy in their contracts, taking profits, and as other traders, sniffing a bottom, buy. The rally picks up speed as demand increases and as buying power begins to absorb all the selling.

But as the market rallies, some traders use the opportunity to add to their existing short position; others who failed to take advantage of the earlier decline establish new short positions. The upward rally or correction is arrested, and the market begins to move downward again (C to D). The market drops below the low of the previous move, gaining momentum as previous longs (who are losers at this point) begin to liquidate—sell back their contracts—thereby accelerating the downswing.

As the market moves downward, it again encounters renewed profit-taking as well as new buying that induces another rally (D to E), which carries

Figure 13-17 Inverse Head and Shoulders

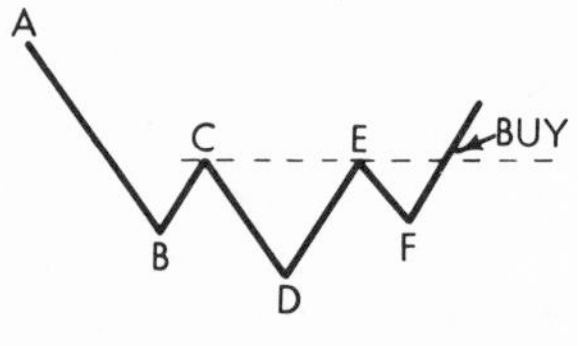

above the downtrend line. At this point new buyers enter the market, and short sellers again start to buy back their contracts.

Prices usually carry to the most recent resistance level (E), the high of the previous move. Traders who recall that this point offered resistance before begin to sell again. Recent buyers who realize that the upward reaction is not following through (even though the downtrend was broken) begin to sell their long positions. The market subsequently begins to react (E to F) but falls short of the previous low. Instead, it rallies under increased buying power, this time carrying above the previous highs of the move. Buying power is at this point more than enough to absorb all selling.

A major reversal, again, ensues. When the market advances above the neckline, the formation *has* been completed. The breakthrough is your signal that an uptrend is beginning. If you are short, you should cover your position. If you had considered taking long positions but were reluctant to do so because the market was in a downward tendency, establish your long positions at this point and place a stop order to sell just below the previous low point, either F or D. Figure 13-18 shows the charting of an actual inverse head and shoulders market situation.

Descending Triangle

Another pattern, usually indicative of a decline, is referred to as a descending triangle. A *descending triangle* is saw-tooth pattern in which the highs encounter successively stronger selling pressure, while the lows

Figure 13-18   Inverse Head and Shoulders

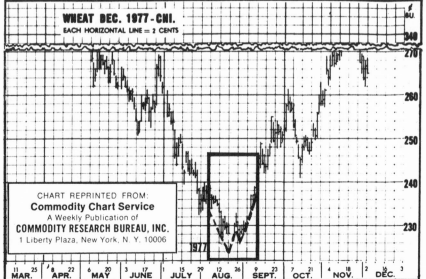

Figure 13-19   Descending Triangle

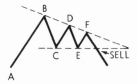

encounter consistently strong support at a particular price level (See Figure 13-19). In a pattern such as this, the support or buying power is limiting the decline to a certain price level, but offerings or selling pressure is cutting off rallies progressively lower; consequently, each subsequent rally falls short of the previous rally.

Figure 13-19 shows the market reaching a high for the current move (B). It then declines to C before selling pressure becomes stronger than buying power at B. However, the market encounters support at C, rallies to D [which is a lower high than the previous one (B)], and declines to E. Buying power once again exceeds selling pressure, and prices rally to F but cannot advance above the previous high (D). Again they decline. This time the market fails to meet support at the C and E level, as it had on two previous occasions. When this level is penetrated, the market has topped out, and the downtrend is beginning.

If you are long, it would be prudent to liquidate your position when C and E are penetrated on the downside! If you had considered a short position but refrained because the trend was up, this penetration is your signal to start selling. Then place a stop order to buy above point F to protect your sale.

Obviously, while the market encountered support at the price level defined by C and E, selling was getting progressively stronger on each rally. Usually when selling pressure is getting progressively stronger, the breakout is on the downside. However, as the highs get lower, a minor downtrend can usually be drawn joining the highs (see the dashed lines in Figure 13-19). If the highs continue to decline below the trendline, wait for the downside breakout into new low ground before selling.

Such a pattern usually develops after an extended advance, and it quite often means that the highs have been reached and an extended decline may ensue. If, however, the price activity fails to remain below the trendline and advances to a point where it breaks through the downtrend line and goes above D or B, a long position might then be contemplated.

Ascending Triangle

An ascending triangle is indicative of a bottoming out formation and portends an advance when completed. An *ascending triangle* is a pattern in which the lows move progressively higher, while the highs encounter resistance at one price level. In a pattern such as this, overhead resistance or selling pressure limits the advance at certain price levels, but demand or buying

246

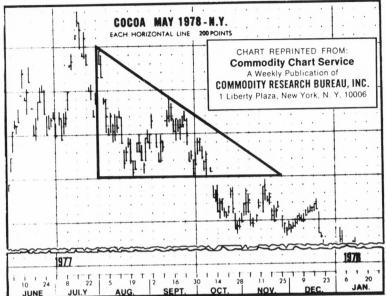

COCOA MAY 1978-N.Y.
EACH HORIZONTAL LINE 200 POINTS

CHART REPRINTED FROM:
Commodity Chart Service
A Weekly Publication of
COMMODITY RESEARCH BUREAU, INC.
1 Liberty Plaza, New York, N. Y. 10006

power gets progressively stronger on each dip. Consequently, subsequent dips do not carry as far as previous reactions (see Figures 13-21 and 13-22).

In this situation, after an extended decline, the market declines to B, then rallies to C, cannot hold, and declines to D—testing the previous low, but not penetrating it. Then the market rallies to E, again encountering increased offerings that force prices lower to F. This decline again falls short of the previous low (D). Obviously, while selling pressure is still sufficiently strong to check the advance at C and E, buying power is getting stronger on each dip—evidenced by the failure of D to penetrate B.

Usually in such a pattern where buying power is getting progressively stronger, the breakout is on the upside. As the lows get higher, a minor uptrend usually can be drawn connecting the lows (see the dashed line in Figure 13-21). If the lows continue to get progressively higher and continue above the trendline, wait for the upside breakout into new high ground before buying. Quite often an extended advance ensues.

If the price activity fails to continue to move above the trendline and deteriorates to a point where it breaks through the trendline, a short position

Figure 13-21 Ascending Triangle

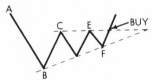

Figure 13-22   Charting of an Actual Market Situation Producing an Ascending
Triangle

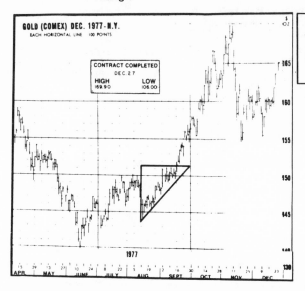

might then be contemplated. A break in the advance develops when the buying power begins to slacken or selling pressure increases.

A trader is therefore prudent to await a move over C and E to confirm that the trend is reversed before buying. Then place a stop order to sell just below point F. If prices decline below the uptrend, penetrating D or B before advancing above C and E, short positions can be made.

Symmetrical Triangle

A combination of an ascending triangle and a descending triangle is known as a *symmetrical triangle* (see Figure 13-22). In this pattern, the highs get progressively lower as the lows of the moves get progressively higher. Each rally falls short of the previous high of the rally, because on each rally, selling pressure or offerings intensify. On the other hand, each dip falls short of the previous low of the reaction, because on each subsequent dip, buying power gets stronger on each dip. In a sense, this is a congestion area—a sideways movement without any clear trend evident. Sooner or later one of these groups (buyers or sellers) predominates and a new trend is established.

In Figure 13-23, the market makes a new high (A), then declines to B as selling pressure intensifies. The market next rallies from B to C as buying power becomes stronger than selling pressure. However, notice that on this rally from B to C, the market cannot advance above A and begins to decline again. This rally from B to C falls short of the previous high of the move, as selling pressure becomes more aggressive than buying power at a somewhat lower level than it had on the previous advance to A. The market now declines

Figure 13-23   Symmetrical Triangle

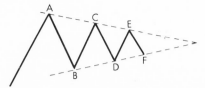

from C to D. On this reaction the market cannot decline below B, and it rallies once again. Buying power is becoming stronger than selling pressure at a higher level than it did on the decline from A to B. Each rally and dip covers a smaller and smaller range, until the market is gradually funneled into a very tight sideways movement.

The breakout can be on the upside or downside. Two minor trend lines can be drawn: one along A, C, E and the other along B, D, F. As they converge, prices must break out one way or the other. If the minor downtrend (ACE) is penetrated on the upside and prices break out above E, an uptrend is very likely beginning and you can establish a long position. Conversely, if the minor uptrend is penetrated on the downside and prices break down below F, a downtrend is beginning and you can establish a short position.

The characteristics of this type of formation are basically the same whether it occurs at the bottom or at the top of a move.

Figure 13-24   Charting of an Actual Market Situation Producing a Symmetrical Triangle

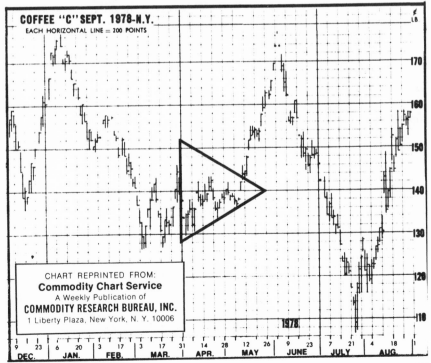

Flags

An *upward flag* is a pattern composed of a flagpole created by a sharp advance and of a flag created by two parallel minor downtrend lines (see Figure 13-25). The flag consists of the channel between the two minor downtrends, a channel in which each high and each low is progressively lower than one before. While the minor trends are both downward and the highs get progressively lower, the market meets good support on each dip, and it declines in an orderly manner.

Figure 13-25   Upward Flag

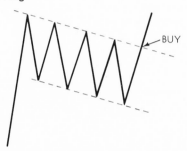

The upward flag usually develops in a major upward trend. The flag is a readjustment to a new price level after a sharp run-up (the flagpole). It is usually not the end of the major move, merely a temporary interruption of it before the upward move resumes. Traders who wish to add to existing long positions or put on new longs should wait for the completion of the flag pattern and the subsequent upward breakout—that is, for a penetration of the minor downtrend line.

A *downward flag* is just the opposite of the upward flag—an inverted upward flag pattern. The flagpole is created by a sharp decline; the staff, by two minor upward trend lines. The flag takes on the appearance of a channel in which each high and low get a little higher than the one before. While the minor trend is upward and the lows get progressively higher, the market meets resistance on each rally (see Figure 13-26). And the market proceeds upwards in an orderly manner.

The downward flag usually develops in a major downtrend. The flag is usually a readjustment to the new price level after an extended sharp decline. It is not the end of a move, but merely a temporary interruption before the subsequent downtrend continues. The flag merely develops a minor uptrend channel within a major downtrend. Traders who wish to add to existing short positions or to put on new shorts should await the completion of the flag pattern and the downward breakout to confirm the resumption of the downtrend. The more congested the pattern, the more reliable the signal.

Figure 13-26 Downward Flag

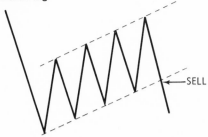

SELL

Gaps

A *gap* is a price area in which no trading takes place. There are two basic types of gaps—an "up" gap and a "down" gap. An *up gap* is an area between one day's high and a subsequent day's low in which no trading takes place. A *down gap* is an area between one day's low and a subsequent day's high in which no trading takes place.

An Up Gap. An up gap occurs when the low of a particular day is higher than the high of the previous day. An up gap occurs if the market opens higher than the previous day's high and remains above the previous day's high during the balance of that trading session (see Figure 13-27).

An up gap is an indication of market strength. Sometimes, when important bullish news develops overnight, the market opens higher than the previous session's high, either because of a surge of aggressive buying, the absence of selling, or a combination of both.

Once an up gap occurs, the market normally moves upward rapidly if the news initially causing the gap is genuine and significant. As long as the up gap area remains open (unfilled)—that is, the market does not trade at or below the high of the trading session preceding the day the up gap occurred—you should trade the market from the long side. If the market reacts and fills in the gap, then the strengthening factors that caused the up gap are no longer prevalent or are insufficient to sustain the upmove; long positions should therefore be liquidated in part or in total. An example of an up gap being filled in is shown in Figure 13-28).

Figure 13-27 Up Gap

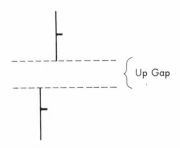

Up Gap

Figure 13-28   Up Gap Filling In

On occasion an up gap has been filled, and the market still proceeded upward. This exception usually occurs when the market advances very rapidly or when the gap between one day's high and a subsequent day's low is relatively small.

A Down Gap.   A down gap occurs when the high of one day is lower than the low of the preceding trading session. A down gap occurs when the market opens lower than the previous day's low and remains below the previous day's low during the rest of that trading session (see Figure 13-29).

A down gap is a sign of market weakness. Should some unfavorable news develop overnight, the market may open lower than the low of the previous day because of heavy selling or the absence of buying. As long as the gap is not filled, you should maintain a short position. When subsequent action results in a rally that fills in the down gap, short positions should be covered, because the weakening factors that caused the gap are obviously no longer dominant. An example of a down gap being filled is shown in Figure 13-30.

There are several other types of gaps such as common gaps, breakaway gaps, runaway gaps, and exhaustion gaps. *Common gaps* are small minor gaps within a congestion area or limited range. A *breakaway gap* is the first up (or down) gap above (or below) the trading range in which the market has been confined. A *runaway gap* is a subsequent gap following a breakaway gap. An *exhaustion gap* is a gap that is filled in by subsequent trading and is usually indicative of the end of a move.

Figure 13-29   A Down Gap

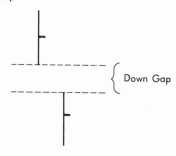

Figure 13-30   Down Gap Filling In

SUMMARY

In the last two chapters, we have covered two very basic approaches to market analysis. Most traders, although they tend to favor one or the other, are forced sooner or later to borrow from both.

Perhaps as you read the next chapter on speculation, you will see why.

Chapter 14

Trading Techniques For the Speculator

Speculators are investors who voluntarily put their capital at risk in the expectation of profits. Basically, they make money by buying when they think prices are low and by selling when they think prices are high.

Their money serves an important economic function by providing liquidity for the market. For every seller, usually there is a buyer and for every buyer, generally there is a willing seller.

Even though the term "speculator" conjures up reminiscences of Yankee trading ships breaking through the Southern blockade and of big capitalists casting large sums of money in desperate gambles, the commodities speculator is no such creature. The speculator is not a gambler. He or she is instead someone who enters into a legally binding and enforceable contract, one that happens to contain an element of risk.

By assuming this risk, speculators live in a more or less happy symbiosis with hedgers. Hedgers are willing to give up a little of their profits from time to time to buy insurance; they are not willing to take risks, because the risk jeopardizes their commercial interests. Speculators, on the other hand, are perfectly willing to assume the risk because a loss is not a threat to their living; a loss is only a partial setback in an overall investment plan.

In a sentence, the relationship between hedgers and speculators typifies the purpose of futures trading—the shifting of risk to those who are willing to assume it.

Speculators have good reason to look to commodities trading for expectation of profits. Commodity trading offers unusual opportunities—for quickly making more money than in almost any other investment venture.

And, contrary to popular beliefs, these profit opportunities are open not only to professional traders and to those with a lot of money, but also to those with limited *risk capital* and to those with no special knowledge of commodity markets. The commodity trader who follows sound trading practices (even an amateur who devotes relatively little time to trading) can realize an average annual return of 100 percent or more on such capital. That kind of return is considerably better than what you can expect from most capital ventures.

Making such large profits possible, of course, is the relatively small margin required to trade in commodities. Instead of the normal 50 percent required to trade in stocks, a commodities trader is seldom required to put up more than 10 percent. Actually, in many cases the margin required to trade in a commodity is no more than 5 percent of the market value of the commodity. Such low margin requirements give traders tremendous leverage.

Commodities become particularly attractive when you consider the many ways in which risk can be curbed and controlled. Usually such high returns are associated with high risks. But don't be fooled: The risks connected with commodity trading are not small, nor should you expect to make money in commodities unless you understand how to evaluate and limit the existing risks. The truth of the matter is that commodity trading falls into a high-risk field—necessarily so. Otherwise large profits would not be possible.

But the risks that exist in commodity trading are not constant risks; given time, they average out the same for all traders. They may be either large or small, depending on the situation and the timing of your market commitments. Because of this, skilled and amateur traders alike who follow sound trading practices are able to make trades that, on the average, carry a relatively small risk and that also have a relatively large profit potential.

Commodity trading can never be reduced to an exact science because prices are influenced by so many factors that cannot be measured precisely. As a consequence, no single method or combination of methods guarantees a profit on every trade. Such a guarantee is impossible, and the experienced trader is well aware of it. But to make *some* profit on a trade, you do not have to forecast tops and bottoms with 100 percent accuracy. Nor do you have to be right in every situation to make money in the long run.

All you can do, therefore, is carefully evaluate and limit risks—and follow sound trading practices. Not even the practices discussed in this book will enable you always to be right on the market. Nothing will. But if followed, they will prevent you from being subjected to serious losses on those occasions when the market does not perform as you expect. At the same time, they should enable you to be right a large enough percentage of the time to make trading in commodities highly profitable.

CONSIDERATIONS BEFORE ENTERING THE MARKET

Four basic rules must be observed if you hope to trade successfully:

1. adopt and follow a definite trading plan, one suitable both to your temperament and to your circumstances;
2. trade conservatively, with money you can afford to risk;
3. never risk all your trading capital on any one situation; and
4. never depend on trading profits to meet living expenses.

Adopt and Follow a Definite Trading Plan

The first rule is extremely important. Frankly, no one can trade profitably over an extended period unless he or she follows a definite trading plan. When you adopt and follow a trading plan, two things are accomplished: First, in deciding on a plan, you are forced to give consideration to certain basic trading principles that may otherwise be overlooked, or at least not given proper attention. Second, by adopting and following a specific plan, you are less likely than otherwise to become involved in trading procedures that are unsuitable to you personally.

With regard to this second point, remember that a certain trading method may work well for one person and not at all for another. For example, suppose a person has a greater-than-average amount of patience. Suppose further that he or she is the kind who wants to know which factors in a situation make a purchase or sale desirable. In addition, he or she doesn't have the time or desire to follow day-to-day market action. Certainly this type of person is best suited to a plan of trading based on the fundamental analysis approach, which takes a long-term view of the market and an optimistic view of its trend. He has the patience to see a trade through to its conclusion, and he probably would not become discouraged by any occasional sizable loss resulting from a situation appraisal that did not work out as expected. Because of his patience, he would no doubt have large profits in those situations in which his appraisals did work out, profits that would far outweigh his occasional losses. And, of course, nothing prevents this type of person from limiting his losses if desired. He could, in other words, supplement his fundamental analysis with just enough of the technical approach to provide stop protection in those instances in which a greater-than-average risk appeared to exist and such protection appeared desirable.

On the other hand, suppose another person's temperament is such that she finds it difficult to maintain a position for any extended period. And suppose, further, that she has no particular interest in appraising situations or in knowing the reasons why prices advance or decline—unless, by chance, the reasons are obvious and customarily covered in the run of trade comment. Obviously this type of person should not attempt to trade on the basis of the fundamental analysis approach. She would be almost certain to lose money if she did (although her failure to trade profitably with this approach does not mean that the fundamental approach is unsatisfactory). Even though lack of patience is a serious handicap for any trader, the impatient trader—the one who is constantly seeking action—will usually do better using price movement analysis than she will using the fundamental analysis approach.

Most of all, every trader must understand that he or she cannot make money trading in commodities on the basis of market news. Occasionally you may find a situation in which profits can be obtained on this basis, but over the long run you are certain to lose money if your trading decisions are influenced by bullish or bearish news and trade commentaries. Usually, such commentary always looks most bullish at the extreme top of a bull move, and it always looks more bearish at the extreme bottom of a bear move. Therefore, if you trade on the news, you will invariably be bullish at the top and bearish at the bottom—just the opposite of what you must do to trade profitably. Market news, as well as the usual run of so-called professional trade comment, is usually nothing more than someone's observation of what is currently taking place. Naturally, when prices are strong, those commenting on the action of the market give emphasis to the bullish factors just as they give emphasis to the bearish factors in a situation in which prices are weak. In both cases the factors commented on usually have already been discounted.

If you have a definite trading plan—based on either the fundamental or the technical approach or a combination of the two—your trading will not be directly affected by day-to-day market news and comments. In using the fundamental approach, the news is important only to the extent that it relates to and alters the basic factors you consider in appraising a situation. And if you use the technical approach, you disregard the news altogether since the theory of this approach is that the price movement alone should be considered in arriving at market decisions.

Trade Conservatively, With Money You Can Afford to Risk

After the lack of knowledgeability or a plan, the tendency to overtrade contributes most to trading losses. Continued success in commodity trading requires conservative trading, with money you can afford to risk. To trade conservatively, you should have trading capital equal to at least double the minimum margin required by your broker. You do not have to deposit more margin than required, but the additional funds that are earmarked for trading purposes should at least be available if needed.

With respect to margin requirements, it has often been said that you should never meet a margin call. In other words, if one's position in the market shows enough of a loss to require additional margin, the position should be closed out rather than be reinforced with additional margin. The rationale, of course, is that the call for additional margin in itself proves that a market position is bad. Although the reasoning holds a certain amount of logic, whether more margin is needed should not be the determining factor in maintaining a position or closing it out. This decision should be made solely on the basis of the forecasting approach and trading plan you are using—together, of course, with how much risk you should take based on this plan.

If you have no trading plan, then by all means close out the position. You should not even be trading without a plan!

Never Risk All Your Trading Capital On Any One Situation

Do not risk everything on any one situation. To do so is to invest recklessly. To make money in commodities with any consistency, you have to program your trading in such a way as to spread your risks over various situations. "Spreading risk" does not mean that you must trade in a number of different commodities at the same time. In fact, for the average speculator, trading in too many commodities at one time is probably a mistake. Pick one or two actively traded commodities, particularly if you have relatively limited trading funds, and confine your trading to them. Get your diversification of risk by participating in various situations over an extended period.

This kind of diversified programming is not always easy, because occasionally a situation comes along that looks particularly attractive. A market position in this situation may appear to have so little risk with such a large profit potential that the trader decides to stake everything on it. In fact, he or she may go so far as to substantially exceed the size of the normal trading commitment. This is a dangerous practice. You only have to miscalculate once to jeopardize the entire trading program.

Provided you use adequate precautions to avoid the taking of a large loss, you can be more heavily committed in situations that appear to have a large profit potential than in those that appear to have less profit potential. But this variation in the size of your trading commitment should not be of the kind that endangers the continuity of your trading program.

Another mistake commonly made by traders is that they increase the size of their trading commitment after they have taken several consecutive profits. There are some compelling reasons for doing so. One is that they have additional money in their account to carry a larger commitment. Another is that, after a period of profitable accomplishment, speculators tend to assume that they have finally found the formula for continuous profits. They reflect on what their profits would have been if they had been trading in larger amounts. Actually, as every experienced trader knows, occasional losses are inevitable. Also, they are more probable after a consecutive run of profitable trades. Thus, increasing the size of your trading commitment after a run of profitable trades is particularly dangerous.

Never Depend on Trading Profits to Meet Regular Expenses

Trading profits simply aren't as regular as paychecks. You cannot depend on profits of fixed amounts at fixed intervals. Remember that profits can be made only as profitable situations develop—a fact that traders too often lose sight of in their desire to obtain a profit.

Also, if you *have to* make a certain amount of money by trading, you cannot possibly analyze situations as objectively if the necessity for profits were not a consideration. Your desire and need for profits will almost certainly cause you to make serious trading errors. Hope and desire have no place in commodity trading. To be successful, a trader must analyze situations in an objective manner as they develop. You must have patience, and you must put yourself in a position to take advantage of profitable situations when they occur. But you should never attempt to force profits out of a situation that doesn't offer them.

Most traders seem to have little conception of how greatly market risks and profit potentials vary from one situation to another. Too often a trader feels that the only advice he or she needs is whether to buy or sell and that this advice can be as easily given at one time or another. The truth of the matter is, of course, that buying and selling advice has to be timed to coincide with favorable buying and selling opportunities—not with the desire of a trader to get into the market.

As a final word, beware of the old trading axiom, which you may have heard: "You will never go broke taking a profit." In a literal sense the statement is true. Many traders have gone broke because they have adopted this axiom as a trading philosophy. Don't make this mistake. If you accept a profit each time it is offered, you will always be accepting small profits. Traders who accept small profits invariably fall into the habit of buying and selling against the immediate price trend in a narrow price range. There is no surer way to lose money trading in commodities. For when prices do move out of their narrow range and into a broad move, the trader who has accepted small profits is usually caught with a sizable loss—a loss that substantially exceeds the small profits previously taken by trading against the immediate price trend.

To trade successfully in commodities, you have to put yourself into a position to accept large profits when they are available. If you do this and at the same time use the techniques outlined in this book to select and limit your risks, you should be well on your way toward becoming a successful trader.

LIMIT YOUR LOSSES AND LET YOUR PROFITS RUN

Not going for big profits is only part of a losing scheme. The biggest failing of the unsuccessful trader is that he or she stays too long with a losing trade and gets out of a winning situation too early. Inexperienced speculators have a tendency to hesitate closing out losing trades. Consequently, what could have been a relatively small loss often turns into a major loss. They are reluctant to admit to themselves that their judgment was wrong and to get out of a position that is not working. They tend to procrastinate and stubbornly hold on, hoping that the market will eventually recover.

While some traders hesitate in taking a loss, others are often too quick to take their profits, fearing that their profits will slip away from them. Although there is nothing basically wrong with taking profits, making a practice of taking small profits—again—requires that your judgment be correct most of the time (which is hardly likely) or that your losses be correspondingly smaller than profits to show an overall profit.

There is no sure-fire method of beating the market—one that guarantees a profit on every trade. However, you do not have to be right on the market every time to make money trading commodities. But you do have to make more money on those trades when your judgment is correct than you lose on those occasions when the market does not perform as you expect. In other words, you can even be wrong more often that you are right and still make an overall profit—as long as you limit losses on your unsuccessful trades and let your profits run on your successful trades. Your dollar return on the fewer successful trades will exceed your dollar loss, even though the unsuccessful trades were more numerous. By limiting your losses and letting your profits run, you tend to gain a lot more when you are right than you lose when you are wrong.

Example: A trader makes ten trades. Out of those ten trades, three are successful and seven unsuccessful. Even though he had seven unsuccessful trades out of ten, he cut his losses short; that is, he liquidated those positions that were not working and took small losses rather than holding on and possibly encountering large losses. Although he had seven losses, they were relatively small, ranging from $175 to $300 on each trade, for a total loss of $1,500. In the case of the three successful trades, he left his profits run; that is, he held on to his positions that were working in his favor until the favorable move appeared to have concluded. He had profits ranging from $825 to $1,525, for a net profit of $1,700 (see Table 14-1).

Table 14-1

Profits		Losses	
Potatoes	$ 850	Cocoa	$ 220
Sugar	825	Soybeans	225
Bellies	+1,525	Wheat	175
Total profits	$3,200	Sugar	225
Total losses	−1,500	Corn	175
		Cotton	300
Net profit	$1,700	Cattle	+180
		Total losses	$1,500

HOW TO INITIATE A POSITION

Although everyone probably agrees that limiting your losses and letting your profits run makes sense and constitutes a logical approach to trading, it is easier said than done. Even those who set out with the idea of limiting their losses and letting their profits run quite often find themselves violating this principle and taking small profits when they are available and letting their losses run heavily against them. Their problem is that they don't have a plan of operation. They have not set up any guidelines as to when to liquidate a position that is going against them or when to refrain from taking a profit on a position that is working in their favor. To avoid making such errors yourself, do the following:

First, make a careful analysis of the *fundamentals* to see which situation has the best profit potential. Use the methods outlined in Chapter 12 to analyze a market to determine whether a market situation is bullish or bearish and whether it warrants buying or selling. After determining the direction of the market trend, you must then project its extent—whether it is of major or of minor importance. The Technical Forecasting chapter can help you on this point. Remember also that support and resistance areas may limit the extent of the move.

Also weigh risk versus profit potential. Enter only those situations in which the profit potential is compatible with the risk you are assuming. For instance, a situation may have a large profit potential, but it may also entail an equally large risk. Such a proposition is less desirable than one in which the profit potential is not as large but the risk is small in comparison.

> *Example*: You anticipate that the extent of an upward move could result in $600 gain. The nearest logical place to put a sell stop order is below the area at which you contemplate buying. That point allows for a $200 loss, and your profit potential is three times your risk. On the other hand, if the profit potential appears to be $200 and the nearest area to place a sell stop results in a $200 loss, your risk versus your profit potential—makes the transaction hardly a worthwhile undertaking.

Secondly, you must determine that the timing is right for entry into the market. You want to take advantage of the high profit potential, but with a minimum of risk. Chart analysis, described in Chapter 13, can be helpful in determining the best time to get in and the best time to get out. In our very fast-moving commodity futures markets, timing is of extreme importance. You might have the right idea, but if your timing is wrong you may encounter heavy losses before the situation begins to work. Getting into a good situation at the wrong time can be just as disastrous as getting into a poor situation.

Sometimes your analysis of the fundamentals indicates that, over the long run, prices will work higher. But the trend of the market may be moving in the opposite direction. Either you have analyzed the fundamentals incorrectly and have overlooked some pertinent factors, or temporary near-term factors are influencing prices contrary to the longer-term outlook.

However, if, after reexamining the fundamentals, they still indicate higher prices, wait until the market trend reverses itself and is moving in the same direction as the fundamentals had indicated before initiating your position.

Establish a long position only when the trend of the market is clearly up or a short position only if the trend of the market is clearly down. If no clear-cut trend is evident or if any doubt is in your mind as to what the trend may be, don't establish a position. When in doubt, stay out. Be patient and wait for conditions—both fundamental and technical—to be exactly right before initiating a position. The market will still be there tomorrow, with several dozen commodities in which you may trade.

Enter the market only when the fundamental and technical factors agree. When the fundamental and technical factors are not in harmony—that is, when both do not indicate higher prices or lower prices—stay out.

Don't try to anticipate a trend. Wait until a trend has started before initiating a position, then trade with it. Don't attempt to forecast what will happen. Be guided by what has already *begun* to happen.

CONSIDERATIONS ONCE YOU HAVE ESTABLISHED A POSITION

Once you have determined that the fundamental and technical factors for a particular commodity are in harmony and you place an order with your broker, you should at the same time determine how far you are willing to let the market go against you before you abandon the position.

A stop order in this instance is used to minimize your loss in the event your judgment is wrong and the market does not perform as you had anticipated. A stop-loss order is a built-in safeguard for the speculator. When properly used, it acts as a safety valve and may save the speculator from unwarranted excesses of optimism. A chart of the price action of a particular commodity is useful in helping you determine where to place a stop order. You should be cautious not to place a stop too close to the market where a minor reaction will eliminate your position; but neither should you place it too far away from the market where you would suffer a greater-than-necessary loss before it is activated. The amplitude of the daily price fluctuations should be considered in your decision as to where a stop order should be placed.

Example: You decide to buy soybeans at $5.90. Prior to entering into the transaction you decide how much you are willing to let the market go against you before you liquidate your position. You choose to limit your loss to approximately 3 cents. You then place a stop order to sell 3 cents below the market, or at

$5.87. If the market reaches that price, your broker will have a market order to sell at the best price obtainable (see Figure 14-1). The market goes against you, and your sell stop is elected. Your long position is liquidated (sold) at the market price at that time.

Though you have incurred a loss, you have limited it to an approximate predetermined amount. If the market moves in your favor, you can always cancel your original stop and raise the stop to protect your profit.

If the market goes your way, maintain your position as long as the market trend continues in your direction. Maintain it as long as the fundamentals continue to be favorable and as long as the trend of the market continues to be favorable. Don't liquidate unless fundamental information leads you to believe that a reversal in trend is imminent or that the favorable trend is concluded. Do not liquidate a position that is moving in your favor just because you have made what appears to be a good profit: The biggest part of the move might still be ahead. However, once you receive some fundamental news that leads you to believe that a reversal is imminent or have an indication that the trend is changing, get out while the getting is good. Although your successful trades may be fewer in number than your unsuccessful trades, if you let your profits run when you have a good position and limit your losses when you don't, you will come out ahead on balance.

Don't let your position influence your decision to stay or to get out. Fred C. Kelley's famous story of the old man and the turkey trap makes the point:

> He had a turkey trap, a crude contrivance consisting of a big box with the door hinged at the top. This door was kept open by a prop to which was tied a piece of twine leading back a hundred feet or more to the old man. A thin trail of corn was scattered along a path which lured the turkeys to the box. Once inside they found an even more plentiful supply of corn. When enough turkeys had wandered inside the box, the old man would jerk the prop and let the door fall shut. Having once shut the door, he couldn't open it again without going to the box and this would scare away any turkeys lurking outside. The time to pull away the prop was when as many turkeys were inside as one could reasonably expect.
>
> One day, the old man had a dozen turkeys in his box. Then one sauntered out leaving eleven. "Gosh, I wish I had pulled the string when all twelve were there," said the old man. "I'll wait a minute and maybe the other one will go back." But while he waited for the twelfth turkey to return, two more walked out on him. "I should have been satisfied with eleven," the trapper said. "Just as soon as I get one more back I'll pull the string." But, three more walked out. Still the man waited. Having once had twelve turkeys, he disliked going home with less than eight. He couldn't give up the idea that some of the original number would return. When finally only one turkey was left in the trap, he said, "I'll wait until he walks out or another goes in and then I'll quit." The solitary turkey went to join the others and the man returned empty handed.[1]

[1] Fred C. Kelly, *Why You Win or Lose: The Psychology of Speculation* (Wells, Vermont: Frazer Publishing Company, 1930).

Figure 14-1

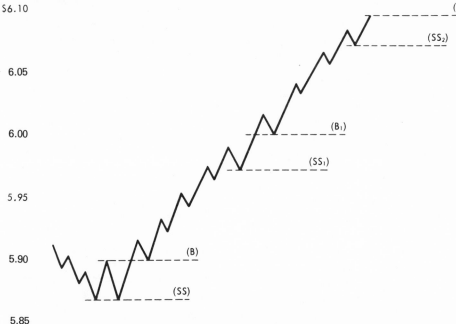

Many traders, unfortunately, do the same thing in commodities. When they have bought at $5.90 and have seen a contract of soybeans go to $6.00 per bushel, they are reluctant to sell at $5.95. By the time it sinks to $5.90, they would gladly have taken $5.92. When obligated to sell out or deposit additional margin at $5.85 they wonder whatever induced them to wait so long.

This hesitance is quite common, and I'm sure that all of us have made the same mistake at some time or other. It's human nature. Although we realize the trend has changed, we hesitate in closing out the trade, hoping the market will recover. Why? Simply because we have no plan or tactics. Consequently, our profits slip away from us, and our losses, instead of being nipped off, run heavily against us.

When a position begins to work, the trader should remain alert for opportunities to alter the stop protection to protect profits and to prevent them from evaporating.

Example: See Figure 14-1. You buy soybeans at $5.90 (B) and place a protective sell stop at $5.87. The price of soybeans subsequently advances to $6.00 (B$_1$), but you feel prices will move higher and want to hold your position. At the same time, you do not want to lose your profit. To protect your profit, you cancel your original sell stop at $5.87 and raise it to SS$_1$—just below the market at $5.97. You are willing to risk 3 cents of your profit against the possibility of additional profits.

If the market drops to $5.97 (your stop price), your stop order to sell immediately becomes a market order to sell and your broker must sell at the best price he can get. You would be stopped out of your position with approximately a 7-cent profit.

Prices continue to advance from \$6 (B_1) to \$6.10 (B_2) and they do not activate your stop price. You cancel your sell-stop order at \$5.97 (SS_1) and raise it again to \$6.07 (SS_2) to protect your profit, thus keeping pace with the market's advances.

Although raising a sell-stop order to protect a profit on a long position is justified as the market continues to move in your favor, you should not cancel or lower your stop when the market moves against you and approaches your stop price. This policy disregards the very protection that stops are supposed to provide.

In a similar fashion, a buy-stop order can be used to either minimize your losses on a short sale or to protect your profits when a market moves against you (see Figure 14-2).

Example: You sell cocoa short at 147.50 cents (S_1), and you place a stop order to buy above the prevailing market level at 148.50 cents (BS_1) to minimize your risk. If the market does not decline as you expect, but advances instead to 148.50 cents (your buy-stop price), your stop order to buy becomes a market order to buy. Your broker then buys at the best possible price, and your loss is limited to approximately \$300 (the value of a 1-cent move in cocoa).

The market declines, as you anticipated, to 145.50 cents (S_2). You cancel your original stop at 148.50 cents (BS_1) and lower it to 146.50 cents (BS_2) to protect your 1-cent or more profit. The market continues to decline and does not touch your buy stop, so you follow the trend of the market by lowering the stop.

The stop order to buy was initially used to minimize loss in the event that the short sale had not declined as expected. If your judgment had been wrong, you would have been wrong for only a relatively small amount—an amount predetermined by yourself, one that you felt you could afford and that was justifiable in relationship to the profit potential the situation seemingly afforded. You would have limited your loss.

As it turned out, your judgment was correct, and the market moved in your favor. As the market moved in your favor, the stop order to buy was then used to protect your profits. As long as the trend of the market remains in your favor, maintain your position and let your profits run—utilizing a trailing stop at logical places to protect your profits. Don't liquidate a position that is working in your favor just because you think the market is too low (if you are short) or because you think you have a handsome profit. Maintain a profitable position until something definite indicates that the market has actually reversed itself. By maintaining your position as long as the trend remains intact and by using the stop order judiciously, you will not leave a profitable situation prematurely, nor will you allow your profits to evaporate into a loss. You will maintain your position, letting your profits run, and you will not liquidate a profitable position until a favorable trend appears to have been

Figure 14-2

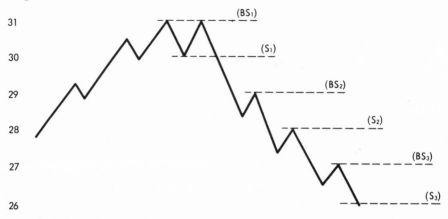

concluded. Don't try to pick tops or bottoms. Let the market tell you when to get in as well as when to get out.

The proper use of stop-loss orders will prevent you from getting out of a good situation too soon and from staying in a bad situation too long. A trader who is taken out of the market by a stop order with the major portion of the profit or with only a moderate loss has capital largely intact to use when another favorable situation develops.

A wise trader usually does not take a position until certain formations are completed or until prices break out of a certain price range, advancing above or declining below a certain price level. At these points consider taking action. If the market has been consolidating in a congestion area with no trend apparent, await a breakout on the topside or the downside to signal the next move before buying or selling.

Figure 14-3

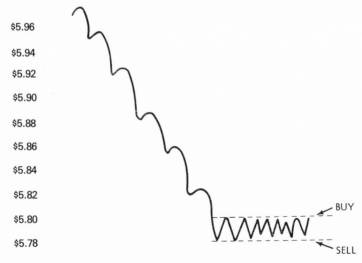

Example: Refer to Figure 14-3. The soybean market is trading over a narrow range between $5.80 and $5.78. Then the price advances above $5.80, signaling a purchase. You are bullishly inclined, so you place an order to buy soybeans at $5.80¼ stop.

If prices had declined below $5.78, they would indicate a short sale. You would then place an order to *sell* soybeans at $5.77¾ stop.

Example: You have thoroughly analyzed the fundamentals, and you feel demand is in excess of supply and wheat prices are going higher. You then look at your chart (Figure 14-4) to see whether now is the time to buy or whether you should wait for a more favorable opportunity.

The trend is up. The market has recently made a new high, then reacted, and is presently resuming its upward move. You could buy at the market, wait for the market to react to a lower level, or wait for the market to make a new high. You wait for the market to make new highs to buy at $2.75 (B). At that time you decide to place a sell-stop order, to protect your long position in the event that the market reverses itself, below the previous low of the move, which was $2.72 (SS). If the market activates the stop price, the uptrend is penetrated and a downtrend is beginning. And you will be out of your position with a nominal loss of approximately 3 cents.

The market advances after you go long to $1.85 ($B_1$). You have a 10-cent profit. The fundamentals are unchanged, and the trend is still up. You should, therefore, stay with your position and ride it as long as the uptrend remains intact. However, you have a nice profit and do not want to lose it. While your original sell stop at $2.72 was justified when you bought at $2.75, it is too far below the market at this point. You cancel your original stop at $2.72 and raise it to $2.82 ($SS_1$). If the market reacts from $2.85 to $2.82, your stop order to sell becomes a market order to sell and your broker executes the order at the best price at the time. And you still have a 7-cent profit.

As long as the price does not touch your sell-stop and continues to advance, you keep moving your sell-stop to a higher level. This practice is

Figure 14-4

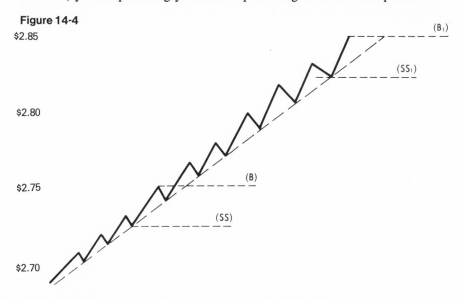

sometimes referred to as a *trailing stop*—that is, keeping pace with the market's advance.

> *Example*: Refer to Figure 14-5. You have analyzed the fundamentals in sugar, and you think that supplies are in excess of demand and that prices should go down. However, when you look at the chart, you observe that the market is in an uptrend. Something is wrong. Either you have analyzed the fundamentals incorrectly, or near-term influences are causing the market to act contrary to what the long-term outlook may be.
>
> While your analysis may ultimately prove correct, this is not the time to take a short position. Wait until the trend reverses itself and is moving in the direction the fundamentals have indicated—that is, downward.
>
> When the uptrend is penetrated on the downside, start to establish your short position (S_1). Place a stop order to buy (BS_1) over the previous high (B). However, you wish to establish only part of your short position at S_1 and wait for further confirmation before establishing the balance of your intended position. The next signal to sell (S_2) is when the market declines below the two previous lows (A and C). When the balance of the position is sold, you cancel the former stop (BS_1) above B and lower your stop to just above D (BS_2). As long as the trend remains down, you should stay short, lowering the buy-stop to protect your profits.

AVERAGING DOWN

When a market moves contrary to an established position, some people tend to add to their long positions. They hope to obtain a lower average price so that when the market recovers, they will break even at a lower price. This is known as *averaging down.* The same principle applies to *averaging up,* but in reverse: Shorts who sell more in an upward trend to break even.

Many traders feel that averaging down permits them to escape unharmed at a lower level. In actuality, averaging down is increasing the risk of a situation that is not working.

Figure 14-5

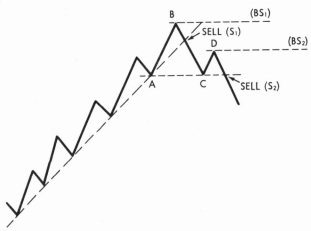

Example: You buy one contract of May potatoes at $4.50. The market goes down to $4.40, and you feel that buying a second contract at $4.40 would give you a lower average price. Your rationale is really, "The deal is bad, so now I'll be able to break even if the price gets back up to $4.45." The danger, however, is that if the market continues to decline to $4.30, you are then losing 15 cents on each of the two contracts, instead of 20 cents on one.

Usually adding to your position is logical only after your first commitment shows a profit.

PYRAMIDING

When the market is moving in your favor, you may at times want to add to your position. This practice is known as *pyramiding*. This can be a highly successful operation, if conducted according to a sound trading plan. Most successful traders generally follow two rules in adding to their positions:

1. Don't add to your position unless your existing position is showing a profit.
2. The number of contracts added to your position should be no larger than your base (generally your initial position), and it should become proportionately smaller as the market continues to move in your favor.

Example: By pyramiding according to these two rules, you increase your commitment as shown in Figure 14-6. You initiate your position by buying five contracts at $4.40. The market advances to $4.45, and you buy an additional four contracts, bringing your total position to nine contracts. Your average price on nine contracts is now $4.42+. The market advances to $4.50, and you buy another three contracts, bringing your cumulative total position to twelve contracts and your average price to $4.44+. As the market advances to $4.55, you buy another two contracts, bringing your total to fourteen contracts and the average price to about $4.46. Again the market gains, this time to $4.60, and you pick up one more contract for a total of fifteen. Your final average price on fifteen contracts is now around $4.47.

By pyramiding in this manner, the average price of all your contracts will be at a level well below the prevailing market. Consequently, a market

Figure 14-6

		Average
$4.60	x	4.47
$4.55	x x	4.46
$4.50	x x x	4.44
$4.45	x x x x	4.42
$4.40	x x x x x	4.40

reaction generally does not seriously jeopardize your position, and a change in trend usually allows you ample time to liquidate at a profit.

Though pyramiding, do not overtrade. Don't use more risk capital than intended on one situation, and don't use all your risk capital.

If, on the other hand, you add to your position (long or short) in increments larger than your base or previous purchase or sale (as illustrated in Figure 14-7), your average price will be relatively close to your most recent purchase price. Consequently, any minor reaction can quickly reduce your profits—if not wipe them out altogether.

> *Example*: You buy one contract at $4.40 and two additional contracts at $4.45 as the market moves in your favor. Your average purchase price is $4.43. As the market proceeds upward to $4.50 you buy three more contracts, then four more, then five more. Even though you are adding to your position only as the market moves in your favor, it is not the most prudent method of adding to your position, as you can see from the way in which your average cost works out in Figure 14-7.

Another popular variation of pyramiding is to initiate a small position, one or two contracts, when you feel that the market has established a trend as shown in Figure 14-8. As the market moves in your favor, you increase the number of contracts at each successive higher price level until your base is established. However, once your desired base (that is, the maximum number of contracts to be bought at a particular price level) is completed, further additions should be no larger than the base. Even though this method of pyramiding in its early stages appears somewhat contrary to the method employed in Figure 14-6, it is in basic conformity with the two primary rules of correct pyramiding.

LOCKING IN A PROFIT

In commodities trading you can lock in a profit on a long position—if the market moves in your favor—by selling a more distant delivery month. By

Figure 14-7

		Average
4.06	x x x x x	4.52
4.55	x x x x	4.50
4.50	x x x	4.46
4.45	x x	4.43
4.40	x	4.40

Figure 14-8

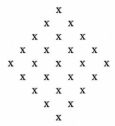

selling a different delivery month with a later maturity, you hope to achieve a long-term capital gain on your long position, with its commensurate tax advantages.

> *Example*: You buy September wheat on February 1 at $2.70, and by June 1 you have a profit of 20 cents per bushel, or the dollar equivalent of $1,000 per contract. You are uncertain as to the future course of the market and contemplate taking profits. However, you would like to maintain your long position in an attempt to achieve long-term capital gains. If you hold a long position for six months and a day or longer, the maximum tax is 25 percent of the total gain.[2] Since you had the position for only four months as of June 1, you must maintain your position for another two months and a day to qualify for long-term capital gains.
>
> To protect your profits, you sell the more distant December delivery as a hedge against your long September. This situation is referred to as *locking in a profit*. You are now long and short, long the September and short the December.

Although you no longer have an outright price risk once your profit is locked in, you still have a risk that the spread difference may work against you. However, the risk of a changing price relationship is usually considerably smaller than the risk of a price change.

Once your profit is locked in, you stand a chance of ending up with a long-term capital gain if your long position is at a higher level than your original purchase price and if the original purchase has been held for more than six months.

> *Example*: On June 1 the September delivery is $2.90, and the December delivery is $2.95. By selling December short, you reduce your risk from one of price change to one of price relationship. If the market declines, you lose part of your profit on your long September position, but you make a corresponding profit on your short December position.

If you maintain this spread position for six months and one day, and if the price of the September delivery remains above your original purchase price, you will be able to get long-term capital gains treatment (once you liquidate your long position) on your profit in the September delivery. Any profit on your short December position is treated as short-term gains.

[2]For U.S. taxpayers only and under certain conditions.

Example: After locking in your profit, the September declines from $2.90 to $2.80 and the December declines from $2.95 to $2.85. You still have a profit of 20 cents, but only 10 cents of it on the long September. The other 10 cents profit is on the short December. You bought September at $2.70, and you sold at $2.80, resulting in a 10-cent profit; you sold December at $2.95 and covered at $2.85, resulting in a 10-cent profit. Although your total profit is still 20 cents, only the 10-cent profit on the long September that you held for six months and one day gets long-term capital gain tax treatment. The 10-cent profit on the short December is short-term. *All short positions are short-term.* Short positions never qualify for long-term capital gain tax treatment, regardless of how long they are held.

On the other hand, let's assume the market continues to advance after you sell December to lock in your profits. By the time you liquidate, the price of September is $3.10, and you have a 40-cent profit, on which you will get long-term capital gain treatment. Assuming also that the December advanced by a corresponding amount (20 cents) to $3.15 and that you buy back the contract, you would have a short-term loss of 20 cents on your short December. You still have, however, an overall profit of 20 cents, the net result of a long-term capital gain of 40 cents on your long September position and a short-term loss of 20 cents on your short December position.

SELLING THE PREMIUMS AND BUYING THE DISCOUNTS

In addition to buying the right commodity at the right time, you must decide on the proper delivery. In other words, you may decide that silver prices are headed higher and that this is the moment to buy. However, you still have to answer one question—which delivery month should be bought? March, May, July, September, or December?

If you are contemplating a long position in an inverted market, buying a distant delivery within the same year is usually more advantageous than a nearby delivery selling at a premium. Of course, the nearby delivery could always widen its premium over the distant delivery. However, if the nearby delivery widens its premium, more than likely the distant delivery will also advance. On the other hand, if the market declines, the nearby deliveries are liable to decline more than the distant deliveries. Your risk is usually considerably less in buying a distant delivery rather than a nearby delivery, which is selling at a premium.

If you are contemplating a short position in an inverted market, selling a nearby delivery is usually more advantageous for just the opposite reasons.

If you are contemplating buying in a normal (carrying-charge) market, buying the nearby delivery rather than the distant delivery is usually advantageous. If the nearby is at full carrying charge to a distant delivery and the distant delivery advances, the nearby delivery has to advance as much as, and possibly more than, the distant delivery. When the market is at full carrying charge, a distant delivery cannot decline less than a nearby delivery because the distant delivery usually cannot be at a premium larger than the amount of the carrying charges above the nearby delivery. On the other hand, if the market advances, the nearby delivery could advance more than the distant delivery. There is no limit to the premium that the nearby can move to above the distant delivery.

If you buy a distant delivery when it is at its maximum premium above the nearby delivery, the distant delivery can decline. But the nearby need not necessarily show a corresponding decline. In fact, the nearby delivery could advance while a distant delivery declines. Although the distant delivery advances, the nearby has to advance as much as, if not more than, the distant delivery, thereby allowing maximum leverage.

If you are considering selling in a normal market, selling the distant deliveries that are at a premium is usually more advantageous for just the opposite reasons as mentioned above.

CONCLUSION

Maybe at this point you feel that, though the practices we've discussed make sense, you would probably miss many opportunities.

Well, you're right. You may well miss many opportunities, but the chances of your success should be considerably enhanced by following a sound trading procedure. And there are so many good opportunities that you don't have to trade for the sake of trading. It's much better to be cautious and miss a few opportunities that might have proven profitable than to lose money by taking a poor risk. The idea is to wind up a year with a profit.

Don't let success or failure allow you to forget these rules. One of the most common pitfalls in commodity trading occurs when a speculator makes a fast profit on an initial venture and is induced to conclude that commodity trading is simple. There is no feeling like walking on water! As a result the trader either forgets that a logical trading technique is necessary or forgets the rules. By the same token, the trader who suffers setbacks often overlooks sensible trading procedures in pure desperation.

Commodity trading is *not simple,* but it can be *very rewarding.* Many years of experience have proved that sensible, conservative trading techniques, along with a fundamental knowledge and a familiarity with the technical aspects of trading, constitute the best approach for successful trading. An experienced statistician and an alert technician working together constitute about as formidable a team as can be found, but only if they continually recognize the importance of always keeping their fingers on the public's pulse. Statisticians may determine the price at which a commodity *should be* trading. However, in the final analysis the price of a commodity is determined by what a buyer is willing to pay and by what a seller is willing to accept. That much is simple.

And one other thing is simple: Be certain that you are undertaking an intelligent speculation. In addition, be fully aware of the risks involved as well as the possible gains. And translate them into a practical trading program that will eventually bring you the profits you seek—money making money.

Chapter 15

Spreading—Sophisticated Speculation

In addition to buying or selling contracts outright or as a hedge against cash commodities, a trader can use futures markets for spreading or straddling operations. In commodity parlance, the terms "spread" and "straddle" are synonymous. Spreading is another form of arbitraging, similar to hedging. However, hedging is an arbitrage between cash and futures, whereas spreading is an arbitrage between futures and futures.

Spreading is the purchase of one commodity futures against the sale of another. A spreader buys the delivery that appears underpriced and simultaneously sells the delivery that appears overpriced. A trader undertakes this dual transaction when he or she feels that the two futures contracts are not in line with one another and expects that later the *spread relationship*—the difference in price between the two—will change. When it changes, the trader realizes a profit or suffers a loss because of the adjustment in the relative prices of the two contracts.

There are four basic types of spreads:

1. *Interdelivery Spreads.* This type of spreading operation involves the purchase and sale of *different delivery months* in the same commodity in the same market: for example, the purchase of October cotton and the sale of December cotton.
2. *Intermarket Spreads.* This spreading operation involves the purchase and sale of the same commodity in the same or different delivery months but in two *different markets*: for example, the purchase of September wheat on the Kansas City Board of Trade and the sale of September (or any other delivery month) wheat on the Chicago Board of Trade.
3. *Intercommodity Spreads.* This spreading operation involves the purchase and sale of *different, but related, commodities* in the same or different markets and in the same or different delivery months: for example, the

purchase of March corn on the CBOT and the sale of March oats on the CBOT. Another example is the purchase of March wheat on the Minneapolis Grain Exchange and the sale of May corn on the CBOT.

4. *Commodity Product Spreads.* This type of spread involves the purchase of the raw material and the sale of the derived processed products, or vice versa: for example, the purchase of March soybeans on the CBOT and the sale of March soybean oil and March soybean meal on the CBOT; or the sale of March soybeans and the purchase of March soybean oil and March soybean meal on the CBOT.

INTERDELIVERY SPREAD

In a Normal Market

An interdelivery spread, sometimes referred to as an *intramarket spread,* is the purchase and sale of the same commodity in the same market but in different delivery months. These spreads take advantage of a disparate price relationship between different delivery months. To do so, you make sales in the delivery month that is relatively high and purchases in the contract month that is relatively depressed. You take a profit by liquidating both contracts when the prices return to what is considered their normal alignment based on existing or prospective conditions, or suffer a loss if prices remain out of line.

There are four types of interdelivery spreading situations:

1. buying a nearby delivery and selling a distant delivery in a normal market, when the deferred delivery is at a premium to the nearby, in anticipation of a narrowing in the spread difference;
2. selling a nearby delivery and buying a distant delivery in a normal market, when the deferred delivery is at a premium to the nearby, in expectation of a widening in the spread difference;
3. buying a nearby delivery and selling a distant delivery in an inverted market, when the nearbys are at a premium to the deferred deliveries in the hope of a widening in the spread difference; or
4. selling a nearby and buying a distant delivery in an inverted market, when a nearby is at a premium to the deferred, in anticipation of a narrowing in the spread difference.

How does a trader make money doing all this? Let's take each type of interdelivery spread one at a time and see how.

Buying the Nearby, Selling the Distant in a Normal Market

Example: On October 19 the price of the March corn delivery is 9 cents below the July delivery—March is $2.16½ and July is $2.25½ per bushel. You feel that the price of the March delivery is underpriced in relationship to the July—or that the July is overpriced compared to the March delivery—and you expect the spread difference to narrow. In other words, you feel that either the March delivery will gain relative to the July delivery or the July will decline relative to the March delivery. You simultaneously buy the March delivery and sell the July delivery.

After establishing the spread transaction at a 9-cent difference, the price difference between the two contracts narrows to 4 cents by December 9, and you decide to take profits. You simultaneously liquidate both contracts (called *unwinding* the spread) and realize a profit of 5 cents. When you liquidate, or close out, the spread, you do just the opposite of what you did originally. Since you originally bought 5,000 bushels of March corn and sold 5,000 bushels of July corn, now you sell 5,000 bushels of March corn and buy 5,000 bushels of July corn. Your profit is calculated as follows:

October 19	Buy 5,000 bushels March corn @ $2.16½	Sell 5,000 bushels July corn @.........$2.25½
December 9	Sell 5,000 bushels March corn @ $2.25½	Buy 5,000 bushels July corn @.........$2.29½
	Profit +$.09	Loss −$ .04

Net profit is 5 cents per bushel, which is the equivalent of $250, less commission.

Watch the Spread, Not the Trend. The relationship between the two prices counts more than the prices themselves. Although both contracts advanced in price, the July delivery rose less than the March delivery; put another way, the March price increased more than the July delivery. The March delivery, the one that you were long, turned higher and resulted in a 9-cent profit. On the other hand, the July delivery, the one that you had previously sold short, also rose and resulted in a 4-cent loss. You made more money on your long March than you lost on your short July; thus, you realized a 5-cent profit on balance.

A profit could just as well have resulted if the market had declined. Even if both contracts decline in price, as long as the July declines more than the March delivery, a profit results.

Example: You buy March and sell July when July is 9 cents over the March. As March thereafter loses 4 cents relative to July, the spread difference is said to narrow from 9 to 4 cents. The March declines 4 cents, while the July delivery declines 9 cents, thus resulting in an overall profit of 5 cents, less commission.

October 19	Buy 5,000 bushels March corn @ $2.16½	Sell 5,000 bushels July corn @....$2.25½ + 9¢
December 9	Sell 5,000 bushels March corn@.......$2.12½	Buy 5,000 bushels July corn @....$2.16½ + 4¢
	Loss −$ .04	Profit +$ .09 + 5¢

Net profit is 5 cents per bushel, which is the equivalent of $250, less commission.

When placing an order to initiate or liquidate a spread, you specify only the price difference between the two contracts. For instance, in the preceding two examples, the instructions to the broker would read, "Buy March corn and sell July corn when July is 9 cents over March." Specifying the exact price at which one contract should be bought and the level at which the other should be sold is not necessary. To do so might handicap the broker in trying to fill the spread order. As a brief example, you would not place a spread order to buy March corn at 2.16½ and to sell July corn at 2.25½. If the order were placed in this manner, the broker might be able only to buy the March delivery and not to sell the July within the prescribed limit. Conversely, the July delivery might get sold, but the March might not be executed. Either way, you would wind up with an outright long position, not the intended spread position.

The particular price at which each delivery is executed matters little to a spreader. The only concern is that the spread is set at a particular price difference. Likewise, the price at which each delivery is liquidated is of little consequence as long as the spread is closed out at the desired difference. In the first example, the trader took profits when the spread had narrowed to 4 cents by telling the broker to "Sell 5,000 bushels of March corn and buy 5,000 bushels of July corn when July is 4 cents premium." The final results would be no different if each contract had to be liquidated at a higher or a lower price than in the example—just as long as it was at a 4-cent difference.

By the same token, a spreader is not necessarily concerned with which way the market moves once the spread is established. The only interest is in either the narrowing or widening of the price difference between the two contracts. Whether the market advances or declines is of little consequence. A profit can be as easily made in a rising market as in a declining market. In our examples, the only important development is that the spread narrows—that the March gains more than the July or that the March declines less than the July. Regardless of trends, what counts is that the profit on one delivery is larger than the loss on the other. The net profit, or loss, results from the combined changes in the price of the two deliveries.

If the spread between the two contracts widens instead of narrows, a loss results on the transaction. If in the first example the March delivery had declined more than the July delivery or the July had declined less than the March, a loss would have resulted.

Example: The March delivery, which you are long, declines 4 cents, whereas the July delivery, which you are short, declines 2 cents. The widening results in a 2-cent loss. You establish the spread by buying the March and selling the July when March was 9 cents under the July. Then, at a later date, you liquidate the spread—sell March and buy July—when the March is 11 cents under the July. With this widened spread, you thus incur a loss of 2 cents on the transaction, which is the equivalent of $100 per spread.

October 19	Buy 5,000 bushels		Sell 5,000 bushels	
	March corn @ $2.16½		July corn @........$2.25½	
December 9	Sell 5,000 bushels		Buy 5,000 bushels	
	March corn @ $2.12½		July corn @........$2.23½	
	Loss	−$ .04	Profit	+$ .02

Net loss is 2 cents per bushel, which is the equivalent of $100, plus commission.

A loss also results if the nearby delivery fails to advance as much in price as the distant delivery. Both contracts may even advance in price and still yield a net loss if the spread difference widens.

Example: Initially you put the spread on (buy March and sell July) when July is 9 cents over March. Then you take the spread off (liquidate) when July is 11 cents over March: You thus suffer a 2-cent loss on the deal. In other words, if the short July delivery advances 4 cents but the long March delivery advances only 2 cents, a 2-cent loss is incurred.

October 19	Buy 5,000 bushels		Sell 5,000 bushels	
	March corn @ $2.16½		July corn @........$2.25½	
December 9	Sell 5,000 bushels		Buy 5,000 bushels	
	March corn @ $2.18½		July corn @........$2.29½	
	Profit	+$ .02	Loss	−$ .04
	Loss	−$ .04		

Net loss is 2 cents per bushel, which is the equivalent of $100, plus commission.

Limiting Risks. When a nearby delivery is purchased and a distant delivery sold, your risk is somewhat limited. The maximum premium a distant delivery can be above a nearby delivery is limited to the monthly carrying charges. In our illustrative spread, between the March corn and the July corn, there are four months' carrying charges—March, April, May, and June. (Do not include July because you can deliver from the first notice day onward.) Assuming the monthly carrying charges for corn to be 5 cents per bushel, the total carrying charges from March to July are 20 cents per bushel. Thus, the maximum premium that the July delivery can go above the March delivery is 20 cents. (See the "Cash and Future Price Relationships" chapter for the reasons.) Because the March was purchased and the July sold when the July was already at a 9-cent premium to the March, the most you could lose on the spread is 11 cents. In other words, the most that the July could gain relative to the March is 11 cents, which is the difference between current spread difference (9 cents) and full carrying charges (20 cents).

Although the premium on a distant to a nearby delivery is limited, the premium on the nearby to a distant may advance without limit. Hence, when you buy a nearby and sell a distant delivery that is at a premium, your risk is limited to the difference between the current spread difference and full carrying charges. Your profit potential, however, is unlimited. The nearby delivery can be lower in price than a deferred delivery when the spread is established, but as time passes the nearby delivery may gain on the deferred delivery and may even move to a premium over the deferreds.

> *Example*: The spread involving a long March and short July is established when the March is 9 cents under the July. As time passes, the March gains on the July, then goes to a premium of 5 cents to the July. The unwinding results in an overall profit of 14 cents, less commission.

October 19	Buy 5,000 bushels		Sell 5,000 bushels		
	March corn @ $2.16½		July corn @......... $2.25½		
November 15	Sell 5,000 bushels		Buy 5,000 bushels		
	March corn @ $2.36½		July corn @......... $2.31½		
	Profit	+$ .20	Loss	−$ .06	

Net profit is 14 cents per bushel, which is the equivalent of $700 less commission.

Selling the Nearby, Buying the Distant in a Normal Market.

In the preceding examples, you purchased the nearby delivery and sold the distant delivery when March was at a discount to the July. You can also do just the opposite. If, however, you sell the nearby delivery and purchase the distant one when the nearby is at a discount, your profit potential is limited because the nearby can widen only to the amount of the carrying charges. Your risk, on the other hand, is unlimited.

Such a spread is undertaken when you expect the spread difference to widen. In other words, you expect the nearby to decline relative to the deferred or the deferred to gain relative to the nearby.

> *Example*: You sell March and purchase July when the March is at a 16-cent discount to July. The most March can decline relative to the July is from 16 cents to 20 cents. In other words, the March can decline farther relative to July, but it cannot go to a discount larger than 20 cents. Even though the short March delivery declines 15 cents, your profit on the spread is 4 cents. The discount of the March compared to July, or the premium on July compared to March, is limited to carrying charges. Consequently, your profit potential is limited to 4 cents, the difference between the spread of 16 cents when it was established and the full carrying charges of 20 cents.

October 19	Sell 5,000 bushels		Buy 5,000 bushels		
	March corn @ $2.15		July corn @ $2.31		
November 15	Buy 5,000 bushels		Sell 5,000 bushels		
	March corn @ $2.00		July corn @ $2.20		
	Profit	+$ .15	Loss	−$ .11	

Net profit is 4 cents per bushel, which is the equivalent of $200, less commission.

However, since your risk is unlimited, you can lose considerably more than you stand to gain.

Example: As time passes, March gains on July. The discount on the March disappears, and March goes to a 4 cent premium above July. Consequently, although your profit potential is limited to 4 cents, your risk is unlimited because there is no limit to which a nearby can go premium to a distant delivery.

Sell 5,000 bushels			Buy 5,000 bushels	
March corn @ $2.15			July corn @ $2.31	
Buy 5,000 bushels			Sell 5,000 bushels	
March corn @ $2.37			July corn @ $2.33	
Loss	−$ .22		Profit	+$ .02

Net loss is 20 cents per bushel, which is the equivalent of $1,000 plus commission.

In an Inverted Market

The previous examples assumed the market is normal, that the nearby deliveries are lower in price (at a discount) than the distant deliveries. But spreading opportunities also exist when the market is inverted, when the nearby deliveries are higher in price than (at a premium to) the deferred delivery months. Spreads can be initiated by buying a nearby delivery and selling a distant delivery, which results in a profit if the nearby delivery widens its premium over the distant delivery. A profitable spread can also be established by selling a nearby delivery and buying a distant delivery in anticipation of a narrowed premium to the distant delivery.

Buying the Nearby, Selling the Distant in an Inverted Market

Example: The March delivery is at a 5-cent premium to the July delivery. You think that the March delivery will widen its premium above the July, so you decide to buy the March and sell the July. If March advances relative to July, you will make a profit.

You buy the March delivery at 2.16½ on October 19, then sell it at 2.25½ on December 9, realizing a profit of 9 cents per bushel. On these same dates, you sell July at 2.11½ and cover your position at 2.16½, resulting in a 5-cent loss. Despite this 5-cent loss on your short position in the July delivery, your profit of 9 cents on the long March is more than enough to produce a net profit. Your overall profit on the transaction is 4 cents, less commission.

October 19	Buy 5,000 bushels		Sell 5,000 bushels	
	March corn @ $2.16½		July corn @......... $2.11½	
December 9	Sell 5,000 bushels		Buy 5,000 bushels	
	March corn @ $2.25½		July corn @......... $2.16½	
	Profit	+$ .09	Loss	−$ .05

Net profit is 4 cents per bushel, which is equivalent to $200, less commission.

The results are the same even if prices decline, as long as the March delivery declines less than the July delivery—as long as the July loses ground relative to the March.

Example: The prices of March and July both decline, but the July declines more than the March. On October 19, you bought March at 2.16½ and shorted July at 2.11½. On December 9, you sell March at 2.11½, resulting in a loss of 5 cents, and cover the July at 2.02½ on December 9, resulting in a profit of 9 cents. The gain on the July is more than enough to offset the loss on the March, and thus the transaction yields a 4-cent profit on balance.

October 19	Buy 5,000 bushels March corn @ $2.16½	Sell 5,000 bushels July corn @ $2.11½
December 9	Sell 5,000 bushels March corn @ $2.11½	Buy 5,000 bushels July corn @ $2.02½
	Loss −$ .05	Profit +$ .09

Net profit is 4 cents per bushel, which is equivalent to $200 less commission.

If after establishing the spread, however, the nearby loses ground relative to July, you would suffer a loss.

Example: The premium on the March narrows from 5 cents to 1 cent, a 4-cent loss results.

October 19	Buy 5,000 bushels March corn @ $2.16½	Sell 5,000 bushels July corn @.... $2.11½ + 5¢
December 9	Sell 5,000 bushels March corn @ $2.25½	Buy 5,000 bushels July corn @.... $2.24½ − 1¢
	Profit +$ .09	Loss −$ .13

Net loss is 4 cents per bushel, which is equivalent to $200, plus commission.

The results are the same even in a declining market.

Example: The March delivery that you are long declines farther than the July delivery that you are short. While the short position in July results in a 1-cent profit, it only partially offsets the loss of 5 cents encountered on the long position in the March delivery. You lose 4 cents on the bushel.

October 19	Buy 5,000 bushels March corn @ $2.16½	Sell 5,000 bushels July corn @ $2.11½
December 9	Sell 5,000 bushels March corn @ $2.11½	Buy 5,000 bushels July corn @ $2.10½
	Loss −$ .05	Profit +$ .01

Net loss is 4 cents per bushel, which is the equivalent of $200 plus commission.

In this case, the loss resulted because the long position declined farther than the short.

Risk is also limited in a spread long the nearby and short the distant in an inverted market.

Example: The March does not gain relative to the July, but the most it can go below July is to full carrying charges. That is, March can go only to a 20-cent discount to July. Since the March is purchased at a 5-cent premium to the short July, the maximum potential loss is 15 cents. The largest discount that the March can sell below July is 20 cents, the cost of carrying the actual commodity from March to July.

Selling the Nearby, Buying the Distant in an Inverted Market.
You can sell the nearby and buy a distant delivery when the nearby is at a premium, in anticipation of a narrowing in the spread difference. In other words, if you feel that the nearby delivery's premium to the deferred will narrow, sell the nearby and buy the distant. If your judgment is correct and the premium on the nearby over the distant narrows, you will make a profit.

Example: You sell March and buy July in an inverted market. March is at a premium to July. Later, on December 9, you unwind the spread for a net 3-cent profit.

October 19	Sell 5,000 bushels March corn @ $2.16½	Buy 5,000 bushels July corn @.........$2.11½	
December 9	Buy 5,000 bushels March corn @ $2.26½	Sell 5,000 bushels July corn @.........$2.24½	
	Loss −$ .10	Profit +$ .13	

Net profit is 3 cents, which is equivalent to $150, less commissions.

Although both deliveries advanced, the long delivery, July, gained more than the short March. Both deliveries advanced, but the spread difference narrowed because July advanced further than March: While July advanced 13 cents, March gained only 10 cents.

In this type of spreading situation your profit potential is limited to 25 cents: That potential is equal to the original spread plus the 20-cent maximum carrying charge (which is the most that March can discount to July). Your risk, however, is unlimited because the nearby delivery, which you are short, can go to any extreme above the distant delivery.

INTERMARKET SPREADS

Spreading opportunities also are latent in the same commodity, one that is traded on two different futures exchanges. Wheat, for instance, is traded on three different futures exchanges: the Chicago Board of Trade, the Kansas City Board of Trade, and the Minneapolis Grain Exchange.

The intermarket spreader operates on much the same principle as the interdelivery spreader—buying low and selling high. Only the intermarket spreader uses exchanges the way the interdelivery spreader uses months. The spreader buys on a market that seems low and sells on one that seems relatively high. However, several differences must be taken into consideration in analyzing intermarket spreading possibilities:

1. transportation cost between the two markets,
2. the value of the class and grade of the commodity deliverable on each futures exchange, and
3. local supply and demand conditions of different deliverable grades in each respective market.

Transportation Costs

Grain normally moves from west to east. In other words, wheat moves from the major surplus-producing areas of the West, either Kansas City or Minneapolis, to the deficit-producing areas of the East. Consequently, the price of wheat in Chicago is usually higher than the price of wheat in Kansas City or Minneapolis because of the transportation cost.

The Kansas City-Chicago spread normally stays at a difference that represents part of the freight cost to ship the wheat from the Southwest to the Chicago area. Minneapolis may be lower than Chicago for the same reason, but in years of spring wheat scarcity it trades higher than Chicago. Only an unusual set of conditions can put the Kansas City price to a premium over Chicago, but actual or artificial scarcities created by government-support loans have created such a spread condition. The reason is that in the Southwest, there is ample storage space to take the loan, but in the East, the source of soft red winter wheat supplies, the loan cannot always be so generally taken.

Different Deliverable Grades

Each market tends to reflect the price of the type of wheat grown most abundantly in that particular area. The Kansas City Market is primarily a hard red winter wheat market, whereas Minneapolis is a spring wheat market and Chicago is a soft red winter wheat market. More specifically, the futures market in each area tends to reflect the price of grades of wheat deliverable on its particular exchange. For example, hard winter wheat that is deliverable on the Kansas City Board of Trade cannot be delivered on the Minneapolis Grain Exchange, which calls for delivery of spring wheat. Both classes of wheat— winter and spring—are deliverable on the CBOT. However, not all numerical grades are deliverable: Winter wheat is deliverable on the KCBT and the CBOT, but the CBOT does not allow No. 3 winter wheat to be delivered; by the same token, No. 2 spring wheat, deliverable on the Minneapolis Grain Exchange, is not deliverable on the CBOT. Therefore, the price of wheat in each of the three markets may reflect a different class of wheat. Consequently, the difference among the three classes may vary considerably from one another, depending upon supply and demand conditions for each particular class.

Local Supply and Demand Conditions

Although wheat is produced in many parts of the country, growing conditions may be altered within the same season by the vagaries of weather. While the Southwest may produce a bumper crop, the crop in the mid-West around Chicago, because of unfavorable weather, may be relatively poor. Similarly, the crop in the Northwest around Minneapolis may be good, and the crops in either or both Southwest and mid-West may be poor.

For instance, when hard red winter wheat supplies are relatively small in the Southwest and soft red wheat supplies are relatively large in the areas near Chicago, the price of Kansas City futures tends to gain relative to Chicago futures. Thus, as an intermarket spreader, you would buy Kansas City futures and sell Chicago wheat futures. By the same token, when spring wheat supplies are relatively large, the price of Minneapolis futures decline relative to Chicago futures or even to Kansas City, particularly if hard wheat supplies are ample. If supplies of hard red winter wheat in the Southwest are relatively large and if soft red wheat supplies are relatively small, the price of Kansas City futures tends to gain relative to Chicago futures. Thus, you would buy Kansas City futures and sell Chicago wheat futures.

Example: The price of Kansas City December wheat futures are $2.50, and the price of Chicago December wheat futures are $2.60. You feel the price of Kansas City wheat, although at a discount, is high compared to Chicago wheat. You base your analysis on the two futures' respective supply-and-demand conditions and on the possibility that the spread difference between the two markets will widen. You sell Kansas City wheat futures and buy Chicago wheat futures when Chicago is at a 10-cent premium. You make a nickel on the bushel when, indeed, the spread widens. After initiating the spread at a 10-cent differential, the difference widens to 15 cents by July 5, when you decide to take profits. To close out your spread, you do just the opposite of what you did originally—you buy K.C. and sell Chicago.

June 1	Sell 5,000 bushels K.C. December wheat @ $2.50		Buy 5,000 bushels CBOT December wheat @ $2.60	
July 5	Buy 5,000 bushels K.C. December wheat @ $2.40		Sell 5,000 bushels CBOT December wheat @ $2.55	
	Profit	+$ .10	Loss	−$ .05

Net profit is 5 cents per bushel, which is equivalent to $250, less commission.

You made a profit because the spread grew wider, incidentally in a declining market. Yet even prices in both markets advance instead of decline, a profit results—as long as the price of K.C. futures do not gain as much as the price of Chicago futures.

> *Example*: The markets and your spread are the same as in the previous example, but this time prices advance. The Chicago futures advance more than Kansas City's. This time, you buy back the K.C. contract on July 5 at 2.60, resulting in a loss of 10 cents. At the same time, you sell Chicago wheat on July 5 at 2.75, for a profit of 15 cents. The 15-cent profit on the Chicago side of the transaction offsets the 10-cent loss on the K.C. side. Hence, you make a profit of 5 cents on the transaction.

June 1	Sell 5,000 bushels K.C. December wheat @ $2.50	Buy 5,000 bushels Chicago December wheat @ $2.50
July 5	Buy 5,000 bushels K.C. December wheat @ $2.60	Sell 5,000 bushels Chicago December wheat $2.75
	Loss −$ .10	Profit +$ .15

> Net profit is 5 cents per bushel, which is equivalent to $250, less commission.

The basic principles that apply to interdelivery spreads apply to intermarket spreads. You need not pay so much attention to the prices or to the trends on the various markets as you must *to the spreads* among them.

A footnote to intermarket spreading: The liquidity of the various markets must also be taken into consideration. The influence of large traders, particularly hedgers, may at times have a significant influence on the spread differences between two markets. Although one market may be more attractive as a hedging vehicle than another from a pricing standpoint, the volume of trading and the resultant liquidity might be the more important consideration, particularly if a large quantity is hedged. Hedgers tend to place their buying or selling on the CBOT because it is a broad, liquid market. Then, when market conditions permit, they move their hedges from the Chicago Board of Trade to the Kansas City Board of Trade.

INTERCOMMODITY SPREAD

Various commodities that have similar uses bear a relationship to each other. For instance, since corn and oats are interchangeable animal feeds, their respective prices should reflect this relationship. When corn prices are higher than oats', the use of corn in livestock feeding tends to slacken, and the use of oats tends to increase. This shift in utilization causes the price of oats to gain on the price of corn, until a normal price relationship is reestablished.

> *Example*: A bushel of oats weighs 32 pounds, whereas a bushel of corn weighs 56 pounds. Therefore, on strictly a weight basis, a bushel of oats should be worth

approximately 57 percent of the value of a bushel of corn. However, the feeding value of oats per pound is about 3 percent better than that of corn. Consequently, the price of oats is normally about 60 percent of the price of corn on a bushel basis. Therefore, when the price of oats is 60 cents per bushel, the price of corn should be about $1 per bushel.

The spread between oats and corn is usually at its widest during the July-August period as the pressure from the oat harvest causes oat prices to decline relative to corn prices. Corn prices, on the other hand, do not necessarily have to decline in connection with oats, because the corn harvest does not begin until October. Corn prices might actually show a divergent tendency during July-August, since bad-weather scares are common to the growing corn crop. Hence, oat prices during the summer months are usually low relative to the price of corn, sometimes declining to less than 50 percent of the value of corn, a situation that offers attractive spreading opportunities. The purchase of December oats and the sale of December corn during the oats harvest period (July-August) is usually a popular spread.

As time passes and we approach the fall, oat prices usually begin to firm up as the pressure from the harvest movement of oats abates; corn prices usually begin to lose ground to oat prices as the harvest period for corn gets underway (October-December). As the price relationship between oats and corn becomes more normal, you take profits on the spread by selling December oats and buying December corn.

Example: You buy December oats in July when it is approximately three-fourths the price of December corn, which you sold. By November 1, the spread narrows so that the premium on corn is reduced from 55 to 48 cents, for an overall profit of 7 cents per bushel. You buy December oats on July 1 at 1.50 and sell them on November 1 at 1.72, resulting in a 22-cent profit. On July 1 you sell December corn at 2.05 and cover your position on November 1 at 2.20, realizing a loss of 15 cents. Combining the profit on your long oats position and the loss on your short corn position, you have an overall profit of 7 cents.

July 1	Buy 5,000 bushels		Sell 5,000 bushels	
	December oats.......$1.50		December corn @ $2.05	
November 1	Sell 5,000 bushels		Buy 5,000 bushels	
	December oats @ $1.72		December corn @ $2.20	
	Profit	+$ .22	Loss	−$ .15

Net profit is 7 cents per bushel, which is the equivalent of $350, less commission.

COMMODITY/PRODUCT SPREADS

Offering profit spreading opportunities is the price relationship between the raw material and its products. For example, generally soybeans are not used as much in their natural state. Rather they are crushed into two products—soybean oil and soybean meal. The oil is an edible vegetable oil used in shortening, margarines, and salad oils. The meal is a high protein feed used to feed livestock. While soybean prices are closely related to those of their products, soybean oil and meal prices are each affected by influences within their own spheres—not necessarily by factors affecting either of the other. However, the price movements of soybeans, soybean meal, and soybean oil all tend to parallel each other. Nonetheless, the values of the products widen or narrow in relationship to soybeans from time to time.

The physical relationship between the price of beans and the value of its oil and meal is called the *gross processing margin*. When you crush soybeans, you get oil and meal. A bushel of soybeans weighs 60 pounds and yields approximately 11 pounds of oil and 48 pounds of meal; about 1 pound is moisture and waste lost in processing. Calculating the gross processing margin is made difficult because soybean prices are quoted one way, and its products are quoted in other ways. Soybeans are quoted in dollars and cents per bushel, while soybean oil is quoted in cents and fractions of a cent per pound, and soybean meal is quoted in dollars and cents per ton. All three quotations must be converted to one common denominator for comparison basis. The normal procedure is to convert oil and meal prices to soybean prices on a "per-bushel basis."

To calculate the gross processing margin, determine the dollar value of both the soybean oil and soybean meal obtained from a bushel of soybeans, then compare the combined value of the products, oil, and meal, to the price of soybeans.

1. *The value of the oil*: Multiply the price of soybean oil by 11; this factor is approximately the number of pounds of soybean oil a 60-pound bushel of soybeans yields when crushed.
2. *The value of the meal*: Multiply the price of soybean meal by 48, which is approximately the number of pounds of meal that a bushel of soybeans yields. Then divide the answer by 2,000 to put it on a comparable basis with soybean oil. Because meal is quoted on a dollars and cents basis per ton and soybean oil is quoted *per pound*, this step gives you the dollar value of 48 pounds of soybean meal obtained from a bushel of soybeans.

   A simpler and faster method of calculating the dollar value of soybean meal obtained from a bushel of soybeans is to multiply the price of soybean meal by the reciprocal .024. This one-step calculation produces the same results as dividing the price of meal by 2,000 then multiplying the result by 48.
3. *The composite value*: The dollar value of oil is then added to the dollar value of meal, which gives you the combined value of the products obtained from a bushel of soybeans.

The combined value of the products is then compared to the price of soybeans. If the combined value of the products is larger than the price of soybeans, the gross processing margin is "plus," or "positive"; and if the combined value of the products is less than the price of soybeans, the conversion margin is "minus," or "negative."

> *Example*: The price of March soybean oil is 21 cents per pound, the price of March soybean meal is $161.00 per ton, and the price of March soybeans is $6.03 per bushel.
>
> To determine the gross crushing margin, multiply the 21 cents by 11, the number of pounds of oil that a bushel of soybeans yields when crushed; this operation gives you the dollar equivalent, $2.31. Next, multiply the price of soybean meal, $161, by .024; this operation gives you the dollar equivalent, $3.86, of 48 pounds of soybean meal obtained from a bushel of soybeans. Then the dollar values of the oil and meal are added together, giving you the combined value of the products, $6.17.
>
> This figure is then compared to the price of March soybeans, which is $6.03 per bushel. Since the combined value of the products, $6.17, is higher than the price of soybeans, $6.03, the gross processing margin is a positive 14 cents. If you buy soybeans at $6.03 and sell the oil produced from the beans at 21 cents per pound and the meal at $161 per ton, the gross profit will be 14 cents per bushel. If the total value of the products were less than the price of soybeans, you would lose, not profit.

	Price Per Bushel
1. 21 cents × 11	$2.31
2. $161 × .024	3.86
3. Combined value of products	6.17
4. Price of soybeans	6.03
5. Gross crushing margin	+$ .14

If the gross crushing margin is a positive number, as in the previous example, and you feel that the value of the products will decline relative to the price commodity, buy the commodity futures and sell the product futures. This type of transaction is called a *crush spread*. If the gross crushing margin narrows, as you anticipate, and you decide to liquidate the spread, you will realize a profit on the transaction.

> *Example*: All the calculations for the previous example stand. In anticipation of a narrowing crushing margin, you buy March soybeans and sell March oil and meal. After making the spread, the value of the products remains unchanged, but the price of soybeans advances from $6.03 to $6.09. Hence the difference between the total value of the products, $6.17, and the value of soybeans, $6.09, now yields a gross margin of plus 8 cents. You make a 6-cent profit per bushel on the transaction.

More realistically, the value of the products usually advances with the price of the commodity.

Example: The price of soybean oil in the original example advances from 21 to 22 cents per pound, the price of soybean meal advances from $161 to $166 per ton, and the price of soybeans advances from $6.03 to $6.32 per bushel. The relative values are as follows:

	Price Per Bushel
1. 22¢ × 11	$2.42
2. $166 × .024	3.98
3. Combined value of products	6.40
4. Price of soybeans	6.32
5. Gross crushing margin	+$ .08

Although the price of all three commodities advance, the price of soybeans advances more than the combined values of the oil and meal. The price of soybeans advances 29 cents per bushel ($6.32 − $6.03 = $.29), whereas the equivalent dollar value of oil and meal advances only 23 cents per bushel ($6.40 − $6.17 = $.23). Thus, you realize a profit of 6 cents per bushel ($.29 − $.23 = $.06). The commodity that you were long (soybeans) gained relative to the products (soybean oil and soybean meal) that you were short, resulting in a narrowing of the spread differences.

The results are approximately the same even if prices of all three commodities decline, as long as the value of soybeans does not decline as much as the total value of the products. Also, whether you are long or short products against soybeans, one product may advance more or less than the other without jeopardizing your position; only the total value of both products in relation to the value of soybeans is the crucial factor.

	Price Per Bushel		Profit
1. 20¢ × 11	$2.20	Decrease of soybean products	$.13
2. $160.00 × .024	3.84	Decrease of soybeans	.07
3. Combined value of products	6.04	Net gain	$ .06
4. Price of soybeans	5.96		
5. Gross crushing margin	+$ .08		

Example: The combined dollar value of the products declines 13 cents per bushel (from $6.17 to $6.04), whereas the value of soybeans declines only 7 cents per bushel ($6.03 to $5.96), resulting in a profit of approximately 6 cents per bushel.

If you think that the value of the products will gain relative to the commodity, buy the products and sell the commodity. This transaction is referred to as a *reverse crush spread*. Even though the commodity is already lower than the products, you expect it to decline farther in relation to the products. In other words, you anticipate an improvement in the gross crushing margin.

Example: The gross crushing margin is plus 14 cents, and you believe that the margin will widen. You therefore buy the oil and meal and sell the beans. Your judgment is correct, and the gross margins widen from 14 to 22 cents—that is, the combined value of the products gains 8 cents relative to the price of soybeans. So you decide to liquidate the spread and take profits. Even though all three commodities advance in price, the combined value of the products advances 23 cents per bushel, whereas the value of soybeans advances only 15 cents per bushel. Thus, you realize a profit of approximately 8 cents per bushel.

Price Per Bushel	Profit
1. 22¢ × 11 .... $2.42	Increase in products .... $.23
2. $166.00 × .024............... 3.98	Increase in commodity .... .15
3. Combined value of products... 6.40	Net gain .... $ .08
4. Price of soybeans 6.18	
5. Gross crushing margin..... +$ .22	

The value of the commodities you were long, oil and meal, gained relative to the value of the commodity you were short, soybeans, resulting in a widening of the spread difference. If prices had declined, the results would have been the same—as long as the soybeans declined more than the combined value of the products.

Figuring the gross crushing margins gives you a rough idea of the profitability or unprofitability of a particular spread transaction, but you should not rely on the calculations alone for precise results. When the spread is done on a one-to-one basis, the dollar gain or loss is somewhat different than the dollar gain or loss based on the cents per bushel of actual crushing margin profit or loss. The method used in the examples is based on the assumption that when a contract of soybeans (5,000 bushels) is crushed, it yields a contract of soybean oil (60,000 pounds) and a contract of soybean meal (100 tons).

Actual yields, however, are somewhat less. When you crush one contract of soybeans, it does not yield exactly one contract of soybean oil, 60,000 pounds. It only yields 55,000 pounds of oil (5,000 bushels × 11 = 55,000 pounds of oil), which is less than one full contract. Similarly, when you crush one contract of soybeans, it does not yield exactly one contract of soybean meal, 100 tons, but rather 120 tons (5,000 bushels × 48 = 240,000 pounds, or 120 tons), which is more than a contract of meal. Consequently, the cent-per-bushel method of figuring a profit or loss is a little distorted as a result of this imbalance between actual product yields and product contract sizes.

Figure the profit on the preceding example by both ways: by the long and correct way and by the cents-per-bushel methods for comparison.

Example: You originally sell soybeans at $6.03 and buy soybean oil at 21 cents per pound and soybean meal at $161 per ton. You buy the soybean contract back at $6.18 per bushel, for a 15-cent-per-bushel loss, or the dollar equivalent of $750. On the other hand, you sell the oil at 22 cents for a 1-cent-per-pound profit, or the dollar equivalent of $600 per contract. Also, you sell the soybean meal at $166 for a $5 per ton profit, or the dollar equivalent of $500 per contract.

The combined profits of $600 on the oil and $500 on the meal result in an overall profit of $350. *Note*: The actual $350 profit does *not* correspond with the apparent cents-per-bushel profit indicated by the gross margin, 8 cents, which appeared to be $400.

TAX STRADDLES

Spread and straddle transactions can also be utilized for reducing or postponing taxes on capital gains. Under certain circumstances, commodity straddles can be used to transfer short-term capital gains from one tax year into the next or to convert them into long-term capital gains. Long-term capital gains can be achieved only through long positions held for six months and one day or longer. Profits made from a short position in futures do not qualify for long-term capital gain benefits. No matter how long they are held, they are always short-term gains.

SPREAD MARGIN REQUIREMENTS

Most commodity exchanges require a smaller margin deposit for a spread position than for an outright long or short position: Usually the margin required is for only one side of the spread, and in some cases only one half one side, even though two contracts are involved (see Chapter 5). The risk inherent in the fluctuation in the price difference between two contracts is generally considerably less than that of an outright long or short position. Because the risk in spreads is less than outright long or short positions, margin requirements are usually smaller.

Although the risk in a spread position is supposedly less than in an outright purchase or sale, a spreader must keep risk in line with profit possibilities. Be careful not to overextend or to take on a larger position than warranted, because of the lowered rate of margin.

SPREAD COMMISSIONS

Besides a reduced rate of margins for spread transactions, many exchanges allow a reduced commission rate for spread transactions. Even though a spread involves two contracts, one long and one short, the rate of commission is less than the rate of commission on two outright contracts but higher than the commission on one contract.

Example: *The roundturn rate of commission for a nonmember on an outright purchase and sale of 5,000 bushels of wheat is $30. You go long Chicago March wheat and short Chicago May wheat, but you do not pay a commission of $30 on your long leg and another $30 commission on your short leg. You pay only a roundturn spread rate of commission of $36 which is more than the commission on one contract but less than the commission on two contracts.

Every exchange except the Chicago Mercantile Exchange requires that both legs of the spread—long and short—be established simultaneously and liquidated simultaneously in order to qualify for the reduced rate of commission. On only the Chicago Mercantile Exchange, spreads may be put on one leg at a time or taken off one leg at a time and still qualify for the reduced commission rates. *But both legs must be put on during the course of a single trading session and taken off during the course of a single trading session.* For instance, if you buy March corn on the CBOT on Monday and sell a contract of July corn on Tuesday, these transactions constitute a spread for margin purposes; however, they are not considered a spread for commission purposes. You would be required to pay the full rate of commission on each leg, even if both legs are liquidated simultaneously.

When *only one side* of the spread is liquidated, a regular roundturn rate of commission is charged on the liquidated side. The remaining side will also be charged the regular full roundturn rate of commission when it is liquidated. For example, if you are long Chicago March wheat and short Chicago May wheat, and you liquidate your long position in the March delivery but retain your short position in the May delivery, you pay the regular roundturn rate of commission of $30 on the liquidated long March position. When you cover your short position in the May delivery, you pay another regular roundturn rate of commission of $30.

In the event that a delivery is made against the long leg of your spread, you are charged half the spread rate of commission on the delivery and the full roundturn commission when the other leg is liquidated. For example, if you are long Chicago March wheat and short Chicago May wheat, and you receive delivery on the long March contract, you are charged $18 commission, one-half the nonmember roundturn spread rate of commission of $36. When you eventually cover the short position in the May delivery, or even if you make delivery against the May, you pay the full roundturn rate of commission of $30. As a result of breaking up the spread, you pay a total commission of $48, rather than $36. On all New York exchanges, this rule applies to deliveries.

In addition, on New York exchanges if you lift a leg by liquidation of one side of a spread, you are charged one-half the spread commission on the liquidated contract and a regular commission on the remaining position when closed out. For example, as a nonmember client you establish a spread long

*Commissions as stated are subject to negotiation.

July copper and short September copper. If you liquidate your long July leg, you are charged $25.20 commission, one-half the spread rate of commission of $50.40 for a nonmember. If you cover the short position in the September delivery or if you make delivery against the short position when the month of September arrives, you are charged the full roundturn rate of commission of $36 on that leg. As another example, you put on a spread long March wheat and short July wheat—or any other type of interdelivery spread—then switch the long March to long May to avoid delivery against the March contract. But you want to maintain a spread long May short July, you are charged one-half the spread rate of $18 for the switch from March to May. When you liquidate the spread, you pay the spread rate of $36.

Intermarket or intercommodity spreads do not qualify for reduction in commissions. For example, when you buy Kansas City wheat and sell Chicago wheat, you pay the full roundturn rate of commission on each side: $22 commission on the long leg and $30 on the short leg, whether you establish and liquidate them simultaneously or not.

There is also a special spread rate of commission for commodity/ product spreads, that is, the purchase of soybean futures and the sale of soybean oil and soybean meal futures, or vice versa. The regular roundturn rate of commission for 5,000 bushels, one contract, of soybeans for non-members is $30. For one contract of soybean oil, it is $33, and for one contract of soybean meal, it is $33. However, if you establish a spread long soybean futures and short soybean oil and soybean meal, the roundturn spread rate of commission is only $62, not the $96 it would be if each leg were established independently. Likewise, you are entitled to a spread rate of commission, if you sell soybean futures and buy soybean oil and soybean meal on a spread basis. The spread rate of commission of $62, however, applies only to spreads on a one-to-one-to-one basis—that is, one contract of soybeans against one contract of soybean oil and one of soybean meal. Spreads established in varying units so that they are balanced on a yield-per-bushel basis are treated differently. For instance, if you go long ten contracts of soybeans against nine contracts of soybean oil and twelve contracts of soybean meal nine of the spreads are charged the spread roundturn rate of commission of $62 each. The odd contract of soybeans is charged the regular roundturn rate of $30, and the odd three contracts of soybean meal are each charged the regular roundturn rate of commission of $33. Therefore, the total commission on such a spread is $687.

You are entitled to no reduction in the rate of commission if a client enters into a spread of long oil and short meal, or vice versa. If you buy March soybean oil and sell March soybean meal, you pay the regular roundturn rate of commission of $33 on the soybean oil and another $33 on the soybean meal position. Likewise, no concession in commission is given if you enter into a spread long soybeans and short either soybean oil or soybean meal, or vice versa.

CONCLUSION

Spreading is perhaps the most artful form of commodities trading. While it contains elements of risk like outright speculation, it subtley involves a certain amount of self-protection like hedging.

With spreading, we complete a section of the book devoted to the tactics of commodities trading. With the chapters of the remaining section, we will cover the exciting and relatively new area of commodities trading. We will also go into some greater detail on government programs and market analysis factors.

In effect, we have covered the basics and are going on to glimpse a bit of the overall strategic situation.

Part Three

Commodities Strategy

Chapter 16

Open Interest and Volume of Trading

Open interest and volume of trading figures are two statistical areas that many investors prefer to leave to the technical market students, since they are supposedly more concerned with a market's strength or weakness than a fundamentalist. The fundamental market analysis, however, is just as concerned (or at least should be) because these figures frequently have a bearing on the analyst's findings. If open interest and trading volume numbers confirm a conclusion formed on the basis of your fundamental analysis, you have added reason to assume your analysis is sound. On the other hand, if these figures contradict your conclusions, you might want to carefully reexamine your appraisal of the fundamental factors. You may or may not alter your opinion, but you *will* be alerted to a possible market risk that was not apparent on the basis of a straightforward fundamental analysis. These figures, therefore, can be of use to any commodity futures user.

VOLUME OF TRADING

Volume of trading is the total of purchases *or* of sales, not of purchases and sales combined. Since two must be party to each futures contract (the seller and the buyer), the total of all purchases is equal to the total of all sales.

> *Example*: Mr. Able buys one contract of March sugar from Mrs. Baker. The volume of trading is one contract not two contracts. Although Mr. Able buys one contract of sugar for future delivery and Mr. B sells one contract, only *one* contract unit of sugar is involved.

The volume of trading in a commodity is compiled from data required in daily reports from exchange clearing members. Each clearing member of each exchange makes a daily report of all purchases and sales of commodity futures that it clears. A compilation of these reports gives the volume of trading in each commodity, for each market, and for each day.

OPEN INTEREST

A futures contract is said to be *open* when it has been neither liquidated by an offsetting transaction nor fulfilled by delivery. Open contracts are collectively referred to as *open interest.*

The amount of open interest for each commodity and contract market is obtained every business day by a tabulation of reports made by exchange clearing members. Again, the aggregate of all long open contracts equals the aggregate of all short open contracts that are reported. The open contract figures shown are for *one side only,* not for the long and short sides combined.

When trading in a new delivery month begins, no contracts exist. For example, when trading in the May 1979 corn delivery began in March 1978, there were no May 1979 contracts in existence. A commodity is unlike a "new issue" of stock in this respect. But as soon as someone executes an order to buy and someone else executes an order to sell short, one contract has been created. As other new buyers and other new sellers consummate trades, other contracts are created. This process of contract creation can go on to infinity.

> *Example*: Mr. Able establishes a long position by buying one contract of December cattle from Mrs. Baker, who sells short one contract of December cattle; one contract is thus created. The open interest is now one contract. Then, another trader, Ms Chillingsworth establishes a long position by buying one contract of December cattle from Mr. Dimlit, who is selling short; thus the open interest increases to two contracts, and the volume of trading totals two contracts for the day. Still another new buyer, Mr. Earner, and another new seller, Mrs. Flax, consummate a trade—and another contract is created. The open interest amounts to three contracts, and the volume of trading follows by exactly the same amount—three contracts. Mr. Able, Ms Chillingsworth, and Mr. Earner are each long one contract for a total of three contracts and Mrs. Baker, Mr. Dimlit, and Mrs. Flax are all short the same amount—one contract each for a total of three contracts.

Buys	Sells
Able	Baker
Chillingsworth	Dimit
Earner	Flax
Three contracts	Three contracts

If Mr. Able decides to liquidate his long position by a subsequent sale on the same day, and if Mr. Gloo, a new buyer, purchases the contract that Mr. Able is selling, the open interest remains unchanged at three contracts. Mr. Able merely transfers his contractual obligation to Mr. Gloo. Thus, Mr. Gloo replaces Mr. Able on the longside of the market.

Buys	Sells
Chillingsworth	Baker
Earner	Dimit
Gloo	Flax
Three contracts	Three contracts

Mr. Able, who originally bought and then sold, satisfies his contractual obligations. He has to neither take nor make delivery. The difference between his purchase and sales prices comprises his profit or loss. The open interest remains unchanged at three contracts.

But the volume of trading now totals four contracts.

On the other hand, however, if the contract that Mr. Able is liquidating is purchased by Mrs. Flax, a previous short who is covering her contract, the open interest decreases to two contracts. The volume of trading, however, still totals four contracts. Both Mr. Able and Mrs. Flax are closing out their previously established contracts.

Buys	Sells
Chillingsworth	Baker
Earner	Dimlit
Two contracts	Two contracts

Ms Chillingsworth and Mr. Earner are each still long one contract for a total of two contracts, and Mrs. Baker and Mr. Dimlit are still short one contract—each side for a total of two contracts.

Open interest increases only when a new purchase and a new sale are consummated. It does not change a position, long or short, is simply transferred to another; no new contract is created. It decreases when a buyer and seller mutually close out their positions. Open interest also decreases when a short makes delivery and a long accepts it. By taking delivery, a long closes out the futures positions and initiates a cash position. And by making delivery, the short fulfills the contractual obligations and no longer has a position in futures.

THE STATISTICS

The Commodity Futures Trading Commission issues open interest and volume of trading statistics for commodities that it regulates. These figures are expressed in standard units of trading. Both types of figures are published daily in the financial sections of most large newspapers. And, of course, they are always available from a brokerage firm. Because of data compilation, open interest and volume figures reflect the transactions two days prior to the date line of the newspaper. Usually the figures are broken down by commodity and then again by delivery month; for each month, the volume, the open interest, and the net change in open interest are listed.

In Table 16-1, the "volume" column represents the total of all purchases or of all sales for that particular day—Day X. Total volume of trading on that day was 45,495,000 bushels, which means that 45,495,000 bushels were purchased and 45,495,000 bushels were sold.

Table 16-1   Volume and Open Interest Report for Corn

	Volume (1,000 bushels)	Open Interest (1,000 bushels)	Net Change Open Interest
March	22,455	75,370	−5,290
May	11,380	85,490	+ 30
July	10,030	81,120	+1,090
September	840	17,635	+ 75
December	790	5,585	+ 475
Total	45,495	265,200	−3,620

The "Open Interest" column, 265,200,000 bushels, indicates that the total number of corn contracts outstanding as of the end of trading Day X amounted to 265,200,000 bushels (265,200,000 bushels were held by longs and 265,200,000 bushels were held by shorts). The open interest in the March delivery was 75,370,000 bushels, the open interest in the May delivery was 85,490,000 bushels, and so on.

The figures under the column "Net Change Open Interest" reflect the change in open interest from the previous trading session for each delivery. For example, the open interest in the March delivery at the close of trading on Day X was 75,370,000 bushels, which was down 5,290,000 bushels from the previous session. The open interest in the May delivery increased 30,000 bushels from the previous session. Although the open interest in all the deliveries (except the March delivery) increased on that day, the total open interest decreased by 3,620,000 bushels because the decrease in the March delivery was larger than the increase in all other deliveries combined.

Since open interest figures represent contracts outstanding as of the close of trading each day, day trades are obviously not included in the open interest tabulations. These day trades (both purchases and sales), however, are included in volume of trading figures.

SEASONAL INFLUENCES ON OPEN INTEREST AND VOLUME OF TRADING

The open interest in a commodity tends to increase and decrease in a more or less fixed seasonal pattern. This seasonal change follows the same general pattern as seasonal changes in the visible supply of a commodity—that is, in the amount in commercial storage. In the case of wheat and oats, for example, the open interest and the visible supply tend to be at a seasonal low just ahead of the new crop harvest in June and July; then both increase to a peak sometime in September or October. This peak coincides with the time that commercial warehouse stocks are largest and with the time that it becomes necessary to start using these stocks to meet domestic and export requirements. From this peak the open interest and the visible supply then decline seasonally to a low that is reached just ahead of the new crop movement. In corn and soybeans, the open interest and the visible supply reach a low in late August or September, increase to a peak in December or January, and seasonally decline into late August or September again.

These seasonal changes in the open interest result from changes in hedging requirements. The hedging volume increases as surpluses of a commodity are put into storage; the handlers, naturally, are turned to the futures markets to protect their investments.   The hedging volume decreases as the commodity is taken out of storage to meet requirements.

These purely seasonal changes in the open interest are relatively unimportant in detecting technical market strength or weakness. The changes in the open interest that are most important in such deductions are the net changes after allowed for seasonal trends. There is no way to measure these net changes precisely, but you can usually determine whether open interest changes are greater or less then purely seasonal phases. You can also tell if the deviation from the usual seasonal tendency is substantial or if it is relatively small.

Volume of trading has no seasonal tendency—at least none of importance. Trading volume tends to increase slightly during the period of heaviest new crop movement, but this is not pronounced enough to be of any particular concern.

INTERPRETING CHANGES IN OPEN INTEREST AND VOLUME OF TRADING

Total open interest figures for a particular commodity—not the figures for individual futures—are the ones used in determining probable price trends. The same rule holds true for volume of trading. Changes in open interest and in volume of trading have forecasting value only when considered in connection with price change. Those who chart daily open interest and volume of trading figures usually do so at the bottom of a price chart showing daily high, low, and closing prices. Volume of trading is shown by vertical bars extending up from the base of the chart, and open interest is shown by dots (usually connected by a continuous line) extending across the chart from left to right on a separate scale just above the volume scale and below the price scale. Figure 16-1 illustrates how this chart is done.

The guidelines for forecasting probable market action on the basis of open interest and volume of trading figures are listed below and shown in Table 16-2:

1. If the open interest and prices are both up—this is a sign of new buying and a technically strong market.
2. If the open interest is up and prices are down—this indicates short selling or hedging and a technically weak market.
3. If the open interest and prices are both down—this indicates long liquidation and a technically strong market.
4. If the open interest is down and prices are up—this indicates short covering and a technically weak market.
5. If the volume of trading expands on price strength and declines on price weakness—this indicates the market is in a technically strong position and should sell higher.
6. If the volume of trading expands on price weakness and declines on price strength—this indicates the market is in a technically weak position and should sell lower.

Table 16-2   Significance of Open Interest Changes

	Open Interest	Prices	Activity	Market
I	↑	↑	New Buying	Technically Strong
II	↑	↓	New Selling	Technically Weak
III	↓	↓	Long Liquidation	Technically Strong
IV	↓	↑	Short Covering	Technically Weak

I. If open interest is increasing, new commitments are being initiated. Commitments by new buyers and new sellers are more numerous than commitments by old sellers (who are buying back their contracts) and old buyers (who are selling their contracts). While an increase in open interest indicates both new buying and new selling, buyers are more aggressive than sellers as evidenced by advancing prices, which is considered a sign of technical strength.

II. In the second market situation, open interest is also increasing—indicating that new contracts are being established. However, in this case the increase in open interest is accompanied by a decrease in price, which means that sellers were more aggressive than buyers—considered an indication of technical weakness.

III. On the other hand, if open interest is declining, commitments by old buyers and old sellers are more numerous than commitments by new buyers and new sellers. Declining prices, along with a decrease in open interest, show that the old buyers (now sellers) are more aggressive in their liquidation of long positions than the old sellers (now buyers) in their covering operations, which is considered a sign of technical strength.

IV. In the fourth case, open interest is again decreasing, signifying that old buyers and old sellers are closing out commitments. However, in this situation prices are increasing, suggesting that the old sellers (who are covering their shorts by buying back their contracts) are more aggressive than the buyers and signifying a technically weak market.

Figure 16-1   Typical Chart Showing the Open Interest and Volume of Trading

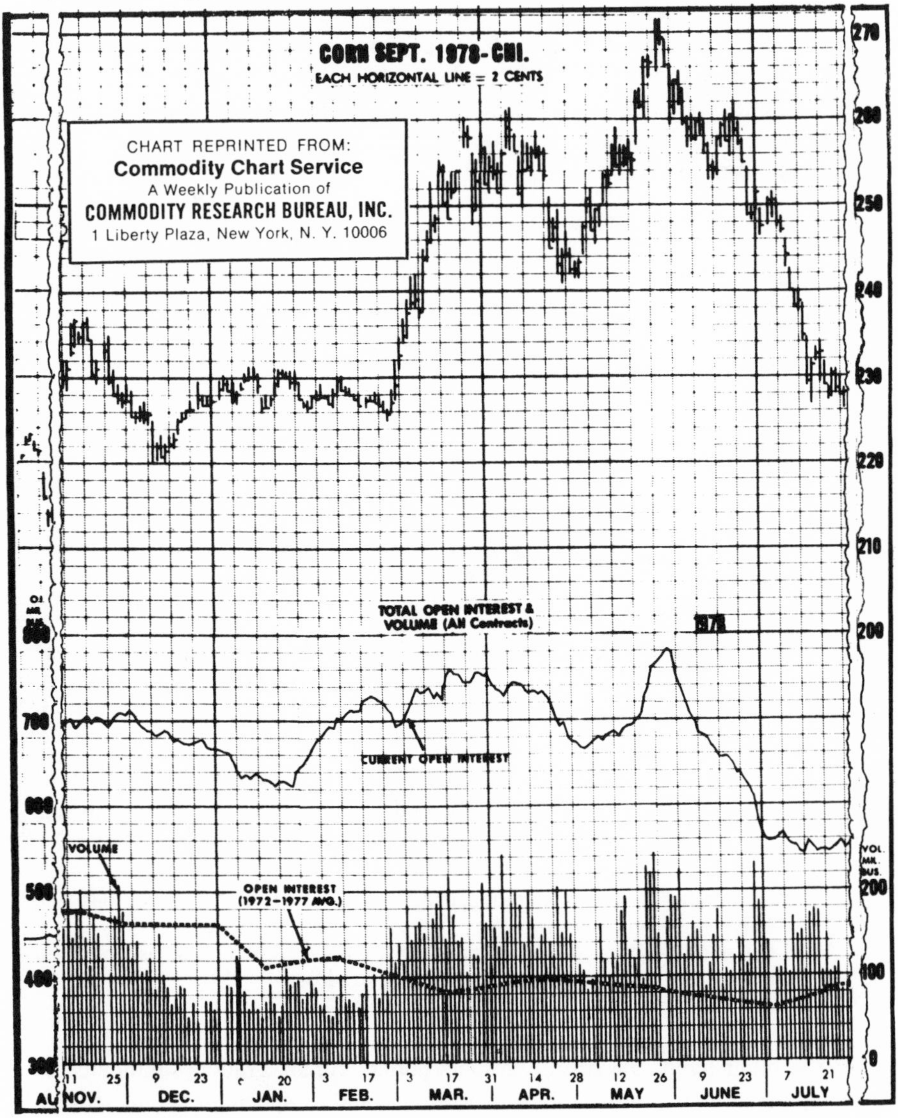

OTHER STATISTICS

The CFTC also issues monthly reports entitled "Commitments of Traders in Commodity Futures." These reports give a breakdown of the outstanding contracts of large and small traders in CFTC commodities at the end of each month.

A *large trader* is one who holds a position on any one contract market and in any one futures of a commodity that equals or exceeds the quantities specified in Table 16-3. Any trader whose position in one future of any commodity reaches a reportable level, as specified by the CFTC, is required to report daily to the CFTC all trades and positions in that commodity. In making this report, the trader also classifies his or her position as speculative (including straddling) or as hedging. Data on commitments of large traders are obtained from such reports.

Table 16-3   Guide to Reporting Levels

Commodity	Quantity
Wheat, corn, soybeans	500,000 bushels
Oats, rye, barley, flaxseed	200,000 bushels
Cotton	5,000 bales
Silver bullion	100 contract units
Soybean oil, soybean meal	50 contract units
Live cattle, live hogs	50 contract units
Sugar	50 contract units
Copper	50 contract units
Gold	50 contract units
Silver coins	50 contract units
All other commodities	25 contract units

Commitments of *small (nonreporting) traders* are derived by subtracting the large traders' positions from the total of all open positions. Commitments of nonreporting traders, being a residual item, include both speculative and hedging commitments.

Table 16-4 is a typical CFTC monthly report showing commitments of corn traders in commodity futures at the end of the month. The open contracts under "Large Traders" fall into three categories:

1. the number of open commitments held by speculators who are on one side only, either long or short;
2. the open positions held by speculators who are on both sides, long and short—that is, those who hold spreads or straddles;
3. open positions (long or short) held by hedgers.

On the other hand, the open contracts under "Small Traders" indicate the aggregate amount of long and short positions held by speculators and hedgers combined.

For example, the first line of data, "Long or short only," indicates that large speculative traders were long 31,625,000 bushels and large speculative traders were short 4,005,000 bushels as of Month Y. The figures to the right of

Table 16-4   Commitments of Corn Traders on the CBOT

CORN *(In thousands of bushels)*

Classification	Monthly		Net Change from Previous Month	
	Long	Short	Long	Short
LARGE TRADERS				
Speculative				
Long or short only	31,625	4,005	+2,035	+1,755
Long and short (spreading)	21,300	21,300	−6,010	−6,010
Total	52,925	25,305	−3,975	−4,255
Hedging	73,015	135,094	+1,230	− 738
Total reported by large traders	125,940	160,399	−2,745	−4,993
SMALL TRADERS				
Speculative and hedging	61,838	27,379	−5,143	−2,895
TOTAL OPEN CONTRACTS	187,778	187,778	−7,888	−7,888
Percent held by: Large traders	67.1	85.4	+ 1.3	+ 0.9
Small traders	32.9	14.6	− 1.3	− 0.9

these show the net change in open contracts from the end of the preceding month; the figure of +2,035 means that large-scale speculation with long positions increased by 2,035,000 bushels from the end of the previous month, as large-scale speculation in short positions increased 1,755,000 bushels. The second line, "Long and short (spreading)," indicates the quantity of corn spreads held by large speculators. Since a spread or straddle involves both a long and a short position, the longs outstanding must be equal to the short commitment.

The third line, "Total," is the total of long and short open positions held by large speculative traders. "Hedging," indicates the number of bushels in large-scale trading that represented hedges. The fifth line, "Total reported by large traders," is the aggregate of large-scale speculative and hedging positions.

"Speculative and Hedging," under "Small Traders," shows the long or short positions held by small traders; that is, by those holding open contracts totaling less than 500,000 bushels in one future delivery on one market. The open positions of small speculators and hedgers are combined and not distinguishable, since there is no breakdown for each group. However, the major portion of both the long and the short positions of small traders probably represent speculative rather than hedge positions.

The seventh line, "Total open contracts," is the aggregate of the open contracts held by large traders and small traders. "Percent held by large traders" indicates the percentage of long and short positions held by large traders, along with the net change from the end of the preceding month. The final line, "Percent held by small traders," indicates the percentage of long and short positions held by small traders.

CONCLUSION

Admittedly a bit dry, these figures can represent the "fine tuning" on your analysis, be it technically or fundamentally oriented. They can serve as a sounding board for your conclusions. Learn to use them, and you will undoubtedly have that much more of a competitive edge on other traders.

Chapter 17

Government Price Support and Disposal Programs

At one point or another, you may have asked what ever happened to "free enterprise?" Why does the government have to become involved in an economic system that is supposed to be based on entrepreneurial ventures— for better or for worse?

The answer is that with improved communications and transportation, this world has become much more interdependent in this century than ever before. A crop failure is no longer a localized and contained problem; it can have, if serious enough, even international implications. If some control is not exerted over supply and demand, prices and transactions, the very least that could happen is that many farmers would quit farming. The worst is that people could starve in some parts of the world while overabundant foodstuffs rot in other parts.

Another part of the answer is that the government *is* part of the economy. Like it or not, governmental policies have a tremendous effect on loan rates, banking in general, investments, import/export, labor-management negotiations, income management and taxation, and dozens of other spheres in our daily lives. For the government to ignore the agricultural aspects of this kaleidoscopic economic scene would be inconsistent, not to mention fool-hardy. The federal government plays too great a part in the macro-economic stageplay to forego the role.

So while the particulars of the government's involvement up to now have not been essential to your understanding of the commodities market, you might now be interested in knowing why the government becomes involved in price support programs and what it does with the commodities it accumulates during the course of these programs.

THE GOVERNMENT PRICE SUPPORT PROGRAM

To prevent sharp declines in farm income during periods of agricultural surpluses, the government instituted a program of supporting the levels of farm prices. Price support program operations have been carried on by the Commodity Credit Corporation (CCC), an agency of the United States Department of Agriculture, since 1933. During most of this period since then, the level of support has been either directed or authorized by specific price legislation. Passage of the Agricultural Adjustment Act of 1938, which made support mandatory for certain commodities, increased the importance of price support in stabilizing prices of farm commodities. During World War II and the Korean Conflict, the program was used to encourage increased agricultural output by minimizing price risks. Recent legislation is designed to make some export commodities more competitive in world markets through market price support at or near world price levels. At the same time, grower's incomes are protected by supplementary price support payments.

HOW PRICES ARE SUPPORTED

Prices are supported in four different ways:

1. loans,
2. purchase agreements,
3. purchases, and
4. incentive payments.

Loans and purchases constitute by far the most important support methods, constituting 76 percent and 16 percent, respectively, of the total program's funding.

Loans

Loans support prices in two ways:

1. by providing farmers a cash return for the commodity at the support level; and
2. by strengthening market prices of the commodity through withdrawal of supplies from the market.

Loans give farmers an opportunity either to market their crops or to keep them under loan, whichever course is more advantageous. If the market price rises above the loan-plus-charges level, farmers have the privilege of paying off their loans, and selling their commodities in the open market.

If the price fails to rise above the loan level, however, the nonrecourse character of the loan agreement makes it possible for them to deliver the commodity to CCC and thereby discharge their obligation in full instead of repaying the loan. Producers are not obligated to make good any decline in the market price of the commodity that they have put up as collateral. Therefore, when market prices are generally below the loan rate and producers choose not to pay off their loans in order to redeem their commodities for their own use or for sale in the market, the bulk of the loan stock is usually delivered to the CCC.

The wheat, corn, cotton, and other commodities acquired by the CCC in this way go into storage and become a part of the price support inventory. If market prices rise above support prices, producers can still pay off their loans and market their commodity.

The loan program tends to even out marketings. Farmers are inclined to market their crops at harvest time, sometimes creating market gluts, undue burdening of the transportation system, and lower prices. The loan program gives farmers an opportunity to hold their crops without risk for later marketing. That flexibility tends to spread marketing over the season, thereby reducing the extent of price swings.

General Procedure for Obtaining a Loan on Grains. The farmer applies for a loan on a supported commodity at the county Agricultural Stabilization and Conservation Service (ASCS) office. The local ACSC Committee first makes sure that the farmer is eligible—that is, in compliance with the provisions of the farm program. If the commodity is farm-stored, a field inspector checks farm bins and cribs to make sure the farmer is providing safe storage, measures the quantity stored, takes a sample of the commodity for grade and analysis, and puts a seal on the bin or crib. If the farmer's commodity meets all requirements, the committee makes out a note and chattel mortgage.

After signing these documents, the farmer may obtain a loan from a lending agency approved by the CCC (usually a local bank), through the committee, or directly from the CCC.

The farmer may either repay the loan any time before it becomes due or turn the collateral over to the CCC. In the latter case, the producer notifies the county ASCS office that he or she wishes to turn over the commodity to the CCC. On loans that are redeemed, a nominal interest rate per year is charged for the period the loan is in effect. No interest is charged when the commodity is delivered to satisfy a loan. In such cases, the CCC pays any interest charges that might be due a lending agency.

Procedure for Obtaining a Loan on Cotton. The producer delivers the ginned fiber to a warehouse approved by the CCC and obtains a warehouse receipt. Or, if warehouse space is not available and arrangements can be made with railroads and others, a bill of lading in lieu of a warehouse receipt is acceptable. But to obtain a loan, the producer must be in compliance with any established cotton program provisions for the farm, and he or she must have the cotton classed by a board of cotton examiners of the Department of Agriculture. The board, after classing samples of the cotton, sends the producer a form indicating the class—that is, the grade and staple length.

The producer is assisted by an approved clerk in the preparation of a note and loan agreement form. Presenting the loan agreement form, together with the warehouse receipt or bill of lading, to the lending agency or directly to the CCC, the farmer receives the loan. Producer members of a cooperative marketing association obtain loans through the association at the same rate, and in much the same manner, as through lending agencies. The association may then tender to the CCC any documents covering the cotton acquired as collateral from producer members; the association then receives a loan on that cotton from the CCC.

Producers may also obtain loans on farm-stored cotton, although very few loans of this type are made and even then only when commercial warehouse space is short. The loan procedure for farm-stored cotton is very similar to that for grain. The county ASCS office inspects the storage facilities and aids the producer in completing loan documents. The loan is evidenced by a note secured by a chattel mortgage covering the cotton. With the note and the mortgage, the producer obtains the loan from a lending agency or the CCC.

In disposing of loan cotton, producers have three choices (provided they have not obtained their loans as members of a cooperative marketing association):

1. They may sell equity in the cotton that is under loan, the equity representing the difference between the amount due on the loan and the value of the cotton. In selling the equity, the producer signs an equity transfer in the presence of a witness authorized by the county ASCS office. The buyer of the equity must present the equity transfer to the ASCS office within fifteen days; the buyer must also repay the loan within five business days after the warehouse receipts are received by the bank designated by the equity purchaser to receive repayment of the CCC loan. Otherwise, title to the cotton reverts to the producer. Almost all producers who redeem cotton under loan do so by means of the equity transfer.
2. They may repay their loans and sell the cotton in the open market.
3. They may decide not to repay the loan and not to redeem the cotton, inasmuch as the loans from the CCC are nonrecourse.

Impoundings and Redemptions.   Loans are available from the government for periods of nine to ten months following the harvest. Loans generally mature 10 months from the first day of the month when the loan is made. For example, a farmer may apply for a loan on corn anytime from the harvest in October until the following June 30. The loan may be repaid and the

The following table shows quantities of the 1977 crops put under support loan* as of June 30, 1978, compared to the 1976 crops as of June 30, 1977.

Table 17-1 Grains: Price Support Activities as of June 30, 1978 and June 30, 1977[a]

Sorghum in hundredweight—others 1,000 bushels

Grain	Quantities placed under loan	Quantities repaid or redeemed	Quantities remaining under loan	Quantities in reserve
		1977 crop		
Barley	83,430	28,088	33,939	21,403
Corn	1,400,738	297,749	655,090	87,899
Oats	78,903	19,979	32,938	25,986
Rye	913	618	295	—0—*
Soybeans	97,146	65,124	32,022	—0—*
Wheat	582,072	276,600	174,404	131,068
Sorghum	115,665	42,477	67,285	5,903
		1976 crop		
Barley	18,019	10,432	5,535	2,052
Corn	274,541	91,856	172,995	9,690
Oats	4,371	2,764	1,256	352
Rye	144	60	84	—0—*
Soybeans	22,491	15,181	7,309	—0—*
Wheat	468,276	54,184	202,318	210,722
Sorghum	11,756	4,413	6,371	971

*No program.

Referring to Table 17-1 the 1977 crop shows that as of June 30, 1978 there were 1,400,738,000 bushels of corn placed under the loan program. The next column gives the quantities redeemed, 297,749,000 bushels; the quantities remaining under the loan 655,090,000 bushels. The last column shows the quantities under the reserve program, previously called reseal, which is 87,899,000 bushels.

Note: Under the support program of the 1977 Act, the reserve aspect is similar to the reseal program with only one exception: The producer now determines the time to redeem the commodity and has three to 5 years to do so. Under reseal, there was a one-year restriction as to the redemption clause.

collateral redeemed anytime after the farmer obtains the loan until the following July 31. Loans are made only on commodities that are produced during the current marketing year and that are already in existence and stored.

Impounding and redemption figures, released monthly by the CCC, give a composite picture of price support activity for each commodity supported by loans. During the course of any month, impoundings may be taking place in one area while redemptions are taking place in another area. Consequently, only the net amount placed under loan or removed from the loan is important in analyzing its influence on the supply-demand relationship, which in turn influenced the price of the commodity. As can be seen from Table 17-2, redemptions at the end of July were 38 million, which means that 5 million were outstanding at the end of the redemption period. If farmers have not repaid their loan by July 31, they merely default and the CCC becomes the owner of the collateral put up against the loan. In the period shown in Table 17-2, the CCC acquired 5 million, the amount still under loan and not repaid, when the redemption period expired.

Table 17-2 Impounding and Redemption Reports by Month over the Course of a Marketing Season

	Impoundings	Redemptions	Loans outstanding
October	10	—	10
November	20	—	20
December	25	2	23
January	30	5	25
February	33	10	23
March	36	15	21
April	39	22	17
May	41	28	13
June[1]	43	35	8
July[2]	43	38	5

[1]End of period for which loan is available.
[2]End of period when loans may be repaid.

GRAIN RESERVES

Farmer-Held Reserve

The legislation requires the Secretary to administer a producer-held storage program for wheat and, at his discretion, a similar program for feed grains. This is to be accomplished through an extended price support loan program of 3 to 5 years duration. Producers will receive storage payments and the Secretary may adjust or waive interest charges on farmer-held reserves.

The quantity of wheat held is not to be less than 300 million bushels or more than 700 million bushels. The maximum amount may be adjusted upward, however, to meet any commitments assumed by the United States to an international agreement on grain reserves. For feed grains, reserve quantities were not specified.

When the market price is between 140 and 160 percent of the current price support level for wheat or a level determined by the Secretary for feed grains, storage payments may be discontinued to encourage producers to redeem loans and market their grain. But if a producer redeems his loan before the market price for wheat reaches 140 percent of the current loan, he will be subject to penalty: the Secretary is required to recover storage payments and to assess penalty interest or other charges.

The loan may be called when the wheat market price reaches 175 percent of the current loan level. Again, the Secretary determines the level at which the feed grain loan will be called.

Whenever a 3- to 5-year extended loan program is authorized, the Commodity Credit Corporation (CCC) resale price for Government-owned stocks must be set at not less than 150 percent of the current loan level. Otherwise, the CCC resale price will be not less than 115 percent of the then current price support loan level.

RESERVE PROGRAM

The reserve program gives farmers the opportunity to obtain an extension of the current price support loan on farm-stored grain and to earn storage payment. It allows them to maintain ownership of corn after the last redemption date of, for example, July 31. The farmers keep their corn in storage on their farms. The CCC pays them the current storage rate per bushel per year for doing so. In other words, if the farmer elects to put the corn into reseal after the redemption date, rather than deliver it to the CCC, and does not redeem the corn prior to next season's maturity date, he or she earns a certain amount per bushel for the entire year. This program gives the farmer the opportunity of having more time to wait for higher market prices that might develop, instead of making settlement as soon as the loan period is up. The monthly impounding and redemptions reports may appear in a different format that summarizes marketing season. Table 17-2 shows that during the first month of the new crop season for corn (October) 10 million bushels of corn were placed under loan. There were no redemptions during that month, which means that 10 million bushels were outstanding under the loan at the end of that month. At the end of November, a total of 20 million bushels had been placed under loan (the cumulative amount placed under loan during October and November), which means that an additional 10 million bushels went under loan during November. There were no redemptions during November so 20 million bushels were outstanding under loan. At the end of December, the quantity placed under loan (during the October-December period) was 25 million bushels. Redemptions (that is, loans repaid) comprised 2 million bushels. The 2 million bushels redeemed from the loan are subtracted from the impounding of 25 million, leaving 23 million bushels outstanding under the loan. At the end of January, impoundings had accumulated to 30 million bushels, with 5 million in January. Redemptions also totaled 5 million bushels for the season; some 3 million bushels were redeemed during the month of January. Deducting the redemptions of 5 million from the total impoundings of 30 million leaves 25 million outstanding under loan. The procedure for February through June is basically the same.

Since June 30 is the end of the impounding period for corn (the end of the period during which loans may be taken out), no further impoundings can take place. Consequently, impoundings at the end of July are the same as those at the end of June. However, redemptions may continue until July 31.

Any farmer who decides to redeem the commodity from the reserve program may do so by repaying the original loan plus interest. In addition, if the farmer redeems it prior to the second year's redemption deadline, the storage payment is pro-rated. In other words, if the farmer puts corn into the reserve program on July 31, 1979 and redeems it on, say, December 31, 1979, he or she repays the 1978-79 loan plus a nominal interest. The farmer redeems the corn from the reserve only if the storage space is needed for other grains or if the price level advances enough to pay the loan, cover the interest, and still provide a profit.

The CCC, however, may call the loan in at any time it desires, or it may choose not to extend the reseal program for a particular crop year. In other words, if a reseal program runs for, say, four years, the CCC may cease the program for the crop for the first of the four years, while extending it for the other crop years. In effect, corn under reseal is potential supply that would find its way onto the market if the market price advanced high enough to cover repayment costs and provide a profit.

How Price Supports are Determined.   Government support prices are based on a percentage of parity. The levels of support are varied each year to maintain a basic relationship between the minimum prices farmers receive for their commodities and the prices they pay for other goods and services. In other words, government supports attempt to maintain a parity between prices for agricultural commodities and other prices.

Parity prices are therefore prices that farmers should receive for their commodites so they may buy the same amount of goods and services these commodities purchased in a given base period. The base period for most commodities is the average of 1910–14. Thus if 5 bushels of corn bought a pair of shoes during the base period, 5 bushels of corn would buy a pair of shoes today if prices were at 100 percent parity. However, if more than 5 bushels of corn are needed today, the price of corn is less than full parity.

The parity price for any agricultural commodity is determined in three steps:

1. compute the average price received by farmers for a specific commodity during the most recent ten years, and
2. divide this average by the index of prices received by farmers for all farm products during the same ten years. This calculation yields an adjusted base price.
3. Then multiply the adjusted price by the current parity index, which is an index of prices currently paid by farmers for goods and services as compared to the base period, 1910–1914.

The result of step 3 is the parity price. The parity price is then multiplied by the percentage of parity established by the Secretary of Agriculture in order to find the loan level for that commodity. This figure then becomes the national average support price.

The Food and Agriculture Act of 1977, more popularly known as the "farm bill" is a 4-year bill that becomes effective in 1978.

Target Price and Loan Program Continues

The 1977 Act continues the dual target price and loan rate system, providing price and income support protection to farmers. Target prices are used to establish a basis for providing deficiency payments to producers who participate in the wheat, feed grain, cotton, and rice programs. Deficiency, or target price payments vary inversely with market prices. No payments are made if the market price is at or above the target price; if the market price is below the target, payments are based on the difference, but in no case can the payment rate exceed the price support loan-target price differential. Payments will be made on the farm program acreage, a new concept.

Nonrecourse loans continue to be a basic part of the farm program. With these loans, a producer complying with farm programs can commit any quantity of his crop as collateral for a loan from the Commodity Credit corporation (CCC). The total amount that can be borrowed from CCC is equal to the quantity of the crop placed under loan times the loan rate. Nonrecourse loan contracts are written with an expiration date. Upon or anytime prior to expiration, producers may retain possession of their crop by repaying the loan amount plus any interest that has been incurred. If producers choose not to redeem their loan, the CCC takes title to the commodity as full payment for the loan, including interest payments.

The 1977 Act specifies target prices and loan minimum for wheat and corn for 1978 and a target price adjustment formula for 1979–81 wheat and corn crops; a minimum target price for cotton for 1978 through 1981; loan minimums for wheat, corn, and a formula for determining cotton loan prices.

A target price adjustment provision will apply to the 1979–81 wheat and corn crops. The adjustment provision will begin in 1978 for cotton. With a minimum target price of $0.52 a pound specified for upland cotton in 1978.

Price Support Loans for 1978–81 Crops

Nonrecourse price support loan levels for cotton, beginning with the 1978 crop, will be set at the lower of (1) 85 percent of the preceding 4 marketing years' moving average spot market price for Strict Low Middling 1-1/16" (SLM 1-1/16") upland cotton at average U.S. locations or (2) 90 percent of the average adjusted price for the first 2 weeks of October of the "five lowest priced growths" of the growths quoted for Strict Middling 1-1/16" (SM 1-1/16") cotton, c.i.f. (cost, insurance, freight) Northern Europe. The Secretary must announce the loan level for any crop of cotton by November 1 of the year preceding the marketing year for which the loan is to be effective and cannot thereafter reduce it.

Downward Adjustment in Loans

Loan levels for wheat and feed grains may be adjusted downard in any marketing year if the average market price in the previous year falls to within 105 percent of the loan level. The adjustment is limited to 10 percent per year, or a lower limit of $2.00 a bushel for wheat and $1.75 a bushel for corn. This variable loan concept is included to maintain domestic and export markets for grain.

Program Acreages Instead of Allotments

National program acreages for wheat, feed grains, and upland cotton will be determined by the Secretary and will represent the estimated acreage needed to meet domestic and export needs (less imports) plus any desired adjustments in stocks. The national program acreage for each crop will be determined by dividing the estimate of projected utilization by a national average program yield to give the needed harvested acreage. Farm program acreages for deficiency payment purposes will be based on current plantings. This represents a significant departure from prior law, which based farm allotments and bases on historical planting patterns. The allotment system for the above crops is terminated beginning with the 1978 crop.

Set-Aside

Paralleling changes in the allotment system are changes in the provisions for set-aside programs. As in previous legislation, the new law extends to the Secretary of Agriculture the authority to implement set-aside if he determines supplies are likely to be excessive. However, instead of being based on a percentage of historical allotments, set-aside in any year will be based on a farmer's acreage planted for harvest in that year.

Payment Limits

For wheat, feed grain, and upland cotton, the 1977 Act revised the payment limit upward. In the 1973 legislation, the limit on payments to wheat, feed grain, and upland cotton producers was $20,000. The limit is now $40,000 for the 1978 crop and $45,000 for the 1979 crop. For 1980 crops, the payment limit for wheat, feed grain, upland cotton, and rice combined will be $50,000. Payments for disaster loss will be excluded from the payment limitation beginning in 1978.

Nonrecourse loans will continue to be available to wheat and feed grain producers. The minimum loan level for the 1978–81 wheat crops was set at $2.35 per bushel. Corn's price support loan minimum for 1978–81 was established at $2.00 per bushel. The maximum loan level for wheat cannot exceed 100 percent of parity.

Soybeans

The 1977 Act requires the Secretary to establish a loan and purchase program for 1978–81 soybean crops. The Secretary is given discretionary authority in establishing the loan level. Previously, as a "nonbasic" agricultural commodity, soybeans were under a support program implemented at the discretion of the Secretary of Agriculture.

Set-aside of soybean acreage cannot be required as a condition of eligibility for price support.

Target price payments are not authorized for soybeans.

Criteria.   In determining whether to supply support and the level, the Secretary of Agriculture must consider the following factors:

1. the supply of the commodity in relation to the demand,
2. the levels at which prices of other commodities are being supported and, in the case of feed grains, the feed values of such grains in relation to corn,
3. the availability of funds,
4. the perishability of the commodity,
5. the importance of the commodity to agriculture and the national economy,
6. the ability to dispose of stocks acquired through price support oeprations,
7. the need for offsetting temporary losses of export markets, and
8. the ability and willing of producers to keep supplies in line with demand.

Some commodities are supported even though supports are not mandatory. These commodities can be supported at any level between zero and 90 percent of parity.

For operating purposes, the national average support price is broken down to reflect location, quality, or type differentials for each commodity in all the counties where it is produced. In other words, a loan based on grade, type, and staple is established for each commodity in each county. The government does not announce terminal loan rates for Chicago for corn, oats, and soybeans. However, the Chicago equivalent of the loan may be approximated by adding transportation and handling cost to the average Illinois county loan.

If farmers store the grain on their own farms, they will receive what is known as the *gross loan*—that is, the full loan rate. On the other hand, if they store the grain under loan in commercial warehouse facilities, they receive the gross loan less storage costs (known as the *net loan*) until the end of the loan period.

Purchase Agreements

A *purchase agreement* is, as the expression indicates, an agreement on the part of the CCC to purchase from a producer later in the marketing year, at his or her option, a stipulated quantity of a commodity at the support price.

Producers obtain a purchase agreement though the ASCS county office by signing a document specifying the maximum amount of the commodity they elect to sell to the CCC. The CCC agrees to purchase at the applicable rate, which is equal to the loan rate, any quantity of an eligible-quality commodity the producer elects to sell, up to and including the maximum quantity covered by the agreement.

> *Example*: A producer signs a purchase agreement covering 5,000 bushels of corn. He may sell no corn to the CCC, or he may sell any quantity up to and including 5,000 bushels. But after specifying that 5,000 bushels is the maximum quantity, he may not sell more to the CCC.

Loans and purchase agreements provide support at exactly the same level. A loan suits the needs of the producer who requires money immediately and who can meet loan storage requirements. A purchase agreement, on the other hand, provides a convenient, inexpensive form of price insurance for the producer who does not have an immediate need for cash, who is not able to meet loan storage requirements, or who is not willing to encumber the commodity as is required under a loan operation.

The CCC is also authorized to buy such commodities as soybean oil, eggs, meat products, and lard in the open market in an effort to raise prices. The commodities purchased by the CCC under this type of program are used for domestic and foreign donation programs.

Wool and Mohair

The 1977 Act extends the National Wool Act of 1954 through December 31, 1981, and thus continues to require the Secretary of Agriculture to provide supports for wool and mohair.

Incentive Payments

The payment method of support, authorized by the national Wool Act, may be used only for shorn wool, pulled wool (the wool removed from the carcasses of slaughtered sheep and lambs), and mohair. Payments on domestic production of shorn wool are called *incentive payments,* because

Congress, in enacting the payment type of program, declared it a policy "to encourage the annual domestic production of approximately 300,000,000 pounds of shorn wool, grease basis."

Under the program a grower sells the shorn wool in normal marketing channels, obtaining at that time a sales document describing the transaction. The sales document and an application for payment are filed with the grower's ASCA county office. Payments are made to producers by the county office as rapidly as possible after the rate of payment is determined at the end of the marketing year.

The rate of payment is based on differences between a previously announced incentive price and the United States average price received by producers for wool sold during the marketing year.

> *Example*: The announced incentive price for a particular marketing year is 65 cents a pound for shorn wool. Growers actually receive an average price of 52.1 cents. To bring actual prices to the incentive level, the U.S. Department of Agriculture makes payments amounting to 24.8 percent of producers' sales returns, which raises average U.S. wool prices to growers to the 65-cent incentive level. Each grower of shorn wool receives 24.8 percent of the price received on the sale.
>
> Obviously, the higher the price obtained in the open market, the higher the payment. The producer who sold wool at an average price of 50 cents a pound gets a payment of 12.4 cents a pound, whereas another producer who markets wool at 40 cents a pound gets a payment of only 9.9 cents a pound.

Price Support for Shorn Wool

Support rates for shorn wool were raised to 85 percent of the formula rate and are to be effective for the marketing years beginning January 1, 1977, and ending December 31, 1981. The formula rate for shorn wool is determined by multiplying 62 cents by the ratio of (1) the average of the parity index for the 3 calendar years immediately preceding the calendar year in which the support price is determined and announced to (2) the average parity index for the 3 calendar years 1958, 1959 and 1960.

Although the National Wool Act authorized support of mohair prices, market prices were high enough in the first seven marketing years under the act to make actual support operations unnecessary. If it becomes necessary to carry on actual support operations for mohair, the support method used will be the same as is used for shorn wool.

WHY MARKET PRICES MAY BE LESS THAN SUPPORT PRICES

Market prices of supported commodities sometimes drop below support levels for several reasons. If all the producers of a supported commodity participated in the program to support prices of that commodity, the price of the commodity would obviously be equal to or higher than the support level. Failure to participate in the program, then, is a major reason that market prices of some supported commodities sometimes drop below the support level.

Lack of Adequate Storage. Insufficient storage—both farm and warehouse—can be an obstacle to a producer's participation in the program. To obtain a price support loan, a producer must store in facilities approved by the CCC, either privately owned or commercial space. Producers participating through purchase agreements need not store in approved facilities, but they still need safe storage while the commodities must be held prior to sale to the government. Many producers, including share tenants, lack adequate farm storage. To obtain support, these producers must store part or all of their commodities in commercial warehouses. When space is not available (as sometimes happens during periods of peak marketings or overall storage shortages), producers must sell their commodities at the best prices obtainable. If such marketings reach sizeable volume, they tend to depress prices below support levels.

Quality. The crop may not be of good storing quality, and commercial warehouse operators may refuse to accept it. Thus a producer must elect either to run the risk of both quality deterioration and shrinkage by storing the commodity on the farm or sell at the market price. When storage space is scarce, warehouse owners may be even more reluctant to handle grain of questionable storability—which further aggravates the problem.

Potential Gain. The quantity of a commodity owned by a particular producer may not be large enough to encourage participation in the program.

Inconvenience. If supplies are considered ample and a price increase during the loan period is not likely, producers may be reluctant to undertake the paperwork involved in completing a storage loan or to run the risks of a loss of quality. In such circumstances, they are willing to sell in the open market at prices slightly below the loan level.

Disagreement with Price Support. Not all producers agree with the concept of price support. To the extent that this group may be of significant size in any marketing area, prices in that area may be held down by their failure to take part in the support programs.

Sales by Nonfarmers. Only an eligible producer (that is, any legal entity producing the supported commodity, such as a landowner, landlord, tenant, or sharecropper) can obtain price support. From time to time at the end of the marketing season or over the course of a full marketing season, considerable quantities of a commodity may be owned by nonproducer groups. Such noneligible interests may sell stocks in a weak or falling market in order to minimize or stop their losses. These operations depress prices even more.

PRODUCTION ADJUSTMENT PROGRAMS

Congress has authorized a number of programs that include the objective of adjusting the production and marketing of farm crops. Adjustments recommended may be either upward or downward. Among those programs administered by the Agricultural Stablization and Conservation Service are:

1. national program acreages and allocation factor,
2. voluntary diversion programs,
3. cropland adjustment program, and
4. cropland conversion program.

National Program Acreage

The national program acreage for wheat for a particular crop year must be announced by the Secretary no later than August 15 of the preceding calendar year. National program acreages for feed grains must be announced by November 15 of the preceding year. The national program acreages may be adjusted at a later time, with the adjustment based on the most recent information, for purposes of calculating the program allocation factor.

Announcement of the national program acreage for cotton is to be made by the Secretary no later than December 15 of the year preceding the program year. While the Secretary may later adjust the national program acreage for purposes of computing the program allocation factor, such national program acreage cannot be reduced below 10 million acres.

Program Allocation Factor

The program allocation factor for wheat and feed grains may range between 80 and 100 percent. The exact percentage is determined by dividing the national program acreage by the number of acres that the Secretary estimates will be harvested in the current year. The allocation factor is used for determining the farm program acreage. In practice, the program acreage allocation factor does not need to be determined until the sixth month of the current marketing year.

A program allocation factor for cotton is determined by dividing the national cotton program acreage by the number of harvested acres as determined by the Secretary. The allocation factor may not exceed 100 percent. No minimum allocation factor was specified.

Voluntary Diversion Programs

These programs seek to divert acreage from crop production to an approved conservation use. To participate in commodity diversion programs, producers sign up to reduce their acreage of the commodity by at least a minimum amount below farm base acreages or allotments. Payments are made under commodity diversion programs to help farmers maintain their incomes while reducing their acreages to keep production in line with needs.

Since 1961, substantial reductions in grain surpluses have been achieved through feedgrain and wheat acreage diversions. The acreage diversion program, which has been successful for grains, has been broadened to include cotton. In the first two years of operation the cotton surplus was reduced substantially. Participation in allotment and acreage diversion programs (when they are in effect for a crop) are conditions for price support eligibility.

Aerial photographs provide base maps for measuring the area planted and thus determine farmer compliance with acreage diversion and other programs.

The Cropland Adjustment Program and the Cropland Conversion Program

These programs supplement the commodity acreage diversion programs by offering farmers an opportunity to take acreage out of production for longer periods of time than provided by the annual commodity programs. The program seeks to shift cropland that produces actual or potential surplus into long-term (five to ten years) conservational, recreational, and open space uses, for both farm and nonfarm benefit.

Accepted agreements are paid at a rate determined according to the diverted crop and to the productivity of the crop on the farm. Additional payments may be made, when offered, under agreements that permit free public access to designated acreage for hunting, trapping, fishing, and hiking. Participants agree to divert all or at least one of their bases or allotments, and they can then divert other crop bases and allotment.

COMMODITY DISPOSAL AND INVENTORY OPERATIONS

Commodities acquired under the price support program are made available for movement into consumption channels both at home and abroad, as needs require, to carry out the *ever-normal granary concept* and to keep CCC inventories at manageable levels.

The ever-normal granary principle has been an integral part of farm programs since their beginning in the 1930s. When production exceeds needs, farm income is protected from undue market-depressing effects of the surplus by adding price-supported commodities to ever-normal granary stocks under storage loans or CCC ownership, thus stabilizing farm market prices. The complementary purpose of the ever-normal granary provides for using these built-up stocks to stabilize consumer prices by moving commodities into use in times when supplies are low relative to need or when demand is strong through unusual circumstances. In many instances, the strengthening of demand relative to supply results directly from production adjustment programs that bring output down. By filling the gap between reduced production and current needs, the government reduces the surplus.

Commodities acquired under the price support program are moved into consumption in various ways. Some are sold for domestic use and some for export. Some sales are for cash, others under credit arrangements, and some indirectly for foreign currencies. Some are used, under a "payment-in-kind" subsidy program, to stimulate commercial exports. Some are bartered for strategic and critical materials produced abroad or for goods and services to fill U. S. government needs abroad. Some are transferred to other government agencies for such uses as food for the Armed Forces, for veterans' hospitals, and for foreign relief programs. Some are transferred to other agencies for eventual donation to school lunch programs, and, through approved U.S. welfare organizations, to needy people in the United States and foreign countries. Some, such as feed grains, are used to finance acreage diversion programs and price support payment through payment-in-kind. Cotton is similarly used to finance the cotton program. Some grains are either sold at reduced prices or donated to livestock producers in areas where feed is short due to drought, flood, hurricane, or other natural disasters.

Domestic Sale

In pricing commodities for domestic use, the CCC must stay within certain legal guidelines. With the exception of limited, specific emergency programs, the CCC's selling prices on commodities for domestic use are never below the current market price for the same quality of the commodity.

In addition, Section 407 of the Agricultural Act of 1949 prohibits domestic "bargain sales" of storable CCC-owned commodities. It provides that the CCC shall not, in general, sell any storable commodity in the domestic market at less than 115 percent of the current support price for the commodity, plus reasonable carrying charges. Aside from definite exceptions set by law, the CCC makes domestic sales of storable commodities only at this price level or higher—never below the current market.

The objective of this provision is obvious. If the CCC made a general practice of selling storable commodities below support levels, such sales would tend to drive market prices down below support prices. This, in turn, would result in more price support activity—with more commodities coming into the inventory.

Exceptions to the 115 percent provision are sales authorized by the feed-grain and cotton programs. These programs provide for making price support and acreage diversion payments to producers "in kind" from CCC stocks of feed grains and cotton. These payments are primarily in the form of certificates at levels reflecting the support loan rate plus reasonable carrying charges. This permits an orderly movement of the surplus of these commodities into use as production is brought down below needs. Thus, the Section 407 provision requiring a domestic sale price for storable commodities at 115 percent of the support price does not apply in these sales. However, these sales are not made at prices below the market.

Section 407 also exempts from the minimum price restriction any storable commodities in danger of loss or waste through deterioration or spoilage that can render the commodity unsuitable for further storage. The CCC has followed a consistent policy of pricing these commodities at not less than the market price for a comparable quality. Despite the huge quantities taken into the inventory, spoilage losses as a result of complete deterioration have been negligible. Commodities in danger of deterioration are sold before any appreciable loss occurs.

Under certain disaster conditions, feed grain can be donated and sold at less than the current support rate to supplement feed supplies for farmers. Under other disaster circumstances, feed grains can be sold at the support price.

Export Movement

The Section 407 minimum pricing provision does not apply to sale of CCC commodities for export. Generally, the CCC follows a practice of selling commodities for export at world price levels or at domestic market prices with export payments, if needed, to keep competitive in world markets. In both instances, steps are taken to isolate most sales for export (particularly grain) from domestic channels to prevent their moving into domestic use. Exporters are required to file a proof of export. In addition, delivery of grain and most other commodities is made at a port location, which insures movement abroad.

The CCC has moved very large volumes of its holdings into useful channels of consumption, both at home and abroad.

METHODS OF DISPOSITION

Sales for Dollars

Sales for dollars, both for domestic and export use, have been the biggest single outlet for CCC-owned farm products.

As noted, some domestic sales are made at the so-called formula prices—that is, 105 percent above the support price plus carrying charges. Some are under the payment-in-kind provisions of commodity programs. Some are sold at reduced prices to meet needs in disaster areas. Other commodities in danger of deterioration are sold at the market price for comparable quality. Also export sales are made in some instances at domestic market prices and in others at prices somewhat below domestic market price levels to enable American exporters to compete in foreign markets on a more even basis with commodities produced in other countries.

Credit Sales for Dollars

To stimulate export sales for dollars, the CCC sells some of its commodities on credit. The CCC Export Credit Sales Program provides short-term credit, and long-term credit is available under authority of Title IV, Public Law 480.

CCC Credit Program

Under authority of the CCC charter, commercial sales of CCC-owned commodities are made under the CCC Export Credit Sales Program on a deferred payment basis for periods up to a maximum of three years. The Credit Sales Program also provides deferred payment terms in connection with certain agricultural commodities exported from private stocks, in addition to CCC commodities. Exporters who ship from private stocks receive an Export Commodity Certificate (CCC-341) for an amount equal to the port value of the commodity sold under the credit program.

Interest is charged at a rate announced each month by the CCC. All sales under the program are made to United States exporters who pass the credit on to foreign buyers. An assurance of payment from United States or foreign banks is required.

Public Law 480 Credit Program

Title IV of Public Law 480 provides that long-term supply and dollar credit sales agreements for delivery of farm commodities may be entered into with (1) United States or foreign traders and (2) governments of friendly nations. While the law permits a ten-year delivery period for credit sales, supply periods generally are limited to not more than three years.

Title IV provides for repayment in dollars with interest. Repayment may be made in annual amounts over periods of not more than twenty years from the date of the last delivery of commodities. Interest rate and payment periods are set in relation to the purchasing country's financial situation, terms of AID dollar loans for economic development, and other related factors. Under private trade sales, payment periods are set on the basis of the particular project or purpose for which the credit is to be utilized.

Emphasis in the agreements is on the use of credit to expand dollar markets for United States farm products, to develop foreign markets for these products, and to assist in the economic development of nations.

Eligible commodities include those under price support and other commodities not price supported but eligible for export financing under P.L.480. The agreements require that cash dollar exports of the United States be safeguarded with assurances that sales will not unduly disrupt world prices for agricultural commodities or normal patterns of commercial trade.

Financing and operating procedures applying to Title IV, P.L. 480 sales agreements are generally similar to Title I, P.L.480 procedures described in the following paragraphs in connection with sales for foreign currencies, with the exception that payment is made in dollars.

Sales for Foreign Currencies Under Title I, P.L.480.

Substantial quantities of agricultural commodities are sold abroad for foreign currencies under Title I, P.L.480, as amended—also called the Agricultural Trade Development and Assistance Act of 1954. By authorizing sales for foreign currencies, Title I enables the United States to overcome a big obstacle to agricultural export trade—dollar shortages among importing nations. Transactions under Title I require the following steps:

1. A foreign importing country enters into an agreement with the United States to purchase agricultural commodities in this country and pay for them with foreign currencies.
2. The importing country applies for purchase authorizations providing for dollar financing of the commodity sales and specifying the conditions under which the financing will be done. When authorizations are issued, the importing country designates certain banks in its country and in the United States to participate in the program.

   The CCC issues letters of commitment to the United States banks in the amounts requested by the importing country. Each letter of commitment names the foreign bank as well as the American bank and constitutes commitment by the CCC to reimburse the United States bank for payments made under letters of credit for the account of the foreign bank.
3. A commercial importer or the government in the importing country buys United States commodities from an American exporter who, in most instances, acquires them from United States commercial stocks. The importer pays for them in foreign currencies at the foreign bank. The American exporter, however, receives payment in dollars from the United States bank.
4. The American bank is reimbursed by the CCC. Foreign currency that paid for the transaction is deposited by the foreign bank to the account of the United states in the foreign country. The foreign currency is used abroad by the United States to develop new markets for American farm products. It can also be used to procure military equipment, materials, facilities, and services for the common defense, to pay U.S. obligations abroad, and to finance

international educational exchange activities. The currency is also used to finance the purchase of goods or services for other countries, and it is loaned or granted to importing countries for economic development purposes.

5. To the extent that the CCC is not otherwise reimbursed by government agencies utilizing foreign currencies accruing under Title I transactions, the CCC is reimbursed through appropriations for commodities disposed of and costs incurred under such transactions.

Prices of some United States commodities are higher than "world" prices. To make it possible for American exporters to compete on even terms in foreign markets (thus enabling United States producers to share in world markets and helping the American balance of payments), the Department of Agriculture, through the CCC, makes export payments amounting, per unit, to approximately the difference between the U.S. price and the world price.

The payment-in-kind export program consists of export payments in the form of commodities to maintain and stimulate commercial exports of United States farm commodities. As CCC inventories decline, the program is phased out.

How the Export Payment Program Works.   In the case of wheat, for example, the exporter purchases from regular commercial sources the wheat for shipping and registers the export sale with the U.S. Department of Agriculture. On this wheat, he or she receives an export payment. Wheat export payment rates, except for durum, are set and announced daily by the USDA. Payment rates for durum wheat are established by competitive bids of exporters who submit bids for an export payment rate per bushel and indicate the quantity for export. The payments are made on virtually all wheat exports, including shipments under the International Wheat Agreement. If the wheat is shipped in the form of flour, the exporter also gets the export payment in cash. Payments on flour shipped under the International Wheat Agreement are also made on cash basis.

Barter.   Since 1949, large quantities of CCC-owned farm products have been "swapped" for strategic and other materials produced abroad. More recently, substantial quantities of farm products have been bartered predominantly for the procurement abroad of materials, goods, equipment, and services for United States agencies that reimburse the CCC rather than spend those dollars abroad.

Procurements abroad through barter divide into (1) strategic materials for stockpiling and (2) goods and services for U.S. government agencies. Procurement through barter has included such items and services as airplane parts and repairs, post exchange supplies, port handling and transportation services for the Department of Defense, and cement, fertilizer, and sugar for AID. In reducing the need for dollar payment for these items by United States agencies abroad, the barter transactions help the United States balance of payments.

Barter transactions are carried out through regular commercial trade channels by private American firms. Barter contracts generally run from periods of a few months up to two years, during which the contractor both delivers materials and exports agricultural commodities received in exchange. Contractors are required not only to furnish cash or irrevocable letters of credit for the total value of any farm products received in advance of delivering material or making procurement arrangements, but also to pay interest (at the rate in effect for the CCC Credit Program when the barter contract is made) for any period during which the value of farm products received exceeds the value of the contractor's performance.

Transfers and Donations

Over one-fifth of the CCC's dispositions—primarily food commodities—have been donations for recipients in the United States and foreign countries. Some of the donations have been handled by other government agencies and some by the Department of Agriculture itself, with reimbursement to the CCC. Substantial quantities of food from CCC stocks have been donated by other agencies, however, with no reimbursement to the CCC. The USDA distributes food to:

1. nonprofit lunch programs in schools of high school grade and under,
2. American Indians on reservations,
3. charitable institutions, such as hospitals, homes for the aging, and other institutions for the needy,
4. state and local public welfare agencies,
5. organizations providing relief for victims of disasters such as drought, floods, and other natural disasters, and
6. voluntary agencies distributing donated foods to people in need in various parts of the world.

THE INTERNATIONAL WHEAT AGREEMENT

Wheat is one of the most important food commodities in many areas of the world. Large volumes move regularly in international trade. A few countries produce more wheat than they need for their own consumption, have supplies for shipment beyond their own borders, and are therefore classed as wheat exporting countries. A large number produce less than their needs, depend upon shipments from other areas, and are classed as wheat importing countries. Both groups have special problems: The exporters need primarily to be assured of stable markets from year to year; the importers need stable supplies. Additionally both need and seek reasonable price stability.

The International Wheat Agreement was designed to help solve these problems, which have been of concern to wheat trading countries for years.

The main objective of the agreement is to assure markets for wheat from exporting countries and supplies of wheat to importing countries—both at equitable prices. Importing countries are obligated to purchase from member exporting countries specified percentages of their total commercial imports. The United States and other exporting countries are obligated to sell member importing countries quantities up to historical commercial levels at the agreement maximum price.

The International Wheat Council conducts an annual review of the world wheat situation in the light of information obtained about national production, stocks, prices, trade, surplus disposal, and so on. The council then informs member countries of the effects these factors have on international trade in wheat and flour.

Early in the crop year, the exporting members report to the council the estimated quantities of wheat they will have available for export during the year. Likewise, the estimated commercial wheat and flour import requirements of the importing countries are reported to the council by those countries each crop year. Both import and export members must later submit reports of actual imports and exports of wheat and flour.

The agreement also provides for action to be taken by the IWC in the event of crop shortages in exporting countries, as well as for relieving an importing country of its purchasing obligations in case of balance of payments difficulties.

Participating in the IWS does not restrict wheat exports is any way. The United States is free to export any quantity of wheat to any country to which exportation is not prohibited by statutes or by the U.S. Department of Commerce under the Export Control Act of 1949.

CONCLUSION

If farmers could plow and plant with the unqualified confidence that their crops will fetch at least a moderate profit without any government support at all, surely both the American farmer and the United States government would be a lot happier.

And if each country could produce exactly enough foodstuffs to feed its own population, no international agreements on exporting and importing policies would be necessary.

But soil and seasons, blight and vermin, frost and drought—the unexpected in general—do not permit such ideal situations. And so a buffering influence is needed to catch prices when they plummet and to contain them when they skyrocket, to supply where there is a need and to hold back where there is too much.

If the government did not provide such services, someone would undoubtedly be screaming that, "There ought to be a law!"

Chapter 18

Financial Instruments as Commodities

Money in the form of metals emerged as a commercial convention about three thousand years ago, proving all the more the probably even older adage that, "Necessity is the mother of invention." Undoubtedly the practical necessity of breaking away from a barter exchange system led to the invention of an intermediate element by which trade could be expanded. Money, an accepted unit and common denominator, facilitated the immediate exchange of goods but also added a time dimension to trade—the value of goods sold one time could be "stored" in units of money and used to purchase other goods at a later time. This feature, in turn, permitted investment, the division of labor, and industrialization—which ultimately produced a general standard of living that would not have been possible in a barter economy.

Futures trading in money-denominated instruments certainly will not have an impact on the course of commerce equal to that of money itself, but it is having an increasingly noticeable impact on the way financial decision-makers view futures markets. Their interest is the first step toward using financial futures, and actual use should provide a foundation of knowledge and experience that will likely cause changes in the way certain financial transactions are evaluated or structured.

THE GROWING VOLUME OF SUCCESS

The reason for this growing interest is simple enough: Success always attracts attention—and financial futures have been very successful. One measure of success is *quantitative,* in terms of trading volume and open interest.

For instance, trading in Government National Mortgage Association

(GNMA) futures began on October 20, 1975. Total trading volume during the first twelve months for GNMA futures was 114,000 contracts. Compare that with the first year's trading volume of 46,275 contracts in cattle futures, a very successful market recently established at the Chicago Mercantile Exchange, or with the 41,000 first-year trading volume in plywood futures, previously the most successful new contract introduced by the Chicago Board of Trade. In open interest, also, the GNMA market set a record-breaking pace. In way of comparison, cattle and plywood accumulated end-of-first-year open interest figures of 3,322 and 2,847, respectively: Open interest in GNMA futures at the end of the first year was 4,201. And GNMA futures growth did not diminish: In the month of May 1978, total volume was 60,140 contracts—up 103 percent from May of the previous year—while May 1978 open interest was 27,480—up 108 percent from the prior year.

Ninety-day U.S. Treasury Bill (T-Bill) futures were introduced on January 6, 1976. Their trading volume (111,200) nearly matched that of GNMA futures in the first twelve months, but their open interest fell short after reaching only 3,504, then ending the first year at a respectable 2,686. After eighteen months, however, T-bill futures volume exceeded GNMA futures' eighteen-month volume: 257,700 for T-Bills compared to 234,800 for GNMAs. During the month of May 1978, T-Bill futures traded 38,930 contracts, up 21 percent from May 1977. May 1978 month-end open interest at 20,280 contracts was up 185 percent from the prior May's month-end total.

The emerging superstar of financial futures, however, is the long-term U.S. Treasury Bond (T-Bond) futures contract. At the end of the ninth month after trading began on August 22, 1977, T-Bond futures had traded a total of 109,400 contracts, 32 percent ahead of the pace set by GNMA futures in a comparable period of time. And T-Bond open interest was 9,735—two and a half times the level for GNMAs at the same point of market maturity.

The only damper on this success story consists of the 90-Day Commercial Paper Futures, opened for trading on September 20, 1977. The possible or probable reasons for its lack of growth compared with the other financial futures is beyond the scope of this chapter. Suffice it to say that, in their early days, the market's daily volume seldom exceeded 50 contracts and open interest seemed to be stalled around the 700 to 750 level. However, the Chicago Board of Trade applied to the Commodity Futures Trading Commission for a 30-Day Commercial Papers Futures contract. This and other trading modifications are likely in an effort to develop more interest in what could be a viable commercial hedging medium.

THE SWEET QUALITY OF SUCCESS

Another measure of success for financial futures is that it attracts competitors. By this measure, too, the Chicago markets have succeeded. The

American Stock Exchange has formed a subsidiary, the Amex Commodities Exchange, for the primary purpose of drawing to New York futures trading in fixed-income debt instruments. Trading in a GNMA futures contract slightly different from the one trading at the Chicago Board of Trade began on the New York market in September of 1978, and the Amex has already announced plans to trade U.S. Treasury Bill Futures in January 1979 and U.S. Treasury Bond Futures in May 1979. All these plans, of course, are subject to approval by the Commodity Futures Trading Commission.

PRECONDITIONS FOR FINANCIAL FUTURES

The primary economic justification for any futures market is that it provides an easy and efficient mechanism for the transfer, or hedging, of price-level risks arising in the normal course of business. Traditionally, price-level risks in the "normal course of business" have been identified almost exclusively with the production and distribution of agricultural and industrial commodities. But the success of financial futures acknowledges the price risk in the *financing* of production and distribution. It also demonstrates that the concept of price-level risks (and hedging) can be expanded to include the price of financial instruments.

Not too many years ago, the business and financial communities would have found it very difficult to recognize a serious interest rate risk or to accept hedging on an organized futures exchange as a viable alternative to bearing that risk. The reasons for this attitude were easy to understand. High-grade corporate bond yields in 1964 were at about the same level as in 1932, and from 1957 to 1966 they had not varied much on either side of a 4- to 5-percent range. And though short-term interest rates were admittedly more troublesome, the cycles were still relatively long and gradual, providing both investors and borrowers ample time to adjust. Also, the level of short-term rates as late as 1968 did not exceed the highs set nearly forty years before.

The first shock to this tranquil scene came in late 1968. Pressures had been built up by the government's deficit spending on the Viet Nam War and the Great Society programs, and this pressure eventually squirted out in the form of rapidly escalating prices and extraordinary demands on the credit markets. As an example of just one sector of the economy, the housing industry took an awful beating: The interest rate on three-month U.S. Treasury Bills rose from 5.1 percent in September 1968 to 7.1 percent in September 1969, and then to 7.9 percent in January 1970—a 55 percent rise in fifteen months. Such returns were too good to resist. Individual investors directed savings away from home-financing institutions and directly into money market securities, such as 3-month bills, thus producing a contraction in housing construction and an increase in home mortgage rates. Housing starts fell from a 1.73 million annual rate in November 1968 to a 1.28 million rate one year later, and the national average home mortgage interest rate during that same period of time rose one full percentage point, from 7.23 percent to 8.25 percent.

Interest rate risk was taking on a cold, hard meaning.

If 1969–70 was a shock, then 1973–75 was closer to an earthquake. The causes or details of the events can be dispensed with, in light of a few startling facts regarding interest rate volatility: The 90-day U.S. Treasury Bill rate ballooned from 3.2 percent in February 1972 to 8.7 percent in August 1973. Housing starts hurtled from 2.68 million in February 1972 to 889,000 in December 1974. The commercial bank prime lending rate reached 12 percent in late 1974, then fell to just under 7 percent during the next nine months. Federal Funds (overnite bank reserves) after trading near 14 percent in mid-1974 fell to under 5 percent one year later. The maximum interest rate on FHA-insured mortgages, 8.5 percent in August 1973, was 9.5 percent in August 1974 and 8.0 percent in March 1975.

By 1975, interest rate risk was being taken very seriously.

HEDGING INTEREST RATE RISK

To understand the mechanics of hedging interest rate fluctuations, keep in mind the *inverse* relationship between interest rates and the market value of a fixed-income financial instrument: As interest rates *rise,* prices *fall*; as interest rates *fall,* prices *rise.*

> *Example*: A new issue bond pays a fixed dollar amount of interest each year. The buyer pays par (or 100 percent of the maturity dollar value) for this $100,000, 8 percent bond that returns $8,000 a year in interest. At a later time, the investor finds it necessary to sell that same bond. However, interest rates have *risen* to 8.5 percent, and so the resale value of the bond has *fallen.* The higher interest rate in other words, a new bond pays $8,500 a year in interest while the old bond pays only $8,000. Therefore, the owner of the old bond has to offer it at a discounted price, say $90,000, in order to give a new buyer the higher yield prevailing in the market. The new buyer of the old bond receives the annual $8,000 plus $10,000 more than the $90,000 purchase price when the bond matures and pays its maturity value of $100,000. The $10,000 *discount* effectively *raises* the yield.
>
> Conversely, if interest rates *fall* and a new bond pays only $7,500 a year interest, then the old bond's value has *risen* to a premium, to $110,000, because buyers will pay a higher price for the right to receive $8,000 a year. The $10,000 *premium* effectively *lowers* the yield.

If bonds trade in the market at a discounted price, then current yields must be above the bond's stated interest rate. If bonds trade in the market at a premium price, then current yields must be below the bond's stated interest rate.

SELLING HEDGE (GNMA FUTURES)

The specific information regarding the trading of GNMA futures is contained in Figure 18-1.

> *Example*: In March, a mortgage banking company is processing mortgage loans that will permit it to deliver in about thirty days at $1 million principal amount GNMA certificate bearing an 8.5-percent interest rate. This certificate is the equivalent of the "cash" commodity.
>
> In the futures market, the currently quoted dealer price for an April delivery is 96-24 (96 and 24/32 or $967,500), to yield 8.91 percent. If yields rise and the mortgage company does not either sell for actual delivery or hedge in the futures market, then the value of the GNMA will fall. The company decides to hedge in the futures market, as follows:

	Cash	*Futures*
March 15	$1 million 8.5% GNMA planned delivery in 30 days, April dealer bid 96–24 (8.91%)	Sell 10 June GNMA futures 92–25 (8.99%).
April 19	Sell $1 million 8.5% GNMA immediate delivery 96–16 (8.95%)	Buy 10 June GNMA futures 92–17 (9.03%)
	Loss $2,500	Gain $2,500

A few things shown in this illustration require elaboration. First, notice the wide discrepancy (or apparent discrepancy) between the cash market prices (96–24 and 96–16) and the futures prices (92–25 and 92–17). Why sell in the futures market at 92–25 when the cash market bid is 96–24? The futures price is *always* for an 8-percent certificate, while the cash market is for an 8.5-percent certificate. On a yield basis there is far less difference.

Second, there *is* a significant yield difference between April dealer deliveries (8.91 percent) and June futures (8.99 percent). The futures have the higher yield, or lower price, because prices for financial futures, unlike the prices in physical commodities, are usually lower for deferred deliveries. June futures are therefore lower-priced than April cash. And yet the June futures are higher-priced than September futures, September futures are higher priced than December futures, and so on.

Why? The fixed-dollar amount of interest for long-term GNMAs and bonds is usually more than the short-term cost of financing the bond. An 8-percent bond pays $2,000 interest per three-month period, but if short-term funds to finance ownership of the bond can be borrowed for three months at a 6-percent rate (of $1,500), there is a $500 "positive" carry. The futures market *takes away* that positive carry by pricing more distant months at successively lower dollar amounts (or at successively larger dollar discounts).

Finally, the hedge in the example is a "perfect" hedge—the loss and

Figure 18-1 (a)

Financial Futures Contract Summary

March 15, 1978

GNMA FUTURES
8% Coupon With Yield Equivalent Delivery

EXCHANGE: CHICAGO BOARD OF TRADE

TRADING HOURS: ~~8:50 AM to 1:30 PM (Chicago)~~ 8:30 AM to 2:00 PM (Chicago)

TRADING UNIT: $100,000 PRINCIPAL GNMA CERTIFICATE, 8% STATED INTEREST RATE

GNMA Certificates, modified pass-through mortgage-backed securities, guaranteed for timely payment of principal and interest by the Government National Mortgage Association (GNMA), as described in Standard Prospectus HUD 1717.

PRICE QUOTATIONS: Points and 1/32nds of 100 percent of $100,000

A typical price quotation for GNMA Futures would be 95-20, meaning 95 and 20/32nds or 95.625% of $100,000. Given that price, the buyer would pay and the seller receive $95,625 for a $100,000 principal amount GNMA Certificate.

MINIMUM PRICE FLUCTUATION: 1/32nd, or $31.25 per $100,000

PRICE MOVEMENT DAILY LIMIT: 24/32nds, or $750 per $100,000

The "normal" limit for any trading day is 24/32nds above or below the previous day's settlement price; however, these limits are expanded under predetermined conditions and there is no limit on the expiring contract during the delivery month, e.g., there would be no price movement limit on the June 1978 contract during the calendar month of June 1978.

EXPIRING CONTRACT TRADING TERMINATION: Eighth-to-last business day of month

There is no trading in the expiring contract during the last seven business days of the delivery month.

DELIVERY PERIOD: Any business day during the contract's delivery month

It is the seller's option to initiate the delivery process. Actual delivery in settlement of a "sold" futures position can be made on any business day during the delivery month. The buyer, holding a "bought" futures position, is selected to take delivery by the Exchange.

DELIVERY INSTRUMENT: Collateralized Depository Receipt (CDR)

Anyone may deliver a CDR in settlement of a "sold" futures position, but only those firms previously approved by the Chicago Board of Trade may originate, or create, a CDR.

DELIVERY SUBSTITUTION: Deliverers at their option may collateralize CDRs with GNMAs other than 8%, provided the GNMAs delivered bear the same yield as 8% GNMAs when calculated at par and under the assumptions of a 30-year mortgage prepaid in the 12th year. (see conversions on back of this page)

Figure 18-1 (b)

GNMA STATED INTEREST RATE	CONVERSION FACTOR	AMOUNT EQUIVALENT TO $100,000 of GNMA 8s
6.50	1.121233	$112,123.30
7.00	1.078167	$107,816.70
7.25	1.058201	$105,820.10
7.50	1.038062	$103,806.20
8.00	1.000000	$100,000.00
8.25	.982198	$ 98,219.80
8.50	.965018	$ 96,501.80
9.00	.931677	$ 93,167.70

32nds	DECIMAL	32nds	DECIMAL
1	.03125	17	.53125
2	.06250	18	.56250
3	.09375	19	.59375
4	.12500	20	.62500
5	.15625	21	.65625
6	.18750	22	.68750
7	.21875	23	.71875
8	.25000	24	.75000
9	.28125	25	.78125
10	.31250	26	.81250
11	.34375	27	.84375
12	.37500	28	.87500
13	.40625	29	.90625
14	.43750	30	.93750
15	.46875	31	.96875
16	.50000	32	1.00000

Bache Halsey Stuart Shields Incorporated, 141 W. Jackson Blvd., Chicago, IL 60603

gain offset exactly. Simplifying hedge illustrations in this manner is more or less a convention, but would-be hedgers should recognize that in actual practice hedges are more likely to be on one side or the other of perfect. This less-than-perfect feature should not detract from the value of hedging, however, because even a partial loss recovery by hedging is far better than no loss recovery at all.

BUYING HEDGE (T-BOND FUTURES)

While the hedger selling futures is usually trying to protect the value of something owned, the hedger who buys futures is trying to establish a price relationship for something *intended* to be owned (see Figure 18-2).

Example: In April, the investment committee of an insurance company concludes that long-term interest rates are at an attractive level and that a larger portion of the company's portfolio should be invested in 20-year maturities. The investment manager is directed to buy $5 million in bonds from cash in-flows over the following three months with an objective of averaging approximately the current market yield of 8.36 percent.

The investment manager subsequently buys $2 million in bonds for immediate delivery at 8.34 percent and $3 million in bond futures at 8.41 percent, intending to buy bonds for immediate delivery as the cash becomes available. The manager is hedging the intended purchases in case yields should fall.

	Cash	*Futures*
April 2	Buy $2 million bonds yield $8.34%	Buy 30 June bond futures 96–03 (8.41%)
May 9	Buy $1 million bonds yield 8.31%	Sell 10 June bond futures 96–13 (8.38%)
June 19	Buy $2 million bonds yield 8.34%	Sell 20 June bond futures 96–23 (8.35%)
	$5 million bonds bought at 8.33% average (3 basis points under objective)	$3 million bonds bought at 8.41% (5 basis points over objective)

This very simple illustration does not get into any of the fine points of dollar values for bonds actually bought or conversions of futures to specific deliverable bonds. However, it is conceptually valid and demonstrates the advantage of buying bond futures when long-term rates are higher than short-term rates. Because June delivery futures were at a higher yield than the immediate delivery bonds in the dealer market, the buyer has an advantage, just the opposite of the disadvantage to the seller discussed in the GNMA

Figure 18-2 (a)

Financial Futures Contract Summary

March 15, 1978

U.S. TREASURY BOND FUTURES

EXCHANGE: CHICAGO BOARD OF TRADE

TRADING HOURS: ~~8:35 AM to 1:40 PM (Chicago)~~ 8:20 AM to 2:10 PM (Chicago)

TRADING UNIT: $100,000 FACE VALUE U.S. TREASURY BOND, 8% COUPON

TRADING UNIT MINIMUM MATURITY: 15 years to call or maturity, whichever occurs first

A deliverable bond must have at least 15 years remaining to the call date, if callable, or maturity date from the first day of the futures delivery month.

PRICE QUOTATIONS: Points and 1/32nds of 100 percent of $100,000

A typical price quotation for U.S. Treasury Bond Futures would be 96-04, meaning 96 and 4/32nds or 96.125% of $100,000. Given that price, the buyer would pay and the seller receive $96,125 for $100,000 face amount bond (assuming no adjustment for coupon or maturity).

MINIMUM PRICE FLUCTUATION: 1/32nd, or $31.25 per $100,000

PRICE MOVEMENT DAILY LIMIT: 24/32nds, or $750 per $100,000

The "normal" limit for any trading day is 24/32nds above or below the previous day's settlement price; however, these limits are expanded under predetermined conditions and there is no limit on the expiring contract during the delivery month, e.g., there would be no price movement limit on the September 1978 contract during the calendar month of September 1978.

EXPIRING CONTRACT TRADING TERMINATION: Eighth-to-last business day of month

There is no trading in the expiring contract during the last seven business days of the delivery month.

DELIVERY PERIOD: Any business day during the contract's delivery month

It is the seller's option to initiate the delivery process. Actual delivery in settlement of a "sold" futures position can be made on any business day during the delivery month. The buyer, holding a "bought" futures position, is selected to take delivery by the Exchange.

DELIVERY INSTRUMENT: Specific security by Federal Reserve book-entry transfer

The futures "seller" wires a deliverable bond to a Federal Reserve member bank designated by the futures "buyer" in exchange for Federal funds on the same day.

DELIVERY SUBSTITUTION: Deliverers at their option may deliver any deliverable bond with price adjustment for other-than-8% coupon and actual time to call or maturity. (see conversions on back of this page)

Figure 18-2 (b)

ISSUE		DELIVERED IN			
		Jun 78	Sep 78	Dec 78	Mar 79
7 7/8s	02-07	0.9869	0.9868	0.9870	0.9869
7 5/8s	02-07	0.9605	0.9605	0.9608	0.9608
8 1/4s	00-05	1.0254	1.0255	1.0251	1.0252
8s	96-01	1.0000	0.9998	1.0000	0.9998
8 3/8s	95-00	1.0345	1.0341	1.0340	1.0336
7 7/8s	95-00	0.9887	0.9885	0.9888	0.9887
8 1/2s	94-99	1.0441	1.0440	1.0434	1.0432
3 1/2s	1998	0.5523	0.5547	0.5569	0.5593
3s	1995	0.5463	0.5496	0.5532	0.5566

The futures price is multiplied by the appropriate factor to determine the delivery price of a specific bond. A less-than-one factor for a less-than-8% issue decreases its delivery price while a greater-than-one factor for a greater-than-8% issue increases its delivery price.

June 1978 Futures Price		8 1/4s 00-05		Delivery Price
97-07 (97,218.75)	x	1.0254	=	99,688.11

selling hedge. In a perfectly steady interest rate environment, the seller of futures should expect to have a loss as the discounted later delivery price rises to the current market, while the buyer of futures can expect a gain by that same process. The gains and losses reverse themselves in an "inverted" market where later delivery prices are at a premium to the current market.

BUYING HEDGE (T-BILL FUTURES)

Treasury bill futures are evaluated by what is called an *index*, which is a substitute for price. Thus the objective is to buy low and sell high. This goal differs from the dealer market practice of trading in discount yield where the objective is to buy high and sell low (a "high" discount is a "low" price). The index instead of actual price also makes trading much simpler. An index change from 91.85 to 91.86 would be a price change from $979,625 to $979,650. The following discussion uses "price" in the index sense, but of course the index is not the actual price of the delivered bill (examine Figure 18-3).

Futures prices for 90-Day U.S. Treasury bills are lower for later deliveries, as they are for GNMA and bond futures prices, but for slightly different reasons. Here the reason relates to a smaller section of the yield curve, which extends from 90-day out to about two-year maturities. A *positive slope* in the yield curve—that is, lower yields for shorter maturities and higher yields for later maturities—forces T-Bill futures to be priced at successively lower levels for deferred deliveries. This will be brought about by arbitrage traders selling T-Bill futures against longer maturity bills and notes.

T-Bill futures can be used to lock in a yield on bills intended to be bought.

Example: Ninety-day bill rates in September and October of 1976 showed a strong inclination to fall, and the general outlook was for continued movement in that direction. In October 1976 an investor anticipates buying 90-day bills early in December 1976 and wants to hedge that purchase in the futures market to establish the current yield level for the later investment. The complete transaction is shown below.

	Cash		Futures	
October 21	Current 3-month bill at 4.85%		Buy 2 December T-Bill futures 94.99 (5.01%)	
December 9	Buy $2 million 90-Day bills at 4.43%		Sell 2 December T-Bill futures 95.53 (4.47%)	
	Loss	$2,100	Profit	$2,700

This unusually favorable result was caused by the significant fall in bill rates that actually occurred in late 1976 and by the movement of the

Figure 18-3 (a)

Bache Halsey Stuart Shields Incorporated

Financial Futures Contract Summary

March 15, 1978

90-DAY U.S. TREASURY BILL FUTURES

EXCHANGE: International Monetary Market (Chicago Mercantile Exchange)

TRADING HOURS: 8:35 AM to 1:35 PM (Chicago)

TRADING UNIT: $1 Million 90-Day Maturity U.S. Treasury Bill

The market trades a $1 million face value bill with 90 days to maturity from the delivery date of the particular contract, therefore the maturity of the bill will always be three months later than the contract delivery month, e.g., the June 1978 futures contract could be settled by delivering a September 21, 1978, maturity bill.

PRICE QUOTATIONS: I.M.M. Index

The I.M.M. Index is 100.00 minus the 90-day discount. A typical futures quotation would be 93.50, meaning a discount 6.50%. Given that quotation and discount, the seller would receive and the buyer would pay $983,750 for $1 million face amount bill with 90 days to maturity.

MINIMUM PRICE FLUCTUATION: One Basis Point (.01), or $25 per $1 Million

PRICE MOVEMENT DAILY LIMIT: Fifty Basis Points (.50), or $1,250 per $1 Million

The "normal" limit for any trading day is 50 basis points above or below the previous day's settlement price; however, these limits are expanded under predetermined conditions and there is no limit on the expiring contract during the last day of trading, e.g., there would be no price movement limit on the June 1978 contract on June 21, 1978.

EXPIRING CONTRACT TRADING TERMINATION: Wednesday following the third auction of

13-week Treasury Bills in the delivery month

DELIVERY PERIOD: The business day following the last trading day

DELIVERY INSTRUMENT: Specific security by Federal Reserve book-entry transfer

The futures "seller" wires a deliverable bill to an approved Chicago bank designated by the futures "buyer" in exchange for Federal funds on the same day.

DELIVERY SUBSTITUTION: Deliverers at their option may deliver U.S. Treasury Bills with 90, 91

or 92 days to maturity and receive payment reflecting actual maturity. (All bills in a $1 million

delivery unit must have uniform maturity dates.)

Figure 18-3 (b)

Dollar Value of 1 Basis Point Discount Per $1 Million

Days to Maturity	1 Basis Point Dollar Value	Days to Maturity	1 Basis Point Dollar Value
10	$ 2.78	120	$ 33.33
30	8.33	180	50.00
45	12.50	225	62.50
60	16.67	270	75.00
90	25.00	360	100.00

If a $1 million bill with 100 days remaining to maturity rises 5 basis points in yield, the dollar value of the bill falls $138.90 (5 basis points x $27.78).

I.M.M. Index	Percent		Amount	
	90-Day Discount	Bond Yield	$ Discount	$ Principal
97.00	3.00	3.06	7,500	992,500
96.00	4.00	4.10	10,000	990,000
95.00	5.00	5.13	12,500	987,500
94.00	6.00	6.18	15,000	985,000
93.00	7.00	7.22	17,500	982,500
92.00	8.00	8.28	20,000	980,000

The dollar amount of discount for 91- or 92-day maturity bills delivered in the futures market can be calculated by the following:

90-day discount 5.00%, discount amount $12,500.00

For 91-day maturity, $\frac{91}{90}$ x 12,500 = $12,638.88

For 92-day maturity, $\frac{92}{90}$ x 12,500 = $12,777.77

Bache Halsey Stuart Shields Incorporated, 141 W. Jackson Blvd., Chicago, IL 60603

December futures to a very small price discount as it approached termination of trading. Needless to say, such a result should not be expected with any regularity.

A seller of T-Bill futures seeks protection against rising interest rates—on bank borrowings under a "floating" rate pegged to the prime lending rate, or for financing in the form of banker's acceptances, certificates of deposit, or commercial paper.

COMMERCIAL PAPER

A borrower or investor may also consider commercial paper futures as a hedging medium, either to lock in rates on intended investments or to hedge against higher borrowing costs (see Figure 18-4). The commercial paper futures market trades a *rate*. Someone who buys T-Bill futures to establish an investment interest rate is a *seller* of commercial paper futures; someone who sells T-Bill futures as a hedge against rising interest rates is a *buyer* of commercial paper futures. One way to remember the proper direction is to recall that *selling* the rate is *buying* the price, and *buying* the price is *selling* the rate. This role reversal goes even further: traditionally the futures seller is the one supposed to make delivery; in commercial paper futures, the buyer of futures makes delivery.

THE DETERMINATION OF INTEREST RATE LEVELS

Interest is the price of money, and, like other prices, it is determined substantially by supply and demand. The supply is usually referred to as *loanable funds,* a good phrase not only because it is understandably descriptive but also because it avoids possible confusion with the word "supply." The term "money supply" means something different from loanable funds. The other factor is called *demand for funds.*

Supply and Demand

Traditional supply-demand theory dictates that the lower the price, the greater the demand. But an increase in demand without new supply causes price to be used as a rationing device and prices rise. This, in turn, brings forth new supply and prices fall. As prices fall, however, this attracts demand again, and the cycle is repeated until an equilibrium is established between supply and demand at a so-called market-clearing price—in this case, a rate of interest equally acceptable to both marginal lenders and borrowers.

This process is a reasonably accurate description of what actually

Figure 18-4 (a)

Bache Halsey Stuart Shields Incorporated

Financial Futures Contract Summary

March 15, 1978

90-DAY COMMERCIAL PAPER FUTURES

EXCHANGE: CHICAGO BOARD OF TRADE

TRADING HOURS: 8:30 AM to 1:35 PM (Chicago)

TRADING UNIT: $1 MILLION 90-DAY COMMERCIAL PAPER

Deliverable commercial paper must satisfy four requirements: (1) Rated A-1 by Standard & Poor's Corporation, (2) Rated P-1 by Moody's Investor Services, Inc., (3) Approved by the Chicago Board of Trade and (4) Mature on a business day not more than 90 days from the date of delivery.

PRICE QUOTATIONS: Points and basis points of annualized discount

A typical price quotation in commercial paper futures would be 7.00, meaning a 7.00% annualized discount on $1 million for 90 days. Given that rate, the discount amount is $17,500 per $1 million.

MINIMUM PRICE FLUCTUATION: One basis point (.01), or $25 per $1 million

PRICE MOVEMENT DAILY LIMIT: Twenty-five basis points (.25), or $625 per $1 million

The "normal" limit for any trading day is 25 basis points above or below the prior day's settlement price; however, these limits are expanded under predetermined conditions and there is no limit on the expiring contract during the delivery month, e.g., there would be no price movement limit on the March 1978 contract during the calendar month of March 1978.

EXPIRING CONTRACT TRADING TERMINATION: Eighth-to-last business day of month

There is no trading in the expiring contract during the last seven business days of the delivery month.

DELIVERY PERIOD: Any business day during the contract's delivery month

It is the buyer's option to initiate the delivery process. Actual delivery in settlement of a "bought" futures position can be made on any business day during the delivery month. The seller, holding a "sold" futures position, is selected to take delivery by the Exchange.

DELIVERY INSTRUMENT: Financial receipt

DELIVERY SUBSTITUTION: Deliverers at their option may deliver a financial receipt backed by commercial paper with less than 90-day maturity but payment will be calculated on the basis of 90 days.

Figure 18-4 (b)

COMMERCIAL PAPER APPROVED FOR DELIVERY

The Chicago Board of Trade has approved as deliverable the commercial paper of the following companies:

American Express Credit Corp.	Kraft, Inc.
Associates Corp. of North America	Merrill Lynch & Co.
Bell Telephone Co. of Pennsylvania	Michigan Bell Telephone Co.
Chesapeake & Potomac Telephone Co. (D.C.)	Mobil Oil Corp.
Chesapeake & Potomac Telephone Co. of Md.	Montgomery Ward Credit Corp.
Chesapeake & Potomac Telephone Co. of Va.	Mountain States Telephone & Telegraph Co.
Chesapeake & Potomac Telephone Co. of W. Va.	New Jersey Bell Telephone Co.
Cincinnati Bell Inc.	New York Telephone Co.
C.I.T. Financial Corp.	Northwestern Bell Telephone Co.
Commercial Credit Co.	Ohio Bell Telephone Co.
Diamond State Telephone Co.	Pacific Northwest Bell Telephone Co.
E. I. DuPont De Nemours & Co.	J.C. Penney Financial Corp.
Ford Motor Credit Co.	Sears Roebuck Acceptance Corp.
General Electric Co.	Shell Oil Co.
General Electric Credit Corp.	South Central Bell Telephone Co.
General Motors Acceptance Corp.	Southern Bell Telephone & Telegraph Co.
Gulf Oil Corp.	Southwestern Bell Telephone Co.
Walter E. Heller & Co.	Standard Oil Co. of California
Household Finance Corp.	Western Electric Co.
Illinois Bell Telephone Co.	Wisconsin Telephone Co.
Indiana Bell Telephone Co., Inc.	

Anyone holding commercial paper notes issued by the above companies may deliver that commercial paper in satisfaction of a previously "bought" futures position. The limitation as to approved companies applies only to the issuer of the commercial paper, it is not a restriction at to deliverers. For example: ABC Corporation is not an approved issuer and therefore could not deliver its commercial paper; however, ABC Corporation could deliver the commercial paper issued by any of the approved issuers. Obviously, an approved issuer company could deliver its own commercial paper as well as the commercial paper issued by any other approved issuer.

Bache Halsey Stuart Shields Incorporated, 141 W. Jackson Blvd., Chicago, IL 60603

happens as the price of money is determined by the marketplace. Take the case of manufacturing companies whose sales are increasing along with a growing economy. The companies' needs to pay greater administrative costs and to finance larger work-in-progress inventories and accounts receivable represent a *demand for funds,* and the companies' banks comprise a source of *loanable funds.* As this growth sequence continues, the banks become "loaned up" and, without reserves to support further lending, they have to borrow to supplement their reserves. If this practice is widespread, then competition among banks for a limited amount of loanable funds raises the cost of bank borrowing which then forces up the price of loanable funds offered to the manufacturing companies. At some point the manufacturing companies encounter prohibitive interest costs and reduce sales to a level that does not require as much borrowing.

The sequence then reverses as banks have no need to borrow and eventually have excess reserves. As demand for loanable funds diminishes through the system, prices (interest rates) fall.

A similar sequence occurs in the long-term bond market. Manufacturing companies require additional or modernized plant and equipment to meet the growing sales volume. The companies sell bonds to raise long-term funds appropriate to the long-term investment nature of the facilities. As more and more companies do this, their demand for funds force up the price of loanable funds. Some new supply might become available as short-maturity investors shift to the rising long-term rates. But sooner or later the price of long-term funds rises to a level at which the borrowers become unable to pay the fixed interest costs and still operate the new facilities at a profit. When they stop borrowing, the escalation of interest rates subsides and eventually interest rates can be expected to fall.

These generalizations merely explain what is easily observable by looking at historical trends of interest rates and aggregate economic output, the broadest measurement of which is Gross National Product (GNP). They also explain to those who watch financial futures why the markets quite often rise or fall in price immediately after a news release shows an unexpectedly large change in some measure of economic activity. If, for example, the index of leading economic indicators is reported to have declined, financial futures prices might rise on the assumption that a declining volume of economic activity will cause interest rates to fall. Or a report that unemployment fell might cause financial futures prices to fall on the assumption that the economy is absorbing more workers and that therefore the demand for loanable funds will increase (that is, interest rates will rise).

Inflation

Another factor that in recent years has become increasingly important to interest rate levels is inflation. Inflation is particularly important to long-term rates because the principal amount to be received some number of years in the future is subject to great depreciation in terms of real purchasing power. Expectations of increasing inflation cause bond prices to fall while signs of declining inflation cause bond prices to rise. For this reason, the financial futures markets generally are sensitive to monthly reports on both the Consumer Price Index (CPI) and Producer Price Index (PPI).

Governmental Determinants

Beyond the more or less "natural" events reflecting thousand or millions of individual decisions to borrow or not to borrow, to lend or not to lend, two other more centralized factors play an important role in the determination of interest rates: first is the fiscal policy of the United States Government, and second is the monetary policy of the Federal Reserve Board.

Fiscal policy refers to government spending and taxation, that is, the sources and uses of money by the federal establishment. Deficits arise when the government spends more than it has to spend, thus requiring that it borrow from the private sector. Borrowing by the United States Treasury to finance past and current deficit spending can be an important element in the determination of interest rates.

Unique about Treasury borrowing is that it cannot be postponed or cancelled because interest rates are too high. Unlike private sector decisions, which are constrained by economic measures of investment return, previous legislation and political decisions determine the level of government spending; the Treasury has no choice but to obtain any amount of funds necessary at the administratively determined time for disbursement.

Another aspect of Treasury operations that affects interest rates is the *maturity* of the funds borrowed.

Example: The Treasury had allowed the average maturity of its debt to decline during the years preceding 1974. As a result, the Treasury was in the short-term market constantly just to refund, or roll-over, its maturing debt. Also in 1974, an unusually heavy demand for short-term financing arose from the private sector. The combined demand for funds pushed short-term interest rates to the highest levels in the nation's history.

Fairly commonly, therefore, the financial futures markets move in response to both the amount and maturity of debt offerings announced periodically by the Treasury.

Monetary policy refers to the management of the nation's banking system by the federal Reserve Board to achieve broad national economic objectives related to price stability, employment, and balanced international trade. While this area is large and complex, possibly the most important segment of monetary policy consists of decisions by the Federal Reserve to effect the price of bank reserves and the amount of "money" in the economy.

Although the term "money supply" itself is controversial, it will be used here with its commonly accepted definition of being currency held by the public plus demand deposits (checking accounts) at commercial banks.

Money supply is the fuel, so to speak, that allows the economy to maintain its growth—sustainable real growth or, if there is too much money supply, unsustainable and inflationary growth. The Board of Governors of the Federal Reserve have been very mindful in recent years of the detrimental long-term consequences of excessive money supply growth. For this reason, "The Fed" has become a major factor in the day-to-day (sometimes minute-to-minute) determination of interest rates.

The leading edge of the Fed's activity is its open market operations through which it buys securities (raising bank reserves) or sells securities (lowering bank reserves). The impact is almost immediate. The commercial banks are then left with more reserves, so they can expand their lending at the same or possibly lower interest rate, which tends to expand money supply; or they are left with less reserves, so they have to restrict their lending or raise the interest rate, which tends to shrink money supply. When the Fed buys securities, it has the effect of increasing the supply of loanable funds; selling securities, on the other hand, has the effect of decreasing the supply of loanable funds. From a borrower's point of view the bank loan (demand deposit) is the supply of loanable funds; but from the bank's perspective the loanable funds are the reserves required to support the demand deposit. Therefore, scarce reserves lead to a higher price for bank loans which deter some borrowers and slow the growth of bank loans, demand deposits, and money supply.

The financial futures markets respond to open market activities very quickly, particularly if the Fed's action signals a change in the interest rate level of federal funds or overnight borrowing of bank reserves.

> *Example:* The Fed has been selling securities (draining reserves) whenever Fed funds traded on the open market at 7-7/16 percent, and it has been buying securities (supplying reserves) whenever Fed funds traded at 7-9/16 percent. Thus, the "target" is 7½ percent, the mid-point between pushing up the cost of reserves (7-7/16 percent) and pushing down the cost of reserves (7-9/16 percent). If, on a certain day, the Fed enters the market to sell securities with funds at 7-9/16 percent, financial futures prices drop immediately because it is assumed that the Fed has taken action to push up the target: The lower limit is now 7-9/16 percent, not 7-7/16 percent, and the target probably is 7-5/8 percent instead of 7½.
>
> Of, if funds trade in the other direction, and the Fed waits until the market rate is 7-5/16 percent before selling securities, financial futures prices rise. Then it is assumed that the new target is 7-3/8 percent.

The financial futures markets have become quite sensitive to economic news and the Fed's daily activity. These markets on occasion are guilty of over-reacting, but frequently what at first appears to be an over-reaction compared with prices in the dealer market is later confirmed as the dealers move into line with futures.

CONCLUSIONS

This chapter provides an introduction to a new and rapidly growing segment of the commodity futures trading industry. While trading a financial instrument is new and certainly different, all the concepts, techniques and mechanics of trading are very similar to those employed in other commodity markets. Simply apply what you know about commodities to the trading of financial instrument futures, with a few twists.

The most important differences between traditional commodity futures and financial futures relate to fundamentals. The unique supply and demand factors that enter into the price movements and price levels of financial futures is one such difference. Also, financial futures require a new mathematics. Those who want to fully understand financial futures must be prepared for "bond yield equivalents" and "yield maintenance" prices as well as some familiarity with price value differences related to maturities. Although seemingly forbidding, this somewhat different arithmetic is no more difficult in practice than a number of calculations now common with grains or metals.

All present indications show that financial futures will continue to grow and that the markets will expand to include trading in new contracts. This zeal for growth should provide a vast frontier with its challenges and achievements for those who choose to be pioneers.

Glossary

Accumulate: To establish and to add to a position over a period of time.

Acreage Allotment: Government-imposed limitations on planted acreage for some basic crops. Its purpose is to maintain or achieve a balance between production/supply and demand for several commodities.

Acreage Reserve: An arrangement under which farmers agree to withdraw a stated acreage of cropland from production for a specified number of years. This is a conservation measure under the Soil Bank Program, and it provides for annual compensation for any loss of income.

Actuals: Physical commodities, as distinguished from futures contracts; also known as cash commodities.

Afloats: Commodities loaded in vessels that are in harbor or in transit but have not arrived at destination.

Animal Unit: The amount of grain feed necessary for an animal to attain full growth.

Arbitrage: The simultaneous purchase of one commodity contract against the sale of another to take advantage of a price disparity. When this procedure involves actuals and futures, it is known as *hedging*. On the other hand, if only futures are involved, it is known as *spreading*. [*See also* Spread (Straddle).]

Associated Person: A person associated with any futures commission merchant (or with any agent of a futures commission merchant) as a partner, officer, or employee or any person occupying a similar status or performing similar functions, in any capacity that involves (a) the solicitation or acceptance of customers' orders (other than in a clerical capacity) or (b) the supervision of any person or persons so engaged.

At the Market: A type of order to buy or sell at the best price obtainable when the order reaches the trading floor. Speed of execution is the most important consideration.

Basis: The relationship between the cash (spot) price and futures (usually the current delivery month) price of a commodity at a definite time at a specific location. To be "long" the basis or "short" the basis refers to hedging an already established position in the cash market by taking an equal and opposite commitment in futures. A basis that is "under" or "over" a specified futures month refers to the relationship of the cash price to that futures month. In a normal market, the basis is under to reflect carrying charges; in an inverted market, the basis is over and does not reflect carrying charges.

Basis Grade: The grade or grades specified by the exchange as deliverable on a futures contract. Other grades may be tendered for delivery subject to a discount or premium to the contract, or basis grade.

Bear: A speculator who expects the market to decline.

Bid: An order to buy a specific amount of a commodity.

Board Order. *See* Market-If-Touched (MIT) Order.

Break: A rapid, significant decline in price.

Broad Tape: A reporting system (news wire) providing news on prices, weather conditions, and commodity markets.

Broker: One who effects transactions on an agency basis and is paid a commission or fee. A floor broker is responsible for executing orders on the floor of an exchange. The term "broker" may also be used as a synonym for "account executive."

Brokerage: The fee or commission charged by a floor broker for executing customer orders, a commission fee.

Bucket, Bucketing: Accepting orders without any intention of executing them. Bucketing may also refer to the illegal use of margin deposits without disclosure to the customer.

Bulge: A rapid, significant advance in price.

Bull: A speculator who expects the market to rise.

Buy In: Covering a previous sale by an offsetting purchase. Also known as short covering.

Buying Hedge: *See* Hedging.

Buy (or Sell) on Close: An order to buy or sell within the closing price range. Such an order guarantees execution within the closing range if executed at all.

Buy (or Sell) on Opening: An order to buy or sell within the opening price range. This order guarantees execution within the opening range if executed at all.

C&F: Cost and freight paid to port of destination.

CIF: Cost, insurance, and freight paid to destination.

Call: A trading period designated by an exchange for the purpose of establishing a particular futures price. This can be an opening or closing call.

Call, Buyer's: The purchase of a specified quantity and specified grade of a commodity at a predetermined number of points above or below the price of a futures delivery month, allowing the buyer a certain period of time during the delivery months to fix the price either by purchasing for the seller's account or by indicating to the seller when he or she wishes to fix the price.

Call, Seller's: Same as a buyer's call except that the seller has the right to determine when the price shall be fixed.

Calls and Puts: Options to buy or sell a specified quantity of a commodity or security at a fixed price during a stated period.

Cargo: The load capacity of an ocean vessel.

Carload: The capacity of a railroad car. A variation of this is *cargo*.

Carrying Charges: The expenses incurred in owning and carrying a spot commodity. These include storage costs, insurance, and interest. In normal market situations, the price differential between futures delivery months of a commodity reflects these charges. These charges may also include transportation, grading, sampling, and so on, when computed in connection with delivery against a futures position.

Carryover: A portion of current supplies representing surplus or carryover from a previous marketing season.

Cash Commodity: Spot commodity. (*See also* Actuals.)

Cash Forward Sale: The sale of a cash commodity for delivery at a later date. Price may be fixed at the time of the agreement, or there may be an agreement to determine the price at the time of delivery on the basis of prevailing local cash price or on some futures price. One who effects a cash forward sale under the later arrangement still needs protection against a price decline that may occur between the time of the original agreement and final settlement on price Also known as "deferred delivery" or just "forward sale."

Certificated Stocks: Supplies that have been approved as deliverable grades and have been stored at warehouses or delivery points designated as regular by the exchange upon which the commodity is traded.

Commodity Futures Trading Commission (CFTC): An independent federal regulatory agency empowered under the Commodity Futures Trading Commission Act of 1974 with regulation of all commodities trading on all domestic contract markets. The commission consists of five commissioners, one of whom is chairperson. All are appointed by the president subject to senate confirmation The Commodity Futures Trading Commission replaced and assumed all powers of the Commodity Exchange Authority.

Commodity Product Spread: *See* Spread (Straddle).

Commodity Solicitor: A registered commodity representative employed by, and soliciting business for, a futures commission merchant. Also called an account executive or customer's man. (*See also* Associated Person.)

Congestion: In technical analysis, a price range within which buying power and selling pressure are about equal, resulting in a sideways movement of prices.

Consignment: An arrangement under which the seller places an unsold shipment of a commodity with an agent for sale at the best possible price. Title to the commodity rests with the seller until it is disposed of in accordance with the terms of the agreement.

Contract Grades: Commodity standards specified in the rules of an exchange that must be met when delivering a physical commodity in satisfaction of a futures contract. For most commodities, there may be deliverable grades other than contract grade, but these are deliverable at a discount or premium, depending on quality.

Contract Market: An exchange designated by the CFTC to conduct futures trading.

Controlled Account: A commodity account controlled by someone other than the owner or customer. Present requirements are that a controlled account: (1) be handled by a solicitor who has a minimum of two years experience in commodities trading, (2) prior written authorization (power of attorney) be given, and (3) have a minimum of $5,000 equity at all times. Also known as a "discretionary account" or "managed account."

Corner: In its extreme form, it is the acquisition of more contracts requiring delivery than the existing supply of a commodity can meet. More commonly, it represents securing significant control of a commodity, enabling price manipulation.

Coupon Rate: The rate of interest that the issuer of a bond will pay the purchaser.

Covering: Offsetting a previously established futures short position by a purchase. Also known as "evening up" or "liquidation."

Crop Year: In grains, generally the time period from one harvest to the next. The beginning and ending dates vary with the commodity. It is important to note that new crop futures trading does not necessarily begin and end on dates coincidental with the crop year harvest-to-harvest dates.

Current Delivery: A futures contract that will mature and become deliverable during the current month. Also called "spot month."

Customer's Man. *See* Commodities Solicitor.

Day Order: An order that, if not executed during the day it is entered, automatically expires at the end of that trading session.

Delivery: Tender of a commodity either by (1) issuing a warehouse receipt or a bill of lading, (2) issuing a shipping certificate for some commodities, or (3) delivery of actuals against a futures contract.

Default: (1) The failure to make or take delivery of the physical commodity as required under a futures contract.
(2) Under the farm loan program, it is a decision not to repay a government loan, instead surrendering the crop that has been pledged as collateral.

Deferred Delivery: *See* Cash Forward Sale.

Delivery Month: A futures contract month.

Delivery Notice: Written notice from a seller through the clearing house stating intention to make delivery on a short futures position on a particular date. This notice also specifies quantity, grade, and place of delivery. A notice precedes and is distinct from a warehouse receipt or shipping certificate, which are instruments representing transfer of ownership.

Delivery Points: Locations designated by a futures exchange at which the physical commodity covered by a futures contract may be delivered in fulfillment of the contract.

Delivery Price: The settlement price of the trading session during which the buyer of a futures contract receives a delivery notice from a seller (through the clearing house). Also the price the buyer must pay for the commodities represented in the futures contract.

Differentials: The premiums paid for grades better than the basis grade and the discounts allowed for grades lower than the basis grade. Differentials are fixed by contract terms of an exchange; however, in cotton, commercial differentials apply.

Discretionary Account. *See* Controlled Account.

Distant Delivery: Distant futures delivery months as distinguished from nearby futures delivery months.

Elasticity of Demand: The phenomenon of price change creating an increase or decrease in the consumption of a commodity. If price change has little or no effect on consumption, it is known as inelasticity of demand.

Elasticity of Supply: The phenomenon of price change creating an increase or decrease in the production of a commodity. If supply is unresponsive to price change, it is known as inelasticity of supply.

Evening Up: *See* Cover.

Excess: The amount by which equity exceeds margin requirements in an account. Excess above original margin levels may be withdrawn or used for additional commitments; this is not true of excess above maintenance margin levels.

Ex-Pit Transactions: Trades made outside the trading pit or ring. There are two types: (1) a transfer trade that involves the transfer of a customer's account between brokerage firms; or (2) an exchange of cash for futures involving the purchase of cash commodities in exchange for a futures contract, at a price difference mutually agreed upon. The second is a technique used by commercial accounts to close out a hedged position.

Feed Ratio: An indicator of profit margin or lack of it in the cost of feed-to-market-weight sales price of an animal; such as steer/corn ration or hog/corn ratio.

First Notice Day: The first day on which notices of intention to deliver against a short futures contract can be presented by sellers through the clearinghouse. The first notice day varies with each commodity and exchange, but it usually precedes the beginning of the delivery period.

FOB: Free on board, indicating that all costs of putting a commodity aboard a carrier have been paid.

Forward Sale (or Purchase): *See* Cash Forward Sale.

Free Supply: Supply of a commodity in the open market, exclusive of government stocks or controlled stocks being processed.

Fundamental Analysis: Analyzing price trends using the underlying factors of supply and demand. Among these are items such as weather forecasts, price support programs, political developments, population, floods, drought, labor problems, the economy, acreage yields, substitutes, and so on.

Fungibility: Interchangeability. Futures contracts for the same commodity and delivery month are fungible because contract specifications are standardized by the exchange where the commodity is traded.

Futures Commission Merchant (FCM): Individuals, associations, partnerships, and corporations engaging in soliciting or in accepting orders for the purchase or sale of any commodity for future delivery (on and subject to the rules of any contract market) must be registered with the Commodity Futures Trading Commission.

Futures: Contracts calling for delivery at a later date, in which the contract specifications are identical in terms of size, deliverable grades, and so on. All futures trading is subject to the rules of the exchange on which the commodity trades; consequently the terms of all trades in any one commodity in the same delivery month are identical. The significant distinction between futures and cash is the offset privilege of a futures contract prior to making or taking delivery. That is, anyone who enters into a futures contract is contingently liable for the full value of the contract only if he or she allows the contract to expire.

Give-up: A contract executed by one broker for the client of another broker that the client orders to be turned over to the second broker. The broker accepting the order from the customer collects a wire toll from the carrying broker for the use of the facilities.

Good 'Til Cancelled (GTC): An order instruction to the broker that it is to remain in effect until executed or cancelled. In futures trading, a GTC order has a cancellation provision built into it, in that the order automatically expires at the end of the trading session on the last day of trading when that delivery expires. Also known as an "open order."

Grain Futures Act: A federal statute enacted June 22, 1923 for the purpose of regulating grain futures trading, administered by the USDA. In 1936, the act was amended, creating the Commodity Exchange Authority, and the act has since been referred to as the Commodity Exchange Act. (*See* Commodity Futures Trading Commission)

Gross Processing Margin (GPM): The price relationship between the raw material and the value of products derived from it. In soybeans, it is the difference between the cost of soybeans and combined sales income of soybean oil and soybean meal, which results from the processing of soybeans.

Hardening: A gradual firming of price; a slowly advancing market.

Heavy: A market condition characterized by overhanging sell orders without a correesponding number of buy orders; prices demonstrate an inability to advance, and more often they display a tendency to decline slowly.

Hedging: Taking the opposite position in the futures market of a position held in the cash market. The expectation in hedging is that a loss in one market will be offset in part or in whole by a gain in the other. A bona fide hedger seeks a profit as well as protection, in that he or she hopes the basis (price difference) between cash and futures will move (narrow or widen) favorably. As defined by the CFTC Ruling, a hedger is one who deals in the physical commodity. Hedging theory rests on the principle that the cash and futures prices of a commodity move in the same direction, though not necessarily by the same amount. There are two basic types of hedges:

1. A *Buying Hedge* is a long futures position versus a short cash position. Its main purpose is to protect against a price increase in the cash market. For example, a manufacturer who has agreed to deliver finished products at a predetermined cash price puts on a buying hedge by taking a long futures position on the raw material he will need. Since a buying hedger is someone who will eventually have to acquire the physical commodity, in our example, the manufacturer—who will need the raw material at some point—will have the choice of either taking delivery on the long futures position or of offsetting the futures and buying the raw material in the cash market, whichever is more profitable. In a normal market, a buying hedge closed out after a widening of the basis results in a profit. The buying hedge is used primarily by business concerns that have made cash forward sales at specified prices. Also known as a "long hedge."

2. A *Selling Hedge* is a short futures position versus a long cash position. Its main purpose is to protect against a price decline in the cash market. For example, a grain elevator operator who has an inventory of wheat sells a futures contract against that inventory to protect against falling prices in the cash market. In this way, the hedger can either use the inventory to deliver on the short futures position or offset the futures and sell the wheat in the cash market, whichever is more profitable. The selling hedger is someone who will eventually sell or deliver in the cash market. If a cash forward sale is made with the agreement that the cash price will be determined at some point in the future (at time of delivery), there is still a need for a selling hedge inasmuch as the seller may be concerned that the cash price may decline between the time of the agreement and the delivery date. On the other hand, if a cash forward sale is made at a fixed price at the time of the agreement, the seller has no inventory to protect and would not, therefore, sell futures.

In a normal market, a selling hedge that is closed out after a narrowing of the basis results in a profit to the hedger. The results of a selling hedge are also referred to as "contribution to carrying charges," since you cannot incur carrying charges unless you have an inventory of the physical commodity. Also known as a short hedge.

Incentive Payment Plan: A United States government subsidy paid to domestic wool growers.

In Sight: The amount of a particular commodity at locations near producing areas. The term implies that reasonably prompt delivery can be made.

Intercommodity Spread: *See* Spread (Straddle).

Interdelivery Spread: *See* Spread (Straddle).

Intermarket Spread: *See* Spread (Straddle).

Inverted Market: A futures market characterized by the nearby futures selling, at a premium to distant futures and by cash prices at a premium to nearby futures. This type of market develops when demand for immediate delivery exceeds actual (physical) supply; the costs of carrying the commodity are not reflected in prices.

Invisible Supply: Stocks in the hands of wholesalers, manufacturers, and producers, which cannot be counted but are theoretically available for market.

Job Lot: Unit of trading less than a round lot.

Last Trading Day: The final day during which trading may take place in a particular futures delivery month. Settlement of futures contracts outstanding at the end of last trading day can only be settled by delivery of physicals, or in some instances by monetary settlement if delivery is not possible.

Letter of Warning: A written notice issued by the CFTC to an individual or firm, an order to cease and desist an improper practice or violation of law.

Licensed Warehouse: A warehouse designated as regular for delivery by the exchange upon which a commodity is traded. Only such designated warehouses may be used to store a commodity for delivery. Also referred to as a "regular" warehouse.

Life of Contract (Delivery): The period of time from the first trading day in a futures month through last trading day.

Limit: *See* Price Limit.

Limited Order: An order that has some restriction upon execution, such as price or time.

Limit Order: An order to buy or sell at a specific price or better.

Limit (Up or Down): The maximum price advance or decline from the previous day's settlement price permitted in one trading session by the rules of the exchange.

Liquidation: Usually understood to mean the specific liquidation or offsetting of a previously held long position. *See* Covering.

Liquid Market: A market characterized by the relative ease of buying and selling, by many buyers and many sellers.

Loan Program: United States government agricultural price support operations. A program under which farmers commit their crops to the government with the assurance that they will receive a certain minimum loan price. If the price of the commodity rises above the loan price, the farmers may sell their crops in the open market. If the price of the commodity falls below the loan level, the nonrecourse character of the loan makes it possible for farmers to deliver their crops to the CCC (Commodity Credit Corporation), discharging their obligation in full.

Long: One who purchases futures contracts or who owns actuals. A net long is a trader whose total purchases exceed total sales in open futures contracts.

Long Hedge: *See* Hedging.

Long the Basis: A hedge consisting of ownership of actuals versus short futures in a particular commodity. (*See* Hedge, selling.)

Lot: A unit of trading (round lot, job lot).

Margin: Money or collateral deposited by both buyers and sellers of futures contracts that serves as a performance guarantee. It is not a down payment nor is it part of the purchase payment.

> 1. *Original Margin.* The amount of money required by a brokerage house when a futures position is established. It is the same for long or short positions. Generally, a speculator is subject to higher margin requirements than a hedger or spreader. A hedger deposits less margin than a speculator because the hedger has equal and opposite commitments in the cash and futures markets and is, therefore, subject to less risk. A spreader deposits less margin than either a net position speculator or hedger because a spreader has equal and opposite commitments in futures only,

and price volatility between futures is less than between cash and futures. Minimum margin is set by an exchange, but a brokerage house may set higher minimums.

2. *Maintenance Margin.* The amount of margin or equity that must be on deposit at all times. When a customer's equity falls below maintenance level, most exchanges require the broker to issue a margin call for an amount that will bring the equity back to the original margin level.

Managed Account: *See* Controlled Account.

Margin Call: A written communication from a brokerage firm to a customer calling for additional money that will bring the equity to a minimum level. The clearing house of an exchange can also issue margin calls to brokerage houses calling for additional deposits. For clearing purposes, a member of the clearing house generally carries two accounts, a house account and a customer's account.

Market-If-Touched (MIT) Order: An order to buy or sell when the market reaches a specified price. An order to buy becomes a market order when the commodity sells (or is offered) at or below the order price; an order to sell becomes a market order when the commodity sells (or is bid) at or above the order price. An order to buy is placed below the current market price; an order to sell is placed above the current market price. Also known as "board order."

Market Order: An order to buy or sell at the best price available and as soon as possible after the order reaches the trading floor of the exchange.

Market Quota: Government restriction on the amount of a commodity a producer is allowed to sell.

Maturity: Period between first notice day and last trading day of a commodity futures contract; the period within which settlement of a futures contract can be made by delivery of actuals. In financial instruments, it is the time period the issue deems necessary to redeem the bond, note, bill, or the like.

Member Rate: The commission rate charged members of an exchange for execution of futures orders on the exchange for the member's account. These rates are normally less than rates charged to nonmembers.

Nearby: The futures delivery month traded with maturity closest to the present calendar month. The futures contract with maturity closest to spot or cash trading.

Net Position: The difference between open contracts long and open contracts short held in any one commodity by any individual; or the difference held by a FCM with a clearing house.

Nominal Price: Generally, an average between bids and offers. Nominal price is quoted when no actual trading takes place during a trading session. Nominal price is quoted in lieu of a settlement price.

Notice Day: Any day on which a notice of intention to deliver may be issued on a specified delivery month.

Offer: A price at which a trader is willing to sell.

Offset: The procedure by which a futures commitment is closed out by an equal and opposite transaction. It can also mean the practice of commission merchants of setting total longs against total shorts for the purpose of determining net long or net short position.

Omnibus Account: An account of one commission merchant carried by another commission merchant for clearing purposes. In such an account, the transactions of customers are combined and treated as one account. Although the account stands in the name of a person or firm, it is used for clearing trades of one or more undisclosed customers of the merchant originating the account.

On Track: A type of delivery agreement whereby the buyer agrees to pay freight charges from the seller's location to destination. The seller, however, pays all costs involved in getting the commodity loaded and on track.

Open Contracts. *See* Open interest.

Opening Range: Range of prices at which transactions took place during the period designated as "the opening" of trading by an exchange.

Open Interest: Futures contracts that have been neither offset by an equal and opposite transaction nor fulfilled by delivery. Since all open interest long is equal to all open interest short, open interest figures show one side only. Open interest increases when a new seller sells to a new buyer; it decreases when both the buyer and the seller are covering previously established positions (old buyer and seller). In other situations, open interest remains unchanged. Also known as "open contracts."

Open Order: *See* Good 'Til Cancelled.

Open Outcry: Method of trading required in the exchange trading pits or rings. All futures trades must be made by open outcry with the exception of ex-pit transactions.

Option: A term erroneously applied to a futures contract.

Overbought: A market condition characterized by speculators drastically increasing their long positions. A technical analysis opinion that prices have risen too sharply and too quickly in relation to underlying fundamental factors.

Oversold: A market condition characterized by speculators drastically increasing their short positions. A technical analysis opinion that prices have fallen too sharply and too quickly in relation to underlying fundamental factors.

Parity Price: A theoretical equal relationship between farm product prices and all other prices of goods. It is issued monthly by the USDA, and it shows what the grower of a commodity has to receive to obtain the same purchasing power today as during some base period.

Pit: An area or space on the trading floor of a grain exchange where trading in futures is conducted. The equivalent of the ring on most exchanges.

Point: Unit expressing minimum price change. Synonymous with "minimum price fluctuation."

Position: A market commitment, long or short.

Position Limit: The maximum number of contracts, net long or net short, in any one future or in all futures of one commodity combined, that may be held open by one person in certain regulated commodities according to the provisions of the Commodity Exchange Act. Also a limit on positions, held by one person, established by an exchange. Other than the CFTC Regulation.

Position Trader: A commodity trader who holds contracts for an extended period of time, as distinguished from a day trader who initiates and closes out a position on the same day.

Premium: The excess price of one futures contract over another. Also the additional payment for delivery of higher than required grades of a commodity against a futures contract.

Price Limit: The maximum daily price fluctuation on a futures contract during any one trading session. Price limits are determined by the exchange upon which the commodity is traded. Also known as "limit." (See Variable Price Limit.)

Primary Market: Key distribution centers at which physical commodities are originally accumulated for commercial distribution.

Private Wires: Electronic communications networks leased by a commission merchant for private use.

Provisional Price: In cotton, a tentative price set on call cotton until a final price is fixed.

Public Elevators: Storage facilities for grain, licensed and regulated by federal and state agencies. Grain of the same grade but owned by different persons is usually commingled, or mixed together. Some elevators are designated as regular for delivery by exchanges dealing in commodities stored at these elevators.

Purchase and Sale (P&S) Statement: A statement sent by a commission house to a customer when a customer's position has changed. It shows the number of contracts involved, the prices at which the contracts were purchased or sold, profit or loss, and commission fees.

Pyramiding: Adding to existing position as the market moves favorably allowing profits on existing positions to be used as margin on new commitments.

Rally: An upward movement of pride after a decline.

Range: The difference between the highest and lowest prices recorded during a given trading session, week, month, life of contract, or any given period.

Reaction: Price decline following an advance.

Regular Warehouse: *See* Licensed Warehouse.

Regulated Commodities: Commodities subject to the provisions of the Commodity Futures Trading Commission Act of 1974.

Reporting Limit: Position sizes set by the Commodity Futures Trading Commission and/or exchanges at or above which traders must file daily reports to the CFTC and/or to the exchange on position size, delivery month, and purpose of trading.

Resting Order: Any order to buy below the current market price or sell above the current market price, such as limit, MIT, and GTC orders.

Restricted Stocks: Quantities of a commodity off the market for a period of time; stockpiles resulting from defaulted loans and/or periods of government controls.

Retender: The holder of a futures contract who has been issued a notice of intention to deliver through the clearing house has the right to sell an equivalent amount of futures represented in the notice during the same day and return (retender) the same notice to the clearing house, along with the name of the party that bought the contract. Retendering can be accomplished only with certain commodities and only within a specified period of time.

Round Lot: Trading unit corresponding or equal in size to the futures contract in that commodity: for example, 5,000 bushels in grains, 100 bales of cotton.

Roundturn: A completed transaction involving an initiating of a position and an equal and opposite offset. Commissions on commodities transactions are usually roundturn.

Scalper: A speculator on an exchange floor who trades in and out of the market on very small price fluctuations. The scalper, trading in this manner, provides market liquidity; however, he or she normally avoids thin markets and inactive months to avoid becoming locked in.

Seller's Option: The right of the seller to select commodity quality and time and place of delivery within the limits prescribed by the exchange upon which futures contracts are traded.

Selling Hedge: *See* Hedging.

Settlement Price: The daily price at which the clearing house clears all the day's trades. It may also refer to a price established by the exchange to settle unliquidated contracts that, because of uncontrollable circumstances, could not be liquidated in the trading ring. (*See also* Clearing Price.)

Short: The selling side of an open futures contract; also refers to a trader whose net position shows an excess of open sales over open purchases.

Short Hedge. *See* Hedging.

Short the Basis: A person or firm who has sold the cash or spot commodity at a fixed price and has hedged that sale with a purchase of futures.

Soften: The process of a slowly declining market price.

Soil Bank: *See* Acreage Reserve.

Speculator: A person entering the futures market for a purpose other than hedging. Although spreading is a sophisticated form of speculation in that only futures are involved in trading, more commonly a speculator is simply a commodity trader who is outright long or short in futures attempting to forecast price movement for profit.

Spot Commodity: *See* Actuals.

Spot Month: *See* Current Delivery.

Spot Price: The price quoted for the actual physical commodity.

Spread (Straddle): The purchase of one futures delivery month against the sale of another futures delivery month of the same commodity; the purchase of one delivery month of one commodity against the sale of that same delivery month of a different commodity; or the purchase of one commodity in one market against the sale of that commodity in another market. The purpose of any of these transactions is to take advantage of distortions in normal price relationships. The term "spread" is also used to refer to the difference between the price of one futures month and the price of another month of the same commodity. There are four basis types of spreads:

1. *Interdelivery Spread.* The purchase and sale of the same commodity, in the same market, in different delivery months. Also called an intramarket spread.
2. *Intermarket Spread.* The purchase and sale of the same commodity, in the same or different delivery months, in two different markets.
3. *Intercommodity Spread.* The purchase and sale of different but related commodities; in the same or different markets, in the same or different delivery months.
4. *Commodity Product Spread.* The purchase of futures raw material and the sale of the derived processed products futures, or vice versa.

In order to determine the type of spreading transaction, look first to the commodity/commodities involved. If the commodities are different, it is an intercommodity spread. If the commodity is the same but the markets are different, it is an intermarket spread. If the commodity is the same and the markets are the same but the delivery months are different, it is an interdelivery spread. Note that a spread involves futures only. In transactions other than grains, a spread is known as a straddle.

Straddle: A spread in a commodity other than grains.

Switch: Liquidation of a position in one delivery month and simultaneously initiating a similar position in another delivery month.

Technical Analysis: An approach to forecasting commodity prices based on the study of price movement itself without regard to underlying fundamental market factors.

Technical Rally: Price variations arising from factors other than those affecting supply and demand for a commodity.

Tender: Delivery against a futures position; issuance of a warehouse receipt, shipping certificate, or other instrument representing transfer of ownership.

Terminal Elevator: In the movement of grains, a storage facility located at a point of accumulation or distribution.

To-arrive: An agreement specifying that the price of the transaction will be based on delivery at the destination point. The seller pays the freight in shipping it to that point.

Transferable Notice: A notice of intention to deliver that may be passed on to an eligible buyer.

Transfer Trade: A trade for the purpose of transferring a customer's account from one brokerage firm to another. It is executed outside the trading pit.

Variation Margin Call: A margin call issued to a member of the clearing house during trading hours. Its purpose is to bring the member's margin up to a minimum level relative to changing prices and net position.

Variable Price Limit: A price limit schedule, determined by an exchange, that permits variations other than the normally allowable price movements for any one trading day.

Index

A

Accounts, handling of, 68–70, 74–75
  confirmations, 69–70
  customer statements, 69
  duties of broker, 68–69
  purchase and sale statements, 70
    information in, 74–75
Accounts, opening new;
  guaranteed accounts, 66
  individual speculator;
    customer agreement, 49
    supplement to, 49
    new account report, 46–47
  joint and business accounts, 55–62
    accounts with power of attorney, 60, 62
    corporate accounts, 60
    joint, 55
    partnership accounts, 57–58
    right of survivorship, 55, 57
    sole proprietor company account, 57
    tenants in common, 57
  know your customer, 45–46
  omnibus accounts, 66
  regulations on:
    confidential, 50
    customer in care of other person or entity, 50
    Part 17, 54
    and prior written consent, 52–55
    Rule 407, 52–53
    Rule 406, 53
    two or more accounts with one name, 49
    trade or hedge accounts, 62, 65
    unacceptable accounts, 66, 68
Accounts, transferring of, 68
  ex-pit transactions, 68
Advances, in market, 167–68
  example, 167–68
Averaging down, 268–69

B

Bar charts, 225–26
  example, 226
Buying, 187–91
  example, 188–89
  ex-pit transactions, 190
  by exporter, 189–90
  price protection, 190–91
  purposes, 188
  replacement of inventory, 190
  uncovered forward sales, 188
  uncoveredness, 187
Buying power vs. selling pressure, 228–38
  congestion areas, 233–34
    nature of, 234
    and subsequent trends, 234
  downtrend, 231–33
    example, 232
  example, 229
  sound practice, 233

Buying power vs. selling pressure (*continued*)
  taking a count, 235–36
    examples, 235–36
  uptrend, 229–31
    example, 230

C

Cash and future prices in delivery month,
  171–73
  arbitraging, 172
  example, 172, 173
Changes in open interest and trading volume,
  interpretation of, 303–05
  guidelines, 304
Chart analysis, 223–24
  market psychology, 224–25
  stampedes, 225
  trader sentiment, 225
Clearing house, 144–57
  and accounts, 150
  function of, 144, 145
  membership of, 145
  net positions, calculation of, 149–50
  original margin, 147
  substitution, principle of, 145–46
    example, 146
  trade register, 150
  transactions, guaranteeing of, 146–47
  variation, 147–49
    example, 149
    net position at day end, 143
    settlement price, 148
Close-out instructions, 78
  examples, 78
Commodities; 4–5, 19–20
  facts about, 25–31 (tables)
  and futures contracts, 4–5
  and risk, 4
  and speculator, 4
Commodity accounts, types of, 44–45
  nonregulated, 44
  regulated, 44
  spot cash, 44–45
Commodity clearing house, security of, 150–
  52
  clearance fees and surplus, 151
  commissions, 156
  delivery, making and taking, 152–155
    examples, 153, 154
    notice of, 152
  delivery responsibilities, 156

  guaranty fund, 150
  provision against loss, 151–52
  transferable vs. nontransferable, 155–56
Commodity disposal and inventory programs,
  324–26
  domestic sale, 325–26
  ever-normal granary concept, 324
  export movement, 326
  Sec. 407, 326
Commodity exchanges, 7, 21
Commodity prices, technical approach to forecasting of, 223–53
Commodity product spreads, 287–92
  actual yields, 291–92
  crush spread, 289–90
    reverse, 290
  gross processing margin, 288
Competitive executions, 106–07
  closing bell, 107
  cross orders, 106
  errors, adjustment of, 107
  opening, 106–07
Contract by itself, 21–22
  quantity, 22
Crop futures, old and new, 178
Crop scarcities, 220
  concern about, 220
  damage as bullishness, 220
Crop years, 178
Customer, death of, 79–80
  joint tenant, 79
  partner, 80
  principal and power of attorney, 80
  tenant in common, 80
Customer give-up, 79

D

Day trade margin requirements 88
  examples, 88
Deflation, 221
Deliveries, 134–42
  background, 134–35
  delivery points, 142
  grades, deliverable, 141–42
  period of, 138
  right of appeal, 136
  at seller's option, 137–38
  standardization of controls, 135
  switching forward, 138–39
    tables, 139–41
  time element, 136–37

Discount buying, 272–73
Disposal, methods of:
    barter, 329–30
    CCC credit program, 327
    credit sales for dollars, 326–27
    export program, 329
    PL 480 program, 327–28
    sales for dollars, 326–27
    sales for foreign currencies, 328–29
    transfers and donations, 330

E

Erroneous reports, 78–79
Exchange trading floor, 104
    floor broker, 104
    floor trader, 104
    scalper, 104

F

Federal legislation, 10–18
    Commodity Exchange Act, 10–11
    Commodity Futures Trading Commission,
        11–18
    nature of, 11–12
    powers of:
        advertising of commodity market per-
            formance, 17
        associated person, 12
        commodity exchanges, 13
        Commodity Pool Operator, 13
        Commodity Trade Advisor, 12–13
        confirmation of trades, 17
        contract markets, 13
        discretionary accounts, 16–17
        hedging, 16
        investor, protection of, 15–16, 17
        registration, 12
        reporting levels, 15
        risk disclosure, 17
        speculation limits, 14 (table)
        suitability, 17
        supervision, 16
        transaction activities, regulation of, 13–
            15
Financial instruments as commodities, 332–
51
    buying hedge, T-bill futures, 342–45
    buying hedge, T-bond futures, 339–42
    commercial paper, 345
    commercial paper futures, 333

financing of production and distribution,
    334
GNMA futures, 333
historical factors, 334–35
interest rate risk, hedging of, 335
selling hedge, GNMA futures, 336–39
T-bills, 333
Fluctuations, minimal, 23–24
Futures, buying and selling, 7–9
    cash market, 7
    clearing house, 8
    delivery, 8
    example, 9
    futures market, 7
    going long vs. going short, 7
    hedgers, 8
    offset, 8
    resale of contract, 8
    summary, 9
Futures, contract, defined, 20–21
    and contract creation, 20
    covering, 21
    going long vs. going short, 20
    liquidation, 20
Futures contracts, history of:
    cash market, 6
    mid-nineteenth Century, 5
    purchase of contracts, 6
    scheduled arrival, 6
    to-arrive contracts, 5–6
    yearly cycle, 5
Futures relations, opportunities in, 173–76
    between different futures markets, 176–77
    between raw materials and products, 177
    between related commodities, 177
    examples, 175, 176
Futures and different times, relations between,
    173
    examples, 173

G

Government price support and disposal pro-
    grams, 309–31
    Commodity Credit Corporation (CCC),
        310
        how it supports prices, 310
        impoundings and redemptions, 312–14
        loans, 310–14
            on grains, 311
            on cotton, 311–12
        grain reserves, 314
        reasons for, 309

H

Hedging, 180–205
  basis, 181
  buying, 181
  example, 181–82
  selling, 181
  and speculator, 181
  and supply, 180
  and risk, 180
Hedging in practice, 191–202
  buying and basis narrowing, 195–96
  buying and basis widening, 196–97
  buying in inverted market, and narrowing
    basis, 200–01
  buying in inverted market and widening
    basis, 202
  perfect hedges, 191
  sale and basis narrowing, 191–92
  sale and basis widening, 192–95
    examples, 193, 194
  sale in inverted market and widening basis,
    198—200
    example, 198–99
Hedgers, 182–83
  conditions, 183
  cross-commercial hedges, 183
  definition, 182
  requirements for, 182
  types of, 182
Hedges, summary, 204–05
Hedges, trade of, 202–04
  examples, 203, 204
  and expiration date, 202–03

I

Inflation, 221
Interest rate levels, 345–50
  government fiscal policy, 349
  inflation, 348–49
  monetary policy, 349–50
  money supply, 350
    example, 350
  supply and demand, 345–48
Intermarket spreads, 283–86
  different deliverable grades, 284–85
  local supply and demand conditions, 285–
    86
  transportation costs, 284
International Wheat Agreement, 303–1

L

Losses, limiting of, 260

M

Margin calls, procedure for, 90–93
  maintenance requirements, 93
    example, 93
  original margin calls, 90–91
    example, 91
  rule call, 92
    example, 92
  variation margin calls, 91–92
    examples, 92
Margin transactions, 81–82
  examples, 82
  maintenance margin, 81–82
  rate of margin, 81
  variation call, 81
Market factors, basic:
  crop carryover, 210
  export, 210
  imports, 210
  new crop, 209
  parent commodities, 210
  seasons, 210
  supply and demand, 209
  USDA statistics, 209
  uses, 210
Market analysis, basic guide to, 221–22
  free supply and demand, balance, 222
  price level, 222
  seasonal tendency, 222
  special factors, 222
  total supply and demand balance, 221–22
Market, inverted, 168–171
  illustrated, 169–70
Market, normal, 164–68
  calculation of carrying charges, 164–66
    example, 165
  convergence of prices, 166
  declining market, 166–67
    example, 167
Market prices, how they can be less than
    support prices, 321–22
  disagreement with price support, 322
  inconvenience, 322
  lack of storage, 322
  potential gains, 322
  quality, 322
  sales by nonfarmers, 322

O

Open interest, 300–01
Orders, 99–103
    account number, 102
    action code, 100
    description, 100
    duration, 101
    exchange, 100
    placing, mechanics of, 103
    price, 101
    production unit, 101
    qualification, 101
    quantity, 100
    registered representative, 102
        example, 102
    secondary information, 101
Orders:
    board, 113–15
    cancellations, 131–32
        cancel former order, 132
        straight cancel, 132
    combination, 125–27
        alternative, 125–26
    contingent, 127
    immediate or cancel, 123
    limit, 111–12
        to buy, 111
            example, 112
        to sell, 112–13
            example, 112–13
    market, 109–11
        examples, 109–10
        order to buy, 110
        order to sell, 110–11
    market-if-touched, *see* board
    on-the-close, 128–29
        limit, 129
    on-the-opening-market, 128
        limit, 128
    scale, 124–25
    spread, 129–30
    stop, 115–20
        to buy, 116–17
        to sell, 117–18
    stop-limit, 118–20
        to buy, 119
        to sell, 119–20
    stop-and-limit, 120
    switch, 130–31
    time, 121–23

        day, 121
        off at a specific time, 122
        open, 122–23
        time of day, 122
        week and month, 122

P

Pattern identification, 239–52
    ascending triangle, 246–48
    bottom, 240
    descending triangle, 245–46
    double bottom, 241–42
    double top, 240–41
    downward flag, 250
    down gaps, 252
    head and shoulders, 242–44
    inverse head and shoulders, 244–45
    neckline, 244
    symmetrical triangle, 248–49
    top, 240
    up-gaps, 251–52
    upward flag, 250
Point and figure chart, 227–28
    example, 227–28
    nature of, 227
Position, initiation of, 261–62
    anecdote, 263
    buy-stops, 264
    common error, 262–63
    considerations after, 262–68
    example, 261
    sell-stops, 264–65, 266–67
    trailing stop, 268
    trends, 261–62
Premium selling, 272–73
Price forecasting, 206–22
    fundamental analysis approach, 207–08
        advantages of, 207–08
        factors in, 207
        seasons, 207
        supply and demand, 207
Price quotations, 23–24
Price relations between cash and futures, 161–79
    basis, 161
    carrying charge market, 162
    cash price, 161
    futures price, 161
    inverted market, 162
    seasonal influences, 163

Price relations (*continued*)
  supply and demand, 162–63
Price tendencies, normal:
  and prevailing price level, 221
  rule of thumb, 221
  and seasons, 221
Prices:
  quotations, for CBOT commodities, 105
  reporting and dissemination, 104–05
  symbols, commodity and delivery month,
    105
Production adjustment programs, 323–24
  acreage allotments, 323
  cropland adjustment program, 324
  cropland conversion program, 324
  marketing quotas, 323
  voluntary diversion programs, 323–24
Profit, locking of, 270–72
  examples, 271, 272
  running of, 260
Pyramiding, 269–70
  examples, 269, 270

Q

Quotations, daily, 33–34
  and maximum daily range, 33–34 (table)

R

Resistance levels, 238–39
Reserve program, 315–21
  downward adjustment of loans, 318
  Food and Agriculture Act of 1977, 317
  incentive payments, 320–21
  parity prices, 316
  payment limits, 318–19
  price supports, how determined, 316–17
  price support loans for 1978–81, 317
  program acreages, 318
  purchase agreements, 320
  set-aside, 318
  shorn wool, 321
  soybeans, 319–20
  wool and mohair, 320
Roundturn rate of commission, 39–42
  day trade commission, 42
  examples, 41–42
  foreign rates, 42
  member rates, 42
  straddles, 42

S

Seasonal influences, 302–03
Selling, 183–87
  and carrying charges, 186–87
  consignment, 184
  deferred shipment agreements, 184
  example, 185
  and insurance of price, 187
  by manufacturers and processors, 186
  mechanics of, 184–86
  purposes, 183–84
Sell-out, procedure for, 93–94
  due notification, 93
    example, 94
  funds receipt from customers, 94–95
    example, 95, 96
    transfer of from stock accounts, 96
    transfer of funds to stocks, 96–97
  payouts, 97
  rules, 97
Speculative account requirements, 82–90
  concessions in house requirements, 85
  house requirements, 83–84
  margin requirements, changes in, 84
    example, 84
  minimum commodity exchange speculative requirements, 82
Speculation, rules of, 254–74
  preconsiderations:
    committment increase, 258
    conservative trading, 257–58
    market news, 257
    profits vs. expenses, 259
    spreading or risk, 258
    temperament, 256
    trading plan, 256
  risks, 255
  speculators, 254
Spreading, 275–94
Spreads:
  commodity products, 276
  intercommodity, 275–76, 286–87
  interdelivery, 276–83
    in normal market:
      buying near, selling distant, 276–80
      risk limits, 279–80
      selling near, buying distant, 280–81
      watching spread, 277
    in inverted market:
      buying near, selling distant, 281–83

Spreads (*continued*)
        selling near, buying distant, 283
    intermarket, 275
Spread commissions, 292–94
    legs of, 293
    roundturn rates, 293, 294
Spread margin requirements, 88–89, 292
    examples, 89
Statistics, 301–02
Supply scarcity, free, 215–18
    artificiality of, 215, 216
    breakdown, 218
    crop as collateral, 216
    examples, 216, 217, 218
    nonrecourse loans, 216
    redemptions, 216–17
Supply surplus, free, 219–20
    bearishness of, 219
    tables, 219–20
Supply scarcity, total, 213–14
    breakdown, 214
    example, 213
Supply surplus, total, 214–15
    example, 214–15
Supply and demand, balance, 210–13
    calculation of, 211
    Commodity Credit Corporation, 211
    government purchases, 210–11
    price levels, 212–13

    seasons, 212
Support levels, 236–38
    example, 237
    psychology in, 237

T

Tax straddles, 292
Time and sales, 107–08
Trade account requirements, 85–87
    examples, 86
Trader commitments in commodity futures,
        305–08
    large traders, 306
    reporting levels, 306
    small traders, 306
Trading hours, 22
Trading limits, daily, 35–39
    first notice day, 39
    maximum daily range, 35–37
    and previous settling price, 37
    purpose, 37
    spot months, 39
    variable daily price limits, 37–38
        function, 38–39
Trading, volume of, 299–300
Transactions, 45
    regular, 45
    straddle, 45